Children and the Faces of Television

Teaching, Violence, Selling

Children and the Faces of Television
Teaching, Violence, Selling

Edited by

EDWARD L. PALMER

Department of Psychology
Davidson College
Davidson, North Carolina

AIMÉE DORR

Annenberg School of Communications
University of Southern California
Los Angeles, California

ACADEMIC PRESS

A Subsidiary of Harcourt Brace Jovanovich, Publishers

New York   London   Toronto   Sydney   San Francisco

ACADEMIC PRESS, INC.
111 Fifth Avenue, New York, New York 10003

United Kingdom Edition published by
ACADEMIC PRESS, INC. (LONDON) LTD.
24/28 Oval Road, London NW1 7DX

Library of Congress Cataloging in Publication Data
Main entry under title:

Children and the faces of television.

Includes bibliographies and index.
1. Television and children--Addresses, essays, lec-
tures. 2. Television programs for children--Addresses,
essays, lectures. 3. Television advertising and children--
Addresses, essays, lectures. 4. Violence in television--
Addresses, essays, lectures. 5. Television in education--
Addresses, essays, lectures. I. Palmer, Edward L.
II. Dorr, Aimee.
HQ784.T4C49   791.45'01'3   80-1099
ISBN 0-12-544480-X

PRINTED IN THE UNITED STATES OF AMERICA

82 83   9 8 7 6 5 4 3 2

Contents

List of Contributors   xiii
Preface   xv

Part I

THE TEACHING FACE OF TELEVISION   1

1

The Teaching Face: A Historical Perspective   5

KENNETH G. O'BRYAN

Television's Perceived Promise   6
Educating with Television   6
Rise of Networks and Consortia   14
The Past Made Present   15
References   16

2

Current Emphases and Issues
in Planned Programming for Children   19

BARBARA FOWLES MATES

Current Trends in Producing Children's Educational Programs   20
Current Concerns and Issues   26
Conclusions   30
References   30

3

Content Development for Children's Television Programs   33

VALERIE CRANE

Content and Format of Different Types of Children's Programming   33
Factors Influencing the Development of Children's Programs   36
Summary and Conclusions   46
References   47

4

Effects of Planned Television Programming   49

BRUCE A. WATKINS, ALETHA HUSTON-STEIN, AND JOHN C. WRIGHT

Cognitive Skills   49
Prosocial Behavior   56
The Process of Learning from Television   60
Enhancing Children's Learning from Television   63
Conclusion   65
References   66

5

Children, Television, and Social Class Roles:
The Medium as an Unplanned Educational Curriculum   71

GORDON L. BERRY

Television as a Communicator of Social Class Lifestyles   72
Social Learning and Television: Representations of Social Class Roles 74
Television as an Unplanned Curriculum   78
References   81

6

Realities of Change

83

SAUL ROCKMAN

Educating with Television 84
Decisions and Influence 87
Funding: The Ultimate Political Issue 89
Technology and Change 94
References 97

7

The Future of Television's Teaching Face

99

PETER J. DIRR

Three Aspects of Television's Teaching Face 99
Projections for the Future 100
Unanswered Questions 104
References 108

Part II
THE VIOLENT FACE OF TELEVISION

109

8

Television Violence: A Historical Perspective

113

ELI A. RUBINSTEIN

Early Background 113
The Eisenhower Commission 114
The Surgeon General's Program of Research 115
Other Early Research on Television Violence 118
The Consensus on the Effects of Television Violence 120
Public Campaigns against Television Violence 121
Policy Changes 123
Conclusion 125
References 125

9

New Emphases in Research on the Effects of Television and Film Violence

GEORGE COMSTOCK

New Emphases in Research on the Effects
of Television and Film Violence   129

The Emerging Evidence   129
The Present State of Knowledge   131
The Psychology of Entertainment and Behavior   137
Emerging Directions in Research   141
Conclusion   143
References   144

10

The Violent Face of Television and Its Lessons

GEORGE GERBNER AND LARRY GROSS

The Violent Face of Television and Its Lessons   149

Television and Society   149
Concerns about Violence   154
Teaching the Social Order   155
Coping with Power   160
References   162

11

Concomitants of Television Violence Viewing in Children

MONROE M. LEFKOWITZ AND L. ROWELL HUESMANN

Concomitants of Television Violence Viewing in Children   163

Concomitants of Viewing Violence   164
The Processing of Observed Violence   171
Summary and Conclusions   176
References   178

12

Some of the People Some of the Time—But Which People? Televised Violence and Its Effects

AIMÉE DORR AND PETER KOVARIC

Some of the People Some of the Time—But Which People?
Televised Violence and Its Effects   183

Kinds of Effects and Measures and Their Import   184
Methods for Studying Individual Differences   184
Individual Difference Variables   186
Evaluation of Studies of Individual Differences   193
Implications for Practice and Policy   195
References   196

13

The Political Environment for Change 201

PERCY H. TANNENBAUM AND WENDY A. GIBSON

Background and Setting 202
Points of Intervention 208
Some Remaining Thoughts 216
References 217

14

Research Findings and Social Policy 219

ALBERTA E. SIEGEL

Research and Its Utilization 220
Causes for Television Industry Responses to Research 222
Television Reform 226
Social Change and Satisfaction 230
References 230

Part III

THE SELLING FACE OF TELEVISION 233

15

Children's Television Advertising: History of the Issue 237

RICHARD P. ADLER

The Evolution of Children's Programming and Advertising 238
Development of the Children's Television Advertising Issue 240
The Emergence of Research on Children's Television Advertising 245
References 248

16

Children and Television Advertising:
Policy Issues, Perspectives, and the Status of Research 251

JOHN R. ROSSITER

The Nature of Policy Issues 251
An Analysis of Policy Issues to Date 255
The Status of Research 266
Summary and Outlook 269
References 271

17

The Nature of Television Advertising to Children   273

F. EARLE BARCUS

The Amount of Time Devoted to Advertising   274
The Types of Products Advertised to Children   275
Selling Techniques in Children's Advertising   276
Appeals in Children's Television Advertising   279
Value Lessons in Children's Advertising   281
Ethical and Other Issues in Children's Television Advertising   282
Summary   284
References   284

18

Effects of Television Advertising on Children   287

CHARLES K. ATKIN

Impact of Advertising on Product Preferences   288
Nutrition Learning from Food Advertising   294
Side Effects of Children's Advertising   297
Effects of Noncommercial Spot Messages   302
Implications of Research Findings for Advertising Regulation   302
References   303

19

Individual Differences in Children's Responses
to Television Advertising   307

ELLEN WARTELLA

Children's Attention to Television Advertising   308
Children's Comprehension of Television Advertising   312
Effects of Television Advertising on Product Decision Making   318
Summary   319
References   320

20

The Politics of Change   323

ROBERT B. CHOATE

Development   323
The Present   333
References   336

21

The Future Is Inevitable: But Can It Be Shaped in the Interest of Children? 339

EMILIE GRIFFIN

Quantitative and Qualitative Change	340
Influences of Advertising on Programming	341
The Future of Advertising	343
Reprise	351
References	352

Index *353*

List of Contributors

Numbers in parentheses indicate the pages on which authors' contributions begin.

*RICHARD P. ADLER (237), Motion Picture/Television Division, Department of Theater Arts, University of California, Los Angeles, Los Angeles, California 90024

CHARLES K. ATKIN (287), Department of Communication, Michigan State University, East Lansing, Michigan 48824

F. EARLE BARCUS (273), School of Public Communication, Boston University, Boston, Massachusetts 02215

GORDON L. BERRY (71), Graduate School of Education, University of California, Los Angeles, Los Angeles, California 90024

ROBERT B. CHOATE (323), Council on Children, Media and Merchandising, Washington, D.C. 20036

GEORGE COMSTOCK (129), Newhouse Communications Research Center, Syracuse University, Syracuse, New York 13210

†VALERIE CRANE (33), Media Division, Public Affairs Research Institute, Wellesly, Massachusetts 02181

PETER J. DIRR (99), Education Office, Corporation for Public Broadcasting, Washington, D.C. 20036

*425 Seale Avenue, Palo Alto, California 94301
†Present address: Research Communications Associates, Chestnut Hill, Massachusetts 02167

AIMÉE DORR (183), Annenberg School of Communications, University of Southern California, Los Angeles, California 90007

GEORGE GERBNER (149), Annenberg School of Communications, University of Pennsylvania, Philadelphia, Pennsylvania 19174

WENDY A. GIBSON (201), Institute of Child Development, University of Minnesota, Minneapolis, Minneapolis, Minnesota 55455

EMILIE GRIFFIN (339), 110 Audley Street, Kew Gardens, New York 11415

LARRY GROSS (149), Annenberg School of Communications, University of Pennsylvania, Philadelphia, Pennsylvania 19174

L. ROWELL HUESMANN (163), Department of Psychology, University of Illinois at Chicago Circle, Chicago, Illinois 60680

ALETHA HUSTON-STEIN (49), Department of Human Development, University of Kansas, Lawrence, Kansas 66044

PETER KOVARIC (183), Annenberg School of Communications, University of Southern California, Los Angeles, California 90007

MONROE M. LEFKOWITZ (163), State of New York, Office of Mental Health, Albany, New York 12229

BARBARA FOWLES MATES (19), Department of Communication Arts, C. W. Post Center, Long Island University, Greenvale, New York 11548

KENNETH G. O'BRYAN (5), Addiction Research Foundation, Toronto, Ontario, M5S 2S1 Canada

SAUL ROCKMAN (83), Agency for Instructional Television, Bloomington, Indiana 47401

JOHN R. ROSSITER (251), Graduate School of Business, Columbia University, New York, New York 10027

ELI A. RUBINSTEIN (113), Department of Psychology, University of North Carolina at Chapel Hill, Chapel Hill, North Carolina 27514

ALBERTA E. SIEGEL (219), Department of Psychiatry, Stanford University Medical School, Stanford, California 94305

PERCY H. TANNENBAUM (201), Graduate School of Public Policy, University of California, Berkeley, Berkeley, California 94720

ELLEN WARTELLA (307), Institute of Communications Research, University of Illinois at Urbana–Champaign, Champaign, Illinois 61820

* BRUCE A. WATKINS (49), Department of Communications, University of California, San Diego, La Jolla, California 92033

JOHN C. WRIGHT (49), Department of Human Development, University of Kansas, Lawrence, Kansas 66044

* Present address: Department of Communication, The University of Michigan, Ann Arbor, Michigan 48109

Preface

Young children have been characterized as innocent, naive, and curious. Television, on the other hand, has been thought to be a teacher, a corrupter, a relaxer, and a time waster. Just what television does for, to, or in collaboration with children is now receiving considerable attention from researchers, citizens, and policymakers. Yet, the field has been fragmented by the breadth of issues considered and the spectrum of backgrounds and agendas of the interested parties. As a result, there has been no single source that could introduce one to the various "complexions" of the field, its research, and its issues. Authoritative mentors, a well-equipped research library, and a wide-ranging line of correspondence were needed by anyone attempting to piece it together. Few have access to all these ingredients—either frustrating their pursuit of the field or leaving them with only a pinpoint view of it. This book was begun with the intention of ameliorating that situation.

We have pursued our goal by considering what we like to call the three faces of television content—teaching, violence, and selling. In contrast to some other faces we might have chosen, these three have active research and public policy bases. They have a history, a present, and a future, and we can say something about what they mean to children's lives. Historically, instructional uses of television were the first to command the attention of researchers and policymakers. By the mid-1960s we realized that entertainment programming could also teach and, for a variety of reasons, we turned our attention primarily to the instructional capabilities of televised violence and what we could do about them. Finally, we have begun to consider commercial advertising directed toward children. While the "hottest" policy action right now is in the area of chilren and advertising, policy issues and actions also abound in the other two areas. In all three areas, there is ongoing production and research with actual or potential relevance for both production and policy.

To discuss research, production, and policy for the three faces of television, we have been fortunate to obtain the cooperation and time of people who have considerable expertise and experience in each area. Most are academic researchers who have strings of traditional publications to their names, but they are also people who have participated in one way or another in the production and policymaking processes. Also represented are people who are researchers or managers in production groups, consumer lobbyists, and advertising agency executives. Together, the authors represent a large part, although clearly not all, of the spectrum of backgrounds and agendas of people who work in these areas. We have organized their contributions into three sections (faces, if you will)—teaching, violence, and selling. Each section begins with a review of the history of the area and then moves sequentially through current emphases, content and production, effects, individual differences in effects, and the politics of change. Each section then ends with a look toward the future.

The *historical* chapter identifies and discusses key events in past research, practice, policy, and advocacy for that face of television. The *current emphases* chapter picks up this time-line at the point where contemporary issues come into focus. The *content* chapter describes current programming or advertising characteristics, changes in these over time, present patterns of content consumption, production methods, the decision-making process, and the guidelines that influence such decisions. On the basis of an in-depth literature review, the *effects* chapter presents what is known about the effects of content on the child viewer. The *individual differences* chapter extends the effects of content to dimensions such as age, sex, social class, ethnicity, and viewing patterns. Both the effects and individual differences chapters identify and discuss critical research questions. The *politics of change* chapter examines strategies used by different participants in the change process and considers the contributions of research to this process. A concluding chapter then looks toward the *future* of research, practice, policy, and production for each face of television. We hope that the consistent structure of the chapters in the three sections of the book will lend itself to meaningful comparisons— whether among comparative ancestries, current emphases, or any of the other five topics.

Many people have contributed, directly or indirectly, to this book. We are naturally indebted to the authors. They are first-class formulators of questions and inquiries themselves, and they took the time to produce an original contribution that might both educate and excite the reader. Our respective institutions, Davidson College and The Annenberg School of Communications at the University of Southern California, and our colleagues there and throughout the "invisible college," provided intellectual and moral, as well as tangible, support. In the last category we are particularly grateful to Agnes Uy, who ably and cheerfully supervised the typing and organization of the entire manuscript. With equal cheerfulness and skill, Nancy Catron developed an effective computer indexing program and translated chapter entries to meet computer needs. Other students provided valuable and perceptive insights into preparing the book title and manuscript.

Both of us feel a special indebtedness to Gerald S. Lesser, Director of the Center for Research in Children's Television at Harvard University. He served as an admired and admirable colleague and mentor of one editor (AD) for 6 years. For the other (ELP), the study opportunity he provided, his supportive insights, and his suggested avenues of inquiry proved central to piecing together the "mosaic" that has emerged in this book as three television faces experienced by children. Finally, we acknowledge the support of our spouses and children, who were, in fact, occasionally given last consideration as we worked to complete this book. Their understanding acceptance of such a fate, their loving emotional support, and their assumption of household chores and child care responsibilities are recognized and very much appreciated by us.

Sharing has also been very much a part of the book for us, the editors. It began a number of years ago when one of us (ELP) went to Harvard to learn about children and television and found that such learning could best happen when AD and her colleagues shared a wealth of unpublished and widely scattered materials. It continued when ELP decided that he wanted such information more easily available for others interested in the field and asked AD to join in such an endeavor. And it has persisted to the completion of this volume. With such sharing, we naturally did an Alphonse and Gaston routine about who should be first editor. In the end, first went to him who conceived that such a book ought to exist.

Children and the Faces of Television

Teaching, Violence, Selling

Part I

THE TEACHING FACE
OF TELEVISION

A child experiences. A child learns. Some learning experiences were planned in advance; others occurred simply because the child was there—experiencing behavior, attitudes, joys, and fears. With television, the child experiences and, again, the child learns. When the teaching is an unplanned by-product of the child's having "been there," we call it socialization, incidental learning, or "unplanned educational television." When the teaching is planned, we call it instructional or educational television. This section on the teaching face of television will focus primarily on programming that intends to instruct and is designed to be viewed in school (instructional television) or at home (educational television). There will be only some minor forays into the planned instructional uses of programming—usually commercial—that is not intended to instruct.

The section begins with O'Bryan carefully tracing the growth of televised teaching from its seedling stage, as a part of commercial television, to its flowering stage within both the Public Broadcasting Service and the schools. He outlines the two profiles of television—the master teacher and the high-quality, entertaining educator—and discusses the relative predominance of each profile at different points in time. O'Bryan finds imaginative parallel between the first walk on the moon and the initial walk on Sesame Street, and he creatively considers the aspects of national need, technology, and faith, which he finds common to these two events.

Mates' contemporary chapter focuses more closely on the high-qual-

ity entertaining educator concept. Her discussion is in two parts. In the first part, on current trends, she describes the Children's Television Workshop Model and the hallmark pattern it established for the production of educational programs. She then takes a more comprehensive look at the production process for successful educational programs, particularly the role of research. In the second part, on current concerns and issues, she considers the potential drawbacks of a teaching-while-entertaining format and the criticism that television learning is too passive a behavior. Her attention then moves to issues such as financing, and the relationship between television and the tradition of literacy.

Crane's goal is to enable the reader to understand "the process of content development in programs prepared for children" [p. 33]. At the outset, she describes different types of content and format found in the entire range of programming viewed by children—commercial, educational, and instructional. She then takes a close look at the process of content development and how it is affected by the funding source, the target audience, and the production team. Fully recognizing that she is reviewing an imperfect world, she pinpoints and comments on areas in which greater care and attention will facilitate constructive change in the content available to children.

The Watkins, Huston-Stein, and Wright chapter brings a shift in focus from the production of television content designed to teach to the effects of such content on children. These authors review research on cognitive, prosocial, and attitudinal effects, giving special attention to evaluations of the pacesetting Sesame Street. To explain how television can achieve such learning effects, they examine the concepts of additive exposure and of active processing and selection, the potential contribution made to learning by television form as well as content, and the more general notion of learning media codes. They conclude with a look at both production and environmental variables which have the potential to enhance a child's learning from television.

The title of Berry's chapter clearly indicates the specific avenue he will follow. His chapter, in contrast with the "planned" teaching emphasis in previous chapters, examines television's "unplanned educational curriculum" about individual differences in social class roles. Lower socioeconomic status roles, especially those for minorities, are highlighted. Viewing existing depictions of social class roles from the perspectives of socially desirable behaviors, socially successful behaviors, and behaviors which promote self-esteem, he finds an "audio-visual deficit"—the absence of a balanced representation of lifestyles—and he ponders its contribution to social class differences.

Rockman discovers within his politics of change palette fewer bright, attention-commanding colors than he would expect to find in the corresponding chapters about television's violent and selling faces. He begins by dealing with this contrast and the reasons why he believes it exists. Moving to the nature of political decisions and influence, he finds that adults hold decision-making power in the world of children's television and that the greatest power may ultimately reside with the funder. Several funding arrangements are reviewed and critiqued, and Rockman takes an informed, careful look at their effects on content decision making and their promise for use in developing future instructional programming. He concludes by reviewing the ramifications of technological change.

Crystal balls never come equipped with guarantees of accuracy, and Dirr is well aware of this limitation as he looks toward the future. Like Rockman, he knows quite well the impact technological advances have had on televised teaching. So he couples his projections with a discussion of several unanswered questions—including those on technological change—which make it difficult to project. His chapter begins with a definitional framework of three types of teaching with television, for each of which he sees a place in the teaching face of the future. High-quality programming, technologically sophisticated children, teachers facing new challenge, and a new language and grammar in the schools—these are some of the elements he finds in what he predicts will be decades of turmoil and change.

1

The Teaching Face:
A Historical Perspective

KENNETH G. O'BRYAN

In 1969 two significant events took place: Neil Armstrong set foot on the moon, and *Sesame Street* went to air. Each arose from closely connected points of origin, and both were the culmination of enormously expensive national efforts. Although the costs of the space program dwarfed those of eductional television, the relatively huge investments involved in each effort reflected America's reaction to the threat of Sputnik 1 and to the challenge of new technology. Neither effort has been equalled in scope or significance in the decade since.

What made reaching the moon possible and what prompted the creation of *Sesame Street* were almost identical—a national need to succeed, the development of the required technology, the availability of funds in relative abundance, and an abiding faith in the rightfulness of the enterprise. That faith is no longer so secure, the funds no longer flow, the technology has advanced beyond the need, and the need itself has been severely questioned. What happened to the faith, the funds, the technology, and the need is the subject of this chapter, at least insofar as it applies to the teaching face of children's television.

CHILDREN AND THE FACES OF TELEVISION: *Teaching, Violence, Selling*

Television's Perceived Promise

Two years after Sputnik ignited, the American educator Charles Siep-mann (1958) wrote, "Education needs television, and that desperately. . . . Television, we hold, while not the *deus ex machina* to solve the crisis, is one indispensable tool that we can and must use to extricate ourselves from the grave trouble we are in, but of which all too few still seem to be aware [p. 2]." What was the crisis and why did Siepmann and a horde of educators place such strong faith in the new technology of television for its solution?

Essentially, the educational "crisis" of the 1950s arose from the over-crowding of schools, the shortage of teachers, the low quality of teacher training, and the fear that American education had somehow fallen behind the competitive world in quality and effectiveness. The faith in television as a technology was as much a reflection of the tenor of the times as it was a rational understanding of the strengths and limitations of the medium, its delivery systems, its creative personnel, and its ability to carry educational content.

Indispensable or not, educational television was not without its critics from the earliest stages of its development. The new medium was accused of being robot-like, a danger to the employment and security of teachers, and a robber of the personal, one-on-one relationships that almost all educators believed to be the basis of quality education. The lack of true interaction between the master teacher on the television screen and the individual learner and the inability of the master teacher to vary the pace of the lesson were considered crucial educational prob-lems.

Even more esoteric criticisms were leveled as well. Educational tele-vision was thought to be somehow undemocratic because it created authoritarian figures who directed the activities of children while far removed from their presence.

Costs, the problems of scheduling, the recurrent belief that whatever television could do a film might do better, and the very human fear that master teachers and high-quality educational productions might make an average, regular classroom teacher look incompetent and dull, rounded out most of the major criticisms. Protagonists of educational television might feel that, with minor exceptions, little seems to have changed.

Educating with Television

The teaching face of children's television began with the first com-mercial broadcasts of the new medium in 1940, when puppet shows and short programs for children were broadcast along with cooking demonstrations, sports, news, and the movies on television. The intervention of World War II and the subsequent freeze on licensing by the Federal Communications Commission (FCC) in 1948 delayed the development of more formal educational television (ETV) for both children and adults until two major breakthroughs occurred in 1952: (a) The reservation by the FCC of 242 television channels for education; and (b) the establishment by the Ford Foundation of the Educational Radio and Television Center, later (in 1958) to become the National Educational Television (NET).

The FCC's action was not so extravagantly supportive of ETV as it might at first have seemed. Most of the channels were UHF (ultra high frequency)—a frequency that almost all television sets of the time were unable to receive. Furthermore, the few VHF (very high frequency) channels allotted to educational broadcasters were not usually found in the major market areas. As a result, ETV had a broadcast technology that few could receive. Its producers had little or no experience in the programming needs of its clients, and there was an early shortage of funds. Also, the first producers endured substantial internal criticism and heavy competition from commercial interests whose primary goals were entertainment and profit. Nevertheless, the technology was new and exciting, the need was thought to exist, and there was no lack of supporters. By 1953 the first ETV station was broadcasting, and by the end of the 1950s, 44 stations were on the air.

From the very beginning of educational television, two distinct profiles of the teaching face emerged. One side—the first to be emphasized—grew out of the belief that master television teachers supported by classroom custodians were the answer to overcrowded schools with undertrained or low-competency teachers. The other, now stronger, profile owes its shape and character to the proposition that educational television should be created with the same or better production values and skill levels as commercial television and should be thought of more as an aid to, rather than a replacement of, the classroom teacher. The progressive but still incomplete integration of these profiles has lent modern educational television for children its unique aspect.

Master Teaching on Television

In-school instructional television can be divided into two main characteristic approaches. One of these depends on the use of a closed circuit system in which the central studio of a school or a closely grouped number of schools broadcast a master lesson to the classrooms; the other is a telecast from the ETV station.

In the days before the advent of videotape and telechains, the tele-lesson was shot live, often with very limited equipment and poorly trained production personnel whose output featured the ubiquitous big talking face. Variations in shots and production values generally tended to end at wide shots of the teacher working at the blackboard, holding up a picture or a piece of apparatus, or demonstrating at a bench. Such production techniques as background music, special sound effects, and close-up explorations of materials were generally absent. Many of the special techniques of television were either unknown or ignored as being irrelevant to the instructional content of the tele-lesson. By the commercial standards of the time, and certainly by current standards for successful television, instructional television programming broke most of the tenets of television production.

Instructional television (ITV), however, had the advantage inherent in the novelty of the medium. It intrigued (and probably taught) almost a generation of children who were born before television broadcasts began. At the very least, ITV appeared to do no worse than the regular classroom teacher (Siepmann, 1958). Its supporters were even sure that new technology just around the corner would solve the remaining problems.

For indeed there were problems. Master teachers, it turned out, were not necessarily masterly television performers. In fact, many were uncomfortable in front of the cold glassy eye. Even though the class may have been present in the studio, many master teachers missed the natural warmth of children's reactions, on which their success as teachers had been based.

Research on instructional television in the period to 1960 was focused primarily on the medium's ability to compete with the classroom teacher. Results were generally inconclusive. In an exhaustive review, Kumata (1960) concluded that few differences could be found between television and teacher in terms of the target audience's retention of knowledge. The student's motivation was critical to success whichever approach was used. Kumata also concluded that skillful preparation and careful integration of the subject matter with the teaching style were key factors.

These less-than-shattering findings were similar to those of Schramm (1962) in his review of 393 studies. Two-thirds of the research comparing live teaching with mediated instruction found no difference in amount of resultant learning. Three out of every five of the remaining studies indicated that television did better than the teacher; the other two indicated the opposite was the case.

What did emerge from the early studies was a clear indication that ITV was serving the elementary school audience much more effectively than either the high school or the college-level students. It was at its best in presenting math, science, and social studies lessons and was weaker when dealing with literature and the humanities. In 1980 the research face of ITV looked much the same as it did in 1960.

It is still hypothetical (no one has tested the proposition) that a key reason for the lack of ultimate success of closed circuit instruction was not that the master teacher responded badly to the camera's needs, but that the camera could not react to the teacher. The argument that master teachers were robots may have hit the wrong side of the target in that automation (the technology that the teacher was actually teaching to) rather than students was on the receiver's end of the lesson.

Another major problem that the early closed-circuit programming failed to overcome was the ego of the nonmaster teacher (Berkman, 1977; Gordon, 1970). Explicitly developed to provide a solution to actual over-crowding of classrooms and to perceive incompetency in instruction, the ITV approach was resented by the nonmasters who felt relegated to second-class status, as indeed they were. The ready integration of the lesson into the regular classroom pattern was not forthcoming, and the teachers thought the system was unfair and unreasonable competition.

Of all the problems of early instructional television, the teacher's fear of being upstaged and eventually replaced by television has proven the most difficult to combat. Palmer (1978) noted that overcoming this resistance was a major task for Children's Television Workshop in its development of both Sesame Street and The Electric Company; almost all current ETV broadcasters are very careful not to indicate any "teaching superiority" of the hosts of their in-school productions over what might be expected from regular teachers. Actually—unlike estrogen—ETV has cost few, if any, teaching jobs and probably has not constituted a significant threat to the teacher's hegemony in the classroom or to the level of respect he or she gains from students.

Nevertheless, master teaching as an educational process largely failed in the initial period of educational television, probably because, as Palmer (1978) pointed out, instructional television could not achieve widespread and effective use by *fiat*. Instead, it had to "stand up to the test of the school as a market place of various sources and strategies of teaching. It had to be perceived as a tool with sufficient payoff to warrant the schools' and the teacher's investment of capital, time, energy [p. 125]." Palmer might have added here that it must do all of that and at the same time be competitive with commercial television or lose credibility by com-parison.

Closed-circuit master teacher television did not and probably cannot reach such a level of credibility. By the end of 1959, it was falling far behind the production values of commercial broadcast television, and it is now relatively rarely used in schools.

Education and High-Quality Production

The other profile, the educational television broadcast, was ham-pered in its early development by substantial technological problems. The lack of receivers for UHF and the scarcity of VHF stations prevented widespread broadcast reception. The growth of cable companies and the development and distribution of videotape and playback equipment were still far off. Scheduling of programs for early users was uncertain and fraught with technical difficulties. Consequently, initial growth was stunted.

But ETV had the potential for a better future. It could, and would, develop a production quality that would match and occasionally exceed that of the commercial networks. It would also be able to use the medium to its capacity rather than confine it to the talking face and actions of the master teacher. What it lacked then was a delivery system and also a philosophy. It has almost overcome the first problem now, but the second continues to be, perhaps, its major flaw.

The Delivery System. The most adventurous early attempt at a broadcast delivery system was the creation of the Mid-West Project on Airborne Televised Instruction. Aircraft circling overhead transmitted programs to schools in a six-state area. Technically, the project, which was heavily funded by the Ford Foundation, worked. It continued until the mid-1960s, when new methods of transmission and reception began to render it obsolete.

Ability to transmit and potential to receive ETV programs did not, however, solve the problems associated with either the lack of television sets in schools or the resistance of the teachers, principals, and administrators (the "gatekeepers") to the programs. Moreover, children had, to some extent, habituated to the novelty of television in schools.

At home children were showing an almost overwhelming tendency to reject educational television in favor of commercial programming. By 1960 they were devoting approximately one-sixth of their waking hours to commercial television (Schramm, 1960). Schramm reported that he and his colleagues could find no evidence that children were using educational television above a very minimal amount and that, compared to commercial television, interest in ETV was negligible. Worse, its use declined from its very small base in the preteen years to near extinction in late adolescence.

Clearly, broadcast programming in educational television in the first 10 years had failed to capture the interest of the child and had not significantly improved the performance of the student or the teacher, captive though they were in the classroom during in-school telecasting. The problem was no longer a question of technology, but one of educational and production philosophy—and philosophy had lagged far behind. The development of a philosophy and a subsequent applied art and science of teaching with television were later to prove to be two of the critical keys to potential success of ETV for children.

An effort to improve the quality and usefulness of programming and to increase the amount of available funding was reflected in the formation of the Eastern Educational Network in 1960. This pattern has been followed down the years by the formation of other networks to achieve similar goals.

Whether improvements in program quality were a direct result of the cooperative ventures or whether they arose out of government initiative, such as the passage of the Educational Facilities Act of 1962, is difficult to determine; but there was a general upgrading of production quality during the early part of the 1960s. Nevertheless, ETV offerings to children continued to lack the vigor and pace that their clients demanded of—and received from—commercial television.

At this time the influence on ETV and the financial support of it by the Ford Foundation had become very substantial. As one result, NET was providing some 10 hours per week of educational programming, focusing three-quarters of it on cultural and public affairs and offering the remaining 2.5 hours per week as children's ETV. However, NET was essentially a procurement agency seeking foreign programming for use in the United States. It was also engaged in contracting with independent producers for American programs. Much of the work done was piecemeal, and production quality was low and inconsistent.

Nevertheless, by 1966 NET was supplying almost half the programming for an average ETV station. State and local production accounted for almost a quarter, and the remainder came from exchanges and films. Very little effort had been devoted to the creation of substantial children's programming. That which did exist was usually low budget, generally inferior, television, as compared with commercial programming, and was of doubtful or negligible educational usefulness.

The Philosophy. In 1967 a major event in the history of educational television occurred with the publication of the Carnegie Commission's (1967) report. In it the Commission recommended the establishment of a Corporation for Public Television and increased state and local support for ETV stations. Its recommendations were adopted and the Corporation for Public Broadcasting (CPB) was formed. This has had far-reaching effects on the teaching face of children's television. It brought on a change in philosophy from one of a largely instructional use of ETV for children to one of educational television as an expander of intellectual horizons and a creator of imagination. It demanded the same attention to production quality as its commercial counterpart and required the same levels of funding and professionalism. Out of it came part of the support for the development of the organization which most reviewers will agree gave credibility to children's educational programming and effectively brought public television into the consciousness of the nation.

Children's Television Workshop (CTW) was formed in 1968, and with it came a new theory and practice of children's television that changed not only the instructional/educational face but also forced the commercial networks to temporarily but significantly upgrade their children's productions. The essence of CTW's success was the recognition that television of any type had to withstand the competition of the market place. That was all that commercial programmers had to achieve for success, but for avowedly instructional television, producers also had to create learning. Though not at all incompatible, these two requisites for success had never been effectively integrated in a children's program. CTW's first program, *Sesame Street,* did so, and set the standards for all children's ETV programming in the ensuing decade.

Sesame Street was, and is, such an important feature of the teaching face of television that no historical perspective aimed at interpreting more recent developments can ignore the effects of its structure in bringing about change in ETV production. *Sesame Street* was founded with a unique blend of unity of purpose, adequate (indeed lavish) finance, high-quality research, professional production talent, educational leadership, a penchant for elaborate instructional design, and an almost universally accepted need.

Unity of purpose was especially important to the program's ultimate success. Unlike NET, the local stations, or the independent producers who had multiple objectives and many options, CTW had a defined target audience. It possessed the unencumbered dollars needed and was able to develop a philosophy and teaching technology with which to reach its audience.

Clearly, in the creation of *Sesame Street* its producers recognized that a working interaction between the best that current commercial television could provide in terms of technical staff, producers, directors, and writers would have to be matched with the best of available specialists in learning, psychology, and teaching. The critical requirement was finding a technique that would create a good mix. No one, then or since, has been able to define or recreate the mix, although the ingredients seem to be well known (Lesser, 1974).

That the mix did occur was obvious from the first broadcast of *Sesame Street.* Perhaps the very bringing together of talent, experience, and knowledge was sufficient in itself, or it may have been the excitement generated by the scope and novelty of the enterprise. Whatever it was, the results surpassed the expectations of almost everyone connected with the project, and it became the focal point of public television.

Arising out of *Sesame Street* came a new awareness of the needs of educational programming for children. Gone were the days of the big talking head or the cheap kid's show. *Sesame Street* and Wall Street were in the same neighborhood and not too far apart. It seemed clear that massive success required equally massive investments of time, talent, and dollars, and that a tough, market-oriented approach to production was necessary to gain big audiences. The CTW's approach included the marshalling of special consultants to advise in-house staff on target audience characteristics and on latest teaching methodologies. Teams of researchers were hired to test scripts and to conduct field research on experimental segments and pilot programs. Thus, formative research in ETV was born, to become a required part of all major productions and an acceptable field of scientific study. Technical specialists were contracted to improve production technology. The forebearers of today's instructional designers were hired to write guidebooks for script writers, and the best available producers, directors, and talent were taken from commercial television.

It all worked, and Sesame Street became the model for the teaching face of children's television. It gave credibility to two profiles in that the instructional profile was clearly present and apparently successful, while the television/entertainment profile was equally present and obviously successful. For the next decade, the Sesame Street model would dominate the funding, planning, and creation of educational television for children.

CTW followed Sesame Street with another big success that also made a major change in the nature of the teaching face of television. Like Sesame Street, The Electric Company, which became public television's only other successful big-audience series, was not designed with the classroom audience in mind. It was originally intended for use as a remedial reading program, with or without the teacher. In some ways it was a return to the master teacher approach since it was created on the premise that television can deliver "pedagogically significant effects through forms not otherwise accessible to the classroom. It can serve as a window on the world, thus providing for vicarious field trips; it can employ film, animation, and technical effects not otherwise available to the teacher [Palmer, 1978, p. 128]."

Indeed it could, and so it did. The Electric Company used a very extensive bag of technical devices to present its content. It was in the forefront of computer animation techniques, and it employed a range of laboratory technology and advanced formative research (O'Bryan, 1973) to design its programs. The Electric Company was, in several ways, a more educationally relevant and instruction-oriented program than Sesame Street, and it, too, became a model for the production and design of ETV.

Both the CTW successes had shared a common look. They brought to the teaching face the hard, brassy, painted features of the very talented big-time show girl. Glitter and glamor abounded, and the pace was very fast; too fast for some educators and producers, who sought a softer, more gentle smile in less frenetic surroundings. They found it in Misterogers Neighborhood.

Fred Rogers has been around for a long time in instructional television. His programs would have been a success with or without CTW, but the controversy that developed over the relative values of CTW's up-front, vigorous style and Misterogers' laid-back, apparent warmth and openness has strengthened educational television for children.

The contrast in styles alone generated imitators and refiners. But unlike CTW with the *Sesame Street* and *The Electric Company* batteries of writers, producers, characters, and consultants, *Misterogers Neighborhood* is an intensely personal show with a very personal message. Nonetheless, it is high-quality television production, partly because of the nature and skill of the host and partly because it obeys the principle that ETV must be as well produced as any other programming if it is to be competitive in the battle for the viewer's willing attention. The controversy on the more appropriate way to present content continues to the present writing and is unlikely to be resolved since it is as much a matter of personal style and taste as it is one of educational television production and design. Both are obviously necessary, as are the variations on their themes that are currently being developed.

Rise of Networks and Consortia

The early 1970s were marked by a surge of interest in television for children arising out of the implications of a number of studies and reports on children's viewing patterns. The growing concern over violence in the commercial media, the anger that consumer lobbies directed toward children's television advertising, and the growth of special action groups such as Action for Children's Television led to demands for more and better children's television for both school and general use. Almost everyone agreed on the need for and desirability of alternatives to the commercial cartoons and adult shows which were the favorite television programs of most children. The key problem was how such programs might be produced and who would create and use them.

Although stations from five major centers (New York, Boston, Washington, D.C., San Francisco, and Los Angeles) had provided the bulk of national programming on educational television, they were thought no longer able to satisfy the demand, and alternatives were sought. The decade of the consortia was about to begin.

Station managers had not been slow to grasp the significance of *Sesame Street's* success, although many may not have understood all of the reasons underlying it. They were generally aware that, with very few exceptions, quality productions cost substantial sums and require very talented and creative production. Moves were made to develop production and distribution consortia that would pool resources and share the outcomes.

National Instructional Television formed nine consortia before becoming the Agency for Instructional Television (AIT). Its mandate was the pooling of resources, including money, leadership, and production experience, to achieve mutually agreed on goals. What was very interesting about AIT's approach was its determination that the subject matter of its programming should represent a real priority of the school systems. It also wanted to ensure that it would provide enough programming to be of significant use and that the content would be "new enough to facilitate change in classroom practice but not so new as to be beyond the grasp of teachers and schools [Carlisle, 1978, p. 45.]" In its aims, AIT's approach was a return to the schoolroom as the expression of the teaching face of ETV. But in its essence it may have signaled a return to the master teacher with the critical differences that now he or she was much more multi-faceted and was the subordinate of the classroom teacher.

Massive increases in the cost per minute of instructional television resulted. Whereas programs had once been made for $1500 per half hour, the cost soon reached $1500 per minute. Quality also improved, and with it came the readiness of stations to buy programs designed for national use. There was also an increase in the willingness of teachers to put the programs into their instructional plan.

The growth in availability and quality of production series such as *Ripples, Inside/Out,* and *Bread and Butterflies* was matched by a major advance in the potential for their use. This arose from the rapid development and general acceptance of big regional networks such as Central Educational Network (CEN) and the Southern Educational Communications Association (SECA). Such networks are broader based than state-wide systems such as the Mississippi Authority for Educational Television or Canada's Ontario Educational Communications Authority. They have supplied library services, engaged in upgrading training programs for writers, producers, and instructional designers, and become involved in group buying. All of this has led to a much wider distribution of programs and to the tendency to centralize funds for more adventurous undertakings than would normally be possible for the average state networks.

The system has been further augmented by the development of the Public Broadcasting Service (PBS). PBS is the umbrella organization for public television licensees in the United States. Its advent led to an increase in children's morning programs from 3 preschool and 1 primary grade program series, at its inception, to 24 program series in 1976–1977. These programs were available for instructional use in the classroom or at home for every level from prekindergarten to college extension (Carlisle, 1978).

The Past Made Present

By 1976–1977 most of the technical problems that had beset the early sculptors of television's teaching face were solved. Microwave transmission, cable-casting, satellite development, and videotape rerecording systems had overcome delivery difficulties and most of the scheduling

questions. Production values in the better children's educational television had exceeded those of most of the offerings of Saturday and Sunday
morning commercial programming.

And yet, with the exception of *Zoom, Sesame Street, The Electric
Company,* and perhaps a few local programs such as TV Ontario's *Polka
Dot Door,* Wilbur Schramm's 1959 survey could be repeated today with
much the same look to the results—only the names have changed.

Very few children choose ETV offerings over those of the commercial
networks. Public television has been able to provide no great teaching
program the equal of *Sesame Street.* Even CTW's much heralded *Feelin'
Good* failed, and TV Ontario's *Saturday Morning Supershow,* a collection
of the top ETV shows broadcast against the Saturday network programs,
did not succeed in drawing a significant audience. *Sesame Street* proved
that effective instructional content was not incompatible with audience
appeal. But like the first walk on the moon, it has been followed, never
repeated.

It is tempting to conclude that the wheel has turned full-circle and
that the best that ETV has managed has been to keep its pace—and its
place—well behind commercial television. But such a conclusion would
be inadequate for ETV *has* become an almost "indispensable tool" for
education, even though the dollars, the need, and the technology have
changed.

Teachers no longer suspect ETV to be a threat to their jobs. Its
teaching face is well known and familiar, although it is not yet a member
of the family. Nor is there a crisis of overcrowding in the schools. In fact,
many schools are emptying, and teachers have never before possessed the
formal qualifications they have today. Although the lavish dollars are no
longer available, there are enough funds for quality programming. The
technology may have surpassed the ability of most writers and producers
to use it to its fullest advantage, but the need remains. Fortunately for
ETV, however, it has changed from a crisis-based replacement of
teachers, at which it probably could never have succeeded, to something
much more within its grasp—the provision of imaginative, creative, and
integrated programming in support of and under the control of the teacher.
In effect, the teaching face of children's television has become a servant
rather than the master of the classroom.

References

Berkman, D. Instructional television: The medium whose future has passed. In J. Ackerman
     & L. Lepsitz (Eds.), *Instructional television: Status and directions.* Englewood Cliffs,
     New Jersey: Educational Technology Publications, 1977.
Carlisle, R. (Ed.). *Patterns of performance: Public broadcasting and education, 1974–1976.*

Washington, D.C.: Office of Educational Activities, Corporation for Public Broadcasting, 1978.

Carnegie Commission. *Public television: A program for action.* New York: Harper & Row, 1967.

Gordon, G. N. *Classroom television.* New York: Hastings House, 1970.

Kumata, H. A decade of teaching by television. In W. Schramm (Ed.), *The Impact of educational television.* Urbana: Univ. of Illinois, 1960.

Lesser, G. S. *Children and television: Lessons from Sesame Street.* New York: Random House, 1974.

O'Bryan, K. G. *Research on eye movements and reading instruction on the Electric Company.* New York: Children's Television Workshop, 1973.

Palmer, E. *The Electric Company* and the school market place. In R. Carlisle (Ed.), *Patterns of performance: Public broadcasting and education, 1974–1976.* Washington, D.C.: Office of Educational Activities, Corporation for Public Broadcasting, 1978.

Schramm, W. Television in the life of the child: Implications for the school. In *New teaching aids for the American classroom.* Washington, D.C.: U.S. Department of Health, Education and Welfare Symposium, 1960.

Schramm, W. What we know about learning from instructional television. In *Educational television: The next ten years.* Stanford, California: Institute for Communication Research, 1962.

Siepmann, C. A. *TV and our school crisis.* New York: Dodd, Mead, 1958.

2

Current Emphases and Issues in Planned Programming for Children

BARBARA FOWLES MATES

The insight shaping the current direction of educational television is that its real competition is popular television programs rather than the classroom teacher. If educational television is to be viable in the classroom or outside of it, it must compete successfully in the eyes of children with *The Flintstones* and *Happy Days*. Today's children develop their expectations of what television should be from watching programs of this type, and they will no longer settle for the "home made" atmosphere of a series like the once-popular *Mr. Wizard*. Recent efforts in educational television are most clearly marked by attempts to combine the attractive approaches of commercial entertainment television with desirable educational content.

The balance of this chapter is devoted to describing these efforts and some of the issues that surround them. Programs designed for *formal* educational use (in-school television) and for *informal* use in homes, day care centers, and the like are both included. The educational effects of entertainment programs and of commercial advertisements are not discussed, although the critical influence of these forms on deliberately educational programs will be explored.

CHILDREN AND THE FACES OF TELEVISION:
Teaching, Violence, Selling

Current Trends in Producing
Children's Educational Programs

The Children's Television Workshop Model

Carrying the attractiveness of commercial entertainment television to the educational setting is not an easy task. Several important elements and procedures are involved in making a successful translation, and it is these which are receiving most emphasis in producing educational programs for children. Most were pioneered by Children's Television Workshop (CTW) in the creation of *Sesame Street*. They were refined in subsequent projects by CTW and by others who borrowed and adapted what has come to be called "The CTW Model" (Palmer, 1978). This is essentially a blueprint for collaboration among a professional television production team of producers, directors, choreographers, and so forth, a research team of psychologists and education specialists, and an advisory team of experts in various aspects of the program's proposed subject matter (Palmer, 1974).

Thus, the model prescribes a departure from the usual ways of producing educational programs for television. *Formal* educational programming—referred to as instructional television (ITV)—has typically been in the hands of educators who were untrained in television production and limited by chronically tight institutional budgets. Long accustomed to the polished appearance of high-budget entertainment programs, children are no longer so attracted by such programming.

Elements of Successful Programs

Several important attributes characterize the production of recent, high-quality educational programs for children. Although not all these features apply to every noteworthy program, they do in general represent the current model for successful production.

Involvement of Experts. Expert advisors play a vital role in the creation of programs. They are more thoroughly versed in the subject matter of a program than even the most conscientious staff members could ever hope to be. Also, they are not directly involved in program production and are therefore likely to maintain greater objectivity. Experts at various levels of theory and application are involved. For example, a recent mathematics series, *The Infinity Factory,* used as consultants both theoretical mathematicians from the Massachusetts Institute of Technology and elementary- and secondary-level classroom teachers. Although such consultant involvement is expensive and time consuming, it pays off in establishing a sound theoretical structure and in assuring that the programs will be useful to classroom teachers and children.

Experts may also be invaluable in assuring acceptance of a series, particularly among educators. For example, CTW's series *The Electric Company* met with much skepticism among classroom teachers, reading experts, and communications theorists who felt that to teach reading via television was inappropriate and confusing (Parker, 1974). Many of these fears were allayed when teachers learned that respected experts in the field had contributed to the series and were serving in a continuing advisory role.

Parents, community leaders, and spokespersons for groups with special programming needs (e.g., Hispanic children, the handicapped, and women) also serve as expert advisors. They can provide information and guidance useful to program staff, and they may also be useful in helping to assure utilization of programs by the community.

A Targeted Viewer. Most current educational programs are designed with a specific audience in mind. This audience may be defined by age group (*Sesame Street*), ethnic group (*Villa Allegre*), achievement level, or a combination of these (*The Electric Company*). The narrowness of the target audience varies a great deal, and viewing outside the target audience range, particularly for programs not aimed at school audiences, is assumed. The nature of the program's goals (e.g., reading, science, emotional growth) will obviously dictate the nature of the target audience to some extent.

According to the CTW model, the needs and abilities of the target audience are assessed before program planning gets underway. The intensity of the assessment will depend on the extent to which this audience has been studied in the past. When *Sesame Street* was first created, little research on 3- to 5-year-olds had been carried out, and the CTW research staff had to study their target audience thoroughly. On the other hand, when *The Electric Company* was being developed, children with reading problems had been the subject of much recent research, and so it was only necessary to test ability in the particular areas the series was intended to cover.

With the proliferation of cable television it seems likely that programs will be produced for increasingly specialized audiences. But given the present broadcast situation, programs which are expensive to produce must defray their high costs by servicing as many children as possible while continuing to meet the special needs of target groups effectively. This is a tricky business, requiring inventive programs which ideally can be understood at many levels simultaneously.

A Realistic Curriculum. Sesame Street demonstrated the effectiveness of having a clear set of educational goals and then developing programming to bring about demonstrable improvement in the viewers' skills in those areas (Ball & Bogatz, 1970). The set of goals chosen for a program must reflect the needs of the target audience, but it is equally vital that the curriculum realistically reflect the limitations of the medium. For example, at first it seemed like a good idea to use *Sesame Street* to teach young children about common dangers in their environment such as crossing against the light. But this would typically call for a depiction of the dangerous behavior—which might be imitated—and the harmful consequences—which might be frightening. Goals of this type were therefore dropped from the original curriculum (Lesser, 1974) and only later added in cautious experimental presentations. Clever, experienced writers and producers can often stretch the limits of what can effectively be accomplished with television, but the primary emphasis now certainly is on exploiting the qualities of television as television (see Fowles, 1976, for an example using metalinguistic principles).

An Interpretable Curriculum. The curriculum lays out exactly what is to be accomplished by the program. The CTW model suggests that the items in the curriculum be stated in terms of *behavioral* goals. Briefly, a behavioral goal is expressed in terms of what the child who views the program should be able to *do* after viewing. For example, a hypothetical behavioral goal might be: "The child can list six undesirable outcomes of smoking cigarettes."

Such goals may sound trivial and overly concrete to those not familiar with their use. Obviously, the intention of the goal stated above is that the child should understand that smoking is harmful and should internalize a negative attitude about it. But how can the producers go about effectively presenting these general ideas and attitudes to children? By dealing in specifics they have a better chance of reaching children, who are concrete thinkers, and later determining whether or not they have succeeded.

Behavioral goals have several advantages. They force the persons who write the goals to be concrete and specific, they translate directly into test items (e.g. "Tell me six reasons why somebody should *not* smoke cigarettes"), and they suggest how the goal should be presented in the program. For this particular goal, the requirement that the child be able to *list* the outcomes suggests program content stressing *enumeration* of them. A different goal, such as: "The child can discuss the negative effects of smoking cigarettes," might suggest a presentation with more depth and less repetition.

For some programs a "writers' notebook" is created which serves to build a bridge from the curriculum document to the script writer's imagination by offering detailed suggestions and examples of appropriate ways to realize a particular goal with the target age group. Although some topic areas in educational television do not ultimately lend themselves well to curricula stated in behavioral terms and concretized in a writers' notebook, it still usually helps when producing a program to attempt to formulate such goals for its design. The current emphasis is certainly on having a set of specific, concrete educational aims rather than vague good intentions or general aims for educational programs for children.

Research. Research like that typically employed in the development of high-quality educational products (Baker & Shultz, 1972) was virtually unknown as a component in the development of educational television programs until a decade ago. Since it is expensive and time-consuming, a thorough research undertaking is still not typical for children's programs, but it is generally seen as desirable and even critical to the success of a program.

While many kinds of research can contribute to program development, the most useful is *formative research*. It has the exclusive aim of providing information which will help improve the quality and effectiveness of the program and is a part of the actual process of creating a program. Thus, formative research has certain characteristics not typical of traditional forms of psychological or educational research (Palmer, 1974). It must be planned and carried out quickly and therefore generally must be relatively simple: It must involve minimal preparation of special materials such as tests and be relatively small-scale. The point of a formative research effort is to gather sufficient information from careful testing and cautious interpretation to allow for practical decision making.

The role of formative research in the development and improvement of educational programs for children has evolved as the programs themselves have evolved. As programs have moved toward a more precise "fit" between teaching goals and formats for their presentation, research methods have become more precise in their ability to study the influence of various aspects of format on such viewer outcomes as attention, comprehension, grasp of processes, and retention (e.g., Anderson & Levin, 1976; Flagg, Housen, & Lesser, 1978). Refinement of programs and formative research methods have a leapfrogging effect on one another.

One good illustration of the role of formative research is how eye-movement research was used to improve The Electric Company, a series designed to teach beginning reading to 7- to 10-year-old children with reading problems. Eye-movement recording allows one to trace what a viewer looks at during a television program. It was a natural for use with this series because it was crucial to know where on the screen the viewers would tend to look when print was presented.

Early use of this method revealed that print at the bottom of the screen was easy to ignore and that action, particularly that near the center of the screen, drew attention (O'Bryan & Silverman, 1972). When print was placed near the center of the screen, close to the focus of the dramatic action, attention to it was maximized. Scanning print from left to right, as in reading, was then encouraged with television production techniques emphasizing process and movement and was documented to be effective through eye-movement recordings (O'Bryan & Silverman, 1973). Thus, a research method provided information which helped producers move from a phase of little control over viewers' visual responses to one of significantly greater ability to predict and control.

Currently, research of this formative type is the most interesting and innovative aspect of research connected with children's television (see Crane's chapter in this volume for more specific information on the formative research process). The dominant trend in formative research (insofar as this informal and usually unpublished work can be documented and summarized) is to attempt to identify the role of each element in a program sequence and the effects of element interrelationships on such viewer outcomes as attention, comprehension, and behavior change (see Bernstein, 1978, for one interesting example).

Although formative research is clearly the most pertinent to program development, other work can also make some contribution. Studies that consider more general issues about children and television, such as the general cognitive skills that television techniques can encourage (e.g., Salomon, 1972), can stimulate programming ideas. Studying the social and emotional outcomes of television viewing (e.g., Stein & Friedrich, 1972) can suggest changes in content emphases. Investigating the competence of the medium as a teacher, the relationship between the medium of presentation and the learning outcomes (Collins, 1970; Ide, 1974; Parker, 1974), and the cognitive and emotional significance of receiving substantial doses of one's information from television (Olson & Bruner, 1974; Salomon, 1970) may not contribute directly to the improvement of any particular program, but it will clarify the broader implications of teaching with television.

Summative research, in contrast to the broader work which I have just discussed, is research designed to evaluate an entire series for its educational effectiveness; it, too, can contribute to program development and utilization. It can provide information to demonstrate to funding agencies that a program is worth supporting (or not worth continuing); it can demonstrate to skeptical teachers, parents, and others that a program has some value; and it can provide credibility for the program before the public-at-large and the media. Summative research uses carefully selected samples, skillfully designed tests, and complex statistical analyses. Therefore, it can be extremely expensive and is not feasible in many situations. The summative evaluations of *Sesame Street's* first two seasons (Ball & Bogatz, 1970; Bogatz & Ball, 1971) are the prototypes for such research.

Large-scale teacher surveys for a particular program or group of programs (e.g., Herriott & Leibert, 1972; Leibert, 1973) can also be helpful. Questionnaires can explore teachers' attitudes toward a program, their criticisms of it, their methods of utilizing it, and their patterns of using and not using it. Such information can help to alter a program or teachers' understanding of a program in order to increase its acceptance and appropriate utilization in the schools.

Teaching Strategies for Television

Using Formats Constructively. The important thing about children's television today is that television itself has become an important *plus* in teaching rather than a limiting factor. Formats have been matched to teaching goals so that the strengths of a particular type of television presentation can be used to a specific educational end. For example, Kentucky Educational Television (KET) designed a program called *Contract* which borrows the format of the commercial television game shows popular with children. Built into this game, as in many of the "real" shows, is a necessity for the contestants to read simple passages. Thus, this program polishes reading skills and capitalizes on a format which encourages the viewer to participate by competing with the on-screen contestant.

Through research (e.g., the eye-movement research described earlier) and experience it has become possible to design the television stimulus in such a way as to control viewer response better, at least in certain areas. This ability should increase as research techniques are refined and should be expanding from more obvious areas such as reading and visual search strategies to problem solving and other mental processes which can eventually be given audiovisual analogs via television.

Teaching with Entertainment. Another important aspect of current educational television is the use of successful entertainment production techniques in the service of teaching. Earlier educational programs either were devoid of attempts to entertain or created an artificial and uncomfortable alliance between fun and instruction by inserting a few supposedly amusing elements into an otherwise straightforward educational context. The current marriage of teaching and entertainment is the result of two dovetailing insights. First, children, particularly younger children, find learning to be a gratifying and entertaining experience for its own sake. As long as material is presented in a clear and well-paced fashion, it is not necessary to add sugar coating. Second, many devices employed to entertain children, such as music, rhyme, simple narratives, and various forms of animation, are natural teaching devices needing only appropriate content (Lesser, 1974). Since these devices have the advantage of being familiar to children, new information will be comfortably fitted into an old pattern. This increases learning efficiency (Palmer, 1978).

Current Concerns and Issues

Children's Expectations

Naturally, it has been suggested that it is dangerous to confuse entertainment and education too much, particularly when such programs are brought into the schools. The fear is that children will expect that education should be this way and will not tolerate the necessarily less entertaining teaching that often must go on in the classroom (Carlisle, 1978).

The most obvious way to try to confirm these fears is by measuring children's attention span. Some research has been carried out to determine whether or not viewing fast-paced, entertaining educational programs affects attention span. Salomon (1974) found that viewing *Sesame Street* had an adverse effect on persistence in a tedious school-like task for Israeli children. But the applicability of this finding may be quite limited since the children were not accustomed to *Sesame Street* or to similar American television programs, and the task chosen to measure the effects was an extremely repetitive one.

There is at present no sound evidence available to demonstrate that either educational or instructional television has an adverse effect on classroom performance. Children do not seem to expect that the same standards should apply to the two situations.

Passivity

Those concerned with child development often feel that television encourages passivity by feeding children information for which they might otherwise actively investigate (Fowles & Voyat, 1974). Although this concern relates to television viewing in general, it is critical to an assessment of the role of educational television. If television teaching encouraged passive learning, it would certainly be harmful to a child's advanced education and detrimental to success and satisfaction as an adult. This concern does not lend itself easily to empirical research, but evidence in related areas suggests that television can, in fact, initiate active behavior when the appropriate devices are used (see demonstrations in the area of visual search [O'Bryan & Silverman, 1972, 1973; Salomon, 1972], verbal participation, and classifying activity [Dennis, 1977].

Whether television contributes to the development of passive learning modes in children is indeed a complex issue. Generally, the fact that children may make few *overt* responses while viewing is taken as evidence that little processing is taking place. This interpretation does not allow for the child's *covert* involvement with the material being viewed. In young children we tend to equate motor involvement with active involvement in the educational process, but we make no such equation for adults. In fact, very young children are able to respond to visual stimuli in a much more organized fashion than initially had been thought (Bower, 1977). Since human motor functions develop more slowly than do visual functions, it may be that a sensorimotor focus in teaching may actually impede learning in very young children. Thus, it has not yet been proven that television engenders a passive state in young children, and there is considerable evidence to the contrary.

Classroom Problems

Misuse of television in the classroom is a more concrete problem. The best of current instructional programs are designed to involve the classroom teacher in introducing the program, following up on the material presented, and generalizing it to other relevant contexts. In some cases (e.g., CTW's The Electric Company and WNGT's Our Story) it is possible to obtain materials which have been especially designed to coordinate with the program. In other cases the teacher may be given a program guide or offered a workshop. Seldom are programs with a specifically educational intent produced today without some accompanying print materials about the intentions of the program and how it might be used.

Beyond teacher involvement is the problem of adapting mass audience materials to the unique needs of a particular classroom. Producers of good programs are aware of this potential mismatch problem and try to produce supplementary materials which can help the teacher build a bridge from the television program to the particular needs of his or her classroom. Inventive and experienced teachers automatically do such bridging and may be called on as consultants.

A final potential problem for classroom use of television derives from the facts that teachers and students alike are accustomed to television as an entertainment medium, that they are accustomed to programs where they are not expected to be involved, and that much of their viewing is of programs in which very few demands are placed on the viewer. When such expectations and habits are carried into the classroom, instructional programs may be seen as a rest or a treat by both teacher and student. This means the programs are not used productively and students probably do not learn much. A self-fulfilling prophecy then operates to reinforce the teacher's low expectations for programs. Active involvement and interest in the program on the part of the teacher are vital to the effectiveness of most programs.

Television and the Tradition of Literacy

An interesting issue of a more philosophical nature has arisen as the use of instructional television has increased and as programs have become more "television-like" and less booklike. The question is whether television is further eroding our already imperiled tradition of literacy—and if so, whether this matters or not. The first part of this question is empirical, though complicated. The second part is a question of values.

Television can teach people many things they formerly had to learn about by reading. Early attempts at instructional television were closely tied to the literate tradition. However, as we became more skilled in using the devices of the medium (e.g., animation, chromakey, film, color) to present information, instructional television departed from the older avenues of education. In many ways this is clearly an advantage. First, television can teach many useful things to children before they are old enough to master reading. Second, television can provide information for that rather large segment of our population who have not learned to read well enough to use the skill to obtain information they need. There are many who welcome this as the wave of the future, while others see it as a dire trend (Parker, 1974).

Most people will now admit that, in the future, much of the information needed by people who are not employed in highly technical or professional work will be readily available with minimum reading. Only "survival" reading will be necessary. Then, except for a minority of people for whom the amount required will probably increase, reading will become a leisure activity which is lost to most people. Pragmatists are not bothered much by this; other educators are deeply troubled.

This issue was brought into focus in a particularly interesting way when CTW's program *The Electric Company* came on the scene. *The Electric Company* was not the first instructional program to teach reading, but it was the first national, highly publicized, well-funded effort of this kind. More significantly, *The Electric Company* was the first such program to use the devices of television well to teach reading. Many educators found it bizarre and logically impossible to use the mortal enemy of literacy to teach literacy. Summative research (Ball & Bogatz, 1973; Ball, Bogatz, Kazarow, & Rubin, 1974) subsequently proved that the program did teach basic reading skills. Nevertheless, the Cassandras may be right. With its colorful, dynamic visuals for which print is no match, *The Electric Company* may be teaching basic reading skills but eroding children's motivation to become truly literate. The legitimacy of this concern may be discovered only when the current generation of viewers reaches adulthood, but it is certainly one with which programmers and educators must now cope.

Financing

The funding situation for noncommercial educational programs for children has improved noticeably in recent years. This is especially true for programs designed for in-school use. The Corporation for Public

Broadcasting (CPB) and other national broadcasting organizations have increased their interest in children's television. When CPB recently committed major support to an "Essential Learning Skills" program produced by the Agency for Instructional Television (AIT), it marked the first time CPB had ever helped to fund a formal in-school series (Carlisle, 1978). Federal agencies have been critical in providing funds for many years. *Sesame Street* and *The Electric Company* were heavily supported, and *Sesame Street* continues to get significant support. Many consortia, made up of television stations and other institutions in a given region, have also formed. State departments of education are often responsible for funding local in-school programming, and some educational programs are commercially financed. Finally, private foundations and big business have also provided money for several series, although they are, appropriately, more interested in starting new programs than in providing continuing support.

The problem of funding is more critical for preschool programs, which lack a network of educational institutions to provide at least some of their support. In reviewing this situation, Mielke, Johnson, and Cole (1975) concluded that the United States government must expect to contribute most of the funding for quality preschool programs if these programs are to survive. However, they also noted that while the federal contribution to educational television of all types in fiscal year 1974 was in excess of $1 billion, there was "almost no coordination" within and among agencies distributing the money. Thus, it is far from obvious where production groups should turn in seeking federal money for programs.

To complicate matters, the government has placed more and more importance on the criterion of "cost effectiveness" for expensive programs such as *Sesame Street*. A production company such as CTW must demonstrate that its programming serves a large audience, particularly of those with needs that concern federal agencies. It must also demonstrate that its staff is highly productive and that expensive production techniques (and expensive writers, producers, and researchers) are justified by the educational results.

The cost-effectiveness of a program hinges on its ability to serve the largest possible audience while remaining reasonably effective. This can make it difficult for programs with specialized audiences to gain funding. It has also, however, been at least partly responsible for valuable programming decisions such as those made for *Sesame Street*: to include segments for retarded children and their parents, to emphasize Hispanic language and culture, to include a character who is deaf, and to add more prereading goals.

On the whole, cost-effectiveness is merely a reflection of the fact that the boom of interest in and money for experimental education (especially for the disadvantaged) is ending. Programs must now justify their existence. For the most part this requirement is appropriate. It becomes dangerous only when creativity is truly stifled by the demands of the market place.

Conclusions

Television programs designed to teach children formally or informally have markedly improved in quality in recent years. Most noticeable to someone who views these programs is the fact that they have come to look much more like television as we know it and less like on-camera classrooms. With the help of research, we have learned how to use the unique audiovisual properties of television to gain desirable educational ends while holding the child's attention. We have gained more control over the relationship between the design of a particular program segment and the viewer's response to it. What was once intuitive has been analyzed, understood, and rendered repeatable. At the same time, we are struggling to deal with the real limitations of television and with those limitations that are not necessarily real but that are imposed by skeptics worried about the implications of allowing this medium into the classroom.

The advent of television more than a generation ago has certainly changed the nature of childhood in America. We now accept the fact that it is an integral part of children's lives and thus a very real part of their education as well. Producers of educational programs for children have, after years of fumbling, begun to capitalize on young children's involvement with the medium. Educational traditions have been slow to accommodate these efforts, but recent high-quality programs with documented educational benefits have begun to make significant inroads into the classroom.

References

Anderson, D. R., & Levin, S. F. Young children's attention to Sesame Street. Child Development, 1976, 50, 806–811.

Baker, R., & Schultz, R. Instructional product research. New York: American Book, 1972.

Ball, S., & Bogatz, G. A. The first year of Sesame Street: An evaluation. Princeton, New Jersey: Educational Testing Service, 1970.

Ball, S., & Bogatz, G. A. Reading with television: An evaluation of The Electric Company. Princeton, New Jersey: Educational Testing Service, 1973.

Ball, S., Bogatz, G. A., Kazarow, K., & Rubin, D. Reading with television: A follow/up evaluation of The Electric Company. Princeton, New Jersey: Educational Testing Service, 1974.

Bernstein, L. J. Design attributes of Sesame Street and the visual attention of pre-schoolers. Unpublished doctoral dissertation, Columbia University, 1978.

Bogatz, G. A., & Ball, S. The second year of Sesame Street: A continuing evaluation (Vols. 1 and 2). Princeton, New Jersey: Educational Testing Service, 1971.

Bower, T. G. R. A primer of infant development. San Francisco: Freeman, 1977.

Carlisle, R. *Patterns of performance: Public broadcasting and education 1974–1976.* Washington, D.C.: Corporation for Public Broadcasting, Office of Educational Activities, 1978.

Collins, W. Learning of media content: A developmental study. *Child Development,* 1970, 44, 1133–1142.

Dennis, R. *Prompting viewer participation with televised instruction: Modifications on Sesame Street classifying segments.* Unpublished manuscript, University of Kansas, 1977.

Flagg, B., Housen, A., & Lesser, S. *Pre-reading and pre-science on Sesame Street.* Unpublished manuscript, Harvard University, 1978.

Fowles, B. Teaching children to read: An argument for television. *The Urban Review,* 1976, 9(2), 114–120.

Fowles, B., & Voyat, G. Piaget meets Big Bird: Is TV a passive teacher? *The Urban Review,* 1974, 7(1), 69–80.

Herriott, R. E., & Leibert, R. J., *The Electric Company in-school utilization study: The 1971– 1972 school and teacher surveys.* New York: Children's Television Workshop, 1972. (ERIC Document Reproduction Service No. ED 973 709)

Ide, T. R. The potentials and limitations of television as an educational medium. In D. R. Olson (Ed.), *Media and symbols: The forms of expression, communication and education.* Chicago: Univ. of Chicago Press, 1974.

Leibert, R. J. *The Electric Company in-school utilization study: The 1972–1973 school and teacher surveys and trends since fall 1971.* New York: Children's Television Workshop, 1973. (ERIC Document Reproduction Service No. ED 094 775)

Lesser, G. *Children and television: Lessons from Sesame Street.* New York: Random House, 1974.

Mielke, K. W., Johnson, R. G., & Cole, B. G. *The federal role in funding children's television programming.* Unpublished manuscript, Indiana University, Institute for Communications Research, Department of Telecommunications, 1975.

O'Bryan, K. G., & Silverman, H. *Report on children's television viewing strategies.* New York: Children's Television Workshop, 1972. (ERIC Document Reproduction Service No. ED 126 871)

O'Bryan, K. G., & Silverman, H. *Research report: Experimental program eye-movement study.* New York: Children's Television Workshop, 1973. (ERIC Document Reproduction Service No. ED 126 870)

Olson, D. R., & Bruner, J. Learning through experience and learning through media. In D. R. Olson (Ed.), *Media and symbols: The forms of expression, communication and education.* Chicago: Univ. of Chicago Press, 1974.

Palmer, E. L. Formative research in the production of television for children. In D. R. Olson (Ed.), *Media and symbols: The forms of expression, communication and education.* Chicago: Univ. of Chicago Press, 1974.

Palmer, E. L. *A pedagogical analysis of recurrent formats on Sesame Street and The Electric Company.* Paper presented at the International Conference on Children's Educational Television, Amsterdam, June, 1978.

Parker, H. The beholder's share and the problems of literacy. In D. R. Olson (Ed.), *Media and symbols: The forms of expression, communication and education.* Chicago: Univ. of Chicago Press, 1974.

Salomon, G. Can we effect cognitive skills through visual media? An hypothesis and initial findings. *A-V Communications Review,* 1972, 20(4), 401–423.

Salomon, G. *Sesame Street in Israel: Its instructional and psychological effects on children.* Jerusalem: Hebrew Univ. of Jerusalem, 1974. (ERIC Document Reproduction Service No. ED 122 814)

Salomon, G. What does it do to Johnny? A cognitive functionalistic view of research on media. *Viewpoints. Bulletin of the School of Education, Indiana University,* 1970, 46(5), 33–89.

Stein, A., & Friedrich, L. Television content and young children's behavior. In J. P. Murray, E. A. Rubinstein, & G. A. Comstock (Eds.), *Television and social behavior* (Vol. 2). *Television and social learning*. Washington, D.C.: U.S. Government Printing Office, 1972.

3

Content Development for Children's Television Programs

VALERIE CRANE

The main goal of this chapter is to examine the process of content development in programs prepared for children. Understanding this process is important because it can elucidate opportunities to make systematic changes in children's programming. This chapter begins with a description of different types of content and formats in commercial, educational, and instructional programming for children. Both in-school and at-home programming from preschool through high school levels are considered. Since an analysis of subject matter and format does not provide a full understanding of the content development process, the second part of the chapter deals with three factors which influence development of content—the funding source, the target audience, and the production team.

Content and Format of Different Types of Children's Programming

Commercial Programming

Commercial programming includes series usually prepared for the networks, local stations, and syndication companies to be broadcast on weekday mornings and afternoons and on weekends (primarily Saturday morning). Although most commercial programs are designed only to entertain, some commercially supported series for children are also informational or purposive in nature (e.g., *Fat Albert and the Cosby Kids, ABC Afterschool Specials,* and *NBC News Notes.*)

Over the last 8 years, Earle Barcus of Boston University has performed several content analyses of commercial programming for Action for Children's Television (ACT). In his 1978 study, Barcus analyzed commercial programming aired during October, 1977, including weekend programming available on three networks and three independent stations in Boston, and after-school programming available on ten independent stations across the country. Since series originally prepared for adult audiences comprise much of the after-school television on independent stations, they have been included in Barcus' content analyses. Barcus (1978) found that, as in the past, entertainment programs dominated commercial stations. Informational programs were represented much less frequently on weekends on network stations (16% of their total air time), on weekends on independent stations (20% of their total air time), and on weekdays on independent stations (3% of their total air time). The large number of informational programs noted on weekends on independent stations included three federally funded educational programs and one commercially supported series.

On the average, the subject matter of programs most frequently involved themes of crime, domestic affairs, love and romance, and science and technology. Other themes (e.g., fine arts, literature, nature, and history) were represented infrequently on commercial stations (Barcus, 1978). The format found most frequently on both network and independent stations was animation, particularly cartoon comedy. Situation and family comedies were also well represented on independent stations.

Only slight changes in subject matter and format of commercial programming were noted between 1975 and 1977 (Barcus, 1977). In 1977 cartoon comedy was less frequent on all stations (from 42% in 1975 to 31% in 1977). More frequent were programs with themes of love and romance, scheduled for weekdays on independent stations (from 6% in 1975 to 18% in 1977). Informational programming on weekends by network stations dropped 4%, while independent stations increased such programming from 0% in 1975 to 20% (weekend) and 3% (weekday) in 1977.

In summarizing, Barcus (1978) notes that the subject matter of commercial programs offers a narrow range of choices. While content analyses do not reflect substantive changes in commercial programming from 1975 to 1977, an interview with ABC's vice president of children's programming (Olin, 1979) revealed that since 1972, the children's programming staff at ABC has become increasingly concerned with producing quality television for children. It is hoped that future content analyses will reflect these concerns.

Educational Programming

Educational programming (ETV) for children is defined as series aired on public television stations. They are designed for home viewing but also can be used in the schools. Examples include entertainment series such as *Zoom*; purposive or informational series such as *Sesame Street, The Electric Company,* and *Misterogers Neighborhood*; and multicultural series funded by the Emergency School Aid Act (e.g., *Vegetable Soup, Infinity Factory, Rebop*).

In a study for the Corporation for Public Broadcasting (CPB), Katzman and Wirt (1976) surveyed programming reports from 152 public broadcasters across the country. Based on this input, the authors computed percentages of total broadcasters' hours and of total programs scheduled that were devoted to various types of programming for children. Children's Television Workshop (CTW) programming represented 16% of the home-viewing broadcaster hours and 12% of the total number of programs scheduled. General children's programming (e.g., *Zoom, Villa Alegre, Misterogers Neighborhood*) comprised 10% of total air time and almost 12% of the programs scheduled. Therefore, the total for children's programming was 26% of the total air time and 24% of the programs scheduled. These percentages are well above those for commercial broadcasting, particularly when one averages the higher percentages for commercial programming on weekends with their much lower percentages for weekdays.

The subject matter for educational programming is quite varied and includes bilingual and multicultural education (*Villa Alegre, Carrascolendas,* and *Rebop*), affective education (*Misterogers Neighborhood* and *Sesame Street*), reading (*Sesame Street* and *The Electric Company*), entertainment (*Zoom*), and career education (*Freestyle*). The majority of these series uses a magazine format.

Instructional Programming

Instructional television (ITV) programming consists of series that are broadcast during school hours for in-school use. Like educational programming, ITV has objectives and a curriculum. Since, however, the programs are used in classrooms where follow-up activities are likely, the curriculum is usually more detailed and specific. Examples of instructional programming include *Bread and Butterflies, Inside/Out, Self Incorporated,* and *MeasureMetric*.

Katzman and Wirt (1976) reported that ITV represented almost 15% of public broadcasters' total air time and 27% of all programs scheduled. While ITV programming was available for all grade levels, the bulk of it targeted the first- to fifth-grade audience. ITV subject matter included reading and writing (14%), science (12%), music, art, and theater (12%), literature and humanities (10%), health and safety (9%), and children's basic education (9%).

ITV programs most frequently utilized dramatization (36%), lecture (30%), and demonstration (26%) formats (Katzman & Wirt, 1976). While studying format patterns from 1974 to 1976, Carlisle (1978) noted a decrease in the use of demonstrations and lectures and an increase in the use of dramatizations. This shift in program format suggests that ITV producers are increasingly concerned with presenting educational content in a format which will prove entertaining to the audience. In this sense, ITV and ETV are becoming increasingly similar.

Comparing Types of Programming

Most commercial programming is entertainment-oriented, with some informational programming offered as well. Although some changes have been noted in commercial programming, Barcus (1978) maintains that diversity in content has not been achieved. In contrast, educational and instructional programming are primarily educational, informational, and/or purposive. The subject matter of educational and instructional programming represents many different curricular areas, while commercial programming focuses on a somewhat narrow set of themes. The variety of content offered by ETV and ITV does not, however, obviate the need for more educational and instructional children's series (Seaver & Weber, 1979). In fact, there are too few new series being generated each year to meet the demand.

Commercial programs most frequently utilize animated formats with story-lines, while educational programs favor the magazine format, often with some animated segments. ITV programming differs from both commercial and educational programming by utilizing dramatization, lecture, and demonstrations most often. It is promising to note that ITV is shifting toward more frequent use of dramatization rather than using the traditional lecture and demonstration format.

Factors Influencing the Development of Children's Programs

In the previous section, differences in the content and format of children's programs were noted. These differences can be attributed in part to the intended use of a program—whether it will supplement classroom instruction or be viewed at home without the benefit of follow-up activity. Three other factors—the funding source, feedback from the target audience, and the production team—also account for differences, and their influences will be discussed here.

Financial Support of Children's Programs: The Funding Source

Funding sources influence the type of content and sometimes the format which is developed on children's television projects. Those who provide support vary in the amount and timing of their influence, but a common problem lies in the ability of the funding source to identify areas which reflect the needs of the target audience and not merely the need of a commercial, federal, or state agency to promote its own concern. The funding sources and their influence on commercial, educational, and instructional programming are discussed next.

Commercial Programming. One way to define the scope of commercial programming for children is to identify the amount of programming to be aired. Taking commercial stations in Boston as an example, there are approximately 102 hours of programming to be scheduled each week for children. This gargantuan appetite for programming (Schramm & Alexander, 1973) becomes a key factor in determining the level of quality in the programming. Whereas ABC, for example, has allocated a substantial amount of money for *ABC After School Specials,* which are carefully and expensively developed, there remains the task of filling many more hours of programming at a lower cost per program hour. The need for many hours of programming also means that many commercial productions must be completed relatively rapidly (Rushnell, 1980), while a quality, purposive series can take up to 3 years to develop. Time, therefore, is also an important factor.

While the children's programming department at the network level may have its own budget for production, commercial programs are ultimately paid for by advertisers who buy time to air their commercials for children. Advertisers are concerned with selling products to a large audience. Hence most programming is targeted for a wide age range (2–11 years) in order to maximize the opportunity to sell products. Programs prepared for such a wide age range cannot focus on subject matter involving age-specific social, developmental, or educational objectives. Nor is that the intent. Saturday morning programming is supposed to be fun and entertaining. Programming on fine arts, literature, and the like would not generally be considered competitive in attracting a large audience.

Format as well as subject matter is affected by the funding source. Animation is often chosen because sponsors believe it attracts the largest possible audience. Although animation is costly to produce, it proves less expensive over time as revenues are generated through reruns (Rushnell,

1980). In fact, all programs become more profitable to the network the more times they are aired. Consequently, changes in content, as reflected in formal content analysis, occur slowly, since today's programming incorporates old programming with the new in order to increase profits.

Financial resources at most local stations affiliated with a network are more limited than at the network level, with the result that fewer children's programs originate at the local level (6%, Barcus, 1978). The resources of the local independent stations are even more limited. One major source of relatively inexpensive programming for them is the syndicated reruns of series which were originally developed for an adult audience (e.g., *The Lucy Show*, *Bonanza*, and *Star Trek*).

The commercial broadcasting system is complex and cannot be adequately reviewed in this short discussion. However, the purpose here has been to show that the financial support for commercial programming does affect the format and subject matter of the programs themselves. As long as a large number of programs are demanded in a short time and the first audience of children's programs is the advertiser, substantial changes in the content of children's commercial programs will be slow in coming.

Educational Programming. Most support for public broadcasting comes from state and federal funds. The Office of Education is the primary source of federal funds, while other sources of funding include foundations, CPB, and other private corporations. In the past, the bulk of federal funds has been allocated to CTW and to the Emergency School Aid Act (ESAA) within the Office of Education, which has then distributed funds to various production groups (Mielke, Johnson, & Cole, 1975).

While CTW has developed the objectives and content of their series without intervention from its funding sources, ESAA has consistently directed the content of its series in three ways. First, ESAA funding is allocated to promote multicultural programming, and it specifies those ethnic groups to be addressed. Second, the age levels and, third, the categories of content (including cognitive, affective, or bilingual subject matter) are all designated in the Request for Proposals (RFP) (Mielke *et al.*, 1975).

Other federal agencies which have supported programming include the Department of Agriculture, Bureau of the Handicapped, Bilingual Education (Office of Education, Title VII), National Institute for Education, National Endowment for the Humanities, and National Endowment for the Arts. Obviously, it is the mandate of each of these agencies to support programs which promote its particular concerns. These agencies generally specify the subject matter for a series at the time that proposals are requested, but the direction of content during production is often minimal or altogether absent. However, some funding sources such as ESAA initially only fund the production of a pilot program and then determine whether a project merits further funding. When judging the merit of a program, it can become difficult for staff to separate content issues from the other factors which characterize a program.

Instructional Programming. A number of series which are funded primarily for public broadcasting are also broadcast for in-school use (e.g., *The Electric Company, Vegetable Soup, Freestyle*). State educational agencies are, however, the major source of support for instructional programming. One of the largest producers of ITV programming, the Agency for Instructional Television (AIT), enlists the support of many educational agencies in the United States and Canada. The various organizations become supporting members of a consortium because the content reflects a need within their educational system (Middleton, 1979; Rockman, 1976). In this consortium model of funding, AIT undertakes the difficult task of satisfying not one "sponsor" but sometimes more than forty. Extensive feedback systems are implemented to assure the client that the project is moving on schedule, within the budget, and with every promise of achieving its goals. Some of the most highly utilized instructional programming is achieved with this funding model, and AIT programs are especially effective in meeting the specific needs of the clients. Since there is more opportunity for the AIT clients to participate in program development, there is also the need for an able administration to balance input from many sources and make decisions which meet the needs of all members and of the project as well.

A Link with the Target Audience: Formative Research

The preceding discussion suggests that an important audience for children's programming is the funding source, whether an advertiser or a government agency. Since projects seldom start until the funding mechanisms are established, this is true to some degree. The target audience should, however, be brought into program development—and the sooner the better.

As mentioned earlier, commercial broadcasters rely most heavily on audience ratings—if children watch in sufficient numbers and if advertisers continue to sponsor a program. In some cases, commercial programs with high ratings are compared to those with low ratings, and new programming ideas with the format and content characteristics of the more successful programs are pursued. However, this approach is problematic for a number of reasons. First, many factors other than content and format influence ratings. Second, it provides information on existing programming far too late in the production process. Third, it fails to provide producers with information on which specific elements within a program work or do not work and why. In an industry which places so much importance on viewership, it is surprising that so few program developers directly test their audience's understanding of concepts and material during planning and production phases. So unsystematic an approach to the audience would be unthinkable in the marketing of other products. Even children's commercials are carefully researched to determine their potential for impact on the target audience (Mielke, 1978). So, too, children's programming needs this systematic link from the outset of a project.

One way to provide a systematic link with the target audience is through the use of formative research: "In children's television programming, formative research is, in general, designed to provide diagnostic feedback into the decision-making process for production, so that programming improvements, if needed, can be made before broadcast [Mielke, 1978, p. 17]." Formative research in developing children's television series was first used by CTW with *Sesame Street* (Palmer, 1974). Since that time, AIT (Rockman, 1976) and the Ontario Educational Communications Authority (Nickerson & Gillis, 1979) have also consistently included research as an ongoing, permanent, in-house arm for children's television productions. The success of this formative approach has been documented recently by Seaver and Weber (1979) in a report to CPB on children's programming: "A relatively small number of programs achieve 'success' by any criteria. The 'big hits' of children's programming may have some critical features in common, one feature possibly being careful formative research [p. 35]." Despite the success of these organizations, formative research has not been systematically integrated into production. Two reasons may explain why such an approach has been underutilized: lack of published materials which could be made available to producers and lack of allocation within the production budget. While many consider formative research very expensive, the budget can be based on the scope of the project. If full-time, in-house evaluation is not possible, limited subcontracted formative research is both feasible and economical.

Whatever the staffing pattern for formative research, the key ingredient for success is the process of obtaining systematic feedback from the target audience and translating that feedback into meaningful recommendations and direction for production. In this sense, the link between production and the target audience becomes fixed, and content development continually reflects the needs and demands of the target audience. On the following pages, four phases of the research process will be discussed: (a) preproduction research; (b) production evaluation—in process; (c) production evaluation—pilot testing; and (d) postproduction research.

Preproduction Research. The first step in developing content for a children's series is to ascertain needs: "What kind of content warrants priority?" and "What audience has this need?" The formative researcher can address these questions in the following ways: (a) consultation with content or subject matter experts; (b) examination of existing test data for different potential viewers in the content areas; and (c) review of studies which examine performance in the content areas. Once the needs, content area, and audience are identified, the feasibility of the project for television must be determined: "Is the audience of sufficient size to warrant a television series?", "Can the needs be met with television?", and "Can the project obtain funding?" These questions can be addressed through: (a) examination of demographic data on the audience; (b) continued consultation with experts and in-house project staff; and (c) a search for funding sources.

Once needs are identified, objectives for the series should be developed by content experts and formative researchers. At this point, it is important to survey the target audience to ascertain: (a) knowledge of and attitudes toward the content area; (b) television viewing preferences; and (c) reactions to existing televised materials in the content area (for examples see Cambre & Carroza, 1978; Chen, Katz, Clarke, & Mielke, 1978; and Crane, 1979). Surveys of the target audience can provide in-depth analyses of content and objectives according to age, sex, and ethnic group differences, which in turn provide important direction in the development of script treatments and characters. The evaluation of televised segments and viewing preferences provides further direction in developing characters and program format and in selecting production techniques. These data can then be used to develop a Writer's Manual or Notebook. Such guidelines for writers have been used for both educational (Palmer, 1974) and commercial (Quiroga & Crane, 1978; Rushnell, 1980) productions.

Once ideas are translated into treatments, scripts, storyboards, or inexpensive videotape, they can be analyzed to determine whether objectives are adequately represented, whether positive social values are portrayed, whether unintended messages are present, and whether the characters in the series are balanced with respect to age, sex, and ethnicity. This may be done through a formal content analysis and/or through an informal review of scripts by experts. Recommendations for change are then based on these findings. Testing scripts for comprehension and credibility can be done at this point with small samples of the target audience, using such procedures as: (a) reading or performing scripts for the audience; (b) showing storyboards to groups of children; and (c) showing videotaped storyboard material. While script reading, storyboards, and inexpensive videotape do not have that production quality hopefully characteristic of the series itself, these approaches can determine initial reactions to the content of the material, with little cost and much benefit to producers. These procedures are particularly important when there can be no revision once material is produced.

Production Evaluation—In Process. Once televised material is available in rough-cut form, it can be tested with the target audience. Appeal and comprehension are the two most important considerations in early testing of televised material. Whether a program is highly purposive or primarily entertaining, appeal and comprehension are critical factors in determining whether or not it will hold the attention of an audience. While an appealing and comprehensible program does not guarantee high viewership, an unappealing and confusing one precludes any possibility of success.

If transitional material or final editing are still needed, testing audience appeal and comprehension can provide input for these purposes. On one series, for example, film stories were available for evaluation before transitional segments were filmed in the studio. The content of these transitional segments was based on feedback obtained in testing rough-cuts of the filmed stories. Low points of appeal were edited, and problems with comprehension were clarified either through editing or with transitions (Quiroga & Crane, 1978).

There are a number of methods and techniques for determining the appeal and comprehension of televised material. In an attempt to measure preschoolers' reactions to Sesame Street, Palmer (1974) developed the "distractor method," in which children's eye contact with the television screen was recorded while distracting slides were flashed simultaneously onto a screen at a 45 degree angle from the set. AIT also uses eye contact data, but they are obtained in classroom settings (where its programs are meant to be shown) by trained observers who sit at the front of the room and record the number of students watching the screen at specified intervals of time throughout the program.

School-age viewers can use rating scales to provide information about appeal. With a simple rating scale they can indicate whether they like each segment and character in a program "a lot," "some," or "not at all" or which they liked best and least. Using a computerized adaptation of the Stanton-Lazarsfeld program analyzer (PEAC-Program Evaluation Analysis Computer), viewers can press a button while watching a television program to indicate on a scale of up to 14 points whether they like or don't like what they are watching (Chen et al., 1978; Nickerson, 1979). Inexpensive paper and pencil instruments can be used to provide analogous data, although they do not allow the continuous monitoring, the immediate feedback, or the more than 2-point scale as is possible with PEAC. However, the use of this paper and pencil procedure has been successful and offers a useful alternative (Crane, 1979).

Another important measure of appeal is an interview immediately following a viewing session, during which students can provide more detailed information on what segments and characters were most appealing and why. The interview is also an effective measure of comprehension. In-depth information on different segments and on credibility of plot and characters can be gathered through the use of carefully framed questions.

The PEAC system can also measure comprehension by using multiple-choice items. With this technique, however, the reasons for viewers' responses cannot be determined. Since the reasons are an important part of providing direction for production, PEAC is probably best used in combination with other methods to measure comprehension. A final evaluation technique is stop-action or freeze frame where the program is stopped and students are asked to recall, comment on, and/or answer questions about the segment just viewed. This approach is particularly appropriate for programs in a magazine format since the events in the initial segments may be forgotten during subsequent viewing.

In addition to determining the appeal and comprehensibility of material, specific questions on the production format, ordering of segments, pacing, and credibility of plot and characters can be raised and answered. Analysis of these program elements is very important in determining what techniques work best for the target audience. In fact, the examination and use of recurrent formats have proved useful for producers of Sesame Street and The Electric Company (Palmer, 1978).

Once data are collected from the target audience, feedback must be provided to the production team. Short verbal or written reports are most appropriate for reporting. Recommendations and positive suggestions should be made at this point so that information can be used in the continuing production.

Production Evaluation—Pilot Testing. Evaluation of a pilot program is the most common type of formative research in children's television. It can result in meaningful feedback on the success of production elements, as well as on the appeal and comprehensibility of a program. If, however, format, characters, and objectives cannot be revised past this pilot program stage, the evaluation has limited use for production. Moreover, if the results from testing the pilot program are used by the funding source to determine whether or not production of a full series is worthwhile, then the evaluator is in the difficult position of satisfying two clients (production and the funding source), each with a completely different set of needs.

When pilot testing is carried out, the procedures are similar to those used during the previous "in-process" phase. One important distinction between production evaluation in process and pilot testing is that in the latter a larger, more representative sample of the target audience is usually obtained. Therefore, the interview often becomes too expensive and time-consuming as an approach to gathering data, and paper and pencil instruments administered in schools are often preferred. For programs meant for in-school use, such a test site is, of course, appropriate. In order to test programs in the home setting, some recent RFPs have required field testing using cable systems or local broadcast to homes with follow-up telephone interviews or questionnaires.

Since the findings of the pilot program evaluation are often reported to the funding source as well as to the production team, the reporting process differs from that used in previous stages. For the funding source, a longer and more detailed report is usually warranted. For the production team, qualitative data collected during this phase can be incorporated into a separate in-house report.

Finally, it is important to point out not only what can be measured at this stage but also what cannot. While a television series might be designed to achieve a set of specific cognitive or affective objectives, it is not realistic to expect that a pilot program will achieve these objectives in one short viewing session. However, the script analysis, rough-cut testing, and pilot evaluation together indicate the potential for achieving those objectives by analyzing content and by obtaining data on appeal and comprehension from the target audience. If these procedures are initiated at the outset of a project and are continued throughout, the production team will have maximized its potential for success.

Postproduction Research. Once a series is ready for distribution and broadcast, its impact and the degree to which it achieved its objective can be determined by means of summative evaluation. While this type of evaluation is different in its purpose from formative research, it is briefly included in this discussion because it continues to provide a link with the target audience and because it is an important part of the total research process. Broadcasters can use summative evaluation in making decisions on whether to broadcast a series; teachers can make decisions about how a series might be utilized. While summative evaluation has less utility to the production team (since the content cannot be changed at that point), its results can provide direction for new content if the series continues production. Summative evaluation is even more rare than formative research because new funds are usually directed to new production rather than to a study of the impact of a series. It may become necessary to pursue alternative funding models to ensure that this phase of evaluation takes place.

Mechanisms for Decision Making: The Production Team

So far, it has been suggested that the content development process can be affected by the type of financial support for a project and by the systematic approach to the target audience through the use of formative research. The actual impact that these factors will have on a project is determined by the decisionmakers, in particular, producers and managers (here referred to as the production team).

As stated earlier, one reason that formative research is not systematically implemented in projects is that few producers and managers are familiar with the process. Producers usually follow their intuition and experience in developing program content, even though it has been noted that their intuition and experience can be wrong (Mielke, 1973; Noble, 1975). Since producers have built their confidence on these factors, it can be difficult to convince them to consider formative research results as input for making decisions. Moreover, for many producers formative research represents a new field or discipline and a new language. Nevertheless, formative research has been successfully integrated into the production process, first at CTW (Palmer, 1974) and then by others (e.g., Nickerson & Gillis, 1979; Rockman, 1976).

Project staffing patterns are important to effective working relationships and hence to successful formative research and production efforts. There is, however, no one approach which has proven most effective. With different patterns of staffing, different research tasks may be undertaken by one or any combination of individuals on the team. For example, content experts for a series are sometimes permanent members of the staff and at other times are project consultants. On ITV projects, the content experts and ITV designers become heavily involved in defining objectives and determining subject matter; on other projects, advisory board members or the formative researchers act as content experts.

For formative research to be successful on television projects, it is obvious that cooperation and trust among staff members are crucial. In a study examining the impact of evaluation on eight television projects, the investigators were able to identify other factors which facilitated the formative research effort and maximized the use of input from the target audience (Crane, Quiroga, & Linowes, 1977). Formative research was most successful when incorporated into the production process from the outset of the project, particularly through early staff meetings that set the stage for the research process. It was also observed that evaluators should help production staff to understand the evaluation effort, their role in the project, the specific requirements for evaluation, specific evaluation techniques, and the potential utility of evaluation. All of these efforts were found to be particularly successful when there was support of both managers and producers (Crane et al., 1977).

The success of the formative research effort is determined not merely by surveys and studies of the target audience but also by the degree to which results, conclusions, and recommendations are used by the production team. Therefore, the feedback process itself becomes critical in facilitating the use of evaluation results. There can be a promising proposal, an adequately funded project, and the proper formative research input from the target audience, but the final link in the process is a production team that is able to translate all of the essential elements into a television series.

Summary and Conclusions

This chapter began with a brief overview of the subject matter and formats for commercial, educational, and instructional programming for children. In commercial programming, animation was found to be the most frequent format, with crime and domestic themes represented most frequently when network and independent station offerings were averaged. On weekdays, independent station offerings also included sitcoms (situation comedies) and family drama with domestic affairs, love, and romance themes. Educational programming offers a variety of content areas including cognitive, affective, multicultural, and entertainment subject matter often presented in magazine format. Instructional television also offers programs in a variety of curricular areas with frequent use of dramatization, lecture, and demonstration formats.

Over the past few years there has been a decrease in the amount of animation used in commercial programming and an increase in informational or educational content on independent stations in Boston. Aside from these changes, a narrow range of subject matter has been noted (Barcus, 1978). Changes have been noted in ITV which has shifted its format emphasis from lecture and demonstration to dramatization.

The factors which influence program development were identified as the funding source, the target audience, and the production team. Funding sources generally direct and influence content at least during the initial stages of a project. This raises major concern about the ability of the funding agency to distinguish the needs of the target audience from its own need to promote a content area. An additional funding concern is the limited financial resources available for providing a continual supply of quality educational and instructional series. When the target audience is the focal point in the production process, formative research that provides useful data and has the support of the production team has proven successful in developing content that meets both the needs and the demands of its intended audience.

Although the factors which influence content development were examined separately, they never function separately in a project. They are interdependent and complex, changing not only with each new production effort but also many times within each project. Adequate funding, careful formative research, and a competent, effective production team all maximize the potential for a successful production effort; but with all these factors in place, there are still no guarantees. It is not surprising that in their report to CPB on children's programming. Seaver and Weber (1979) did not offer a formula for successful production; it has been eluding producers for a long time. Nevertheless, it is important to understand how children's programs are developed and the constraints that are placed on those involved in the production process. Changes in children's television can only come at this level—from those who are consistently held accountable for achieving what others have recommended for children's television.

References

Barcus, F. E. (with R. Wolkin). *Children's television: An analysis of programming and advertising.* New York: Praeger, 1977.

Barcus, F. E. *Commercial children's television on weekends and weekday afternoons.* Newtonville, Massachusetts: Action for Children's Television, 1978

Cambre, M., & Carroza, F. *Formative evaluation of the Thinkabout programs.* Paper presented at the meeting of the National Association of Educational Broadcasters, Washington, D.C., November, 1978.

Carlisle, R. D. B. (Ed.). *Patterns of performance: Public broadcasting and education 1974–1976.* Washington, D.C.: Corporation for Public Broadcasting, 1978.

Chen, M., Katz, M., Clarke, H., & Mielke, K. *CTW Science Show research presentation.* Paper presented at the meeting of the National Association of Educational Broadcasters, Washington, D.C., November, 1978.

Crane, V. *Formative research for an arts education television series for 8–12 year olds.* Unpublished report prepared for Children's Arts Education Project, Boston, Massachusetts, WGBH–TV, June, 1979.

Crane, V., Quiroga, B., & Linowes, J. *The impact of evaluation on the production of children's television programs.* Paper presented at the meeting of the National Association of Educational Broadcasters, Washington, D.C., November, 1977.

Katzman, N., & Wirt, K. *Public television programming by category: 1976.* Washington, D.C.: Corporation for Public Broadcasting, 1976.

Middleton, J. *Cooperative school television and educational change. The consortium development process of the Agency for Instructional Television.* Bloomington, Indiana: Agency for Instructional Television, 1979.

Mielke, K. *Decision-oriented research in school television.* Bloomington, Indiana: Agency for Instructional Television, 1973.

Mielke, K. *Television as a teacher of children and youth: Educational use of production variables and formative research in programming.* Manuscript submitted to Office of Assistant Director for Children and Youth, National Institute of Mental Health, Rockville, Maryland, March, 1978.

Mielke, K., Johnson, R. C., & Cole, G. *The federal role in funding children's television programming* (Vol. 1). Washington, D.C.: Office of Education, Department of Health, Education and Welfare, 1975.

Nickerson, R. *Program evaluation using the program evaluation analysis computer (PEAC).* Paper presented at the meeting of the Association for Educational Communications and Technology, New Orleans, Louisiana, March, 1979.

Nickerson, R., & Gillis, L. *Research for decision making during television production: The OECA model.* Toronto, Canada: Ontario Educational Communications Authority, July, 1979.

Noble, G. *Children in front of the small screen.* Beverly Hills, California: Sage, 1975.

Olin, M. Personal interview on content development process at ABC. July, 1979.

Palmer, E. L. Formative research in the production of television for children. In D. Olson (Ed.), *Media and symbols: The forms of expression, communication and education.* The seventy-third yearbook of the National Society for the Study of Education. Chicago: Univ. of Chicago Press, 1974.

Palmer, E. L. *A pedagogical analysis of recurrent formats on Sesame Street and The Electric Company.* Paper presented at the International Conference on Children's Educational Television, Amsterdam, June, 1978.

Quiroga, B., & Crane, V. *Formative evaluation of a local television production for children.* Paper presented at the meeting of the National Association of Educational Broadcasters, Washington, D.C., November, 1978.

Rockman, S. *The use of decision-oriented research in the development of school television materials.* Paper presented at the meeting of the National Association of Educational Broadcasters, Chicago, October, 1976.

Rushnell, S. A. Network non-primetime programming. In S. T. Eastman, S. W. Head, & L. Klein (Eds.), *Broadcast programming: Strategies for winning television and radio audiences.* Belmont, California: Wadsworth, 1980.

Schramm, W., & Alexander, J. Broadcasting. In I. de Sola Pool, W. Frey, W. Schramm, N. Maccoby, & E. B. Parker (Eds.), *Handbook of communication.* Chicago: Rand McNally, 1973.

Seaver, J., & Weber, S. *Children's television programming and public broadcasting: An analysis and assessment of needs.* Washington, D.C.: Corporation for Public Broadcasting, 1979.

4

Effects of Planned
Television Programming

BRUCE A. WATKINS
ALETHA HUSTON–STEIN
JOHN C. WRIGHT

Do children learn from educational programming? If so, what is learned, how is it learned, what television techniques are most successful in teaching, and what situational influences in the viewing environment affect learning? These questions provide the focus for the present chapter, which is organized into four sections. In the first two, the effects of planned programming on cognitive skills and prosocial behavior are examined. In the third section, the processes by which children learn from television are explored. The fourth section presents information about what features of television programs and the child's environment enhance or detract from the effectiveness of educational programming.

Cognitive Skills

Early Research

Attempts to use television in a teaching capacity began soon after commercial television was introduced in the late 1940s and early 1950s. The special attractiveness of the medium and its ability to reach large

CHILDREN AND THE FACES OF TELEVISION:
Teaching, Violence, Selling

numbers of Americans raised hopes of massive educational impact despite the fact that similar hopes for educational radio had gone largely unfulfilled (see Schramm, 1962). Educators during this time compared the effectiveness of televised and face-to-face instruction, both in public schools (Craig, 1956; Lathrop, Norford, & Greenhill, 1953; Michael & Maccoby, 1953) and in adult education (Deutschmann, Barrow, & McMillan, 1961; Rock, Duva, & Murray, 1953).

Fairly comprehensive reviews of the studies during these years were provided by Schramm (1962) and Kumata (1960). They reached several conclusions regarding the effectiveness of instructional television: (a) Only in a few well-defined areas did televised instruction produce learning superior to traditional techniques; (b) when effects were apparent, it was generally the brighter students who were helped by television instruction; (c) while some studies demonstrated short-term positive effects of televised instruction, there was no consensus on its effectiveness for long-term retention; (d) the "motivation" of the student was of prime importance in the learning process; and (e) improvement was most likely for topics which benefited from use of concrete examples (e.g., science, math). In short, televised instruction was useful for certain kinds of teaching, but, on the whole, it was no more or less effective than face-to-face instruction.

Early efforts at televised instruction were distinguished from more recent attempts in several respects. Most were aimed at adults and high school students rather than at the children on whom we now focus. Early televised instruction usually consisted of a classroom lecturer filmed by a television camera. When some of television's potential advantages—such as presentations of microscopic phenomena, graphic and dynamic spatial displays, or modeled examples and demonstrations—were later explored, students responded positively and learned, as compared with classroom controls exposed to live lectures (Kumata, 1960). Finally, with a few exceptions, televised instruction was evaluated in the classroom. It was not intended to compete with commercial television in the home, and it wasn't evaluated there.

Schramm (1962) listed the main objections at that time to the use of television as a teaching medium: It could not stop to answer questions; it did not readily permit class discussion; it could not effectively quiz the students; it was not able to adjust to individual differences in learning capacities; and it tended to encourage a passive form of learning versus an active seeking and manipulation of one's environment. Many of these limitations remain at the end of the 1970s. It appeared that these problems were inherent in the medium and that instructional television was an experiment that had largely failed to fulfill the hopes held for it.

A New Approach to Educational Television

During the 1950s and 1960s, there were a few programs on public and commercial television designed to educate or benefit young children, but they drew small audiences and provided little competition for entertainment programming on commercial television. In 1967 a group of academics, researchers, and television producers joined together to create, develop, and produce a series that would entertain as well as educate children. The goals, techniques, and promises of *Sesame Street* went far beyond what had previously been attempted (see Lesser, 1974, for an account of the development of *Sesame Street*). The series had a major impact on the television industry by attracting a mass audience in numbers well above the early predictions of the creators. Partly as a result of its success, a number of similarly styled educational programs appeared on both public and commercial television in the next several years (e.g., *The Electric Company, Villa Alegre, Big Blue Marble, Schoolhouse Rock*). Existing series, such as *Captain Kangaroo*, also incorporated more educational material and a more heterogeneous format. Instructional programming, too, discarded its reliance on the classroom lecture and began to combine education with entertainment.

Several of these series have been subjected to summative evaluations. Our discussion of cognitive effects will focus on the evaluations of *Sesame Street* and *The Electric Company*, prototypes for many others. These evaluations included large numbers of children, diverse geographical areas, varied viewing contexts (school and home), and carefully designed measurement procedures. Exploring their findings in some detail provides information about what and how television can teach effectively.

Research on Sesame Street

Much of the formative research for *Sesame Street* was concerned with identifying those program attributes that attract and hold children's attention. Children were observed while viewing the show, and the program segments that got high visual attention were then compared to those that got low attention to determine how they differed. Some of the attributes that were associated with high or low attention are summarized in Table 4.1. Armed with this information, producers presumably included in their next efforts more of those attributes which evoked high attention and fewer of those which evoked low attention. The appeal of the programming increased, and with it, the opportunity to learn.

During the first 2 years *Sesame Street* was broadcast, summative

Table 4.1

Program Attributes That Are Positively and Negatively Correlated with Children's Visual Attention to Sesame Street and The Electric Company[a]

Positive correlates (attributes associated with high visual attention)

Functional action (central to theme or plot)
Cognitive content with a sparse plot
Simple, clear language in short speeches
Rhythm and rhyme
Lively music
Children's voices and peculiar voices
Changes in sound and sound effects
Clear plot with semipredictable outcome
Songs and speech that are slow in pace and can be easily understood
Animation
Inviting viewer participation
Childhood conflict situation with build-up of tension
Showing objects being constructed

Negative correlates (attributes associated with low visual attention)

Long or complex speeches
Content which can be understood from audio portion alone
Song and dance numbers
Men's voices
Live animals

[a] Based on Anderson and Levin (1976); Bernstein (1978); Lorch and Anderson (1978); Rust (1971); and Wright, Calvert, Huston-Stein, and Watkins (1980).

evaluations of the extent to which children learned from it were carried out by Educational Testing Service (ETS), an independent research organization. These evaluations were on a much larger scale than previous research and set a precedent for later summative evaluations (e.g., *The Electric Company, Freestyle*). The measures were selected to determine whether or not children had learned the content the series was designed to teach (e.g., letters, numbers, relational terms) rather than to test changes in IQ or more general cognitive functioning. By this procedure, it could be readily discerned whether or not the series was fulfilling its goals. This strategy of teaching and then assessing specific skills is much like measuring academic achievement in traditional education. While measures were also obtained for a wider variety of variables, such as attitudes toward school and vocabulary, these effects were not part of the principal focus of the evaluation.

The basic research strategy was to design a field experiment by creating randomly assigned "experimental" (viewing) and "control" (nonviewing) groups. The experimental treatment, called "encouragement to view," involved contacting mothers to tell them about the series, sending them printed materials, and checking with them periodically to find out whether or not their children were watching. Control groups were not given specific information about the series. During the first year, the unexpected success of the series created havoc with the experimental design because many of the control group children watched it. Therefore, comparisons were made between children who watched frequently and those who did not, regardless of their experimental condition. In the second year, cities were chosen where the series was available only on cable or UHF. Reception capacity was supplied to the experimental group but not to the control group. These tactics were successful in creating differences in the amount viewed.

Overall, *Sesame Street* accomplished its goals. Detailed reports of the evaluative findings can be found in Ball and Bogatz (1970, 1972) and Bogatz and Ball (1971). In comparing children who were and were not exposed to *Sesame Street,* either in classroom or home settings, it was found that those children who watched the series achieved significantly higher performance gains on the ETS assessment tests. Pretest and gain scores for children who watched different amounts of the series are illustrated in Figure 4.1. Children were assigned to quartiles that were determined by how frequently they watched the series. Children in the lowest viewing quartile (Q1), who rarely or never watched, gained less than did children in the highest viewing quartile (Q4), who watched on the average more than five times a week. In Year 2, children who were encouraged to view gained more than did children who were not encouraged.

The series was effective for most of the subgroups tested. Younger children *learned* (i.e., gained) more than older children, perhaps because they had fewer skills to begin with. Disadvantaged children who watched frequently gained as much as did advantaged frequent viewers and gained more than did advantaged infrequent viewers. The patterns for each group are shown in Figure 4.1. The finding that advantaged children who watched *infrequently* gained more than disadvantaged *infrequent* viewers suggests that advantaged children more often have other sources for learning the skills taught. We will return to this issue. Other comparisons indicated equivalent learning by boys and girls, Spanish- and English-speaking children, and rural and urban children (Ball & Bogatz, 1970).

The majority of significant gains occurred for skills taught directly in the series but there was some evidence of generalization to other skills. For example, after the second year, frequent viewers had significantly higher scores on a test of verbal IQ than did infrequent viewers (Bogatz & Ball, 1971). Frequent viewers also showed some evidence of more positive attitudes about school and were rated higher in performance by their first-grade teachers.

With success came criticism. In particular, one group of researchers

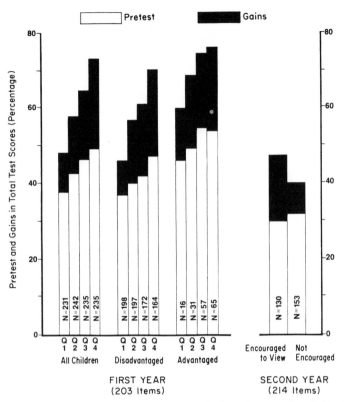

Figure 4.1. *Pretest and gain scores on ETS test totals for advantaged and disadvantaged children by quartiles of Sesame Street home viewing (year 1) and by condition (year 2) in percentages. (Adapted from Ball & Bogatz [1970] and Bogatz & Ball [1971].) Q1 = rarely or never; Q2 = 2–3 times per week; Q3 = 4–5 times per week; Q4 = more than 5 times per week.*

(Cook, Appleton, Conner, Shaffer, Tabkin, & Weber, 1975) reanalyzed the ETS evaluation data and arrived at much more modest conclusions about the effects of *Sesame Street.* They argued that because the experimental treatment, "encouragement to view," provided magazines and printed materials and drew mothers into involvement with the series, effects could not be attributed solely to viewing the series. In fact, the results did show greater gains for children whose mothers were "encouraged" than for the control group in which mothers were not encouraged, even when frequency of viewing was similar. Cook and his colleagues argued that the only true indicator of the effect of the series alone was the comparison of frequent and infrequent viewers in the control group. This comparison showed some significant differences, but, perhaps because of small numbers, they were not as general as those for the encouraged group. The issue remains open. The evaluations indicated that, with or without parental involvement, the series could affect *some* important areas of children's learning and that interest and involvement by an adult could further increase that learning.

A second major criticism was that *Sesame Street* might be increasing rather than decreasing the gap between advantaged and disadvantaged children. Although disadvantaged children who watched the series gained just as much as advantaged children, Cook *et al.* (1975) argued that fewer disadvantaged children *did* watch it often. The net result was that a larger proportion of advantaged children were gaining from the series. This criticism is difficult to evaluate because their audience figures were based primarily on the first two seasons, before the series became well known among disadvantaged groups. More recent audience data assembled by the producer indicate that large numbers of disadvantaged children watch it (Palmer, personal communication). Moreover, "gap filling" was not one of the goals of the series. Instead, it was designed to be an effective teacher of disadvantaged children who, as the evaluation demonstrated, have fewer alternative sources for learning the skills taught. Perhaps critics should work on finding ways to increase viewership by disadvantaged children rather than condemn a program because it teaches too well.

Educators have also criticized the fast-paced format as a possible contributor to hyperactivity, impulsivity, and behavioral problems in the slower-paced environment of public school (Bronfenbrenner, 1976; Singer & Singer, 1979; Sprigle, 1972). However, experimental and field studies have not indicated that such problems result from viewing (Anderson, Levin, & Lorch, 1977; Ball & Bogatz, 1970).

Research on The Electric Company

Soon after *Sesame Street* came *The Electric Company,* a series aimed at teaching reading skills to children in early primary grades who were poor readers. The goals were limited more to academic skills than were those for *Sesame Street.* Three basic reading strategies were emphasized: (a) *blending,* discriminating, and combining phonemes; (b) *chunking,* or recognizing and processing certain letter groups as single units; and (c) *scanning for patterns,* or searching text for units that may affect pronunciation. *The Electric Company* viewers were taught to discriminate vowels from consonants, to scan for typical word structures, to learn strategies of reading for meaning, and to use the context of a sentence to determine the meaning of an ambiguous word.

The summative evaluation of *The Electric Company* (Ball & Bogatz, 1973) was designed to assess whether or not child viewers of the series achieved the curriculum goals. The evaluation research design, sampling procedure, and measurement techniques were parallel to those in the *Sesame Street* evaluation. Again, the specific skills taught in the series were measured with a specially constructed ETS test—The Electric Battery. A standardized reading test was also used to measure generalization. Children participated in a series of experiments either at home or in school. Each assessment section was designed to evaluate and compare the performance of the experimental groups, who viewed or were encouraged to view *The Electric Company* segments, and that of control children, who either did not view (school) or were not encouraged to view (home).

The effects of schoolroom viewing were positive. At all ages, the viewing classes had significantly higher overall performance than did the nonviewers. These effects were most pronounced on The Electric Battery; they were less consistent on the standardized reading test. Like *Sesame Street*, the benefits were especially strong for those skills taught specifically by the series. For first grade children, improved performance, both over their own pretest and compared to control children, was observed on the scales which measured blending, chunking, scanning for patterns, and reading for meaning. For third and fourth grade participants, significant performance improvements occurred in the area of blending and also for some chunking tasks. No effects on the individual scales were observed for the second grade children, although, again, when all scales were totaled, experimental children outpaced controls. At-home viewing produced no significant effects. The evaluators attributed this outcome to the fact that the experimental children who were encouraged to watch at home did not view significantly more than did the controls. In addition, school viewing was accompanied by related curriculum materials and rehearsal by teachers; children who watched at home did not have additional learning aids.

Summary

Evaluations of *Sesame Street* and *The Electric Company* demonstrated that children could learn intellectual skills from television productions that were designed to be both entertaining and instructional. Television was an effective teacher for disadvantaged children and for children as young as 3. Home viewing was effective for teaching preacademic skills to young children, but it was not effective for teaching reading to elementary school-age children. Some skills, such as letter and number recognition, were learned more effectively than others. In all cases, learning from the televised series was enhanced when supplementary learning materials and/or an interested adult were available.

Prosocial Behavior

In the decade of the 1970s there was a notable increase in the production of series designed to teach prosocial behavior and attitudes. Series such as *Inside/Out* and *Ripples* were produced for in-school broadcasting, the Emergency School Aid Act (ESAA) funded such multicultural series as *Vegetable Soup* and *Villa Alegre* for both home and school viewing, commercial networks produced such series as *Fat Albert and the Cosby Kids,* and the Public Broadcasting Service (PBS) carried *Misterogers Neighborhood,* ESAA series, *Sesame Street,* and others. This is not to imply that production of programming designed to affect cognitive skills or to teach traditional academic subjects ceased in the 1970s, but rather to indicate the broadening of the educational goals which television was willing to tackle.

A pioneer in such programming was *Misterogers Neighborhood,* a PBS production that originated in the 1960s. In that program, a friendly adult introduces the viewer to such emotional issues of childhood as birth of a sibling, feelings of anger, and loneliness. Cooperation, caring, helping, empathy, kindness, task persistence, self-acceptance, and other prosocial attitudes and behaviors are demonstrated in live vignettes and in a fantasy "Neighborhood of Make Believe" by puppets and actors. The program is slowpaced, deliberate, and reflective. Mr. Rogers talks directly to the viewer, uses the singular "You are my friend" rather than the plural, refers to the program as a visit with the child, and employs other techniques designed to give viewers a feeling of individual communication with him.

In general, prosocial programming has not been evaluated as extensively as *Sesame Street* and *The Electric Company.* The ESAA series are, because of the legislation under which they were funded, most likely to have undergone some summative evaluation. Even these, however, are likely to be more limited in the size and representativeness of the sample studied and in the length of the viewing period over which effects are assessed. Nonetheless, we do have some information about the effects of such programming. This information is organized here into work on learning and behavioral effects with preschool and then elementary school children and work on attitudinal effects for children of all ages.

Research on Behavioral Effects on Preschool Children

Most research on *Misterogers Neighborhood* was designed to test hypotheses about the ways in which children might learn prosocial behavior from television rather than to evaluate the effects of the series. One of the first studies (Friedrich & Stein, 1973; Stein & Friedrich, 1972) was a 9-week field experiment to compare the effects of daily viewing for 4 weeks of *Misterogers Neighborhood,* aggressive cartoons, or neutral programs on the natural behavior of nursery school children in the classroom. Children who saw prosocial television increased in task persistence as compared with the other two groups. Improved prosocial interpersonal behavior (cooperation, nurturance, and the like) also occurred for viewers from lower social status families. In other studies, similar increases in prosocial behavior have been found using both laboratory and naturalistic observations. In many instances, however, the changes were limited to certain categories of behavior, to subgroups within the sample studied, or to groups who received additional rehearsal or help in understanding the television program (Coates, Pusser, & Goodman, 1976; Friedrich & Stein, 1975; Friedrich-Cofer, Huston-Stein, Kipnis, Susman, & Clewett, 1979; Shirley, 1974; Singer & Singer, 1976; Singer, Singer, Tower, & Biggs, 1977; Stein & Friedrich, 1975a, 1975b).

Although teaching social skills was a secondary goal of *Sesame Street,* some segments emphasized cooperation and taking another person's point of view. Evaluations of these materials indicated that children do learn concepts like cooperation and often imitate the televised behavior if they are put in a situation like the one on television, but no generalized effects on their social behavior have been found (Leifer, 1975; Paulson, 1974).

Research on Learning and Behavioral Effects on Elementary School Children

Commercially made programs with prosocial content and instructional programming for schools are often aimed at elementary school children rather than at preschoolers. One such series, *Fat Albert and the Cosby Kids,* contains episodes dealing with topics such as the arrival of a new baby, divorce, safety, being proud of a father's job even when it is menial, and liking activities that are stereotyped for the other sex. Evaluations by the CBS research department (CBS Broadcast Group, 1974; CBS Economics and Research, 1977) show that elementary school children understand the messages in most of the programs quite well, even when they watch at home under natural conditions. In a more recent study (Watkins, Calvert, Huston-Stein, & Wright, in press), 8- to 10-year-olds recalled most of the content, but 5- to 6-year-olds did not recall it well unless they had some additional help understanding the program messages.

In addition to understanding prosocial messages, children also show increased prosocial behavior in laboratory tasks after seeing commercially-made prosocial programs. For example, W. A. Collins and Getz (1976) found that children from fourth to tenth grade were more helpful to a peer after seeing an action-adventure program containing constructive, cooperative problem solving than after seeing a neutral program or an aggressive program. Similar positive effects occurred when children saw a version of *Lassie* with a prominent theme of helpfulness (Sprafkin, Liebert, & Poulos, 1975). One caution about such findings, however, is that the positive effects of prosocial behavior can be eclipsed and distorted if the same characters are also aggressive. Liss and Reinhardt

(1979) found that young children who saw a version of *Superfriends* in which there were both a prosocial theme and violent treatment of the villain were not only less helpful than those who saw a "pure" prosocial version, but they were also more aggressive than a group who saw straight violence. Apparently the prosocial nature of some of the characters who were also aggressive served to justify their aggressive behavior and make it worthy of emulation.

While the preceding studies all show some prosocial effects in rather carefully controlled testing situations, there is some question about how much these behavioral changes generalize to everyday life. One field-correlational study of prosocial television viewing and natural behavior provided little evidence for widespread effects (Sprafkin & Rubinstein, 1979). Another correlational study in which home viewing was related to self-reported prosocial behavior indicated positive, but very weak relationships between viewing and behavior (Atkin & Greenberg, 1977; Reeves, 1977).

Research on Attitudinal Effects

Television can also influence children's attitudes toward minorities, foreigners, and people who are in other ways "different" from themselves. In two laboratory studies, preschool children expressed more positive attitudes toward children of other ethnic groups or toward general individual differences among children after seeing segments of *Sesame Street* or *Misterogers Neighborhood* that were devoted to those themes (Collins, H. L., 1976; Gorn, Goldberg, & Kanungo, 1976). Early research demonstrated that British children became less ethnocentric after seeing a series of programs on the BBC that presented people from other nations in a positive context (Himmelweit, Oppenheim, & Vince, 1958). In the 1970s the ITT-sponsored *Big Blue Marble* series presented exciting, colorful vignettes about children and adolescents all over the world. A summative evaluation of the reactions of children in fourth through sixth grades indicated that the children liked the program and that their attitudes toward children from other parts of the world became more positive after viewing it. They also became less ethnocentric in the sense that they less often considered U.S. children to be superior to other children and more often thought children in other countries were healthy and happy. A short exposure led to considerable changes in children's perceptions of their world (Roberts et al., 1975).

Summary

We conclude from this literature that children can learn prosocial ideas from television, even at a young age, and that they sometimes put those themes into practice in their own behavior. It is unclear, however, how much the behavioral changes generalize beyond the specific situations or contexts suggested by the television programs or beyond the environment where the children watch the programs. The most pronounced effects have been shown when children are placed in situations that are identical to or very similar to those seen on television (e.g., situations like those shown in the cooperation segments on Sesame Street) or in a laboratory environment where the television program may be unusually salient. When prosocial programs are shown in school, children sometimes generalize to behavior where neither the situation nor the child's response matches the televised content, but such effects are less consistent. We know little about the effects of viewing prosocial programs at home under natural conditions.

The Process of Learning from Television

The fact that children *can* learn cognitive skills and prosocial behavior and attitudes from television raises many questions about *how* that learning occurs. The skills acquired by Sesame Street viewers, for example, are not simple imitative repetitions of program content. Rather, they involve concepts and knowledge which must be generalized beyond specific instances. One of the strengths of the series is that each concept is illustrated repeatedly in a wide variety of ways. The most simplistic explanation for the process by which exposure leads to learning is based on an additive exposure model—children who watch more learn more. Children who see the same concept illustrated repeatedly in different ways may be increasingly likely to assimilate its important elements in a meaningful, durable, and generalizable way.

Active Processing of Televised Material

While some minimal level of exposure is obviously necessary for learning, any comprehensive explanation of the process of learning from television must go beyond an additive-exposure model. In a laboratory study, Lorch, Anderson, and Levin (1979) manipulated exposure to an episode of Sesame Street by providing toys in the viewing room for some of the subjects and no alternative activity for the remainder. Although children who viewed without toys watched almost twice as much as did those with toys, the amount learned from the program was virtually identical for the two groups. Thus, induced exposure to the program did not improve learning. *Within* the treatment groups, however, children who watched more learned more. The authors suggested that the comprehensibility of program material guided attention—that is, children were more attentive when they understood the content being presented. This interpretation and some of the results reported for prosocial programming suggest that learning from television involves active selection and processing by the child, rather than passive reception, and that the match between the program material and the child's level of understanding is an important determinant of learning.

Television Form and Content

Another approach to understanding the process of learning from television has emphasized the fact that television presents information in forms and formats that are different from books, instructional materials in schools, or other sources from which children might learn. Children's learning from television may be a function of their ability to process *both* the form and the content that are presented. Understanding the forms of television should result from general cognitive development and from television viewing experience (Huston-Stein & Wright, 1977; Salomon, 1979; Wright, Watkins, & Huston-Stein, 1978). Salomon (1979) described some television features as filmic codes, or representatives of a complex symbol system, which require decoding before children are able to understand the messages intended. He suggested a series of learning steps that enable children to break the symbolic codes of television in order to extract its content. These theories propose that the forms of television can serve as syntactic organizers and symbols that help the knowledgeable viewer to process the content; they can also be confusing to a naive television viewer. Therefore, general familiarity with the medium should contribute to the child's ability to process televised content.

Children may also learn specific formats that are repeated in a particular series when they view it frequently. Palmer (1978) suggested that these repeated formats become the basis for "learning sets," or expectancies for particular skills or content. For example, when the song, "One of these things is not like the others," begins on *Sesame Street*, regular viewers know that a sorting (or oddity) problem is coming. They are set to think about classes of objects and to look for similarities and differences. Once these expectations have been learned through repeated exposure, the familiar viewer can learn more effectively from a given segment than can the naive viewer, who has to decode all the material presented at once.

Television Form and Mental Skills

In Salomon's view (1979) filmic codes serve not only as vehicles for transmitting content, but also as representations of mental skills or operations in their own right. For example, a zoom-in on one part of a complex array represents the mental operation of analyzing a stimulus into its parts. Showing an object from several different angles may be parallel to the mental skill of perspective-taking. Several experimental studies with older children have demonstrated that they can learn parallel mental skills from these film techniques (Salomon, 1979).

A longitudinal study of "television-naive" children in Israel who were exposed to *Sesame Street* provided further support for the idea that children can learn mental skills from the forms of the series as well as acquire the knowledge presented in the content. When the series was first shown in Israel, children had little experience with television of any kind, particularly programs using the elaborate production techniques employed on *Sesame Street*. Preschool children who saw the series gained knowledge of the content areas presented (e.g., letter matching, relational concepts, and classification). Second and third graders, however, improved not only in their knowledge of some content areas but also in the skills conveyed by the filmic codes (e.g., analyzing complex visual stimuli, perspective-taking). Salomon suggested that the preschool children processed whatever content could be understood without active decoding of the symbolic codes of the medium but that the older children acquired the ability to use those symbolic codes in their own thinking.

Children also used their understanding of media codes to extract the content knowledge from the programs. Before viewing *Sesame Street*, knowledge of those content elements taught by the program was unrelated to mastery of the mental skills needed to understand the media codes. At the end of the broadcasting period, this relationship remained unchanged for the younger children who viewed infrequently. However, for the older children who consistently viewed *Sesame Street*, the relationship between the two steadily increased. Once children became adept at understanding the meaning of the symbolic techniques used in educational television programming, they became increasingly adept at learning the content presented by the medium. When this ability was acquired by the older Israeli children, they became more capable of extracting the program content (Salomon, 1976, 1979).

If television viewing experience contributes to understanding media codes, one would expect American children to show such understanding at an earlier age than would the Israeli children who had had little television experience. The effects of *Sesame Street* on the two cultural groups cannot be directly compared, but one study of older children, fourth and sixth graders, did include a direct comparison (Salomon, 1979). Children's mastery of the mental skills conveyed by television form (e.g., perspective taking, visual analysis) was positively correlated with home television viewing only for Israeli fourth graders. Israeli children actually engaged in more "literate viewing" (i.e., they recalled more television content) than did Americans. This result may indicate that American children of both ages had already gained whatever benefit was possible from television exposure, as had the older Israeli children. Alternatively, this result may reflect a fact about television viewing in the United States that complicates all findings that attempt to relate amount of home viewing to comprehension. The demographics suggest that children in families with higher income, employment, parent education, or intelligence watch less television than do other children (Comstock, Chaffee, Katzman, McCombs, & Roberts, 1978). Thus, those who watch the most television are less advantaged and, in general, less likely to excel on any comprehension test. In Salomon's U.S. sample, this fact may have prevented the expected positive effects of viewing on comprehension from appearing in the data.

In summary, learning from television occurs at several levels. At one level, children learn a variety of skills, behaviors, attitudes, and information—the program content—through active selection and processing of material that is comprehensible to them. At a second level, they learn formats that are specific to a particular program or setting which can serve as learning sets to facilitate understanding of content. At a third level, they learn those more general television forms that provide the syntax or symbolic codes of the medium, which in turn can be used to decode and understand a wide variety of content presentations. These symbolic codes also teach mental skills directly to the extent that they represent mental operations.

Enhancing Children's Learning from Television

Even though television can teach many things at different levels, broadcast television as it existed at the end of the 1970s has several inherent properties that limit its instructional power. It is a one-way medium that transmits information to a child who may sit "passively" receiving. Material is sequenced in a fixed pattern and rate over which the viewer has no control. There is no opportunity for the child to return and review earlier segments or to control the rate of presentation. There is no way to provide individual feedback or to tailor presentations to individual learning needs or histories. Information is presented in a temporal succession, so the child often must integrate temporally separated bits (Wright, Watkins, & Huston-Stein, 1978). Technological changes may remove many of these limitations, greatly increasing the teaching potential of television beyond what we have been able to report today. Within the limitations of the current state of the medium, however, there are a number of variables that may enhance or detract from the effectiveness of educational content. These variables fall into two broad categories: those that are part of the television production itself and those that are part of the child's own living and viewing environment.

Television Program Variables

A number of techniques have been developed by Children's Television Workshop and other production groups to make the viewing child active in the learning process. For example, songs have been presented once by a singer, then the music and visuals have been repeated without the voice so that the child would fill in the words (Palmer, 1978). In a series of experiments conducted by Dennis (1977), pauses were inserted in the middle of segments designed to teach classification and sorting. In one case, a narrator told the child to point to the right answer. This procedure increased preschoolers' active pointing and verbalizing and, in some cases, improved their learning from the segments.

Production features can also be used to increase children's interest in prosocial programming and/or their understanding and likelihood of adopting prosocial behavior. Susman (1976) created versions of a game show in which sharing was verbally labeled by a major character and/or visual attention was focused on that behavior through zooming in when it occurred. Children who saw the versions with verbal labeling shared more than did those who saw unlabeled versions, and visual focusing added slightly to the effect. Such verbal labeling and explanation must be used carefully and sparingly if they are to be effective. In a later study by Watkins (1979), narrated explanations of program themes in a videotape of a *Fat Albert and the Cosby Kids* program produced little improvement in comprehension.

Visual and nonverbal auditory features can be used to improve learning. For example, after seeing an episode of *Fat Albert and the Cosby Kids*, children recalled correctly those central themes that had been presented with high levels of action by the characters and with perceptually salient visual and auditory features (special effects, loud music, and the like). When central content was presented primarily through verbal dialogue, children did not recall it as well (Calvert, Watkins, Huston-Stein, & Wright, 1979).

Environmental Variables

Viewing with an adult who explains, asks questions about, or demonstrates the central content helps children understand and incorporate prosocial themes. Watkins et al. (in press) found that the explanations that had been relatively ineffective when narrated during pauses on the *Fat Albert and the Cosby Kids* program were quite effective when provided by a co-viewing adult. Parent participation in children's viewing also increases learning of cognitive skills from television. In the summative evaluations of *Sesame Street*, children in the "encouragement to view" treatment gained a little more than did the controls even when the amount of viewing was comparable. The possibility that this may have occurred because mothers in the experimental treatment were more involved in the child's viewing and learning from the series was tested experimentally in Israel. Children whose mothers had been encouraged to watch *Sesame Street* with them showed more-improved performance on measures that assess learning of specific series goals than did children whose mothers had not been so encouraged. The effect was particularly apparent for children from lower class homes (Salomon, 1977, 1979).

Although it is fairly clear that adult involvement in the child's viewing increases learning, it is not so clear why that happens. An adult who views with a child may aid learning through serving as a model of attention, interest, or liking; through focusing the child's attention; through verbal labels or clarifications; through eliciting the child's verbal statements about what has happened or will happen; or through indicating how program segments are examples of more general concepts. Available studies do not enable one to determine which of these processes is most important, but it is likely that the conceptual organization provided by verbal labels and explanation is one essential component. Our earlier discussion indicated that simply increasing attention would probably not improve learning greatly but that encouragement to review and anticipate may elicit deeper levels of processing than the child would spontaneously undertake.

Parents may also offer value judgments during viewing that affect the child's acceptance of prosocial educational content. Atkin and Greenberg (1977) found that children who reported that their parents often commented positively about prosocial actions in television programs were more likely to be responsive to those programs than were children whose parents were less involved.

Toys, books, puppets, play materials, and activities can all serve as means for children to rehearse and clarify prosocial television content. In one study of *Misterogers Neighborhood,* children who were told stories with relevant themes after viewing understood the content of the programs particularly well, but those who practiced role playing of program events were most likely to be helpful in a behavioral test (Friedrich & Stein, 1975). Similar patterns emerged from a field experiment in which groups of Head Start children saw a series of *Misterogers Neighborhood* programs in their classrooms. Increased prosocial behavior occurred only in those classrooms supplied with play activities and materials designed to stimulate verbal and behavioral rehearsal of the televised content (Friedrich-Cofer et al., 1979).

Conclusion

Educational messages can be clarified and made memorable to children, not only by presenting them in a novel way on television but also by attending to the entire context of the viewing situation—be it the classroom, an experimental setting, or the home environment. The studies we have just reviewed illustrate that the medium of television is only one facet of the educational experience. It should not be expected that children will learn much through simple observation of television without active involvement in the process. This involvement can be occasioned by the way in which the program itself is constructed (Wright, Watkins, & Huston-Stein, 1978) and by parents and teachers, who help to explain actions, intentions, and motives of characters, sequence and causality in the plot, and the like. By so doing they can involve the viewers in active processing of television information. As an analogy, few would believe that children might easily learn if schools consisted only of books with no instructors. Researchers and educators must be aware that the learning context, of which television is only a part, is a combination of all its components and that all are necessary for efficient learning. This does not argue against the effectiveness of television for presenting educational information in new and creative ways; it only underscores its value within the total learning experience.

References

Anderson, D. R., & Levin, S. R. Young children's attention to *Sesame Street. Child Development*, 1976, 47, 806–811.

Anderson, D. R., Levin, S. R., & Lorch, E. P. The effects of TV program pacing on the behavior of preschool children. *A V Communication Review*, 1977, 25, 156–166.

Atkin, C. K., & Greenberg, B. S. *Parental mediation of children's social behavior learning from television.* Unpublished manuscript, Michigan State Univ., 1977.

Ball, S., & Bogatz, G. *The first year of* Sesame Street: An evaluation. Princeton, New Jersey: Educational Testing Service, 1970.

Ball, S., & Bogatz, G. Summative research of *Sesame Street:* Implications for the study of preschool children. In A. D. Pick (Ed.), *Minnesota symposia on child psychology* (Vol. 6). Minneapolis: Univ. of Minnesota, 1972.

Ball, S., & Bogatz, G. *Reading with television: An evaluation of The Electric Company.* Princeton, New Jersey: Educational Testing Service, 1973.

Bernstein, L. J. *Design attributes of* Sesame Street *and the visual attention of preschool children.* Unpublished doctoral dissertation, New York, Columbia Univ., 1978.

Bogatz, G., & Ball, S. *The second year of* Sesame Street *A continuing evaluation* (2 Vols). Princeton, New Jersey: Educational Testing Service, 1971.

Bronfenbrenner, U. Who lives on *Sesame Street? Psychology Today*, 1976, 10, 14.

Calvert, S., Watkins, B., Huston-Stein, A., & Wright, J. C. *Immediate and delayed recall of central and incidental television content as a function of formal features.* Paper presented at the meeting of the Society for Research in Child Development, San Francisco, March, 1979.

CBS Broadcast Group. *A study of messages received by children who viewed an episode of* Fat Albert and the Cosby Kids. New York: Office of Social Research, Department of Economics & Research, CBS/Broadcast Group, 1974.

CBS Economics and Research. *Communicating with children through television.* New York: Author, 1977.

Coates, B., Pusser, E. H., & Goodman, I. The influence of *Sesame Street* and *Mr. Rogers'*

Neighborhood on children's social behavior in the preschool. *Child Development,* 1976, *47,* 138–144.

Collins, H. L. *The influence of prosocial television programs emphasizing the positive value of individual differences on children's attitudes toward differences and children's behavior in choice situations.* Unpublished doctoral dissertation, Pennsylvania State Univ., 1976.

Collins, W. A., & Getz, S. K. Children's social responses following modeled reactions to provocation: Prosocial effects of a television drama. *Journal of Personality,* 1976, *44,* 488–500.

Comstock, G., Chaffee, S., Katzman, N., McCombs, M., & Roberts, D. *Television and human behavior.* New York: Columbia Univ. Press, 1978.

Cook, T. D., Appleton, H., Conner, R. F., Shaffer, A., Tabkin, G., & Weber, S. J. *Sesame Street revisited.* New York: Russell Sage, 1975.

Craig, C. Q. A comparison between sound and silent films in teaching. *British Journal of Educational Psychology,* 1956, *26,* 202–206.

Dennis, R. W. *Prompting viewer participation with televised instruction: Modifications on Sesame Street classifying segments.* Unpublished report to Children's Television Workshop, University of Kansas, 1977.

Deutschmann, P., Barrow, I., & McMillan, A. The efficiency of different modes of communication. *Audio-Visual Communication Review,* 1961, 9, 263–270.

Friedrich, L. K., & Stein, A. H. Aggressive and prosocial television programs and the naturalistic behavior of preschool children. *Monographs of the Society for Research in Child Development,* 1973, *38,* (4, Serial No. 151).

Friedrich, L. K., & Stein, A. H. Prosocial television and young children: The effects of verbal labeling and role playing on learning and behavior. *Child Development,* 1975, *46,* 7–38.

Friedrich-Cofer, L. K., Huston-Stein, A., Kipnis, D. M., Susman, E. J., & Clewett, A. S. Environmental enhancement of prosocial television content: Effects on interpersonal behavior, imaginative play, and self-regulation in a natural setting. *Developmental Psychology,* 1979, *15,* 637–646.

Gorn, G. J., Goldberg, M. E., & Kanungo, R. N. The role of educational television in changing the intergroup attitudes of children. *Child Development,* 1976, *47,* 277–280.

Himmelweit, H. T., Oppenheim, A. N., & Vince, P. *Television and the child.* New York and London: Oxford Univ. Press, 1958.

Huston-Stein, A., & Wright, J. C. *Modeling the medium: Effects of formal properties of children's television programs.* Paper presented at the meeting of the Society for Research in Child Development, New Orleans, March, 1977.

Kumata, H. A decade of teaching by television. In W. Schramm (Ed.), *The impact of educational television.* Urbana: Univ. of Illinois, 1960.

Lathrop, C., Norford, C., & Greenhill, L. The contributions of film introductions and film summaries to learning from instructional films. *Journal of Educational Psychology,* 1953, *44,* 343–353.

Leifer, A. D. *How to encourage socially-valued behavior.* Paper presented at the meeting of the Society for Research in Child Development, Denver, April, 1975.

Lesser, G. S. *Children and television: Lessons from Sesame Street.* New York: Random House, 1974.

Liss, M. B., & Reinhardt, L. C. *Behavioral and attitudinal responses to prosocial programs.* Paper presented at the meeting of the Society for Research in Child Development, San Francisco, March, 1979.

Lorch, E. P., & Anderson, D. R. *Paying attention to Sesame Street.* Report to Children's Television Workshop, Univ. of Massachusetts at Amherst, 1978.

Lorch, E. P., Anderson, D. R. & Levin, S. R. The relationship of visual attention to comprehension of television. *Child Development,* 1979, *50,* 722–727.

Michael, D. N., & Maccoby, N. Factors influencing verbal learning from films under varying conditions of audience participation. *Journal of Experimental Psychology,* 1953, *46,* 411–418.

Palmer, E. L. *A pedagogical analysis of recurrent formats on Sesame Street and The Electric Company.* Paper presented at the International Conference on Children's Educational Television, Amsterdam, June, 1978.

Paulson, F. L. Teaching cooperation on television: An evaluation of *Sesame Street* social goals programs. *A V Communication Review,* 1974, *22,* 229–246.

Reeves, B. *Children's perceived reality of television and the effects of pro- and antisocial TV content on social behavior.* Unpublished manuscript, Michigan State Univ., 1977.

Roberts, D. F., Herold, C., Hornby, M., King, S., Sterne, D., Whiteley, S., & Silverman, T. *Earth's a Big Blue Marble: A report of the impact of a children's television series on children's opinions.* Unpublished manuscript, Stanford, California, Stanford Univ., 1975.

Rock, R., Duva, J., & Murray, J. *The comparative effectiveness of instruction by television, television recordings, and conventional classroom practices.* NAVEXOS P-850-3. Port Washington, New York: Special Devices Center, United States Navy, 1953.

Rust, L. W. *Attributes of The Electric Company that influence children's attention to the television screen. Unpublished manuscript,* Children's Television Workshop, New York, 1971.

Salomon, G. Cognitive skill learning across cultures. *Journal of Communication,* 1976, *26*(2), 138–145.

Salomon, G. Effects of encouraging Israeli mothers to co-observe *Sesame Street* with their five-year-olds. *Child Development,* 1977, *48,* 1146–1151.

Salomon, G. *Interaction of media, cognition, and learning.* San Francisco: Jossey-Bass, 1979.

Schramm, W. What we know about learning from instructional television. In L. Asheim (Ed.), *Educational television: The next ten years.* Stanford, California: Institute for Communication Research, 1962.

Shirley, K. W. *The prosocial effects of publicly broadcast children's television.* Unpublished doctoral dissertation, Univ. of Kansas, 1974.

Singer, J. L., & Singer, D. G. Can TV stimulate imaginative play? *Journal of Communication,* 1976, *26* (3), 74–80.

Singer, J. L., & Singer, D. G. Come back, Mr. Rogers, come back. *Psychology Today,* 1979, *12,* 56–60.

Singer, D. G., Singer, J. L., Tower, R. B., & Biggs, A. *Differential effects of television programming on preschoolers' cognition and play.* Paper presented at the meeting of the American Psychological Association, San Francisco, August, 1977.

Sprafkin, J. N., Liebert, R. M., & Poulos, R. W. Effects of a prosocial televised example on children's helping. *Journal of Experimental Child Psychology,* 1975, *20,* 119–126.

Sprafkin, J. N., & Rubinstein, E. A. A field correlational study of children's television viewing habits and prosocial behavior. *Journal of Broadcasting,* 1979, in press.

Sprigle, H. A. Who wants to live on *Sesame Street? Childhood Education,* 1972, *49,* 159–165.

Stein, A. H., & Friedrich, L. K. Television content and young children's behavior. In J. P. Murray, E. A. Rubinstein, & G. A. Comstock (Eds.), *Television and social behavior* (Vol. 2). *Television and social learning.* Washington, D.C.: United States Government Printing Office, 1972.

Stein, A. H., & Friedrich, L. K. The effects of television content on young children. In A. D. Pick (Ed.), *Minnesota symposia on child psychology* (Vol. 9). Minneapolis: Univ. of Minnesota Press, 1975. (a)

Stein, A. H., & Friedrich, L. K. The impact of television on children and youth. In E. M. Hetherington, J. W. Hagen, R. Kron, & A. H. Stein (Eds.), *Review of child development research* (Vol. 5). Chicago: Univ. of Chicago Press, 1975. (b)

Susman, E. J. Visual imagery and verbal labeling: *The relation of stylistic features of television presentation to children's learning and performance of prosocial content.* Unpublished doctoral dissertation, Pennsylvania State Univ., 1976.

Watkins, B. *Children's attention to and comprehension of prosocial television: The effects of plot structure, verbal labeling, and program form.* Unpublished doctoral dissertation, Univ. of Kansas, 1978.

Watkins, B., Calvert, S., Huston-Stein, A., & Wright, J. C. Children's recall of television material: Effects of presentation mode and adult labeling. *Developmental Psychology*, in press.

Wright, J. C., Calvert, S. L., Huston-Stein, A., & Watkins, B. A. *Children's selective attention to television forms: Effects of salient and informative production features as functions of age and viewing experience.* Paper presented at the meeting of the International Communication Association, Acapulco, May, 1980.

Wright, J. C., Watkins, B., & Huston-Stein, A. Active versus passive television viewing: A model of the development of information processing by children. In Children's Television Project, *First Annual Report to the Spencer Foundation.* Research report no. 10. Univ. of Kansas, 1978.

5

Children, Television, and Social Class Roles: The Medium as an Unplanned Educational Curriculum

GORDON L. BERRY

The special impact of television on society and its potential for teaching children have led George Comstock (1978) to refer to it as a source of vicarious socialization that tends to compete with the acknowledged agents of socialization in providing influential models that may be emulated. It has also been argued that the power of the medium is so great that children change their attitudes about people and activities to reflect those encountered in television programs. The medium is, therefore, more than mere entertainment for children (Leifer, Gordon, & Graves, 1974). The implication may be that, on television, children can see people and behavior that cause them to pose such questions as: Who am I? Who are they? How am I like them? How am I not like them? Am I good or bad? Are they good or bad? How can I change my behavior, thoughts, and appearance to be more like the models who are validated on television? (Berry, 1979). Answers to these questions become part of a process of self-definition, of learning one's place in life and the place of others. They become part of socialization.

While I would be the first to admit that television can vicariously socialize in many areas, I would like to focus here on its potential for providing social learning about class, status, and roles—individual dif-

CHILDREN AND THE FACES OF TELEVISION:
Teaching, Violence, Selling

ferences par excellence in our society. The ability of the medium to reach a hugh audience and to present a wide variety of images through a real and a fanciful dissection of society into component parts places its instructional impact at the very core of learning about social class roles. The medium offers instructionally oriented content messages to children, messages which are creative, artistic, and professionally developed. However, because the goals of the programs are not usually concerned with the social learning of these messages, television promulgates a set of largely unplanned cognitive and affective concepts about people, places, and behaviors to children who are in the early stages of formulating a perspective about themselves and about social class roles.

Television as a Communicator of Social Class Lifestyles

Most countries of the world, the United States included, maintain some form of social stratification or social class system. The strata within a country's social system may vary, but the process of formally or informally having a classification of the rich, poor, upper, and lower classes is fundamental. Within a given stratification system, there are usually a number of ways individuals can change their status and social class. In the United States a somewhat fluid system provides opportunity for people to achieve some social mobility through individual and group effort. To point out that there is social mobility in American society should not suggest that there is always equal opportunity. Rather, the implication is that a person may modify his or her status and take on different social roles through the acquisition of new skills, knowledge, education, wealth, and other factors judged as having value by the traditional agents of socialization. Regardless of the social mobility and commitments of the country, however, the agencies of socialization tend to validate the social class system to children, youth, and adults, to teach them their place in it, and only occasionally to show them how to change that place.

The continuous teaching and validation processes utilized by the traditional agencies of socialization—such as the family, school, peer group, and religious institutions—are aimed at assisting children to learn the values of their society and to adopt them as part of their behavior pattern. Their techniques include lessons, examples, pronouncements, modeling cues, and reinforcements. The participants and the subprocesses within the socialization process are interrelated, and are aimed at having children—first as children and later as adults—learn, understand, and embrace a set of social roles common to their present or future social class.

A social role may be viewed as a coherent pattern of behavior that tends to be common to those persons who occupy the same position or place in society, and as a pattern of behavior expected of them by the other members of society (Havighurst & Neugarten, 1962). This social role, regardless of social class, has many dimensions, and it changes as the child matures. American society embraces the values and behaviors that certain social classes (or socioeconomic groups) appear to promulgate in their social learning patterns. These values are communicated internally to the members of that social class and externally to other social classes by the agencies of socialization. For example, it may well be that certain social classes have patterns of behavior that include a high dropout rate from school and high levels of unemployment. The social learning being fostered for children within this environment may teach them these social roles, whereas a peer in a different social class may be taught to finish school and get a job.

A number of years ago, the values and behaviors of these two groups would have been very much more localized, and children from the two social classes may have had only casual experiences with the lifestyle of the other. Today, however, the lifestyle and values, correct or incorrect, are quickly portrayed to the wide and diverse audience in our media-oriented society. Compared to the traditional agencies of socialization, the medium of television is a unique newcomer that has emerged within the last 25 years. Its status with and appeal to children and adults as a source of entertainment and information is clearly seen in the statistics from the government report, *Window Dressing on the Set* (Commission on Civil Rights, 1977). This report summarized statistics that showed that in 1975, 112 million television sets were in use in 68.5 million households, and the typical American household viewed 5 hours, 3 minutes of television each day (p. 1).

This widely available and heavily used medium can present broad representations of various social classes, representations which are important in the social learning of children. As a social communicator, it can reinforce in the minds of children selected concepts about social status. Some researchers have suggested that television does more than entertain children; it also communicates information about the social structure and shapes attitudes about ourselves, others, and the world (Liebert, Neale, & Davidson, 1973, p. 18). Since the role of television is so prominent in society, many young people use its information, messages, and portrayals as a way of reinforcing and validating their beliefs, granting television a role comparable to the traditional socializing institutions. Because the children of both the lower and the upper socioeconomic classes are dependent on proper images and portrayals of the various social classes in order to form appropriate attitudes about themselves and about each other, it becomes important to examine television's representations of them. Having done that, and having considered the impact of

these representations, we are in a better position to understand
television's contribution to individual differences based on social class.

Social Learning and Television:
Representations of Social Class Roles

The concepts of social class and of roles generally have rather precise
meanings when used by social scientists. The approach in this chapter is
to combine both concepts in the term *social class roles,* which conveys the
idea that television provides messages related to the values, behaviors,
habits, attitudes, and status of the social classes and to the roles attributable to such factors as sex, age, race, and occupation. To narrow the
focus of the discussion, I will concentrate on lower socioeconomic class
roles to illustrate how the depiction of certain lifestyles may influence the
social learning of children. These roles are quite frequently depicted in
the dramas and situation comedies that children view. Although it is important to be concerned about what such programs teach any child, the
feelings and attitudes of children from lower socioeconomic groups are
crucial because of the potential observational learning and modeling, and
its impact on their self-concept and personal perceptions of their social
class lifestyle.

The lifestyle representations of the lower classes may be particularly
significant for their learning, since evidence suggests that adults, adolescents, and children from these groups view television a great deal and
use its content in special ways. Comstock, Chaffee, Katzman, McCombs,
and Roberts (1978) report that socioeconomic status is a major factor in
the amount of time members of a household spend in viewing television,
with lower-income families viewing longer than higher income households. Similarly, earlier work by Greenberg and Dervin (1972) found that,
in a comparison of the viewing habits of the general population, low-
income adults start watching television earlier during the day, watch
more, continue their viewing at a higher level throughout the day, and end
their viewing later. Lower-class adolescents tend to spend more time
watching television than do those of the middle class, according to these
researchers. One of the most significant observations by Greenberg and
Dervin (1972) was the rationale they offered for their research findings on
the greater use of television by the low-income child:

> The low-income child is more dependent on the mass media, particularly television, as
> a means of contact with the information about the world outside of his immediate
> grasp. Because he has fewer direct contacts with the "real" world and greater frustra-
> tions in his own life, the low-income child gives more of himself to television, believes
> its messages more readily, and is more inclined to perceive that it does more for him [p.
> 51–52].

The seemingly special attraction that television has for the lower socio-economic groups and their use of it to gain information and ideas have some significance for this discussion in that they point to the possibility that many of the misconceptions these children hold about groups and roles may be cultivated through modeling television's images (Bandura, 1978).

In addition to the data on the heavy viewing patterns among the general lower-class groups, there is evidence showing a strong commitment to television on the part of specific minority young people—with most of the data on television use by Black Americans (Bower, 1973; Comstock *et al.*, 1978; Greenberg & Dervin, 1972; Howe, 1977). Since many minority children are part of the lower socioeconomic groups and therefore also likely to be extensive users, one can assume that they have the potential to see their lifestyle represented or misrepresented frequently on television. It is to some of these images of the lifestyle of the lower social class and of American minorities of the lower social class that I should now like to turn to illustrate television's potential for reinforcing in children impressions of differences in people, places, and their own lifestyles.

Table 5.1 offers some examples of some frequent and generalized television representations of the culture and life of lower socioeconomic groups which I have observed in reviewing a number of programs presented on both commercial and public television. My premise is that these representations are so frequently a part of drama and situation comedy fare that they have the potential of providing models and roles for lower-class children. The table considers the representations within four major categories: (a) home and family factors; (b) race and nationality factors; (c) community factors; and (d) career and occupational factors. These categories are not intended to be exhaustive, nor do the examples represent how urban and lower social class portrayals may differ.

The suggestion that these frequent representations of so-called lower-class culture could play a negative role in the social and attitudinal development of children of the lower class is, of course, what makes the portrayals in Table 5.1 important. Such a role could be achieved through the various social learning principles of modeling, reinforcement, and observational learning. To pursue this thesis, it is necessary to turn to the social learning research literature. Kniveton (1976) related this work to television research by observing that one way to learn is to watch how someone else behaves and then to copy that behavior or to perform behavior similar to it. He also noted that to change your behavior to be like the desired model means that the actions of the person being observed are more attractive to you than are those you can think of for yourself (p. 236). The child viewer, therefore, learns through observed behavior and seeks a change in personal behavior as a result of an attractive model.

Table 5.1
Frequent Lower-Class Representations

I. Home and family factors

Frequent disruptions by violence and aggressive behavior between parents and siblings
Female-dominated households, whether or not a male is present
Frequent friction between males and females
High frequency of unwed mothers
Children with little supervision and love

II. Race and nationality factors

"Macho" image preoccupies Latino and Hispanic males
Minority groups—Blacks, Italians, and Hispanics—have the only gangs operating in American cities
Preoccupation with flashy clothes and fancy cars
Inability to delay gratification which leads to promiscuity, crime, and acts of violence
Limited interest in education on the part of the parents and children
Personal and social values that seem to deviate from the norm
Lack of cognitive skills to solve personal and related problems
Homogenous groups of people rather than the heterogeneity within social classes
Minority male as powerless and wanting to be dependent on others

III. Community factors

Crime ridden and disorganized communities
Dirty and unkempt communities
Pimps, prostitutes, and drug pushers valued in the community by most of the people
Hostility toward the police by community people who are noncooperative in trying to combat crime
Community people unbothered by living in poor housing and with crime

IV. Career and occupational factors

Unemployement as the fault of the lower class person who does not value work
Low career aspirations on the part of males and females
Work which does not contribute much to society
Stereotyped jobs held by males and females
Preference for welfare rather than work
Overrepresentation of an athletics career as opposed to other high status careers
Welfare as a way of life

There is a second way in which television's portrayals may play a negative role in the development of lower-class children. This method, I would like to suggest, is somewhat different from the process whereby children simply imitate those whom they feel are successful models. For example, there is a popular notion that low-income children idolize the "pimp" and "numbers runner" because they have money and big cars. It may very well be that one force in the child's life that reinforces the positive role of these two criminal characters is television and that this occurs despite any punishment the characters receive at the end of the story. If so, it would occur because these global representations of the aspects of the lower socioeconomic lifestyle cause the child to believe that they are indeed correct images. The child then embraces these socially retarding messages as a cultural given. The result would be the acceptance of such representations, not because these models appear to be successful (or successful and then unsuccessful) on television, but because these models and the social conditions seem to be frequently validated by this highly attractive socializing medium.

Furthermore, we come to an interesting proposition about a third mechanism that may explain the connection between viewing and behaving. The proposition is that to the extent that television confirms generalized social class models and social conditions, the medium increases the possibility of lowering the child's self-esteem, present and future aspirations, and personal motivation (McCarthy, Langner, Gersten, Eisenberg, & Orzeck, 1975). Without suggesting any value judgment about lower-class status, one can still pose the interesting question of whether or not these "social condition models" of the people and the lifestyles of the lower class negatively motivate members of the lower socioeconomic groups to change their status. This proposition and the preceding one are not based on the direct connection between observed and performed overt action which is so characteristic of the clinical and natural-setting research associated with aggression studies. Rather, the propositions are about the more subtle cognitive process of learning about one's place in life from seeing how one's class, status, and general lifestyle are represented and about the motivational effects of this. Thus, the issue revolves around the concept that televised representations of "social conditions" are generalized social role models, just as individuals may be positive or negative role models.

A case certainly can be made to show that many television representations describe some of the conditions found among lower socioeconomic groups. Because program content is developed by writers and others who generally focus on entertainment, the lifestyle of these groups can be treated and explored without a great deal of attention to cause and effect. In addition, because media other than television provide a somewhat limited and often jaundiced view of the lifestyle of lower socioeconomic groups, representations of poverty, hostility, crime, and social problems become the most frequent portrayals of the community. Representations of individuals within these communities who do not fit the social problems profile are seldom communicated as potential role models for the child viewer. Thus, children do not see a balanced representation of lower-class or under-class lifestyles because television and other media perpetuate a type of "audiovisual deficit view" of that social class.

Of course, no attempt is being made here to call for romanticizing the problems and lifestyle of this social class, nor should we ignore the fact that most media do not portray the middle and upper classes adequately, either, from a sociological perspective. There is a need, however, for programs that offer other role models and increase the frequency of stories representing those low-income people one rarely sees when their communities are portrayed now—providing a more balanced set of social messages to all children.

While all programming tends to take this deficit view of the lower social class, I would argue that commercial programming is perhaps the most powerful such social communicator. However, to say that its potential to serve as a nontraditional socializer and its power to communicate cognitive and affective messages makes it a villain is to miss the point. It is important to suggest that, while one of the major missions of commercial television is to entertain, the effect of that entertainment is to provide social learning messages that reach children just as those associated with the planned curriculum of an educational institution do. The only differences are that commercial programs are not intended to instruct and are essentially unplanned in terms of the learning experiences they provide. However unintended the instructional aspects of commercial television's messages—and indeed, however unintended the ETV and ITV messages which relate to social class—such program content has the qualities of being advisory, informational, prescriptive, and value-oriented in its learning potential. Commercial television programs are curricular learning experiences just like those planned and supervised by the schools.

Television as an Unplanned Curriculum

To refer to television, even gingerly, as a type of unplanned educational curriculum requires some explanation to put the concept into a workable frame of reference. Curriculum, as defined in the context of this paper, refers to a set of learning experiences or activities in which the learner is involved. These learning experiences and related activities are planned and supervised by a person trained to function in this role. Within schools, the persons planning the experiences are teachers, counselors, and administrators. By the same token, the planners of the experiences for a television program are writers, producers, and directors.

Trump and Miller (1968) point out that any definition of curriculum should have vigor, because it is a vital, moving, complex interaction of people and things which includes questions to debate, forces to rationalize, and goals to illuminate. Significantly, both the educator and the television programmer might well agree with the language Trump and Miller suggest. Both might even view their respective curriculum as a means of providing the learner–viewer with a guide or blueprint for identifying and including selected learning or viewing experiences from their respective programs. A set of educational materials designed for children to learn about the social system in the United States or the various social roles one can play in society needs to be well organized; it also needs to have established goals and objectives, to include appropriate scope (i.e., content of the program), to develop elements in sequence (i.e., the order in which experiences and content are presented), and to aim all of these ingredients at arriving at given learning experiences for the student. It is probably true that some of the same planning which goes into the development of worthwhile, effective educational curricula also goes on with creative professionals in the television industry—but of course with different goals.

The analogy between the two socializing agencies of the school and commercial television can, however, only be followed up to a point. A creative person planning to write an entertaining program about a family in an urban depressed area has the liberty to tell that story to an adult audience and to include images that will reach the emotional or humorous side of an individual. The creator may or may not be committed to providing the audience with factually validated sociological or psychological content that will really explain the balanced dynamics of the family relationships, community support systems, or the social and educational aspirations of lower-class adults for their children. The mission—and a legitimate one—is to entertain a broad but unseen audience through the writer's creative artistry. An institution such as a school is, however, committed to tailoring the material to the age-specific needs of children, to those objectives which permit certain content to be absorbed, and to the clear utilization of role models deemed appropriate by this agent of socialization.

The content of the educational curriculum is approved by the major American socializing institutions, and the material is evaluated as part of the curricular development. Evaluation within this system is a process for finding out if the learning experiences developed in the curriculum are producing the intended results; it is a process for identifying the strengths and weaknesses of a given curriculum (Tyler, 1969). This principle of evaluation attempts to ascertain if the curricular messages found within the program objectives are being learned by the student. On the other hand, the messages for a television program also have an evaluation system which uses viewer ratings as a measure of how well they have achieved their goal of attracting a large audience. Both educational and commercial television programs aim for a receptive audience with the exception that television is nondiscriminatory in terms of sex, age, race, and class when it comes to sending messages to its viewers. In addition, television and its entertaining messages are essentially "unplanned" as to the nature of the learning experience, and its planners would not pretend otherwise. Nor would the author suggest that creative expression and storytelling coming from a socializing agency like television have to be similar to those of a socializer, such as the school.

What is important for all of us to consider is the potential social power of television, particularly commercial television, as one of our most significant communications inventions. An invention that presents role models for children, influences their opinions, forms their attitudes, and molds their minds (Hartman, 1978). Commercial television through its presentations aimed at broad-base entertainment has a unique place in our communication system, especially when covering content related to social class roles and social issues. Such content and its specific messages are especially significant when we realize that children may learn social roles and behaviors from dramas and situation comedies without even fully understanding them. Recent research findings (Collins, 1978) indicate that young children from one socioeconomic status group fail to comprehend the images depicting members of other social class groups. This and related findings suggest that children can develop a distorted view of roles and events because of their inability to comprehend fully the storylines that accompany the images of many of the programs.

Social learning about people and places—about social class roles in this paper—can occur from what Bandura (1978) calls direct experience, and, he also notes, they can occur on a vicarious basis by observing the behavior of others and its consequences. Television in our society is especially effective in providing opportunities for vicarious learning, because it opens the world to children and adults with a turn of the switch. As a medium, it has some distinctive features. It has potential effectiveness in communicating to children important concepts that will assist them in their development. Along with its constructive potential, it also provides unplanned learning experiences simply through the creative process of telling a dramatic story or offering a comedy situation. Depending on the messages it provides, it may contribute to maintaining or furthering social class differences in our society.

Just as has been true with the traditional socializers, our charge is to sensitize program planners to the unplanned nature of their messages and to prepare our children to be wise consumers of television and its messages. Children in our schools are taught through the curriculum to understand the dynamics and structure of all socializing agencies and major institutional forces in our society. Television is now one of the major institutions, and I would submit that the creative intent and design of the unplanned curricular messages of television should also be taught to children. If we fail to help children understand this medium and be wise consumers of it, we miss an excellent opportunity to capture the constructive social, educational, and recreational uses of television. We also neglect our adult responsibility in socializing the young people of all social classes to handle the audiovisual messages being presented about their culture and their role in it.

References

Bandura, A. Social learning theory of aggression. *Journal of Communication*, 1978, *28*(3), 12–19.

Berry, G. L. Television and the black child: Some psychological imperatives. In W. D. Smith, K. H. Burlew, M. H. Mosley, & W. M. Whitney (Eds.), *Reflections on black psychology.* Washington, D. C.: University Press of America, 1979.

Bower, R. T. *Television and the public.* New York: Holt, 1973.

Collins, A. Temporal integration and children's understanding of social information on television. *American Journal of Orthopsychiatry*, 1978, *48*(2), 198–204.

Commission on Civil Rights. *Window dressing on the set: Women and minorities in television.* Washington, D.C.: United States Government Printing Office, 1977.

Comstock, G. The impact of television on American institutions. *Journal of Communication*, 1978, 28 (2), 12–28.

Comstock, G., Chaffee, S., Katzman, N., McCombs, M., & Roberts, D. *Television and human behavior.* New York: Columbia Univ. Press, 1978.

Greenberg, B. S., & Dervin, B. *Use of the mass media by the urban poor.* New York: Praeger, 1972.

Hartman, H. D. Television in American culture. *The Crisis*, 1978, *85*(1), 15–18.

Havighurst, R. J., & Neugarten, N. L. *Society and education* (2nd ed.). Boston: Allyn and Bacon, 1962.

Howe, M. J. *Television and children.* Hamden, Connecticut: Linnet, 1977.

Kniveton, B. H. Social learning and imitation in relation to television. In R. Brown (Ed.), *Children and television.* Beverly Hills, California: Sage, 1976.

Leifer, A. D., Gordon, N. J., & Graves, S. B. Children's television: More than mere entertainment. *Harvard Educational Review*, 1974, *44*(2), 213–245.

Liebert, R. M., Neale, J. M., & Davidson, E. S. *The early window: Effects of television on children and youth.* New York: Pergamon, 1973.

McCarthy, E. D., Langner, T. S., Gersten, J. C., Eisenberg, J. G., & Orzeck, L. Violence and behavior disorders. *Journal of Communication*, 1975, *25*(4), 71–85.

Trump, J. L., & Miller, D. F. *Secondary school curriculum improvement: Proposals and procedures.* Boston: Allyn and Bacon, 1968.

Tyler, R. W. *Basic principles of curriculum and instruction.* Chicago: The Univ. of Chicago Press, 1969.

6

Realities of Change

SAUL ROCKMAN

Reviewing television violence and its impact on children is . . . well, sexy. Studying the influence of commercials directed at children is . . . sexy. Analyzing changes in children's instructional television and how they come about is not sexy. Parent and professional groups actively protest to networks and congressional committees about the amount of violence on children's television. They also berate sponsors of children's programs and the Federal Trade Commission (FTC) about the detrimental effects of misleading advertising. But when was the last time you heard about angry parents picketing for better instructional television or read an article by a physician about how important school television could be for the emotional development of a youngster? These things do not happen. This is not to say that the politics of change in children's educational television programs is not a fascinating topic. It is. But it is very different from that of television violence or advertising directed at children.

There are several ways television is used to teach children. For each, there are different decision makers who exert different influences on the programs. Hence, there are different politics involved. Although I will discuss many educational uses of commercial television, my emphasis will be on instructional television (ITV). I will be pointing out the similari-

CHILDREN AND THE FACES OF TELEVISION:
Teaching, Violence, Selling

ties and differences between entertainment programs that teach and instructional programs that are designed to teach. I will review decision making and funding and, along the way, will point out the political and technological changes that influence teaching with television.

Educating with Television

There is widespread belief that all television teaches. I agree. The 15,000 hours of television that a child views by high school graduation will teach him or her a great deal. Neil Postman (1979) argues that commercial television is the primary curriculum for educating the young and that formal schooling is the secondary curriculum. From watching television, children learn about nutrition, both good and bad, and about violence as a means of solving problems; about politics and politicians and about women's roles in society (Comstock, Chaffee, Katzman, McCombs, & Roberts, 1978). But these are not the coursework of schools. The television curriculum is limited and redundant; although it does provide children with a wider view of the world, that view is nonetheless restricted. Schools teach different and equally important things, and television in school helps teachers teach.

Commercial Television at Home

Commercial television is an entertainment medium, not an educational one. However, some programs are designed to be entertaining and educational at the same time. Programs such as *Fat Albert and the Cosby Kids, Schoolhouse Rock, In the News,* and the various after-school specials are designed to be appealing, high-quality, prosocial programming with some educational benefits included. The key element is entertainment, not education; without the ability to draw and hold an audience, no prosocial program can remain on the very expensive Saturday morning air. Nevertheless, the educational content is not an afterthought. It is included by design, and the final credits usually include the name of a child psychiatrist or famous school of education. These are the kinds of programs endorsed by the National Education Association (NEA) and trotted out before meetings of network affiliates, consumer groups, Congress, and the various regulatory agencies. The curriculum is primarily values education, and the high-quality prosocial programming does indeed have an impact on those who view it (CBS Economics and Research, 1977).

However, while these programs are designed to be educational, they are not designed to fit the curriculum of the schools. They are not instructional. There is usually no single subject area for which these programs can be used. They educate incidentally, sometimes accidentally. Contradictory educational messages may even come across in the same program or because of scheduling, such as when a public service announcement about nutrition is followed by a candy commercial. The education is haphazard at best.

Commercial Television in the Classroom

Gaining more acceptance into the classroom, entertainment programs now find a secondary use as adjuncts to the instructional curriculum. As assigned "instructional" viewing, commercial (and public) television programs have been used productively in many classrooms. *Teachers' Guides to Television* and the study guides of Prime Time School Television permit substantial series such as *Roots* and *Holocaust* to be assigned and utilized in the classroom. Sample discussion questions, readings, activities, and assignments provide a curriculum to accompany what would ordinarily be optional, individually selected, evening entertainment. Endorsement by NEA or promotion by the American Federation of Teachers helps increase the audience for these commercial programs (Pines, 1979).

Commercial programs may also provide motivation to read. Dr. Michael McAndrews in Philadelphia demonstrated this by getting poor readers to try scripts of soon-to-be-released television programs. Since then, several networks and syndicators (e.g., CBS Television Reading Program) have been working to provide scripts to participating classrooms. After having read the script, and perhaps acted out the parts, children are "rewarded" by seeing the program at its regular broadcast time. Students, it has been reported, often seek out program-related books to read (e.g., *Little House on the Prairie*) after they have read the script.

Clearly, none of these entertainment programs was designed to be part of a planned instructional curriculum nor were they created with a student audience in mind. The promotion of these programs by educators yields secondary benefits that accrue to the broadcasters. Teacher organizations and foundations see a way to harness beneficially the entertaining powers of television, while the commercial broadcasters insure themselves a larger audience and the self-righteousness that comes from a positive contribution to society. In addition, well-produced programs with proven educational appeal (if not proven educational benefits) have a ready nonbroadcast market which generates revenue and recovers any costs associated with school-related efforts.

Instructional Television

Television that is designed to teach is likely to be a better teacher. Instructional television or school television is linked to the needs and structures of formal education. School television has the educator, not the broadcaster (sponsor), in control of the television content. It differs from Postman's first curriculum, even when compared with commercial television programs used in the classroom.

More than 15 million elementary and secondary students watch instructional television in school, but neither education nor television claims school television as a cause. School television is a very small part of the educational endeavor, and designing television programs to educate is a similarly small part of the television industry. Thus, it should not be surprising that television used for formal instruction has had a long and none-too-glorious history before coming into its own. Until recently, the history of instructional television was filled with a series of unmet promises and a load of unfulfilled potentials (see Wood & Wylie, 1977; and Chapter 1, this volume). In the 1970s, however, it began to demonstrate instructional effectiveness in the classroom (Carlisle, 1978; Rockman, 1976). Much of the television programming now designed for instructional purposes is the technical and aesthetic equivalent of entertainment television, drawing the attention of children and appealing to them in a variety of ways. Instructional programs even win Emmys (e.g., *The Electric Company, Inside/Out*).

Entertainment values are important to students who spend more time before the TV set than in the classroom. The in-school audience is not a captive one; teachers turn off the TV set when students aren't attentive. The requirement for appeal may, in fact, be greater for school television than for entertainment programs. So while I have been drawing distinctions between entertainment programs and instructional programs, I don't wish to leave the reader with the impression that the latter are not entertaining. They aren't *always* entertaining (they aren't always instructive either), but they certainly don't eschew entertainment as one of their goals.

The most important goals, however, for ITV for children are that it relate to the school (or pre-school) curriculum and that its programs be designed to match that curriculum. Programs are designed to teach along with, not in place of, the classroom teacher. Even *The Electric Company,* which was not designed initially for school use, modified the design of its programs and their content in succeeding years to better fit the reading curriculum of the schools (Palmer, 1978). Thus, its utility to the classroom teacher was increased, and it has achieved high and continued use in schools. In contrast, *Freestyle,* designed for both home and school use, did not adequately take into account the needs of the schools and their curricula, nor was there further production which would have allowed for modifications. Its classroom use was therefore not sustained much beyond its initial run. Decisions made at the national level were not consistent with what classroom teachers desired and would use.

Decisions and Influence

Children do not represent themselves when decisions about children's television are made. There are always surrogates speaking on their behalf, always adults. In commercial television, network programmers, producers, advertising agencies, and their clients all have a role in deciding which children's programs will be funded and broadcast. Increasingly, the local stations themselves select children's programs from the many syndicators who offer off-network re-runs and newly created material to fill the after school and early evening broadcast hours. While a standard industry joke has it that children's programming (and, in fact, all of television) is created by children, the truth is that all of it is created by adults. Young people have occasionally been consulted in the development or evaluation of a children's program (Quiroga & Crane, 1978), but it is the exception and may have no relationship to the one criterion that all of commercial television uses to make decisions—the size of the audience the program commands. In commercial television the decisions are economic ones made by adults.

Activists and consumer groups made up of parents and health and education professionals, such as Action for Children's Television, do regularly come forward to speak for children. Through their publicity and organizational and lobbying efforts, the threat of product boycotts may influence sponsors to seek better programming and the threat of legislation or regulation may produce changes such as family viewing time or local access programming. Activist groups thereby force commercial broadcasters to perform up to their statutory obligation to serve the public interest. The motives of activist groups are in the best interests of children, but unfortunately their activities are often negatively directed. They seek reductions in the amount of violence portrayed on the screen or decry the effects of commercials on children's physical and emotional health. However, positive (and economically feasible) programming proposals are rarely forthcoming.

When choices are to be made about the educational uses of entertainment programs, professional educators rather than television programmers or parents make the decisions. By designing print materials for teachers to use with a program, educators help determine the program's impact. Because that impact is more intentional than incidental, parent groups are less involved; they need not be so critical of the products. Professional educators and organizations also influence the actual use of the materials through promotion, dissemination, and endorsements, thereby providing the context as well as the stimulus for educational uses of entertainment programs.

Still, entertainment programming, regardless of its educational value, is created to obtain an audience for the sponsor. No matter how magnanimous the secondary (instructional) use may be, it is the primary one that pays the bills. To commercial broadcasters, television is a means to the sponsor's end—the financial goals are paramount.

To educators, however, television is a means to the viewer's end, and the instructional goal is kept clearly in mind. In instructional television the children again may not speak for themselves, but the surrogates tend to be more child-oriented and possibly more beneficent. People who make decisions about school television seem to care more about children than about the ratings that their program achieves. So far, parents have not seen the need to influence instructional programs, and the federal government defers to the states for the education of children. Within the education profession, challenges might arise on matters of school television's efficacy or content accuracy, but such challenges do not come from the lay public. Schooling is left to educators and to the extent that television in the classroom (or assigned by the teacher for home viewing) is defined as instruction, the professional educator will decide what gets used in the classroom and in what manner.

This professionalization of the decision-making process exists at all levels at which educators are concerned with television. A program is available in an individual classroom because a teacher decided that it could contribute to the educational process in a specific curriculum area. That program was made available to the teacher because a curriculum review committee selected it. The committee members, in turn, could choose to acquire the program because a group of educators at local, state, or regional levels had determined that an instructional need existed for such a program and had elected to initiate the production of it.

While professional educators are the principal decision makers for instructional television, more and more children are helping them make decisions. Instructional television programs are tested almost as much as the commercials on children's entertainment programs are (see, for example, Mielke, Chen, Clarke, & Katz, 1978; Rockman & Auh, 1976; and Chapters 2 and 3 in this volume). The Children's Television Workshop and the Agency for Instructional Television (AIT) consistently stress the use of research and evaluation in the development of children's television. Federally supported television projects, too, have begun to use research in the service of program development (Williams, LaRose, Smith, Frost, & Eastman, 1978).

Instructional television then differs from entertainment television. Those values which are implanted in entertainment television deal with general, prosocial goals and thus lack the well-defined relationship to the curriculum which is maintained by instructional television. This relationship and the teaching success of ITV programs are achieved because of the positive contributions of the professional educator, primarily, and the children, secondarily. Entertainment programming can also be influenced, but by parents and consumer advocates who screen out the negative. Children are directly consulted in the development of commercial television, but only when it comes to designing the commercials.

Funding: The Ultimate Political Issue

The creation of all children's television programs is subject to a version of the Golden Rule—"Those who have the gold make the rules." Thus, as programs are designed, the holder of the purse strings has the ability to influence what will be broadcast. Sometimes it works well; other times, not so well. Some funding arrangements seem better than others; some funders are better than others. But whatever or whoever they are, with money comes the reality of political influence on program content.

While the goals of entertainment and instructional programming may be quite different, their problems are similar. Both require enough money to produce appealing programs, a large enough audience to make the expenditure worthwhile, and enough skill or clout to keep the sponsor from meddling in the program development process. However, because their goals and economic systems differ, their definitions of enough money, enough audience, and enough freedom also differ. In the context of considering the politics and realities of change in instructional programming, "enough freedom" is the crux of the matter. For instructional programming funded by federal agencies, it is a delicate matter indeed.

Federal Funding

The federal government's role in children's educational television has been an evolving one. Education is the constitutional prerogative of states and the agencies to whom they delegate that task. Initially, therefore, most of the federal contribution to school television was for local facilities and equipment. Government money for production was limited so that thoughts of federal curricula would not arise. Questions did arise when, more recently, national and federal agencies began to provide direct support for production, but they were resolved by having restrictions placed on federal involvement in curriculum design. For example, Corporation for Public Broadcasting (CPB) funds have gone to an instructional television series that already had financial support (and content control) from education, and the National Institute of Education (NIE), in its foray into instructional programming, funded a project in which curriculum development was at least nominally vested in a local department of education.

During the 1970s the U.S. Office of Education (USOE) became the largest single funder of children's educational television—from *Sesame Street* and *The Electric Company* (over \$40 million), to the Special Projects Act for such subjects as music, drug addiction, alcohol abuse, and parenting, to the Emergency School Aid Act (ESAA) which has provided more than \$65 million for television projects.

ESAA projects have not focused primarily on the instructional needs of students, nor have they especially sought the contribution of educators. Nonetheless, ESAA holds a special, though not unique, position among the funders of educational television programs. Congress, in its wisdom, has singled out an area of society over which it has authority and has chosen to provide special services. As an agency of last resort and on behalf of public welfare, it steps in where states and local governments have made every effort and failed. In one case, money from a larger pool was set aside to create television programs designed to help eliminate the problems of minority group isolation associated with school desegregation. ESAA series have had an advisory committee represent the minority groups to be served, as a mechanism to minimize government interference. From the producer's point of view, this procedure has met with mixed success.

In the first years of ESAA funding, attempts were made by project officers to review scripts and to influence script content. Several public television stations were producing programs under ESAA funding and they turned to the Public Broadcasting Service (PBS) to help negotiate and enforce a policy that prevents script reviews in federal projects. However, much control is still exerted by the Request for Proposals process. In setting up a federal project, the funding agency can specify the topics it will accept, the audience to whom the television program will be directed, the format, and even some of the evaluation procedures. The project officer takes on a role similar to that of a sponsor in commercial television; she or he is someone who must be satisfied and reassured so that the dollars keep flowing.

Mielke, Johnson, and Cole (1975) have analyzed some of the problems faced in ESAA—a complex, politically motivated, government program. One was that ESAA projects could not always meet the production and content standards established for programs distributed by PBS. Recognizing that they would, therefore, be unable to persuade PBS to distribute many of the series, the ESAA staff chose to develop its own marketing and distribution structure. This marketing effort sought to persuade both commercial and public stations to broadcast ESAA programs on a locally exclusive basis. After administrative and personnel changes in 1979, ESAA shifted its policy from this arms-length posture toward instructional television to a rather chaste embrace. The original choice of commercial and public stations was based on a conviction that school television was an inconsequential effort. Some early ESAA projects had received limited use in the schools (e.g., *Vegetable Soup, Infinity Factory*), but they did not live up to educational expectations and utilization goals. Newer programming efforts, however, seem to align themselves better with established curriculum areas and thus seem to be more attractive to teachers.

The federal government has attempted to fund instructional and educational television from small pieces of categorical programs—ESAA, nutrition, and career education. The dollars are provided to solve specific problems which Congress sees and uses its powers to solve. The federal track record has not been a winning one. For example, NIE made its best guess for a subject area and grade level with *Freestyle*, but it still did not fully consider the school's point of view in developing the project. It gave schools more material on a narrower topic than the schools desired or could realistically use. After the initial, well-promoted semester of use, the series dropped sharply from school television schedules and classroom use.

Freestyle, ESAA, and other federally developed projects were designed to satisfy a goal set at the national, not the local or state, level. The needs of educators, ITV broadcasters, and students were not carefully incorporated into the projects. Such neglect adds to a traditional state and local reluctance to permit federal intervention into curriculum areas, especially when the federal government is the sole sponsor and takes an advocacy role in promoting the programs.

While there are certainly negative attributes to federal sponsorship, Mielke, Johnson, and Cole (1975) have pointed out that the system may not be organized well to capitalize on or produce positive outcomes. USOE has not had a policy or plan for a successful experimental project and has not been set up to quickly fund successive years of a well-received project. Federal projects can be funded from a myriad of divisions, offices, and programs, although regular attempts are made to develop interagency cooperation. Arthur Sheekey of USOE tried it in 1976, CPB tried it in 1977, and Malcolm Davis of USOE tried it again in 1978 (U.S. Office of Education, 1978). But the barrier seems to be the difficulty in obtaining a well-defined commitment from the Department of Education for a centralized office concerned with all television projects. In an era of cooperative efforts and shrinking budgets, no one in the federal bureaucracy wants to relinquish a piece of turf for a cooperatively shared project.

In contrast, CPB's current policy might set a good example. CPB takes the point of view that if education can demonstrate a need for instructional television materials and can support that need with its own funds, CPB can also help. CPB chooses to be neither the sole nor the major funder of an ITV project. Enough outside support, preferably from education, must be present to ensure that curriculum control rests with the educational organization designing the programs. Its experience with AIT's

ThinkAbout project seems to be a useful model. In that project, CPB provided limited production support, in a matching formula, for a project whose curriculum had already been created by state and local educational agencies participating in an AIT consortium.

The Station Program Cooperative (SPC) funding mechanism used by PBS could also work for children's educational programs. This process permits stations to allocate their dollars to a variety of series, where the cost of each series to the station is based on the number of other stations also selecting it. Bidding takes place over several rounds so that buyers can reallocate their funds to acquire the most desirable programs at the lowest cost. Over the past few years, SPC proposals have included 10–15 children's series per year, of which only 3–5 were purchased. Most of the purchases have been for continuations of existing series such as *Sesame Street* and *Misterogers Neighborhood,* and it seems to be very difficult for new series to break in. Thus, the SPC model provides good support for existing series with broad appeal, but it affords no possibilities for the development of new instructional programs.

Consortium Funding

One mechanism to solve the funding problem for new programming has been the consortium. Consortia serving a variety of needs have been around in education and television for decades. Some consortia have been used to produce, not fund, programs. For example, *Freestyle,* with total NIE funding, was cooperatively developed by five institutions working together—a large city school system, a public television station, a large university, a research organization, and a publisher. A more comprehensive consortium model, however, is that developed by AIT and used to create almost a dozen ITV projects in the past decade (Middleton, 1979).

This consortium model incorporates funding, educational decision making, and production into a cohesive yet flexible process. State and local education and television agencies financially support a project, their fees prorated according to school population. This aggregation of dollars allows each contributor to obtain a project that could not otherwise be afforded. Consortium participants are essentially co-owners of the project and share the right to use it without restriction and to duplicate and distribute copies of programs and teacher guides within their jurisdiction. Although the initial proposal is based on needs determination, the funding of the project is basically a free-market decision. Not every state joins every project, nor is participation in one consortium contingent on participation in another. The number of agencies in a project varies according to how many see the need for its product.

What makes the consortium process work well is the opportunity to participate in decision making, for in addition to lower cost and all broadcast and audiovisual rights, consortium members have the opportunity to contribute to the project's development. Individuals representing consortium agencies are educational and television professionals who counsel the project and provide it with access to diverse intellectual resources. The consortium as a committee-of-the-whole (in effect, the sponsor) holds the right of review over AIT (in effect, the executive producer). Through extensive mail communication and periodic meetings, the consortium keeps its collective eyes on the project's progress, insisting on changes when a problem is noted, monitoring and advising until a consensus is reached, and helping plan for implementation and promotion within each member's own areas.

Getting the project used in the classroom is as important as its production. The consortium process creates involvement on the part of educators and school television administrators who then have to work together to get the project used. Their involvement leads to advocacy—a willingness to expend their time and resources to make teachers aware of the programs, to make sure the programs are widely available for use, and to support their continued use. By participating in the cooperative review of a project, from design through production to utilization, consortium participants become publicly associated with the project and committed to its success. The problem of a national curriculum is avoided because, in addition to providing content review, each participant influences the eventual use of the television materials. There are still local screenings for adoption, local reviews, and local control over the distribution and use of the programs.

Funding for consortia, in fact for most of ITV, is based on the aggregation of monies up through the system. Many local schools pay for membership in an instructional television service at a public television station. Often, local ITV agencies contribute to the state ITV organization so that it can purchase programming on a group discount. In turn, the states can participate in consortia on behalf of their constituents. Until recently, this was relatively easy, but a change in federal policy has made state participation more difficult. Federal funds, once controlled centrally by states and used for the benefit of all districts, now flow through the state to school districts and must be reaggregated to have any impact.

For many people associated with school television, the development of consortia has been the major political change in recent years. It provides for the alliance of diverse agencies, each giving up some autonomy for a common goal—a goal that can be locally accepted. But the consortium process has its limitations. There is a greater demand for the high quality instructional series that a consortium creates than there is an ability to fund and produce such series (Mielke *et al.,* 1975; Seaver & Weber, 1979). The inventory of quality programming is diminishing, aging faster than it can be replaced. The number of series offered in the catalogs of the major ITV distributors has leveled off or is being reduced each year. Funding patterns of consortia are beginning to strain the limited financial resources available to state and local ITV sources. States have to decide which of several potential consortia they can join or whether to allocate their dollars for series' rental rather than to consortia. Future production (or lack of it) may reflect funding constraints, not desire or demand.

Mixed Funding

A mixed funding approach similar to CPB's may provide a timely solution, though possibly not a permanent one. As CPB or other agencies can provide matching funds to projects initiated by education and at least partially supported by education, new series can be created. If federal dollars can go for projects more closely matching the perceived and established needs of education—as evidenced by education's willingness to fund them partially—then new series can be created. If television stations, through the SPC, will use some of their programming dollars to match education's dollars for in-school series, then new series will be created and a stronger ITV service will result. The funding issue is a political one. An ever-increasing diversity of funders must cooperatively participate in creating new children's programs, each agency giving up some of its autonomy for a product all can claim as their own.

Technology and Change

At the same time that funding issues are reaching the critical stage, another factor is becoming prominent—technology. With the exception of the book and the chalkboard, television is likely to be the most widely available technology in the schools. As television technology changes, the organizational arrangements to provide television programs to the schools also change. Technological change causes political change.

Twenty years ago, television was a technology sold as a panacea for most educational ills (see Chapter 1 for more discussion of this). The availability of videotape in the late 1950s made what was once a cottage industry more economical and manageable. Instead of each school system or station producing its own live series on the same subject, series of reasonable quality could be shared by broadcasters across the nation. Since the large majority of ITV programming at that time was consistent with curricular needs across the country (Cohen, 1964), ITV libraries could select the best and distribute it to stations and schools who no longer had to produce everything themselves.

Another influential technological event came in the mid-1970s, when videocassette recorders became widely available. While small-format (i.e., less than 2 inch broadcast quality) videotape had been available from the start, it was as difficult to operate as film, had a variety of incompatible formats, and produced a signal of relatively poor technical quality. In contrast, new videocassette machinery was simple to operate, relatively inexpensive and reliable, and it arrived at a time when there was finally a substantial body of television material worth using. It permitted the off-air taping of programs for replay at a convenient time for the individual teacher and the accumulation of more programs than could be broadcast during any 5 hours a day, 5 days a week schedule.

This convenience was limited, however, by the performance rights available for each program. Most producers and distributors of instructional programs permitted users to record and use the programs as many times as desirable within a 1-week period. But as more people tried to use off/air recordings, 1 week's rights seemed too restrictive. Stations insisted on having longer rights to permit their schools the widest and most effective use of ITV materials. In the Fall of 1976 AIT announced a rights policy permitting long-term recording. The two largest regional ITV networks established a policy of a minimum of 1 year's use rights for all programs acquired for network distribution. ITV distributors followed suit or withdrew from the business. Some distributors did not have the rights to offer and no longer made their materials available for broadcasts. Others began to purchase extended rights as they produced or acquired new programming.

The nonbroadcast revolution was beginning. Its purpose was not to change the programming itself but rather to increase the availability of quality programming. Having videocassette recorders in the schools meant that a station could broadcast programs only once a week for recording rather than repeat the same program a number of times to accommodate various viewing schedules. In addition, cassette copies could be made by stations and provided by mail or truck to schools belonging to its ITV service—a supplement to the existing, though changing, broadcast service. AIT has begun to extend this nonbroadcast supplement. By putting multiple 15- or 20-minute programs on a single 1-hour tape, the cost per program can be reduced to the point where a series of fifteen 15-minute programs on videotape costs less than three film copies. In this way, dependence on a broadcast signal is reduced, and programming becomes available at the level of the school or media library.

The first step toward these multiple school television services was the creation of *Sesame Street*. As Katzman (1975) has noted:

The impact of *Sesame Street* and *The Electric Company* on traditional K–12 ITV services cannot be over-estimated. The biggest controversy generated by *Sesame Street* came from the initial request for morning air time in 1968 and 1969. At about half of the PTV stations, this replaced five hours a week of instructional television during school hours. In 1974, roughly a quarter of all air time during hours when local schools were in session was given over to *Sesame Street* and *The Electric Company* plus *Villa Alegre* and *Carrascolendas.* . . .One of the clearest pressures on ITV programming at public television stations is the presence of the CTW programs and the bicultural programs for children. They created demands for air time that were once used for traditional classroom programming produced or acquired at the local level [p. 61].

A powerful children's block that could be programmed for a morning preschool audience as well as for the after-school viewer was an appealing proposition to the broadcaster. Because the PBS children's block could draw a measurable audience, greater constraints were placed on the amount of time that could be given over to a school service. Where ITV was a marginal operation, stations considered dropping the school service entirely. The availability of off-air recording equipment provided some relief for the tight broadcast schedule. Stations could keep the children's block and school television, too.

Videotape and videocassette technologies have made instructional television progressively more economical and feasible. As a result of them, local schools aggregated their ITV funding for a local school broadcasting service, local stations joined together under statewide leadership to obtain price reductions for statewide rentals, and states formed regional organizations which made "group buys." Another technology—satellites—and the low cost of gaining access to them have initiated even more political change and economy of delivery systems.

Satellites make it possible for regional ITV organizations to acquire commonly used materials for distribution nationally. Since local use of these materials is still based on review by local curriculum review and screening committees and since not all stations, states, and regions may participate in the leasing of a particular series, the ever-present apprehension about a national curriculum is minimized. Substantial savings come in needing only one copy of the tape for broadcast. In the 1979–1980 school year a nationally available ITV service was fed daily on Westar I. Twenty-four widely used series were transmitted to stations in all parts of the country. In addition, both AIT and Great Plains National (both ITV distributors) are using satellite time to preview newly available series for local screening committees.

All of these technological changes—videotape, videocassette, and satellite—have brought about a change in the way television stations see their responsibilities. They are but middlemen in the transaction between schools and the producer/distributor of school programs. As the regional networks begin to take on more of the acquisition and distribution responsibilities, stations are seeing parts of their traditional role disappear or be reduced. As this happens they have the opportunity to supply a nonbroadcast service to supplement their broadcast one. In fact, many stations see the demise of the ITV broadcast service and welcome replacing it completely with a convenient, economical system in which the material is available in permanent form. Those whose obligations are to state or local education see audiovisual service as but one way to expand.

The public television stations seem to recognize the rapid changes taking place around them and many plan to become "telecommunications centers." Proposed in 1971 by William Harley, then president of the National Association of Educational Broadcasters, the concept of telecommunications centers was reconfirmed by Hartford Gunn, while PBS Vice Chairman. As stations evolve into telecommunications centers, organizations capable of providing a multitude of television services, they will no longer have to choose between ITV and general audience programming; they can provide both.

Programming and the technology to use it are necessary for instructional television. Corresponding to the need for programming funds is the necessity to make funds available for equipment. With new hardware in place, the ongoing process of using school television programs will be accelerated, and high quality instructional materials can be made available inexpensively and in a variety of formats. No longer is the gray professor behind the podium in front of the gray drape; instructional programs are exciting, powerful, and effective. Cooperative projects make it feasible to create costly instructional programs, and the technology makes it possible to use these programs to strengthen education.

Acknowledgments

While I take full responsibility for the content of this chapter, I want to acknowledge the contributions of several people with whom I discussed the issues: George Aguirre of the Exxon Education Foundation, Edwin Cohen and Bill Perrin of the Agency for Instructional Television, and Chalmers Marquis of the Joint Council on Educational Telecommunications.

References

Carlisle, R. D. B. (Ed.). *Patterns of performance: Public broadcasting and education 1974–1976.* Washington, D.C.: Corporation for Public Broadcasting, 1978.

CBS Economics and Research, Office of Social Research. *Communicating with children through television.* Washington, D.C.: Author, 1977.

Cohen, E. G. *The status of instructional television.* New York: National Instructional Television Library, 1964.

Comstock, G., Chaffee, S., Katzman, N., McCombs, M., & Roberts, D. *Television and human behavior.* New York: Columbia Univ. Press, 1978.

Katzman, N. *Program decisions in public television.* Washington, D.C.: Corporation for Public Broadcasting, 1975.

Middleton, J. *Cooperative school television and educational change: The consortium development process of the Agency for Instructional Television.* Bloomington, Indiana: Agency for Instructional Television, 1979.

Mielke, K., Chen, M., Clarke, H., & Katz, B. M. *Survey of television viewing interests among eight- to twelve-year-olds.* New York: Children's Television Workshop, 1978.

Mielke, K., Johnson, R., & Cole, B. *The federal role in funding children's television programming* (Vol. 1). Bloomington: Indiana Univ., 1975.

Palmer, E. *The Electric Company* and the school marketplace. In R. Carlisle (Ed.), *Patterns of performance: Public broadcasting and education 1974–1976.* Washington, D.C.: Corporation for Public Broadcasting, 1978.

Pines, M. The drive to convince teachers of the educational value of commercial TV. *Phi Delta Kappan,* 1979, *61,* 168–171.

Postman, N. *Teaching as a conserving activity.* New York: Delacorte, 1979.

Quiroga, B., & Crane, V. *Formative evaluation of local television production for children.* Paper presented at the meeting of the National Association of Educational Broadcasters, Washington, D.C., November, 1978.

Rockman, S. School television is alive and well. In D. Cater & N. Nyham (Eds.), *The future of public broadcasting.* New York: Praeger, 1976.

Rockman, S., & Auh, T. *Formative evaluation of "Self-Incorporated" programs.* Research Report # 30. Bloomington, Indiana: Agency for Instructional Television, 1976.

Seaver, J., & Weber, S. *Children's television programming and public broadcasting: An analysis and assessment of needs.* Washington, D.C.: Corporation for Public Broadcasting, 1979.

United States Office of Education. Task Force on Education and Technology. *To support the learner: A report to the Commissioner of Education.* Manuscript draft # 2. November 1, 1978.

Williams, F., LaRose, R., Smith K., Frost, F., & Eastman, H. *Technical report of formative evaluation baseline studies on children's career awareness and sexrole stereotypes for the television career awareness project.* Los Angeles: Annenberg School of Communications, Univ. of Southern California, 1978.

Wood, D., & Wylie, D. *Educational telecommunications.* Belmont, California: Wadsworth, 1977.

7

The Future of Television's Teaching Face

PETER J. DIRR

When the editors of this volume first asked me to write a chapter on the future of television's teaching face, I proposed an outline in the form of a 1999 press release. As I began to compose that press release, I realized how presumptuous I had been in hoping to project the next 20 years' development of television as a teaching/learning force in the world. Yet, project I must, if I am to write about the future. The projections which I offer will be sandwiched between a beginning section on different aspects of teaching with television and an ending section on the forces which make it difficult to project. Hopefully that will diminish my apparent presumptuousness.

Three Aspects of Television's Teaching Face

In thinking about the future, it has been helpful for me to conceive of television's teaching face as a wedge-shaped continuum (see Figure 7.1). At the narrow end is "instructional television," which is intended for use in the classroom and has carefully planned lessons, specific objectives,

CHILDREN AND THE FACES OF TELEVISION:
Teaching, Violence, Selling

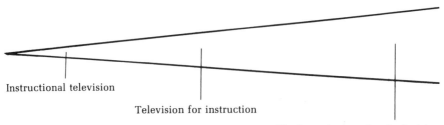

Instructional television

Television for instruction

Unplanned educational television

Figure 7.1. Television's teaching face.

and accompanying curriculum materials. At the broad end is "unplanned educational television," which is any television programming from which people learn. In the middle is "television for instruction" in which teachers adapt noninstructional programming for classroom use. These three categories are neither discrete nor exclusive, but they mark points along a continuum on which it is usually possible to place any educational uses of television.

I suspect that the future of television's teaching face will be different for each of the three points I have demarcated along the continuum, since each point is closely associated with different external forces. For instance, the future of instructional television will be directly affected by changes which take place in schools and formal education, while the future of unplanned educational television will be more directly affected by changes which take place in the entertainment patterns and viewing habits of our society. If that is the case, it is probably simpler to project the future of television at the narrow end of the wedge—instructional television (ITV)—and that is where I'll begin my projecting.

Projections for the Future

The Future of Instructional Television

There is little doubt that the development of ITV has been tied to major changes which have taken place in education during the 30-year history of ITV. This mass medium made its first appearance on the educational scene in the early 1950s when a major goal was to provide universal elementary and secondary school education. Certainly this new medium had the potential of bringing high-quality instruction (the master teacher concept) into every classroom, or living room, throughout the country. It was even viewed by some as being the primary vehicle for achieving universal education.

The goal of universal elementary and secondary school education has now been reached, but not solely or primarily through the use of instructional television. Instead, ITV has become a small part of a larger educational system, as evidenced by data gathered in the School TV Utilization Study conducted in 1977 by the Corporation for Public Broadcasting and the National Center for Education Statistics (Dirr & Pedone, 1979). In this study it was found that 32% of all elementary and secondary school students were receiving a regular portion of their instructional program through television. However, the teacher who used television in the classroom spent only about 1 hour each week viewing one or more lessons with the class and conducting preparatory or follow-up activities. At the elementary school level, most programs were viewed directly off-air from a public television station. At the secondary school level, most programs were taped off the air and used on a delayed basis. And, in spite of the theoretical emphasis which has been placed on individualized instruction in recent years, most teachers (85%) who used television for instruction still used it as a mass medium, in that they had the class view the lessons as a group.

The School TV Utilization Study found that the most highly used series were those which were most widely broadcast on public television stations. A related study conducted by the Corporation for Public Broadcasting (Spergel, 1979) found that, although there were over 1000 K–12 instructional series broadcast by one or more of public broadcasting's 160 licensees, only 137 of those series were broadcast by 10 or more of the licensees. Those 137 series formed the basic core of instructional television programming for the schools.

Given that ITV began more than 20 years ago with the promise of "saving" our educational system and yet is now only a small part of it, what is likely to happen to it over the next 20 years? In terms of programming, the emphasis will continue to be on high quality. There will be fewer low quality and strictly local series produced. The exception to this projection will be those series which are produced by students at the building or district level. Here, we will probably see an increase.

The ways in which programs are used by teachers are likely to change dramatically over the next 20 years. These changes will be brought about by changes outside the schools as much as by any educational revolution. In the first place, the technology of television will undergo dramatic changes in the 1980s, and school-aged children will be among the first to accept and grow up with the new technology. Teachers will have to adapt to it, and for some the adaptation will be difficult.

Continued modularization and further development of the microprocessor will make it possible (and economically feasible) for most homes to have a television-computer-based information-processing system. Children coming to school will be sophisticated in the use of these systems, just as most of today's youngsters are sophisticated in adjusting the color on television sets and many are sophisticated in the use of calculators and television games.

Teachers will be challenged to stay familiar with these technological developments or risk being less sophisticated than their students will be about the information-processing capability of the new media. Good teachers will not be threatened by the hardware, rather they will welcome the opportunity to show students how to harness the full potential of the tools which are available in their homes (and, hopefully, in their schools). The teacher's role, therefore, will be to become a model for the child in problem solving and information processing. And television, more than any of the other related audio and computer hardware, will be responsible for this transformation.

In his or her new role, the teacher will be aided by the availability of a wealth of programming materials. Satellite transmissions and fiber optic cable distribution systems will provide schools with up to 200 channels of audio and video information. By the mid-1980s, the U.S. Copyright Office will have developed simple licensing procedures to facilitate legal off-air recording of any program broadcast over the air or transmitted on cable systems. In addition, prerecorded materials will be available at modest prices on videocassettes and videodiscs.

Doesn't this all sound natural and easy? It won't be. The decades of the 1980s and 1990s will be ones of turmoil for the schools. Their budgets will shrink along with their student populations. Although education will be a no-growth industry, rising personnel costs will compete with the capital expenditures needed to acquire equipment and software comparable to what students will have in their homes.

The resolution of this conflict will not be easy, but it will be driven, in part, by the consumer nature of the hardware and software. Most of the technology and materials used in the schools will be designed primarily for use in the home. Because they will be marketed to a larger population, the cost of these materials to the schools will be lower than that of the materials in use today (which have been developed primarily for the educational–industrial marketplace).

Nevertheless, schools will have to budget adequate sums for equipment, and recent assessments of needs and costs indicate that the sums will not be paltry. In 1978 it was shown (Dirr & Spergel, 1978) that 96% of all instructional programs broadcast by public television stations were produced in color. Yet, two out of three teachers had access to only black-and-white television sets (Dirr & Pedone, 1979). It was estimated that to convert to color sets while maintaining the same classrooms-to-sets ratio (12:1 at the high school level and 5:1 at the elementary school level) would cost $157 million (Dirr, 1979). Furthermore, to place a videotape recorder in each elementary and secondary school which did not have one in 1977 would cost an estimated $75 million. While these costs may decrease when the technology is marketed to a larger population, it still seems likely that they will be substantial and therefore cause conflict in budgetary decision making.

The Future of Television for Instruction

Between now and the end of this century, television will increasingly serve as a bridge between children's lives in the classroom and their lives outside the classroom. In that respect, "television for instruction" (teachers adapting noninstructional programming for classroom use) will become the dominant mode of television use in the classroom. As teachers become models for problem solving and information processing, they will start with the resources which children are likely to have available to them. This will not always (and in some cases, rarely) be programs which were designed as instructional television programs with carefully planned lessons with specific objectives and accompanying materials. Instead, it will often be the teacher's responsibility to lay out the objectives and to provide the child with teacher-made materials (sometimes merely a more detailed educational explanation of the product developer's or manufacturer's instructions). Teachers will thereby make noninstructional programming into instructional programming.

Television and television-related media (e.g., television games, information-processing systems) will be natural vehicles from which children will learn because they will have been in their environment from birth. Children will learn the "language" of these media before they come to school. However, just as English grammar courses are now taught throughout elementary and secondary school, visual literacy and grammar courses will have to be taught in the future.

Visual literacy is a need which is only now being recognized. In 1978 the U.S. Office of Education funded four projects designed to teach critical viewing skills to children in elementary and secondary schools and to adults. Other such projects have been funded by ABC, the PTA, and the Office for Child Development. We need, and can expect to see, many such efforts in the 1980s and 1990s. Implementation of these experimental projects will be an additional responsibility of tomorrow's teachers.

The Future of Unplanned Educational Television

All of television can be considered "educational television" (any television programming from which people learn). Yet, that simple point has been overlooked by most educators for many years. It was only in the early 1970s that the Surgeon General's Report suggested that there might be some association between children's viewing of violent television programs and their consequent antisocial behavior (Surgeon General's Scientific Advisory Committee, 1972). Subsequent studies have shown that the aggressive behavior of some children has, in fact, been learned from television (Murray & Kippax, 1978; Singer & Singer, 1979).

More recently, the National Science Foundation (NSF) and the Federal Trade Commission (FTC) have—among other issues in the area of advertising to children—been concerned about what children *learn* from advertisements which are interspersed among children's television programs. NSF and the FTC have concluded that often children do indeed learn precisely what the manufacturer wants them to learn from the ads (Adler, Friedlander, Lesser, Meringoff, Robertson, Rossiter, & Ward, 1977; Federal Trade Commission, 1978).

During the 1960s, this country learned of the atrocities of the Vietnam War from television coverage of that war. One of the consequences of what we learned was action by some. The rest is now history.

The 1980s and 1990s will see a heightened awareness and appreciation of television's great power as a teaching tool. More Americans are now turning to television as their major source of news. Many also see documentaries (such as a recent program on potential nuclear disasters), science and animal shows (such as *Nova, Jacques Cousteau,* and National Geographic Specials), and historical dramas (such as *I, Claudius; Roots;* and *Upstairs, Downstairs*) as being the most needed types of programs on television. All of these programs are truly educational in a very constructive way, and their educational value can even be increased in the hands of an imaginative teacher. I suspect that the trend to turn to television for this type of education will continue and increase during the 1980s and 1990s.

As previously mentioned, advances in technology will increase channel availability to 200 channels per home. Persons will be budgeting approximately 10% of their annual earnings for their home entertainment/information centers. These will include broadcast programs, programs on demand, and prerecorded (library) programs. Some will resemble today's television programs; others, today's television games; and still others, computer interactive programs. All of them will have at least the potential for teaching.

Unanswered Questions

Most of my projections for the future of television's teaching face have dealt with its future in the United States and have been based on what we know today. I suspect that if the United States were isolated from all other countries, the question would be not *whether* the projections will ever become reality but *when* they will become reality. In that case, timing would be influenced mainly by the ability of our economy to support the technological changes envisioned by those of us who project the future.

But the United States does not function in isolation from the rest of the world. Even today in this country, we depend heavily on Japan for many of our technological advances. We depend on Great Britain for many of our finest public television series. The three commercial networks have international bureaus scattered all over the world. The U.S. government must work cooperatively with the other governments of the world in allocating the use of the sound spectrum and adopting technical standards. Thus, our uses of television for teaching (especially of unplanned educational television) cannot be seen solely as the function of what we as a single nation do.

Our television system today is international by nature. This brings with it some assets and liabilities. On the positive side, it moves us closer to what Marshall McLuhan (Carpenter & McLuhan, 1960) called a global village where what happens in Africa or the Middle East or any part of the world is felt as vividly in the United States as if it had happened within our own village. On occasion in recent years this has been hard for many Americans to deal with, because it has brought into our living rooms cultures, ideals, and values which are foreign to us. It has taught us that others do not always see us as we see ourselves. It has made us acutely aware that we are not as self-sufficient and as independent as we might have once thought.

In the 1980s and 1990s, television will continue to bring us into contact with people who view life differently than we do. We can recoil and retreat from this exposure, or we can use the medium as a learning tool and a vehicle for dialogue. Television can be systematically used as a medium for international education. This is its positive side.

On the negative side, the medium is easy to control. In totalitarian states, it becomes a mouthpiece and propaganda instrument for the ruling faction. This conflicts with our democratic vision of television as a medium for entertainment and education. While the exact line between propaganda and education may be difficult to draw, the unanswered question is whether these two views are irreconcilable. If they are, what are the international implications?

Another set of issues related to television's teaching face has just begun to surface, but it can be expected to persist until the end of this century. It has to do with the impact of television viewing on our brains. Only recently have a few begun systematically to explore the physiological and psychological effects of television viewing on our psycho-neurological system. At present, it is too early to know what results these investigations will yield, but I suspect that improved instrumentation will show that learning from television does affect our brains differently than does learning from print, still photos, or programmed instruction. The results are not likely to indicate that one method of learning is superior to others but rather that specific types of learning are best achieved by specific media. Media choices might then be governed by the type of learning we chose to encourage.

At the more narrow level of instructional television there remain several unanswered questions about how teachers might best use television in the classroom. Some of those questions will remain unanswered until some of the more general issues raised above (e.g., international implications of the medium, psycho-neurological impact of the medium) are resolved. However, the overarching issue of teacher training to use television should be faced head-on in the early 1980s.

The 1977 School TV Utilization Study (Dirr & Pedone, 1979) found that only 17% of all teachers had had any training in the use of television for instruction. This is a condition which should be ameliorated in the early 1980s with our current state-of-the-art knowledge. The issue should not be *whether* teachers should be trained but *how* they can best be trained.

It seems to me that this issue might be brought to a head by teachers themselves. As more and more children come into the classroom from homes where they have home entertainment and information centers, teachers will begin to feel left behind. They will feel the need for training, especially "how to" training on the use of both the hardware and software of new television and information-processing technologies. Once they become comfortable with the technology and its software, they will feel the need for visual literacy training so that they might become adequate models for their students. The unanswered question is, "How can this training best be provided and who will pay for it?" In 1978 it was estimated that it would cost approximately $400 million to provide basic training in the use of television for instruction to every teacher, principal, and superintendent who had not had such training (Dirr, 1979). Obviously, the question of how to provide such training is an important one.

Most of this chapter has dealt with television's teaching face as it applies to elementary and secondary schools. However, we have heard a lot lately about "lifelong learning." There seems to be an emerging, unwritten goal for our country to provide for everyone at least a 2-year college education and continued education throughout life. One national testing organization recently estimated that a child born today will have seven different careers (not just job changes) during his or her lifetime (Educational Testing Service, 1979). If that is the case, it alone makes a good argument for lifelong learning.

There seems to be emerging from the elementary/secondary school concept of individualized instruction a view of learning as a continuum—a process which begins at birth and continues until death. The continuum is a very individual thing (especially in pace and modalities), but it has some characteristics which apply to all of us. One of those characteristics is that learning becomes increasingly self-directed as one ages, with the major increase in self-direction coming after graduation from high school. Formal educational institutions are then available only to assist when necessary and to provide credentials when desired.

Given this view of lifelong learning, it can be seen that television has the potential for playing a major role. The existence of this potential was just being realized in 1979. In that year I counted no fewer than 15 national projects to explore or implement the use of television for adult learning (e.g., the PBS Adult Learner Task Force, the American Association of Community and Junior Colleges' Television Learning project, the National University Consortium for Teaching by Television proposed by the University of Maryland and the Maryland Center for Public Broadcasting, and the Higher Education Utilization Study conducted by the Corporation for Public Broadcasting and the National Center for Education Statistics). This activity should continue well into the 1980s. The major unanswered questions are: "How much of the activity will be broadcast and how much, non-broadcast?"; "What are the respective roles of the TV stations and the educational institutions?"; and "How much of the activity will be user-supported and where will other support come from?"

At the bottom of several unanswered questions lies the issue of support. In times of affluence and an expanding economy, it would have been easy to say that the necessary financial support would be made available and that needed infrastructures would be created. However, my reading of the international economic scene leads me to believe that we are in an international economic crisis and that we will experience very little economic growth during the 1980s. Most change will come about by redistributing resources which will remain at the current overall level rather than increasing. If that is the case, television will undoubtedly experience growth as an entertainment medium as more people stay close to home due to energy shortages. It remains to be seen whether television will also be widely enough perceived as an educational medium to lead large numbers of persons to demand more educational programming from both commercial and public television stations.

If the demand is great enough and if the resources are available, television will grow as an educational resource during the 1980s and 1990s. In that case, I see the 1980s as a decade during which we will systematically investigate the question: "How can the potential of television best be harnessed for educational purposes?" The 1990s would then become the decade during which television will be deployed for education on an international scale.

Today, television is primarily an invisible teacher with an invisible curriculum. It is an invisible teacher, not so much because it is not highly visible in our society—indeed, the television set is the center of attention in many living rooms—but because we have become so accustomed to it in 30 short years that we tend to take it for granted or to overlook its presence.

Television's programming—for all except ITV—provides an invisible curriculum because, although there is no doubt in any parent's mind that children learn from television, there have been very few, if any, systematic, nationwide studies of what children are learning from it. Recent activities of parent and consumer groups have called attention to this condition, but none has yet succeeded in systematically dealing with it. Regardless of the economic conditions of the 1980s and 1990s it is my belief that by the turn of the century television as a teacher will have been carefully studied at all points in my wedge-shaped continuum. It will no longer be able to hide its teaching face behind a veil.

References

Adler, R. P., Friedlander, B. Z., Lesser, G. S., Meringoff, L., Robertson, T. S., Rossiter, J. R., & Ward, S. *Research on the effects of television advertising on children.* Washington, D.C.: United States Government Printing Office, 1977.

Carpenter, E., & McLuhan, M. *Explorations in communication.* Boston: Beacon Press, 1966.

Dirr, P. J. *Estimates of costs for technology improvement in the schools.* Unpublished manuscript, Washington, D.C.: Corporation for Public Broadcasting, 1979.

Dirr, P. J., & Pedone, R. J. *Uses of television for instruction, 1976–77.* Washington, D.C.: Corporation for Public Broadcasting, 1979.

Dirr, P. J., & Spergel, H. K. *A study of public television's educational services, 1975–76.* Washington, D.C.: Corporation for Public Broadcasting, 1978.

Educational Testing Service. *ETS Developments,* Summer 1979.

Federal Trade Commission. *Staff report on television advertising to children.* Washington, D.C.: United States Government Printing Office, 1978.

Murray, J. P., & Kippax, S. Children's social behavior in three towns with differing television experience. *Journal of Communication,* 1978, *28*(1), 19–29.

Singer, J. L., & Singer, D. G. Come back, Mister Rogers, come back. *Psychology Today,* March, 1979.

Spergel, H. K. *A listing of educational series broadcast by public television licensees, 1978–79.* Washington, D.C.: Corporation for Public Broadcasting, 1979.

Surgeon General's Scientific Advisory Committee. *Television and growing up: The impact of televised violence.* Report to the Surgeon General, United States Public Health Service. Washington, D.C.: U.S. Government Printing Office, 1972.

Part II

THE VIOLENT FACE OF TELEVISION

A child experiences violence. A child learns. Mostly we do not deliberately teach our children to be violent or even aggressive. And certainly we do not deliberately do so on television. Yet the messages are there, and our children learn them simply as a by-product of having "been there." Because it is an unplanned curriculum and unintentional teacher, the violent face of television differs considerably from the teaching face in which curricula are planned and teaching is intentional. It also differs in that it has aroused heated policy debates and attempts to change it. Violence is a staple of primetime and children's programming on commercial stations. While many can argue over the definition of violence—a pratfall?, a humorous insult?, an Act of God?, a fistfight?, a war?—all agree it's there. It draws audiences and therefore makes money for stations and networks. It is certainly not intended to instruct viewers. What then are its effects and what are the chances of bringing about any significant reform?

Rubinstein's historical introduction traces attempts to understand effects through research and to examine reform through congressional inquiry. He describes the Eisenhower Commission, its formal assignment and its problems, and provides authoritative review of the Surgeon General's program of study of television and social behavior, discussing its conclusions and its problems. He also looks beyond federally funded research to studies conducted by the commercial networks themselves. He finds a consensus regarding the effects of television violence and examines public efforts to deal with the issue. His concluding section considers the pattern and nature of public policy changes which have occured since the report to the Surgeon General.

In his outline of the current scene, Comstock focuses on newer research on the effects of television and film violence. He gives brief attention to the idea that vicarious experience of violence inhibits its performance or even decreases the drive to perform rather than increasing the likelihood of aggression. He then moves to evidence from laboratory experiments, field experiments, and surveys, describing the strengths and weaknesses of each approach and assessing the conclusions each supports by itself or when aggregated conceptually or through meta-analysis techniques. After reviewing research on the psychology of entertainment and behavior, he concludes with a review of emerging research directions in which he pointedly asks how well entertainment television might do if it taught intentionally rather than incidentally.

Gerbner and Gross view television content as the "first mass-produced and organically composed symbolic environment into which all children are born . . .[p. 150]." They consider it the "modern functional equivalent" to an established religion, and they discuss cyclical/repetitive programming and universal/ritualistic use as two key religious elements. Drawing from their years of message system analysis, they provide a descriptive profile of television characters and violent actions and suggest that the characteristics of those on television and of their relationships are lessons in the American power structure. They then provide a demonstration that these lessons cultivate beliefs in child, adolescent, and adult viewers and conclude with some recommendations for change.

As their article suggests, Lefkowitz and Huesmann look at a variety of concomitants of violence viewing. In addition to longitudinal and cross-cultural studies of aggression, they review research in the areas of socialization and values, physiological responses, and mood. The second half of their chapter considers the processing of observed violence. They discuss observational learning, change in attitude toward aggressive behavior, emotional and physiological responsiveness, and desensitization to violence. They also examine the significant, but infrequently discussed, possibility that viewing televised violence serves as a positive reinforcement for the socially isolated child viewer, thereby increasing the chance for dysfunctional socialization.

Dorr and Kovaric begin their chapter by reviewing the kinds of effects and dependent measures they will examine. They then discuss some significant methodological problems in studying individual differences. In their review of specific individual difference variables, they summarize research findings from studies which have considered the dimensions of age, cognitive ability, sex, ethnicity, social class, personality characteristics, and viewer propensity for aggression. They distill the findings and trends evident within this research and suggest implications these have for practice and policy.

Tannenbaum and Gibson relate the violence issue to some more basic questions regarding children, the existing broadcasting system, and intervention points where change would have the greatest likelihood of occurring. They question whether proposed regulatory cures might not be worse than the current situation and whether children would really be the beneficiaries of change. They make a distinction between statistical and social significance and end by asking whether technological change might not make some current issues obsolete.

Siegel's future perspective takes a fresh, creative look at the relationship between television violence research and television industry reform. She sets the stage by describing how other professions have welcomed relevant research findings from developmental psychology and by contrasting this with the response from the television industry. She then analyzes the reasons for such a difference, including professionalization, continuing education, and training in research. She concludes with an imaginative blueprint for reform within the existing commercial network structure.

8

Television Violence:
A Historical Perspective

ELI A. RUBINSTEIN

Public attention to violence on television has been evident since the early 1950s. Indeed, concerns about violence and the media in general, especially their effects on children, long antedate the advent of television. At the turn of the century there was concern about the effects of dime detective stories and of comic strips. Later, concern was expressed about movies. Research as far back as the 1930s concluded that violence in the movies had a marked effect on an adolescent audience (Charters, 1933). Later, comic strips were again criticized for their bad influence on children (Wertham, 1954).

Early Background

It wasn't until television came along that a major body of research evidence on the effects of violence in the media began to accumulate. One of the first large-scale studies was done in England by Himmelweit, Oppenheim, and Vince (1958). This was a comprehensive examination of the effects of television on children. Among the findings, from a sample of over 1800 British children, was the result that crime and detective stories

CHILDREN AND THE FACES OF TELEVISION:
Teaching, Violence, Selling

did not make children more aggressive. It was noted, however, that programs of violence were not beneficial and that they took up a disproportionate amount of viewing time.

At the same time, public concern was beginning to develop here in the United States where many of these crime and detective stories were being produced. A series of surveys in 1951 by the National Association of Educational Broadcasters found that crime and horror programs comprised 10% of programming time in four large American cities. Shortly thereafter, in 1954, congressional inquiry into the effect of television violence was initiated by Senator Estes Kefauver in a series of hearings by a Senate subcommittee examining the causes of juvenile delinquency. In 1956 that subcommittee issued a report which found that television violence could be potentially harmful to young viewers. Subsequent surveys by the Senate subcommittee in 1961 and 1964 found that the amount of violence on television had increased and that much of it was shown during times when young viewers were a large part of the audience. In its 1965 report, the Senate subcommittee, under the chairmanship of Senator Thomas Dodd, concluded that there had been no reduction in televised violence since 1961 and that televised crime and violence were related to antisocial behaviors among juvenile viewers (Judiciary Committee, U.S. Senate, 1965).

Despite the conclusions by these congressional committees, no definitive body of research data had been accumulated at that time. A comprehensive review of research on the effects of mass communication by Klapper (1960) concluded that no case had been made for the relationship between juvenile delinquency and media crime and violence. He did note that the media were likely to reinforce tendencies, "good or ill," of the viewer. Klapper's position was partially supported by the conclusions of the first major American survey of television and its effects on children (Schramm, Lyle, & Parker, 1961). From a sample of 6000 school children in America and Canada, these researchers concluded that children who were not already somewhat aggressive and who did not confuse fantasy with reality were less likely to be influenced toward violence. Specifically on the issue of juvenile delinquency, they concluded that a disturbed family relationship was a much more likely precursor of delinquency than was the act of watching television violence.

The Eisenhower Commission

The next major event in the examination of television violence was precipitated by the sequence of assassinations of President John Kennedy, Senator Robert Kennedy, and the Reverend Dr. Martin Luther King, Jr. In 1968 President Johnson established a national commission on the causes and prevention of violence. One part of the commission's task was to examine the impact of the mass media on violence.

In recent years, national commissions have been convened to examine and issue findings and recommendations on a variety of issues of major public concern—including television and violence. In most instances, the findings and conclusions of these commissions have stirred up almost as much controversy as they were intended to have resolved. The clearest example of this problem is the Warren Commission, which even 15 years after its conclusions on President Kennedy's assassination is still the target of much criticism. The difficulties of such commissions derive from the facts that a national commission inevitably is given a complex and controversial task, that it operates under much public scrutiny, and that it is given much too little time to complete its task.

The Eisenhower Commission suffered from all these problems. Insofar as its report on violence and the media was concerned, it encountered one further difficulty. Just prior to issuing its final report, it was upstaged by the formation of a new national inquiry—the Surgeon General's program of research on television and social behavior. Despite this last minute and unexpected development, the report on violence and the media from the Eisenhower Commission (Baker & Ball, 1969) provided an important survey of the field. A number of distinguished scientists contributed review chapters to the staff report, and George Gerbner, a leading researcher in the field, prepared a careful content analysis which documented the extent of violence on television. The full staff report concluded that watching television violence taught the viewer how to engage in violent behavior, and a series of recommendations was developed to help make television less harmful to the viewer. Among these recommendations was a comprehensive proposal for a "center for media study," to serve as an independent agency to monitor media performance and to conduct research into the social effects of the media.

The Surgeon General's Program of Research

Before the Eisenhower Commission report was issued in September, 1969, a new national examination of violence on television had been launched. In March 1969, Senator John Pastore, Chairman of the Senate Subcommittee on Communications, requested the Surgeon General to appoint a committee of distinguished scientists to conduct a scientific study to establish whether or not televised violence produced antisocial behavior in children.

The timing of this request has since been looked on with suspicion by viewers of the Washington scene. This reaction is one more hazard of the work of national commissions. Political significance is attributed to every aspect of their operation, including how and when they are convened. In fact, Senator Pastore had been concerned that television violence was not a major focus of the Eisenhower Commission and, understandably, he wanted to initiate an even more comprehensive effort under the scrutiny of his own subcommittee.

For a variety of reasons, including White House support of Senator Pastore's request to the Surgeon General, a program was quickly initiated and an advisory committee convened within 3 months of the Senator's request. By Washington standards this was very rapid implementation of the program. The full story of that program has been well documented elsewhere (Bogart, 1972; Cater & Strickland, 1975; Rubinstein, 1976). There are, however, some points about the entire enterprise that bear repeating.

In all of the previous public concern about and attention to televised violence, relatively little funding had been made available for new research on the basic question of the relationship between television violence and antisocial behavior. The two major surveys mentioned earlier (Himmelweit et al., 1958; Schramm et al., 1961) had been supported by foundation money in England and the United States respectively. The Eisenhower Commission was amply supported by federal funds for its staff work, but very little money was available for new research. The staff report, as already noted, was mainly a series of commissioned review papers. Only the content analysis of television violence by George Gerbner was an effort to obtain new scientific information.

In contrast, the major emphasis in the Surgeon General's program was on producing new scientific evidence. The sum of 1 million dollars was allocated for research. The expectation was that a new body of information would provide compelling evidence for resolving the long-standing question about the relationship between television violence and aggressive behavior. When the program of research was completed in December, 1972, it added over 50 new research papers to the literature. That represented, by itself, about a 20% increase in the published research literature focused directly on television and its effects on children.

The research that was commissioned included laboratory studies, field studies, sociologic examinations of the industry and how it functioned to produce violent programs, and a variety of analyses of how people watch television, of how television affects family interaction, and of how much violent content was included in prime-time programming. The effort was to pursue a number of different approaches rather than do one large-scale integrated piece of research. While this approach has been criticized by some experts, it provided a large body of data with some strongly significant findings.

Another important attribute of the Surgeon General's program was the establishment of the Surgeon General's Scientific Advisory Committee on Television and Social Behavior. The Surgeon General appointed 12 distinguished social scientists to this committee. Their responsibilities were to review and evaluate the research findings and come to a conclusion as to the scientific implications of those findings. It was expected that a conclusion by such a committee would add scientific authority to the conclusions of the individual research reports.

It is pertinent to note that this procedure was modeled after the earlier and notably effective Surgeon General's committee on smoking and health. However, the membership of the present committee included two scientists who were full-time network employees whereas the smoking and health committee had no scientists who were employed by the tobacco industry. The presence of network employees on the committee, plus the blackballing of seven other scientists in the selection of the committee members, raised concerns about the impartiality of the committee. Even the fact that the committee came to a unanimous conclusion that there was evidence of a "causal relationship" between television violence and later aggressive behavior did not eliminate concern that the committee may not have adequately emphasized the strength of the research findings. In any case, there is no question that the findings of the research and the conclusions of the committee received much attention in early 1972 when the committee report and five volumes of technical reports were published (Surgeon General's Committee, 1972).

One of the confusions that emerged about the contents of the two sets of reports was caused by a timing problem. Because of a front-page story headline in *The New York Times* early in February, 1972 that misinterpreted the advisory committee conclusion, the committee report became public before its official release and before the supporting five volumes of technical reports were published. As a result, there were public criticisms of the committee report and claims that its conclusion was not adequately reflective of the actual research findings.

To clarify those conclusions and take steps toward new policy on programming, Senator Pastore held public hearings on the committee report in March, 1972. At those hearings the Surgeon General clearly affirmed the important implications of the committee conclusion and indicated that the evidence warranted "appropriate and immediate remedial action [Commerce Committee, U.S. Senate, 1972]."

Much analysis could be made of the politics of the Surgeon General's program and its impact on the television industry. As indicated earlier, a number of such analyses have already been published. After almost 10 years it would seem that the report had little direct impact on television programming itself but much impact on the entire field of research. Ultimately, it will probably be viewed as a major impetus toward continued scientific investigation of the complex effects of television on the viewer, which in turn cannot help but influence television practices.

Other Early Research on Television Violence

As one of the immediate results of both the Eisenhower Commission's examination of media violence and the Surgeon General's program of research, the television industry was suddenly mobilized to initiate an independent examination of the question. When the congressional inquiries of the 1950s and early 1960s were underway, the official industry response had been that (a) there wasn't that much violence on television; (b) what little there was didn't harm the young viewer; and (c) in any case, the level of violence was being reduced. None of those three points was true, but little change in programming was forthcoming.

In 1968 and 1969, however, with the advent of the two major federal inquiries, both the National Broadcasting Company (NBC) and the Columbia Broadcasting System (CBS) announced they were going to launch major studies of their own. In 1969 NBC began a large-scale panel study, designed to be completed in 5 years, examining the impact of televised violence on young children and adolescents. While some preliminary results have been released, as of the beginning of 1980 the final report of that study had not yet been published.

Also, in 1969 CBS commissioned two major pieces of research, both of which have been published. The first, by Milgram and Shotland (1973), was an ingenious field study designed to measure whether viewers would imitate, in real life, an antisocial act portrayed on a television program. With the cooperation of the CBS network programming staff, one episode of a commercial drama series showed a main character stealing money from an openly displayed charity collection box. People who had seen the program in a theater were then, after being put through a frustrating experience, given an opportunity to imitate the behavior shown on the program. Other opportunities to imitate antisocial behavior were also built into the total series of experiments. Without going into all the details of the research design, the results provided no clear evidence of imitation. The authors concluded that it was a Scotch verdict: not proven. It is important to note that the researchers were highly qualified and well regarded and were given a completely free hand to pursue and complete the research as they saw fit.

In a later study by Belson (1978), an even more complex and comprehensive examination was made of the relationship between heavy viewing of televised violence and antisocial behavior. In this study a large sample of adolescent boys in London was divided into heavy and light viewers of television violence. By a sophisticated statistical procedure, the two groups were equated for a variety of attributes related to aggressive behavior. It was theorized that any remaining differences would have to be due to viewing television violence. Significant results were found, and the author concluded that the viewing of television violence was related to antisocial behavior. What is especially significant in this study—aside from the 8 years it took to complete and the $300,000 it cost CBS—is that it related actual antisocial behavior to viewing television violence. Earlier studies, including one important longitudinal study under the Surgeon General's program (Lefkowitz, Eron, Walder, & Huesmann, 1972), identified primarily aggressive behavior, such as pushing and shoving, as the consequence of viewing violence on television. The Belson study identified, albeit through retrospective self-reporting, actual acts which could be called juvenile delinquency, including property damage and bodily harm to others.

The American Broadcasting Company (ABC), which in 1970 was the smallest of the three networks, commissioned a continuing series of studies by two mental health consultants. A comprehensive report on this work was published by ABC in 1976 (Heller & Polsky, 1976). Over a period of 5 years, Heller, a psychiatrist, and Polsky, a psychologist, pursued a variety of approaches to explore the effects of television violence on children. Altogether, 11 different projects were reported. The subjects included normal and emotionally disturbed children. Unfortunately, the studies were methodologically flawed, and the scientific quality of the research was poor. Most of the statistically significant results supported the relationship between television violence and aggressive behavior. The authors, however, seemed to be biased in the direction of finding television only a very minor contributor to stimulating aggression in children.

These various studies sponsored by the networks are just one part of the significant increase in research on television violence since the report of the Surgeon General's program was published. Indeed, Schramm (1976) noted that the Surgeon General's research produced a "harvest" of new research. This point is vividly documented by the statistics of a major review of the research on television and human behavior completed by Comstock and Fisher (1975). In 1970, just as the Surgeon General's research program began, a citation list of 500 relevant publications was compiled (Atkin, Murray, & Nayman, 1971). Five years later, Comstock and Fisher (1975) were able to cite almost 2400 publications in that same field of inquiry. From about one-third to one-half of that research, especially in the 1975 compilation, was of relevance to the issue of television violence and its effects on the young viewer. Much of that research has been reviewed elsewhere (Comstock, Chaffee, Katzman, McCombs, & Roberts, 1978) and need not be discussed here. While the Surgeon

General's program was not the only stimulus for such increased interest in television and human behavior, it undoubtedly did play a significant role in this development.

The Consensus on the Effects of Television Violence

To the nonexpert in the field it would seem that, in light of all the published research, a definitive answer to the relationship between television violence and later aggressive behavior should have been reached by now. For many expert observers of the field the conclusion is clear: Television violence produces aggressive behavior. And yet, some experts hold that the evidence is far from definitive. Indeed, there are still some observers who believe that viewing television violence can reduce the direct expression of aggressive behavior. This theory goes back to Aristotle, who believed that dramatic presentations provided a stimulus for discharge of feelings by the audience. Known now as the "catharsis" hypothesis, it has been studied primarily by Feshbach (1969) and his students.

There are, thus, three possible theoretical positions on the relationship between television and aggressive behavior: (a) no relationship at all; (b) television reduces aggressive behavior; and (c) television induces aggressive behavior. (An alternative to this direct relationship is the possibility that a "third variable" is related to both television viewing and later aggressive behavior, thus producing the correlation of viewing and behavior.)

Two comprehensive reviews of the literature (Howitt & Cumberbatch, 1975; Kaplan & Singer, 1976) have come to the conclusion that the research does not prove a relationship between television and aggressive behavior. In both reviews, each of the individual published reports purporting to show such a relationship is found to be seriously flawed in methodology, in measurements used, or in statistical analyses. In each instance, the conclusions reached by the investigator are therefore questioned by the reviewers and held invalid. These reviewers thus discount any importance which might be given to the cumulative weight of all this evidence and conclude that the case against television violence has not been proven.

The catharsis hypothesis is not widely held by researchers. It should also be noted that the Surgeon General's Committee quite clearly stated that there was no evidence to support the catharsis hypothesis, nor has there been any subsequent significant research to support this position.

Most experts in the field now agree that there is clear evidence of a positive relationship between television violence and later aggressive behavior. Comprehensive reviews of the literature from those in the Eisenhower Commission report and the Surgeon General's program come down clearly on that side. Subsequently, many experts have confirmed that conclusion after examining the results. Comstock (1976), Rubinstein (1978), and Watt and Krull (1977) are among those who have reaffirmed that conclusion. Indeed, an earlier conclusion by J. L. Singer (1971) that the research did not demonstrate any effects has now been reconsidered by that expert, largely as a result of his own continuing work as well as a later review of the field. He now believes the case has been made against television violence (Singer, 1979).

Even in late 1975, at a major conference on future research priorities on television and children (Ford Foundation, 1976), relatively little attention was given to research on television violence, on the assumption that the scientific question had been answered and other apects of research on television and children deserved greater attention. The reason for this conclusion is that so many of the studies point toward that relationship. Scientifically, it would seem unlikely, even if any one study could be questioned, that there would be such a general consensus by the findings if such a relationship did not, in fact, exist. It is because of this convergence that the Surgeon General's Committee concluded there was a causal relationship between television violence and later aggressive behavior. Studies done subsequently have tended to confirm that conclusion.

Public Campaigns against Television Violence

No history of television violence would be complete without including the many public efforts that have developed to do something about the problem. As already noted, congressional inquiries began in the 1950s, very shortly after television had grown to become a dominant source of home entertainment.

Action by citizens' groups came somewhat later, although one, the National Association for Better Broadcasting, was founded as early as 1949. A recent guide to media organizations (Rivers, Thompson, & Nyhan, 1977) lists over 30 media action groups, many of which concern themselves with television and its impact on citizens. One of the best known and most effective is Action for Children's Television (ACT), which was founded in 1968. Initially, ACT focused much attention on television violence and Saturday morning programming to children. In recent years its major attention has been on television advertising to children (see Chapters 15, 16, and 20 in this volume), although it still serves as an advocate against television violence. In 1974, in still another approach, a research center was established under the sponsorship of the National Council of Churches to develop new knowledge on how to change television programming away from the violent and toward the prosocial. A fully equipped research laboratory in Stony Brook, New York, became one part of a national center known as Media Action Research Center (MARC). In addition to supporting research from its own and other sources, MARC has demonstrated how such public organizations are seeking to effect positive change in television programming through both research findings and other means. While the research laboratory is no longer operational, MARC has developed a number of other projects to effect change. One such activity is a program of workshops, held throughout the country, to train individuals to become more aware of the ways in which television influences the viewer. The workshops involve both training films and a comprehensive set of prepared texts (Logan, 1977). Because of its relationship to many church organizations, the work of MARC receives wide support and has resulted in an updated training program (Logan & Moody, 1979).

In 1976 a very effective effort was initiated by the medical profession. As a result of a lead article on television violence published December 1975 in the *Journal of the American Medical Association,* the American Medical Association (AMA) became actively involved in a major campaign against television violence. The publication of the article (Rothenberg, 1975) was an unplanned event. Rothenberg, a Seattle pediatrician, had earlier given some public lectures on the effects of televised violence on children. In the course of obtaining information on the subject, he wrote an article and submitted it to the journal, which not only accepted it immediately, but also made it the lead article, with a cover picture. Dr Rothenberg summarized the results of about 50 studies supporting the relationship between television violence and later aggressive behavior and called for "a major, organized cry of protest from the medical profession" about this problem.

What is important in this development is the enormous publicity that ensued because of the national influence of the journal and its circulation to over 200,000 doctors. Congressional interest was aroused again, and the AMA initiated a formal effort to persuade the three networks to reduce violence on television. During 1976 and 1977, a number of actions were taken by the Association. Testimony was given before Congressional committees by medical consultants to the AMA, and the Association adopted an official policy identifying television violence as an environmental hazard threatening the health and welfare of young Americans. In early 1977 the president of the AMA wrote letters to 10 major corporations asking them to review advertising policies that supported prime-time television shows containing the most violence. Workshops were sponsored around the country to inform the membership about the problems of television violence, research was supported to monitor the amounts of violence on television, and encouragement was given for concurrent efforts by the National PTA.

The AMA and PTA campaigns accomplished something that all the previous research had failed to accomplish: The level of violence for the 1977 season decreased significantly (Gerbner, Gross, Jackson-Beeck, Jeffries-Fox, & Signorielli, 1978). It is a commentary on how public policy is implemented that the research evidence by itself had not been persuasive, but that public pressure by two influential organizations did produce change. In fact, at about the same time, the J. Walter Thompson advertising agency made a public plea to its clients not to advertise on programs containing television violence because its own survey had shown that the public might not buy products advertised on such programs.

Policy Changes

At the conclusion of the Surgeon General's program in 1972, Senator Pastore characterized the conclusions of the report and the further public affirmation by the Surgeon General of their significance as a "scientific breakthrough." It was generally expected that a marked decrease in the level of violence in programming and much change for the better would occur. In their comprehensive evaluation of the Surgeon General's program, Cater and Strickland (1975) noted that such changes did not occur. It is worth examining what did happen and why.

Cater and Strickland (1975), in commenting on how the Surgeon General's program was organized, noted that any shortcomings in the operation of the program were due to the "way the system worked" and not to the failure of any individuals. Unfortunately, the way the system works is usually the problem in most efforts at policy change.

The whole smoking and health question is a pertinent example, since the Surgeon General's involvement with televised violence was modeled partially on his earlier involvement in reviewing the scientific evidence on the effects of smoking. Even 15 years after the first report on smoking and health, smoking was still labeled by the federal government as a major, preventable cause of death in the United States. A massive public education program had failed to produce a marked decrease in smoking or even an admission on the part of the tobacco industry that smoking was harmful. In a democracy that's the way the system often works, but it means that policy change often takes years to produce.

Insofar as the Surgeon General's program on television and social behavior is concerned, it should be noted that in setting up the program of research he specifically pointed out that no policy recommendations would be made by his scientific advisory committee. This was made explicit not only to emphasize the scientific objectives of the program, but also because the Department of Health, Education and Welfare has no regulatory responsibilities in the federal control of communications.

At the same time, the Federal Communications Commission (FCC), which does have such regulatory responsibility, was supposedly "co-operating" in the Surgeon General's program. In fact, no FCC involvement took place at all during the life of the program. It was only afterward, at the Senate hearings (Commerce Committee, U.S. Senate, 1972), that the chairman and other commissioners of the FCC testified before Senator Pastore about the significance of the research findings. The chairman, Dean Burch, noted that a Children's Unit had been established in the FCC and that public panel discussions would be held to consider how to reduce gratuitous violence and to encourage new and diversified programming for children.

No new action by the FCC resulted from those panel discussions in 1972. It was not until 1975, subsequent to another set of hearings by Senator Pastore (Commerce Committee, U.S. Senate, 1974), that the FCC actively addressed the issue of television violence (Federal Communications Commission, 1975). It was then that "Family Viewing Time" was announced as a means of setting aside some of prime-time for programs suitable for family viewing and presumably suitable for the younger viewer. Even that action was, however, a voluntary one by the television industry rather than a regulation by the FCC.

The FCC's apparent reluctance to regulate—especially directly about violent content—is consonant with that of many other groups. Because the First Amendment guarantees freedom of the press, no direct censorship of programming has ever been advocated by responsible groups concerned with the problem of television violence. While it is true that the First Amendment guarantee has often been used, especially by the television industry, as an argument against any outside pressure toward change, direct censorship or federal involvement in programming control has not been attempted by any major group. The AMA's appeal to major advertisers, mentioned earlier, was officially disavowed by the AMA as any effort toward "boycott." Similarly, researchers who have given public testimony about the dangers of television violence have almost uniformly rejected the idea of federal censorship.

It was against this background that the FCC carefully explained that Family Viewing Time had been adopted as a voluntary industry regulation (Federal Communications Commission, 1975). Despite this fact, the California Supreme Court, in 1977, struck down Family Viewing Time as a restraint against the First Amendment. While there is no official Family Viewing Time now, all three networks still program what they consider to be mainly "family" shows during that evening period.

How can policy changes on the issue of programming televised violence be summarized? If dramatic reduction in the level of violence on television is the prime criterion, the trend from 1972 to 1979 is not indicative of marked change. With the exception of the single year's programming in 1977, following much public pressure, televised violence has not diminished greatly. Indeed, the fall 1978 content analysis by Gerbner and his colleagues indicated that the level of violence rose to near record levels (Gerbner, Gross, Signorielli, Morgan, & Jackson-Beeck, 1979). Nor have Saturday morning programs for children, marked by excessively violent cartoons, changed much for the better.

Conclusion

The full history of television violence is still unfinished. The impact of the published research is growing. Even though policy has not changed greatly, the original question has been answered: Television violence is harmful to the viewer. By extension, the cumulative body of research has shown that television is an important influence, both positively and negatively, in the lives of children. All of these findings have produced an increasing awareness of the basic problem and of the need for change. There are increasing efforts by all parties—the industry, the government, and public interest groups—to find appropriate ways to achieve positive change. This heightened consciousness is important. Hopefully, significant changes in substance will eventually be forthcoming.

References

Atkin, C. K., Murray, J. P., & Nayman, O. B. *Television and social behavior: An annotated bibliography of research focusing on television's impact on children.* Washington, D.C.: United States Government Printing Office, 1971.

Baker, R. K., & Ball, S. J. (Eds.). *Violence and the media. A staff report to the National Commission on the Causes and Prevention of Violence.* Washington, D.C.: United States Government Printing Office, 1969.

Belson, W. A. *Television violence and the adolescent boy.* Hampshire, England: Saxon House, 1978.

Bogart, L. Warning, the Surgeon General has determined that TV violence is moderately dangerous to your child's mental health. *Public Opinion Quarterly,* 1972, *36,* 491–521.

Cater, D., & Strickland, S. *TV violence and the child: The evolution and fate of the Surgeon General's Report.* New York: Russell Sage Foundation, 1975.

Charters, W. W. *Motion pictures and youth: A summary.* New York: Macmillan, 1933.

Commerce Committee, United States Senate, Subcommittee on Communications. *Hearings on Surgeon General's Report by the Scientific Advisory Committee on Television and Social Behavior.* 92nd Congress, 2nd Session, March 21–24, 1972. Washington, D.C.: United States Government Printing Office, 1972.

Commerce Committee, United States Senate, Subcommittee on Communications. *Hearings on violence on television.* 93rd Congress, 2nd Session, April 3–5, 1974. Washington, D.C.: United States Government Printing Office, 1974.

Comstock, G. *Television portrayals and aggressive behavior.* Santa Monica, California: Rand Corporation, 1976.

Comstock, G., Chaffee, S., Katzman, N., McCombs, M., & Roberts, D. *Television and human behavior.* New York: Columbia Univ. Press, 1978.

Comstock, G., & Fisher, M. *Television and human behavior: A guide to the pertinent scientific literature.* Santa Monica, California: Rand Corporation, 1975.

Federal Communications Commission. *Report on the broadcast of violent, indecent and obscene material.* Washington, D.C.: Federal Communications Commission, February. 1975.

Feshbach, S. The catharsis effect: Research and another view. In R. K. Baker & S. J. Ball (Eds.), *Violence and the media: A staff report to the National Commission on the Causes and Prevention of Violence.* Washington, D.C.: United States Government Printing Office, 1969.

Ford Foundation. *Television and children: Priorities for research.* New York: Ford Foundation, 1976.

Gerbner, G., Gross, L., Jackson-Beeck, M., Jeffries-Fox, A., & Signorielli, N. *Violence profile no. 9.* Philadelphia: Univ. of Pennsylvania Press, 1978.

Gerbner, G., Gross, L., Signorielli, N., Morgan, M., & Jackson-Beeck, M. *Violence profile no. 10.* Philadelphia: Univ. of Pennsylvania Press, 1979.

Heller, M. S., & Polsky, S. *Studies in violence and television.* New York: American Broadcasting Companies, 1976.

Himmelweit, H. T., Oppenheim, A. N., & Vince, P. *Television and the child.* New York and London: Oxford University Press, 1958.

Howitt, D., & Cumberbatch, G. *Mass media violence and society.* New York: Wiley, 1975.

Judiciary Committee, United States Senate, Subcommittee to Investigate Juvenile Delinquency. *Hearings on Juvenile Delinquency. Part 16. Effects on young people of violence and crime portrayed on television.* 88th Congress, 2nd session, July 30, 1964. Washington, D.C.: United States Government Printing Office, 1965.

Kaplan, R. M., & Singer, R. D. Television violence and viewer aggression: A re-examination of the evidence. *Journal of Social Issues,* 1976, *32,* 35–70.

Klapper, J. T. *The effects of mass communication.* New York: Free Press, 1960.

Lefkowitz, M. M., Eron, L. D., Walder, L. O., & Huesmann, L. R. Television violence and child aggression: A follow/up study. In G. A. Comstock & E. A Rubinstein (Eds.), *Television and social behavior* (Vol. 3). *Television and adolescent aggressiveness.* Washington, D.C.: United States Government Printing Office, 1972.

Logan, B. (Ed.) *Television awareness training: For new awareness, new decisions, new action.* New York: Media Action Research Center, 1977.

Logan, B., & Moody, K. (Eds.) *Television awareness training: The viewer's guide.* New York: Media Action Research Center, 1979.

Milgram, S., & Shotland, R. L. *Television and antisocial behavior: Field experiments.* New York: Academic Press, 1973.

Rivers, W. L., Thompson, W., & Nyhan, M. J. *Aspen handbook on the media: 1977–79 edition.* New York: Praeger, 1977.

Rothenberg, M. B. Effect of television violence on children and youth. *Journal of the American Medical Association,* 1975, *234,* 1043–1046.

Rubinstein, E. A. Warning: The Surgeon General's research program may be dangerous to preconceived notions. *Journal of Social Issues,* 1976, *32,* 18–34.

Rubinstein, E. A. Television and the young viewer. *American Scientist,* 1978, *66,* 685–693.

Schramm, W. The second harvest of two research-producing events: The Surgeon General's inquiry and *Sesame Street. Proceedings of the National Academy of Education,* 1976, *3,* 151–219.

Schramm, W., Lyle, J., & Parker, E. B. *Television in the lives of our children.* Stanford, California: Stanford Univ. Press, 1961.

Singer, J. L. The influence of violence portrayed in television or motion pictures upon overt aggressive behavior. In J. L. Singer (Ed.), *The control of aggression and violence: Cognitive and physiological factors.* New York: Academic Press, 1971.

Singer, J. L. The powers and limitations of television. In P. Tannenbaum (Ed.), *The entertainment function of television.* Hillsdale, New Jersey: Erlbaum, 1979.

Surgeon General's Scientific Advisory Committee on Television and Social Behavior. *Television and growing up: The impact of television violence.* Report to the Surgeon General, United States Public Health Service. Washington, D.C.: United States Government Printing Office, 1972.

Watt, J. H., & Krull, R. An examination of three models of television viewing and aggression. *Human Communication Research,* 1977, *3,* 99–112.

Wertham, F. C. *Seduction of the innocent.* New York: Rinehart, 1954.

New Emphases in Research on
the Effects of Television
and Film Violence

GEORGE COMSTOCK

The empirical investigation of the possible contribution of television and film violence to the aggressiveness of viewers has covered an enormous terrain in a relatively few years. Progress has been enhanced by two federal commissions and punctuated by controversies and disputes among social and behavioral scientists and between them and broadcasters. Much can be said now that could not have been said two decades ago, and the focus of inquiry, which has been continually shifting, is now decidedly shifting in new directions.

The Emerging Evidence

The first experiments demonstrating that exposure to a violent portrayal increases the aggressiveness of viewers immediately after exposure appeared in a prestigious journal in 1963 (Bandura, Ross, & Ross, 1963a; Berkowitz & Rawlings, 1963). These historically important experiments differed in many respects but were alike in providing the first empirical support for the hypothesis that exposure to television violence increases the aggressiveness of viewers. Bandura and colleagues were concerned with the circumstances which govern the acquisition and display of behavior. Berkowitz and Rawlings were also concerned with the factors that facilitate the display of behavior, but they intended to resolve a specific issue as well. In 1961 Feshbach had reported that mildly provoked college-age subjects had reduced hostile imagery after viewing a violent film episode. He interpreted this as suggesting that exposure to television and film violence would reduce the subsequent aggressiveness of viewers. Berkowitz and Rawlings took a contrary view. They argued that subjects had been so sensitized to the notion of hostility by the vicarious experience that they had suppressed such impulses. To test their interpretation, they ingeniously compared the aggressiveness of mildly provoked subjects toward their tormentor when exposed to a film experience with either justified or unjustified aggression. If inhibition explained the Feshbach results, they reasoned they would find greater aggressiveness after the vicarious experience of justified than unjustified aggression. If catharsis were the correct interpretation, they would find no significant difference since both experiences would be similarly efficacious in purging viewers of their impulses. The support they obtained for their view placed the catharsis hypothesis in inferential jeopardy.

The catharsis hypothesis is often wrongly attributed to Aristotle, but in fact he proposed only that by arousing pity and fear the dramatic genre of tragedy would lead to their catharsis. He said nothing about aggressive behavior, and he was prescient not to do so. The more than 60 relevant experiments published since the early 1960s include few instances in which aggression was reduced by the vicarious experiencing of aggression on film or television. About 90% demonstrate increased aggressiveness after such exposure. The interpretation supported by the experimental study of aggression is (a) that its actual physical and verbal expression will reduce internal tension, and thereby the likelihood of further immediate aggressiveness; (b) that vicarious participation in aggression will not reduce internal tension; (c) that pleasurable reinforcement provided by tension reduction paradoxically will increase the likelihood of actual expression of aggression again when stimuli similar to those associated with the original experience are encountered in the future; and (d) that when vicarious participation reduces aggressiveness, the effect typically is attributable to the inhibition of such impulses (Baron, 1977; Comstock, Chaffee, Katzman, McCombs, & Roberts, 1978; Geen & Quanty, 1977).

It would be wrong to conclude from all this that the expression of hostility or aggression is never reduced by exposure to television or film portrayals of aggression. In fact, the experiment by Berkowitz and Rawlings (1963) suggests that it will do so when the portrayal is sufficiently disturbing to inhibit such responses. There is also the possibility that hostile feelings, which the dependent measure employed by Feshbach (1961) would appear to approximate, are affected somewhat differently than is behavior (Manning & Taylor, 1975). In addition, the available scientific evidence has been strongly shaped by the results of those 1963 experiments, which directed the attention and effort of psychologists away from the mechanisms by which television and film portrayals might reduce aggressiveness and toward those mechanisms by which they increase the likelihood of such behavior. As Feshbach once astutely remarked (in private conversation), experimental psychologists intuitively select the manipulations that will favor the processes they wish to investigate.

The consequence of the predominant interest in the contribution of portrayals to aggression has been that the terrain of contrary effects has been left largely unexplored. The preponderance of outcomes in which violent portrayals increase aggressiveness indicates that a contrary outcome is not common for very many kinds of violent portrayals or types of aggression, not that it is inconceivable under circumstances other than those investigated. That there is much more to be understood is made clear by the experiment of Zillmann, Johnson, and Hanrahan (1973) in which mildly provoked college-age subjects exhibited less aggressiveness toward their tormentor after seeing a violent portrayal with a happy ending than after seeing the same portrayal without such a resolution.

The Present State of Knowledge

The scientific investigation since 1963 of the effects of television violence has added markedly to what can be said with some confidence about its contribution to aggressiveness. There has not only been a substantial body of new experiments, but there have also been studies quite different in character that have gone beyond the inferential limits of the laboratory manipulation.

The Quandary over Generalizability

By the time the Surgeon General's inquiry (1972) into television violence began in 1969, about 50 experiments had been published demonstrating that exposure to violent portrayals increases scores on a measure of aggression immediately after viewing. The Surgeon General's inquiry added more. Although some later would suggest that there was enough evidence on the record to indict television (Bogart, 1972), the experimental findings provided presumptive but insufficient evidence for effects on real-life behavior.

The experiments had three strengths. They provided a catalogue of the particular conditions under which violent portrayals were most likely to influence behavior, they elaborated a plausible, empirically tested rationale for effects, and they established the definite possibility of a causal relationship in real life. By themselves, they were nevertheless insufficient for generalizing to real life with great confidence because of the very character of experimental design, which sacrifices a matching of naturalistic conditions for rigor in control and sensitivity in measurement. The milieu of the experiment is undeniably artificial, perhaps encouraging unusual behavior or conformity to the hypothesized outcome; the television exposure is transitory and abrupt; and there is no possibility of the retaliation that inhibits aggressive displays in real life. In addition, the dependent measures are sometimes ambiguous in character; for example, assaulting a Bobo doll can be construed as play and evaluating an experimenter's competence or administering electric shocks to inform a person of errors on a task can be construed as conforming to a norm of helpfulness.

To this body of experimental evidence with its strengths and weaknesses, the Surgeon General's inquiry (1972) also contributed several surveys in which prior viewing of violent programming was positively correlated with actual aggressiveness among young adolescents, as measured by reports from those most likely to be affected by such behavior—the respondent's peers (Chaffee, 1972; Lefkowitz, Eron, Walder, & Huesmann, 1972, 1977; McIntyre & Teevan, 1972; McLeod, Atkin, & Chaffee, 1972a, 1972b). These same surveys found that a declared preference for violent entertainment was positively correlated with aggressiveness at a far more modest level than was actual exposure to such programming, sharply reducing the likelihood that the relationship between viewing and aggression was attributable to more aggressive youths seeking out violent entertainment. They also found that the relationship remained when school achievement, family socioeconomic status, and sex were taken into account, thus eliminating the possibility that the explanation lay within peculiarities exclusive to some segment of the population who both watched television violence and acted aggressively without the one causing the other. The effect of this new evidence was to greatly strengthen the probability that violence viewing enhanced aggressiveness in real life, for it linked the two in a way not readily explainable other than by the former contributing to the latter.

Such survey evidence by itself is not readily amenable to causal inference. The sole study (Lefkowitz et al., 1972, 1977) that attempted such inference by analyzing the television viewing and aggressiveness of young people at two points in time a decade apart received such methodological criticism (Chaffee, 1972; Comstock, 1978; Howitt, 1972; Howitt & Cumberbatch, 1975; Kaplan, 1972; Kay, 1972) that, despite many arguments that can be offered in behalf of such a conclusion (Eron, Huesmann, Lefkowitz, & Walder, 1972; Huesmann, Eron, Lefkowitz, & Walder, 1973; Kenny, 1972; Lefkowitz et al., 1977; Neale, 1972), its inferential status remains problematical.

It might be thought that the most direct road to concluding whether or not television violence increases aggressiveness in real life would be to conduct a field experiment, in which the rigor of the laboratory ostensibly is transferred to a real-life setting. Historically, such a strategy for arriving at unambiguous conclusions about causal effects in real-life has been disappointing. Milgram and Shotland (1973) manipulated exposure to criminal behavior in a *Medical Center* episode and found no influence when viewers later had the opportunity to commit a similar offense, but a socially significant rate of real-life effects would be far below that required for statistical detection within their design. Feshbach and Singer (1971) reported that violent television led to lower aggressiveness than did neutral fare among the residents of boys' schools, but a likely explanation of their findings is the vehemently expressed frustration of those denied their customary programming (Wells, 1973). Stein and Friedrich (1972) and Leyens, Parke, Camino, and Berkowitz (1975) reported that televised and film violence led to greater aggressiveness, but initial differences between groups seem as likely an explanation as any for the former and the latter employed intact groups whose similarity was not therefore ensured by randomization. Loye, Gorney, and Steele (1977) reported that customary and violent diets of television programming were associated with greater hurtful behavior on the part of husbands than were nonviolent neutral or prosocial diets, but the data were obtained from wives who likely would be aware of what their husbands were watching. Finally, Steuer, Applefield, and Smith (1971) reported increased interpersonal aggressiveness among nursery school children, but—even though their brilliant design evaded most of the problems of the other studies—the fewness of subjects (5 each in treatment and control conditions) would court a contribution by individual differences. Thus, although each of these studies makes its own valuable contribution, as a group they constitute a record that compels caution in relying predominantly on the field experiment.

The strengths and weaknesses of the survey are converse to those of the experiment, be it laboratory or field. The inability to establish time order unambiguously between construed cause and effect and to isolate construed effect as unambiguously attributable to construed cause makes causal inference generally untenable. Panel studies, in which the same sample is measured at different points in time, do not escape from such objections because of the possibility that an unmeasured third variable is responsible for any observed relationships and because there is little agreement on the appropriate statistical procedures for a given set of data. What the survey can do that the experiment cannot is document the existence of a hypothesized relationship in everyday life and, when the requisite variables are measured, eliminate some of the plausible alternative explanations for that real-life relationship.

In the case of television violence, the experiments and the survey evidence in conjunction lead to the conclusion, tentative as always in matters scientific, that television violence actually does increase aggressiveness in real life. The one longitudinal study (Lefkowitz et al., 1972, 1977) remains important for its positive correlations between violence viewing and aggression even if the causal inference offered is rejected, while the field experiments, which on the whole favor the causal interpretation, can be treated as providing ancillary instead of crucial evidence. The survey evidence introduced by the Surgeon General's inquiry (1972) constitutes a very real advance by indicating that what the experiments confirmed in accord with theory is also true in everyday fact.

Meta-analyses

The large number of individual studies concerned with the influence of television and film on behavior has made it possible to analyze these influences quantitatively. Such meta-analyses, as the term implies, go beyond the data of any single study to produce findings reflecting a body of studies as a whole, yet do so by the imposition of a formal method that reserves subjectivity for the interpretation of the quantitative outcome.

Andison (1977) collected all the studies he could find from 1956 to 1976 that examined the relationship between exposure to violent portrayals and aggressive behavior. Each of the 67 studies was scored as to outcome and attributes, thereby giving each an equal weight. Seventy-seven percent were positive in outcome (37% weakly, 34% moderately, and 6% strongly), with exposure associated with increased aggressiveness, about 20% were null, and less than 5% opposite in outcome. The majority of outcomes were positive regardless of age, time period, country of investigation, measure of aggression, or method. The supposition of some that only younger children are affected was not supported by the record: The proportion of positive outcomes was about the same whether the age of those under examination was preschool, elementary school, high school, or college. Especially striking, however, was the less strong pattern that emerged for surveys and field experiments and the measures they typically employ, than for laboratory-type experiments. About 30% of such studies, compared to 13% of the experiments, produced null or inverse outcomes. In part, this pattern may reflect certain properties of laboratory experimentation—the greater sensitivity of the method, the disinclination to submit or for journals to publish null results, and the predominant interest of experimenters in aggression effects. It also most certainly reflects the complexity of the real-life events which surveys and field experiments monitor.

Hearold (1979) in a stunning tour de force statistically aggregated 230 studies. She compared the effects of prosocial, neutral, and antisocial portrayals on prosocial and antisocial behavior by calculating a metric of effect for 1043 comparisons encompassing age and sex in addition to the portrayal and behavior variables. She concludes that the degree to which antisocial portrayals affect antisocial behavior is only slightly less, while the degree to which prosocial portrayals affect prosocial behavior is somewhat greater than that common for medical and educational interventions. Antisocial behavior appears to be encouraged by antisocial portrayals and inhibited by prosocial portrayals, while prosocial behavior appears to be encouraged by prosocial portrayals but not particularly affected by antisocial portrayals. Although trends as children grow older are not without irregularities, they are detectable.

Degree of effect declines somewhat for both boys and girls from the preschool years through ages 9–13, then becomes greater for boys while continuing to decline for girls. The pattern is markedly more pronounced for physical aggression than for the encompassing measure of overall antisocial behavior, with girls decreasing and boys increasing in sharply more disparate fashion. Thus, the Hearold analysis, based on degree of influence, corrects an apparently misleading impression of the Andison study, based on the less sensitive criterion of the presence or absence of statistically significant difference, in regard to the null role of age. Both, however, contradict the popular view that only young children are ever affected. The broad pattern of a decline followed by a forking of trends for males and females presumably reflects first the restraints of socialization increasingly introduced by parents and schooling and later the influence of differing norms for male and female behavior.

When only portrayals with the "ecological validity" of close affinity to entertainment programming were examined, prosocial portrayals continued to have a greater degree of influence on prosocial behavior than did antisocial portrayals on antisocial behavior. However, antisocial portrayals displayed more ability to affect nonportrayed types of antisocial behavior than prosocial portrayals displayed for nonportrayed prosocial behavior; thus, the range, if not the degree, of impact appears to be greater for antisocial portrayals. Because the many studies of antisocial effects have encompassed persons ranging in age from preschool to college while the scant research on prosocial effects has largely been confined to young children, some association between exposure to antisocial portrayals and antisocial behavior has been documented for a wide range of ages while not much can be said about the role of age in regard to prosocial behavior. Girls, however, appear to be more affected by prosocial portrayals than are boys; again, the nurturance of media influence by norms is evident.

The studies examined by Andison (1977) represented data from more than 30,000 persons, and those by Hearold (1979), more than 100,000. The technique of treating each finding as an entity counters the artifacts that might occur in any single study, but such meta-analyses do have several weaknesses. Unlike the reasoning applied in jointly assessing the strengths and weaknesses of evidence from laboratory-type experiments, field experiments, and surveys, meta-analyses depend on the availability of a large body of studies, take account of psychological processes only as these are repeatedly represented in independent studies, and do not escape from whatever contributions politics, fads, trends, and passions may make to guiding research in particular directions. Nonetheless, meta-analyses are invaluable as summaries of a sizable body of studies.

Network-Sponsored Studies

As described in the chapter by Rubinstein, in defensive actions the three networks initiated empirical studies at the end of the 1960s. NBC and CBS emphasized real-life validity by embarking on surveys, and ABC emphasized inferential rigor by a series of experiments. The NBC study consisted of 3½-year longitudinal examination of elementary and high school students in a midwestern and southwestern American city (Milavsky, 1977; Milavsky & Pekowsky, 1973). Aggressiveness was measured by peer report; exposure to violence, by the programming the respondents said they viewed, weighted by a program-by-program measure of violent content. The CBS study (Belson, 1978) involved more than 1500 male adolescents in London. Exposure was measured by the consistent viewing of programming classified in a variety of ways in regard to violent and nonviolent content; aggressiveness was measured by self-report. Causal inference was attempted by ex post facto matching of respondents on variables other than the independent and dependent variable under examination. The ABC studies (Lieberman Research, 1975) involved a series of experiments in which the influence of exposure to various kinds of violent portrayals was tested by subsequent physical aggression displayed in punching an electronic pounding platform especially developed for the research. In all, about 10,000 children 8–13 years of age served as subjects.

The NBC findings cannot be fully assessed until the analysis of data from all respondents is available. If the final results parallel the preliminary reports, the data will certainly reinforce the view that real-life effects are not invariably present and may offer some challenge, given the painstaking methods apparent in the preliminary reports, to the validity of conclusions derived from the previous survey data. The CBS findings are certain to instigate extended controversy over the legitimacy of a causal inference, for the options, techniques, and power of matching are issues of scientific disputation, but, analogous to the longitudinal study (Lefkowitz et al., 1972, 1977) that was part of the Surgeon General's inquiry, it would at least appear to record another positive association between violence viewing and aggressiveness, and, in this instance, between such viewing and seriously harmful attacks against property and other persons. The ABC experiments, which, as do most experiments, employ a proxy for actual aggressiveness against other persons, expand what can be said about the psychological processes behind any effects and give further support to the views of Bandura, Berkowitz, and others that vicarious experience can alter subsequent behavior.

The Psychology of Entertainment and Behavior

The variety of variables investigated in connection with the influence of television and film portrayals is now sufficient to constitute the foundation for a psychology of entertainment and behavior. Although much of the research has focused on aggression, the findings have implications for other kinds of behavior.

Factors on Which Aggressive Effects Are Contingent

Certain aspects of portrayals increase the likelihood of aggressiveness. Those experimentally demonstrated to do so include (a) reward or lack of punishment for the perpetrator (Bandura, 1965; Bandura, Ross, & Ross, 1963b; Rosekrans & Hartup, 1967); (b) depiction of the violence as justified (Berkowitz & Rawlings, 1963; Meyer, 1972); (c) cues, such as attributes of a victim matching those in real life (Berkowitz & Geen, 1966); (d) similarity of a perpetrator to a viewer (Rosekrans, 1967); (e) depiction of violence as malevolent and injurious in intent (Berkowitz & Alioto, 1973; Geen & Stonner, 1972); (f) violence labeled realistic rather than fictional (Feshbach, 1972); (g) violence whose commission pleases the viewer (Ekman, Liebert, Friesen, Harrison, Zlatchin, Malmstrom, & Baron, 1972); (h) highly exciting content, violent or not (Tannenbaum & Zillmann, 1975; Zillmann, 1971); and (i) violence that goes uncriticized (Lefcourt, Barnes, Parke, & Schwartz, 1966).

The influence of a portrayal is also contingent on factors residing in the person and the situation. Hearold (1979) and the many experiments by Bandura (1973) document sex differences, with males often more aggressive than females, that seem to depend on norms discouraging such behavior by females. These norms cease to operate when provocation increases in severity (Baron, 1977), and Hearold's aggregation of findings suggests that they may have far less influence on very young children than Bandura's research had led us to believe. The contingent role of sex norms also suggests that more aggressive persons might be more affected by violent portrayals, for their internal constraints on such behavior would be less strong. The importance of norms is also illustrated by the experiment of Hicks (1968) in which imitative aggression by preschoolers who had seen a violent portrayal was sharply increased or decreased by the subsequent presence in the playroom of an adult who had co-viewed with the child and made positive or negative comments about the portrayed behavior, thereby becoming a symbol of norms and sanctions. That the efficacy of norms depends on their perceived salience is emphasized by the absence of differences in imitative aggression among preschoolers unaccompanied by the negatively or positively vocal adult. Their pervasive importance is, however, illustrated again by the greater effect among accompanied boys than girls, for boys—more ready to express aggression— would be more alert to the prevailing rules about its display. The family, of course, is frequently the source of norms. This is exemplified in the survey finding that the correlation between violence viewing and aggressiveness among young adolescents is sharply reduced when parents emphasize nonviolent means of conflict resolution (McLeod et al., 1972b).

Television is also most likely to serve as a guide for behavior when there is a need for information of a particular kind and an absence of alternative sources of information (Comstock et al., 1978; DeFleur & DeFleur, 1967; Gerson, 1966; Himmelweit, Oppenheim, & Vince, 1958; Lieberman Research, 1975; Tolley, 1973). Effects are also contingent on the opportunity for the behavior in question to be displayed and on the state of excitation or drive impelling any kind of behavior, which may derive from both media and nonmedia sources (Comstock et al., 1978).

Evidence on Effects Other Than Aggression

The hypothesis that television and film portrayals can alter the likelihood of behaving in a certain way gains support from experiments concerned with the modification of phobic reactions. Bandura and Menlove (1968) demonstrated that children's fearfulness of dogs can be reduced by portrayals in which children and canines interact pleasurably, and Hill, Liebert, and Mott (1968) and Poulos and Davidson (1971) demonstrated that a similar alteration could be achieved among children fearful of dentists. The psychological dynamic is presumed to be the extinction of fear and the substitution of a more pleasurable response incompatible with fear. This is analogous to what takes place in the disinhibition of aggression in that in both instances the meaning of a particular act is transfigured for a viewer by its portrayal on television or film.

The hypothesis gains further support from experiments demonstrating that portrayals of prosocial activity can influence the subsequent behavior of young viewers. Helping (Collins, 1974; Rubinstein, Liebert, Neale, & Poulos, 1974), generosity (Bryan & Schwartz, 1971), sharing (Bryan & Walbek, 1970; Elliott & Vasta, 1970; Liebert, Fernandez, & Gill, 1969), cooperation (Baran, Chase, & Courtright, 1979; Stein & Friedrich, 1972), displays of affection (Fryear & Thelen, 1969; Tasch, 1970), acceptance of playmates of other races (Gorn, Goldberg, & Kanungo, 1976), and delay of gratification (Yates, 1974) have all been so enhanced experimentally. These findings, as do those on behavior modification, support the view that the processes responsible for aggressive effects apply generally to other kinds of behavior.

Further support derives from the fact that the use of television in psychotherapy has proven effective. Therapists who have employed it as a means of displaying verbal and physical behavior to a patient argue that its value lies in its capability to convey fully the context and cues associated with behavior and in its undeniable veracity that counters the viewer's defensive mechanisms of revisionist memory and interpretation (Alger & Hogan, 1967, 1969; Bailey & Sowder, 1970; Berger, 1970; Danet, 1969; Hogan & Alger, 1966; Melnick, 1973; Robinson & Jacobs, 1970). Such clinical applications attest to the power that an audiovisual medium can have in presenting an experience that can serve as a standard for altering behavior.

The Nonexempt Status of News

News has escaped much of the anxiety that has been expressed over entertainment, in deference to its presumed status as information and to the service rendered the public by the dissemination of that information. However, the portrayal of violence in the news is distinct from that in entertainment principally because of its typically different placement on the various dimensions that enhance or diminish the likelihood of it having some influence on viewer behavior. News is likely to place high on the dimensions of realism and the presentation of cues found in real life, the factors that enhance the likelihood of influence. In reporting the failure of law enforcement—the successful heist, the provocative caper, the purse snatcher who eludes pursuit—it often presents examples of what, in the language of psychology, are none other than rewarded aggression. At the same time it frequently presents the brutal consequences of violence, it is set—especially at the national level—in circumstances distant geographically, psychologically, and politically from most American viewers, and it presents numerous examples of successful law enforcement. These are factors that diminish the likelihood of influence.

The First Amendment and federal regulatory stipulations testify to the sanctified status accorded news in the public interest, but they do not suspend the principles of psychology. Taking a psychological perspective implies no interest in abridging the rights of newsgatherers. A critical stance toward broadcast reporting is, however, justified given the facts that much of broadcast news is received by its audience as entertainment (Levy, 1978), that news management in part embraces entertainment in the attempt to attract the maximum possible audience, and that visuals—a common means of enhancing influences on behavior—are widely used in news programming but make little contribution to viewer knowledge of the news itself (Katz, Adoni, & Parness, 1977).

Psychology of Television and Film Portrayals

The accumulated evidence sums to a beginning general psychology of television and film portrayals that applies both to entertainment and news, but one which is particularly pertinent to television entertainment because of its predominant place in the media consumption of both adults and children. The behavioral influence of portrayals is contingent on four principal factors:

1. *Social approval.* When portrayals imply that a particular kind of behavior is more or less socially acceptable than a viewer had thought, the meaning attached to an act may be changed and the likelihood of its performance, altered. Justified aggression, malevolent aggression, and the absence of critical comments about aggression exemplify the enhancement of perceived approval by exposure to a portrayal.
2. *Efficacy.* When portrayals imply that a particular kind of behavior is more or less likely to result in reward—whether social, such as approval by others, or material, such as monetary gain—the utility that a viewer assigns to an act may be changed and the likelihood of its performance, altered. Rewarded aggression exemplifies the enhancement of perceived efficacy by exposure to a portrayal.
3. *Relevance.* When portrayals imply that a particular kind of behavior is more or less appropriate to a given circumstance, the meaning that a viewer attaches to that circumstance may be changed and the likelihood of the performance of the act in that circumstance, altered. Labeled realism, cues that match those in the environment, and viewer satisfaction with violence, exemplify the enhancement of perceived relevance by exposure to a portrayal.
4. *Arousal.* When portrayals increase or decrease a viewer's level of excitation, the proclivity to engage in some form of behavior may be altered. Eroticism and violence exemplify the enhancement of arousal by a portrayal—a happy ending following violence its diminution by the same type of manipulation.

The experiment by Worchel, Hardy, and Hurley (1976) illustrates the involved way factors coalesce and interact—or just confound naive expectations. College-student subjects saw full-length versions of either *The Mouse That Roared*, a comedy; *The Wild One*, the violent Marlon Brando motorcycle classic; or *Attica*, an American Bar Association documentary with footage of actual prison rioting. The films were either uncut or interrupted by 10 commercials, and aggressiveness was measured by a competence rating of the experimental assistant. The most plausible interpretation of the results is that the frustration induced by the interruption of the exciting, violent films heightened arousal, thus creating a necessary condition for the aggressive film content to have an influence when compared to the comedy. The results induce caution over the efficacy of arousal by violence alone, since the three uninterrupted films did not differ in their effects, and similarly over the efficacy of commercials to induce frustration, since interruption of the nonviolent film had no effect. Since the two violent films, which differed in actual realism, did not produce different effects, this implies that fictional presentations themselves are arranged on a continuum from high to low apparent relevance. The fact of fictionality predicts little. *The Wild One,* after all, is fiction based on the factual takeover of a California town by a motorcycle gang.

Factors such as those operating in the Worchel *et al.* (1976) experiment come into play not only in regard to aggression but also for other kinds of behavior. However, while the theoretical formulation remains the same, the outcome depends on properties of the behavior in question and on the interpretive ability of the viewer. Violent portrayals have the advantage of engaging the attention of young viewers, and aggression is more often physical and applicable in a wide range of circumstances. On the other hand, prosocial behavior—helping, generosity, and the like—is more abstract, with the opportunity to express any given example being dependent on appropriate circumstances. Thus, it remains plausible—despite the findings by Andison (1977) and Hearold (1979) that positive associations between exposure to violent portrayals and aggressiveness did not decline consistently across the full range of ages—to believe that violent portrayals in everyday circumstances have an advantage over prosocial portrayals in producing immediate effects among very young viewers. This view is consistent with the finding of Hearold that violence generalizes to nonportrayed behavior more readily than do prosocial portrayals. In the long run, as children become better able to generalize from one experience to another and to interpret what they see, the prosocial messages in entertainment programming, including those in violent drama, gain in the possibility of influence. Hearold (1979) supports this view in her conclusions that in the research so far the influence of prosocial portrayals has been more contingent on the measured behavior matching what has been portrayed and that the degree of effect typically has been greater for prosocial portrayals—for they almost invariably have been designed to affect behavior.

Emerging Directions in Research

By supporting the hypothesis that violence viewing increases aggressiveness, the Surgeon General's inquiry (1972) reinforced interest in the psychological processes responsible for the influence of portrayals and brought attention to such issues as the positive influence of prosocial portrayals and the circumstances which mitigate the influence of violent portrayals. Since that 1972 report, additional trends have emerged.

The arousal hypothesis (Tannenbaum & Zillmann, 1975) posits that excitation induced by portrayals may stimulate behavior and implies that increased arousal either from a media or nonmedia source may be necessary for a portrayal to have an observable effect (Comstock *et al.*, 1978). Available evidence strongly supports the view that other processes are also operative: Aspects such as malevolence and justification, which enhance aggression, require some intellectual acrobatics to fit an arousal interpretation; none of the positive outcomes among field experiments is clearly explainable by arousal alone; and arousal says nothing about the learning of new behavior or the alteration of the meaning of acts or circumstances. Yet Krull and Watt (1973), using survey data on viewing and aggressiveness, found that the excitatory attributes, apart from violence, and the violence, apart from excitatory attributes, each related *independently* to viewer aggressiveness. Thus, the growing body of evidence on arousal enlarges the inventory of responsible processes without invalidating previous interpretations.

The desensitization hypothesis posits that portrayals of violence make viewers less responsive to subsequent experiences of violence, including those in real life. The two studies which have demonstrated such a process (Cline, Croft, & Courrier, 1973; Drabman & Thomas, 1974) have, however, only tested responsiveness to violent experiences conveyed by a television monitor. Ignoring the possibility that the effect recorded by Cline and colleagues is attributable to some other, unknown factor, these results support the idea that media exposure produces desensitization to new media experience but provide no evidence for the phenomenon in real-life experience.

The social paranoia hypothesis posits that the pattern of violence in television, which greatly exceeds its frequency in real life (Gerbner & Gross, 1976), leads to a distorted perception of the world emphasizing its malevolent aspects. As Gerbner and Gross describe in their chapter in this book, they and their colleagues have found that adults, adolescents, and children who are heavy viewers quite consistently perceive the real world as more closely resembling televised fiction than do light viewers. Among the propositions they have advanced is that television violence increases a belief in personal vulnerability to crime. Several other investigators (Doob & Macdonald, 1979; Hughes, in press; Stevens, 1978; Tyler, 1978) have explored the hypothesis. Their results are in accord with those of Gerbner and Gross, who found a positive association between amount of television viewing and beliefs and perceptions. However, when other variables—socioeconomic status, age, and sex—were taken into account simultaneously, the relationship with personal vulnerability disappeared, while the relationship with a pessimistic view of the world—such as the trustworthiness of others, the quantity of crimes committed, and the sincerity of public officials—was more robust. Tyler (1978), in addition, found that perceived vulnerability was unrelated to exposure to crime news, but was related to experience with crime personally, or indirectly through the experiences of friends and neighbors. Exposure to crime news was associated with higher estimates of the crime rate. The implication of these varied findings is that feelings of vulnerability and cognitive beliefs are differentially affected by television viewing. They do not wholly discredit the social paranoia hypothesis, but they certainly qualify it. There is much stronger support for the proposition that exposure to television violence cultivates pessimistic cognitions than for the proposition that it cultivates feelings of vulnerability.

The viewer demand hypothesis posits that television violence is the consequence of audience preference. Clark and Blankenburg (1972) found that over a 16-year period the quantity of programs featuring a violent incident peaked every 4 years and correlated positively with the average ratings for such programs in the preceding year. Diener and DeFour (1978) later tested the very specific hypothesis that physical and verbal abuse, as distinct from action and adventure, increases program popularity. They coded such behavior over a season for 11 action-adventure programs and found no relationship between harsh violence and ratings. They also presented two versions of a *Police Woman* episode to subjects and found no greater liking for the version with harsh violence. Programs with violent incidents rise and fall in quantity with the perception by the television business of their popularity. With the increase in quantity, their average ratings fall as the imitators prove less adroit creatively and the audience for the genre is diluted. The industry then temporarily seeks success elsewhere, and the cycle continues. Contrary to what many believe, harsh violence has little to do with the popularity these programs may achieve.

Conclusion

The empirical study of the influence of television and film violence has supported the hypothesis that such portrayals increase viewer aggressiveness and has elaborated the theoretical formulations explaining the influence of portrayals, but there is no compelling demonstration that such portrayals contribute to harmful crime and violence. It would be foolish to interpret such a state of affairs as null evidence, for any linkages are likely to be very complex. Once anecdotes, newspaper accounts, rare events, and reports by prisoners are discarded from consideration, there is little to go on except the kind of empirical evidence so far collected. Even if one is skeptical that effects go beyond the play of children, there is still reason for concern because play itself can be dangerous and ruthless, and it certainly serves as a testing ground for future patterns of behavior. Even if effects seldom transgress the boundary from tolerable interpersonal aggression into proscribed action, one may question whether additional abrasiveness is a social good.

The variability in behavior attributable to differences in portrayals supports the common sense notion that television and film violence is not of one piece, but must be assessed qualitatively. Its demonstrated effects support the television business in its concern—although often motivated only by anxiety over public taste—to excise particular portrayals. The intent of communicators cannot be taken as synonymous with influence, but the finding by Hearold (1979) that both violent and prosocial portrayals have a greater degree of impact when they are specially devised raises the question of whether, were its makers to so desire, television entertainment could not have greater behavioral influence. The answer is yes.

References

Alger, I., & Hogan, P. The use of videotape recordings in conjoint marital therapy. *American Journal of Psychiatry*, 1967, *123*(11), 1425–1430.

Alger, I., & Hogan, P. Enduring effects of videotape playback experience on family and marital relationships. *American Journal of Orthopsychiatry*, 1969, *39*, 86–94.

Andison, F. S. TV violence and viewer aggression: A cumulation of study results 1956–1976. *Public Opinion Quarterly*, 1977, *41*, 314–331.

Bailey, K. G., & Sowder, W.T. Audiotape and videotape self-confrontation in psychotherapy. *Psychological Bulletin*, 1970, *74*, 127–137.

Bandura, A. Influence of models' reinforcement contingencies on the acquisition of imitative responses. *Journal of Personality and Social Psychology*, 1965, *1*, 589–595.

Bandura, A. *Aggression: A social learning analysis.* Englewood Cliffs, New Jersey: Prentice-Hall, 1973.

Bandura, A., & Menlove, F. Factors determining vicarious extinction of avoidance behavior through symbolic modeling. *Journal of Personality and Social Psychology*, 1968, *8*, 99–108.

Bandura, A., Ross, D., & Ross, S. A. Imitation of film-mediated aggressive models. *Journal of Abnormal and Social Psychology*, 1963, *66*, 3–11. (a)

Bandura, A., Ross, D., & Ross, S. A. Vicarious reinforcement and imitative learning. *Journal of Abnormal and Social Psychology*, 1963, *67*, 601–607. (b)

Baran, S. J., Chase, L. J., & Courtright, J. A. Television drama as a facilitator of prosocial behavior. *Journal of Broadcasting*, 1979, *23*(3) 277–284.

Baron, R. A. *Human aggression.* New York: Plenum, 1977.

Belson, W. A. *Television violence and the adolescent boy.* London: Saxon House, 1978.

Berger, M. M. Confrontation through videotape. In M. M. Berger (Ed.), *Videotape techniques in psychiatric training and treatment.* New York: Brunner/Mazel, 1970.

Berkowitz, L., & Alioto, J.T. The meaning of an observed event as a determinant of its aggressive consequences. *Journal of Personality and Social Psychology*, 1973, *28*, 206–217.

Berkowitz, L., & Geen, R.G. Film violence and the cue properties of available targets. *Journal of Personality and Social Psychology*, 1966, *3*, 525–530.

Berkowitz, L., & Rawlings, E. Effects of film violence on inhibitions against subsequent aggression. *Journal of Abnormal and Social Psychology,* 1963, *66,* 405–412.

Bogart, L. Warning, the Surgeon General has determined that TV violence is moderately dangerous to your child's mental health. *Public Opinion Quarterly,* 1972, *36,* 491–521.

Bryan, J. H., & Schwartz, T. Effects of film material upon children's behavior. *Psychological Bulletin,* 1971, *75,* 50–59.

Bryan, J. H., & Walbek, N. Preaching and practicing generosity: Children's actions and reactions. *Child Development,* 1970, *41,* 329–353.

Chaffee, S. H. Television and adolescent aggressiveness (overview). In G. A. Comstock & E. A. Rubinstein (Eds.), *Television and social behavior* (Vol. 3). *Television and adolescent aggressiveness.* Washington, D.C.: United States Government Printing Office, 1972.

Clark, D. G., & Blankenburg, W. B. Trends in violent content in selected mass media. In G. A. Comstock & E. A. Rubinstein (Eds.), *Television and social behavior* (Vol. 1). *Media content and control.* Washington, D.C.: United States Government Printing Office, 1972.

Cline, V. B., Croft, R. G., & Courrier, S. Desensitization of children to television violence. *Journal of Personality and Social Psychology,* 1973, *27,* 360–365.

Collins, W. A. *Aspects of television content and children's social behavior.* Final report, Grant No. OCD-CB-477, Office of Child Development, Department of Health, Education and Welfare, University of Minnesota, July, 1974.

Comstock, G. A contribution beyond controversy. (Review of *Growing up to be violent: A longitudinal study of the development of aggression* by M. M. Lefkowitz, L. D. Eron, L. O. Walder, and L. R. Huesmann.) *Contemporary Psychology,* 1978, *23* (11), 807–809.

Comstock, G. *Violence in television content: An overview.* Syracuse, New York: S.I. Newhouse School, 1980.

Comstock, G., Chaffee, S., Katzman, N., McCombs, M., & Roberts, D. *Television and human behavior.* New York: Columbia Univ. Press, 1978.

Danet, B. N. Self-confrontation by videotape in group psychotherapy. *International Journal of Group Psychotherapy,* 1969, *19,* 433–440.

DeFleur, M. L., & DeFleur, L. B. The relative contribution of television as a learning source for children's occupational knowledge. *American Sociological Review,* 1967, *32,* 777–789.

Diener, E., & DeFour, D. Does television violence enhance program popularity? *Journal of Personality and Social Psychology,* 1978, *36,* 333–341.

Doob, A. N., & Macdonald, G. E. Television viewing and fear of victimization: Is the relationship causal? *Journal of Personality and Social Psychology,* 1979, *37,* 170–179.

Drabman, R. S., & Thomas, M. H. Does media violence increase children's toleration of real-life aggression? *Developmental Psychology,* 1974, *10,* 418–421.

Ekman, P., Liebert, R. M., Friesen, W. V., Harrison, R., Zlatchin, C., Malmstrom, E. J., & Baron, R. A. Facial expressions of emotion while watching televised violence as predictors of subsequent aggression. In G. A. Comstock, E. A. Rubinstein, & J. P. Murray (Eds.), *Television and social behavior* (Vol. 5). *Television's effects: Further explorations.* Washington, D.C.: United States Government Printing Office, 1972.

Elliott, R., & Vasta, R. The modeling of sharing: Effects associated with vicarious reinforcement, symbolization, age, and generalization. *Journal of Experimental Child Psychology,* 1970, *10,* 18–15.

Eron, L. D., Huesmann, L. R., Lefkowitz, M. M., & Walder, L. O. Does television violence cause aggression? *American Psychologist,* 1972, *27,* 253–263.

Feshbach, S. The stimulating versus cathartic effects of a vicarious aggressive activity. *Journal of Abnormal and Social Psychology,* 1961, *63,* 381–385.

Feshbach, S. Reality and fantasy in filmed violence. In J. P. Murray, E. A. Rubinstein, & G. A. Comstock (Eds.), *Television and social behavior* (Vol. 2). *Television and social learning.* Washington, D.C.: United States Government Printing Office, 1972.

Feshbach, S., & Singer, R. D. *Television and aggression: An experimental field study.* San Francisco: Jossey-Bass, 1971.

Fryear, J. L., & Thelen, M. H. Effect of sex of model and sex of observer on the imitation of affectionate behavior. *Developmental Psychology*, 1969, *1*, 298.

Geen, R. G., & Quanty, M. B. The catharsis of aggression: An evaluation of a hypothesis. In L. Berkowitz (Ed.), *Advances in experimental social psychology* (Vol. 10). New York: Academic Press, 1977.

Geen, R. G., & Stonner, D. Context effects in observed violence. *Journal of Personality and Social Psychology*, 1972, *25*, 145–150.

Gerbner, G., & Gross, L. Living with television: The violence profile. *Journal of Communication*, 1976, *26*(2), 173–199.

Gerson, W. M. Mass media socialization behavior: Negro–white differences. *Social Forces*, 1966, *45*, 40–50.

Gorn, G. J., Goldberg, M. E., & Kanungo, R. N. The role of educational television in changing the intergroup attitudes of children. *Child Development*, 1976, *47*, 277–280.

Hearold, S. L. *Meta-analysis of the effects of television on social behavior.* Unpublished doctoral dissertation, Univ. of Colorado, 1979.

Hicks, D. J. Effects of co-observer's sanctions and adult presence on imitative aggression. *Child Development*, 1968, *38*, 303–309.

Hill, J. H., Liebert, R. M., & Mott, D. E. W. Vicarious extinction of avoidance behavior through films: An initial test. *Psychological Reports*, 1968, *22*, 192.

Himmelweit, H. T., Oppenheim, A. N., & Vince, P. *Television and the child.* New York and London: Oxford Univ. Press, 1958.

Hogan, P., & Alger, I. Use of videotape recording in family therapy. Paper presented at the meeting of the American Ortho-Psychiatric Association, San Francisco, April, 1966.

Howitt, D. Television and aggression: A counterargument. *American Psychologist*, 1972, *27*, 969–970.

Howitt, D., & Cumberbatch, G. *Mass media violence and society.* New York: Halsted, 1975.

Huesmann, L. R., Eron, L. D., Lefkowitz, M. M., & Walder, L. O. Television violence and aggression: The causal effect remains. *American Psychologist*, 1973, *28*, 617–620.

Hughes, M. The fruits of cultivation analysis: A re-examination of the effect of television watching on fear of victimization, alienation, and the approval of violence. *Public Opinion Quarterly*, in press.

Kaplan, R. M. On television as a cause of aggression. *American Psychologist*, 1972, *27*, 968–969.

Katz, E., Adoni, H., & Parness, P. Remembering the news: What the picture adds to recall. *Journalism Quarterly*, 1977, *54*, 231–239.

Kay, H. Weaknesses in the television-causes-aggression analysis by Eron *et al. American Psychologist*, 1972, *27*, 970–973.

Kenny, D. A. Threats to the internal validity of cross-lagged panel inference, as related to *Television violence and child aggression: A follow-up study.* In G. A. Comstock & E. A. Rubinstein (Eds.), *Television and social behavior* (Vol. 3). *Television and adolescent aggressiveness.* Washington, D.C.: United States Government Printing Office, 1972.

Krull, R., & Watt, J. H., Jr. *Television viewing and aggression: An examination of three models.* Paper presented at the meeting of the International Communication Association, Montreal, April, 1973.

Lefcourt, H. M., Barnes, K., Parke, R., & Schwartz, F. Anticipated social censure and aggression–conflict as mediators of response to aggression induction. *Journal of Social Psychology*, 1966, *70*, 251–263.

Lefkowitz, M. M., Eron, L. D., Walder, L. O., & Huesmann, L. R. Television violence and child aggression: A follow-up study. In G. A. Comstock & E. A. Rubinstein (Eds.), *Television and social behavior* (Vol. 3). *Television and adolescent aggressiveness.* Washington, D.C.: United States Government Printing Office, 1972.

Lefkowitz, M. M., Eron, L. D., Walder, L. O., & Huesmann, L. R. *Growing up to be violent.* Elmsford, New York: Pergamon, 1977.

Levy, M. R. The audience experience with television news. *Journalism Monographs*, April, 1978, No. 55.

Leyens, J. P., Parke, R. D., Camino, L., & Berkowitz, L. Effects of movie violence on aggression in a field setting as a function of group dominance and cohesion. *Journal of Personality and Social Psychology*, 1975, *32*, 346–360.

Lieberman Research, Inc. *Children's reactions to violent material on television: 5th year report.* Unpublished manuscript, American Broadcasting Company, 1975.

Liebert, R. M., Fernandez, L. E., & Gill, L. The effects of a friendless model on imitation and prosocial behavior. *Psychonomic Science*, 1969, *16*, 81–82.

Loye, D., Gorney, R., & Steele, G. An experimental field study. *Journal of Communication*, 1977, *27*(3), 206–216.

Manning, S. A., & Taylor, D. A. The effects of viewed violence and aggression: Stimulation and catharsis. *Journal of Personality and Social Psychology*, 1975, *31*, 180–188.

McIntyre, J. J., & Teevan, J. J., Jr. Television violence and deviant behavior. In G. A. Comstock & E. A. Rubinstein (Eds.), *Television and social behavior* (Vol. 3). *Television and adolescent aggressiveness.* Washington, D.C.: United States Government Printing Office, 1972.

McLeod, J. M., Atkin, C. K., & Chaffee, S. H. Adolescents, parents, and television use: Adolescent self-report measures from Maryland and Wisconsin samples. In G. A. Comstock & E. A. Rubinstein (Eds.), *Television and social behavior* (Vo. 3). *Television and adolescent aggressiveness.* Washington, D.C.: United States Government Printing Office, 1972. (a)

McLeod, J. M., Atkin, C. K., & Chaffee, S. H. Adolescents, parents, and television use: Self-report and other report measures from the Wisconsin sample. In G. A. Comstock & E. A. Rubinstein (Eds.), *Television and social behavior* (Vol. 3). *Television and adolescent aggressiveness.* Washington, D.C.: United States Government Printing Office, 1972. (b)

Melnick, J. A comparison of replication techniques in the modification of minimal dating behavior. *Journal of Abnormal Psychology*, 1973, *81*, 51–59.

Meyer, T. P. Effects of viewing justified and unjustified real film violence on aggressive behavior. *Journal of Personality and Social Psychology*, 1972, *23*, 21–29.

Milavsky, J. R. *TV and aggressive behavior of elementary school boys: Eight conceptualizations of TV exposure in search of an effect.* Invited address at the meeting of the American Psychological Association, San Francisco, August 29, 1977.

Milavsky, J. R., & Pekowsky, B. *Exposure to TV "violence" and aggressive behavior in boys, examined as process: A status report of a longitudinal study.* Unpublished manuscript, Department of Social Research, National Broadcasting Company, 1973.

Milgram, S., & Shotland, R. L. *Television and antisocial behavior: Field experiments.* New York: Academic Press, 1973.

Neale, J. M. Comment on *Television violence and child aggression: A follow-up study.* In G. A. Comstock & E. A. Rubinstein (Eds.), *Television and social behavior* (Vol. 3). *Television and adolescent aggressiveness.* Washington, D.C.: United States Government Printing Office, 1972.

Poulos, R. W., & Davidson, E. S. *Effects of a short modeling film on fearful children's attitudes toward the dental situation.* Unpublished manuscript, State Univ. of New York at Stony Brook, 1971.

Robinson, M. J., & Jacobs, A. Focused videotape feedback and behavior change in group psychotherapy. *Psychotherapy: Theory, Research and Practice*, 1970, *3*, 169–172.

Rosekrans, M. A. Imitation in children as a function of perceived similarities to a social model of vicarious reinforcement. *Journal of Personality and Social Psychology*, 1967, *7*, 307–315.

Rosekrans, M. A., & Hartup, W. W. Imitative influences of consistent and inconsistent response consequences to a model on aggressive behavior in children. *Journal of Personality and Social Psychology*, 1967, *7*, 429–434.

Rubinstein, E. A., Liebert, R. M., Neale, J. M., & Poulos, R. W. *Assessing television's influence on children's prosocial behavior.* Stony Brook, New York: Brookdale International Institute, 1974. (Occasional paper 74–11.)

Stein, A. H., & Friedrich, L. K. Television content and young children's behavior. In J. P. Murray, E. A Rubinstein, & G. A. Comstock (Eds.), *Television and social behavior* (Vol. 2). *Television and social learning.* Washington, D.C.: United States Government Printing Office, 1972.

Steuer, F. B., Applefield, J. M., & Smith, R. Televised aggression and the interpersonal aggression of preschool children. *Journal of Experimental Child Psychology,* 1971, *11,* 442–447.

Stevens, G. *Cultivation and displacement: Two theories of media effects.* Unpublished manuscript, Annenberg School of Communications, Univ. of Pennsylvania, 1978.

Surgeon General's Scientific Advisory Committee on Television and Social Behavior. *Television and growing up: The impact of televised violence.* Report to the Surgeon General, United States Public Health Service. Washington, D.C.: United States Government Printing Office, 1972.

Tannenbaum, P. H., & Zillmann, D. Emotional arousal in the facilitation of aggression through communication. In L. Berkowitz (Ed.), *Advances in experimental social psychology* (Vol. 8). New York: Academic Press, 1975.

Tasch, M. O. *Modeling of prosocial behavior by preschool subjects of high and low self-esteem.* Unpublished doctoral dissertation, Syracuse Univ., 1970.

Tolley, H., Jr. *Children and war: Political socialization to international conflict.* New York: Teachers College Press, Columbia Univ., 1973.

Tyler, T. R. *Drawing inferences from experiences: The effects of crime victimization experiences upon crime-related attitudes and behaviors.* Unpublished doctoral dissertation, Univ. of California at Los Angeles, 1978.

Wells, W. D. *Television and aggression: Replication of an experimental field study.* Unpublished manuscript, Graduate School of Business, Univ. of Chicago, 1973.

Worchel, S., Hardy, T. W., & Hurley, R. The effects of commercial interruption of violent and nonviolent films on viewers' subsequent aggression. *Journal of Experimental Psychology,* 1976, *2,* 220–232.

Yates, G. C. R. Influence of televised modeling and verbalization on children's delay of gratification. *Journal of Experimental Child Psychology,* 1974, *18,* 333–339.

Zillmann, D. Excitation transfer in communication-mediated aggressive behavior. *Journal of Experimental Social Psychology,* 1971, *7,* 419–434.

Zillmann, D., Johnson, R. C., & Hanrahan, J. Pacifying effect of happy ending of communications involving aggression. *Psychological Reports,* 1973, *32,* 967–970.

The Violent Face of
Television and Its Lessons[1]

GEORGE GERBNER
LARRY GROSS

What children and other viewers learn about violence from television is not necessarily learned from just seeing acts of violence. To understand the full scope of its lessons we need to look at television as a social institution. Once we have done that, we shall sketch some features of the world of television, of the role of violence in that world, and of public concerns about the depiction of violence as the context within which one can best understand those findings of our long-range research project which we will report here.

Television and Society

Television comes to us as a combination of radio, movies, the pulps, games, circuses, comics and cartoons, and a dash of journalism, but it is

[1] The research on which this chapter's discussion is based is a team effort in which our chief associates were Nancy Signorielli, Michael Morgan, Suzanne Jeffries-Fox, Marilyn Jackson-Beeck, and Michael F. Eleey. The research has been conducted since 1967 under grants from the National Commission on the Causes and Prevention of Violence, the Surgeon General's Scientific Advisory Committee, the National Institute of Mental Health, the White House Office of Telecommunications Policy, and the American Medical Association.

none of these. It is the first mass-produced and organically composed symbolic environment into which all children are born and in which they will live from cradle to grave. No other medium or institution since pre-industrial religion has had a comparable influence on what people of a tribe, community, or nation have learned, thought, or done in common.

Although television broadcasting today is private business, it is an officially licensed enterprise operating in the public domain. Television thus becomes an organ of governance as well as of acculturation. The First Amendment's prohibition against "an establishment of religion" did not prevent (in fact, continues to shield) the establishment of its modern functional equivalent. Television relates to the State as only the Church did in former times. Its nearly universal and ritualistic use fits its cyclical and repetitive programming. People attend to television as they used to attend church except that they do it much more often and more religiously.

Universal and Ritualistic Use

Television is now our common and constant learning environment. Over 4 million hours of programming a year are discharged into the mainstream of common consciousness to claim the time and attention of 200 million Americans. Television demands no mobility, literacy, or concentrated attention. Its repetitive patterns come into the home and show, as well as tell about, people and society. Presidents, police officers, doctors and nurses, judges and lawyers, spies, and celebrities are familiar members of a selective and synthetic world that nearly everyone knows most about. Television is a total cultural system with its own art, science, statecraft, legendry, geography, demography, character types, and action structure. The world of television encapsulates those selected features of the larger media culture that lend themselves best to its basic sales and socializing functions.

The television audience is not only the most heterogeneous public ever assembled but also the most nonselective. Most viewers watch by the clock and not by the program. Viewing is a ritual governed by styles of life and time. Different kinds of programs serve the same basic formula designed to assemble viewers for the most profit and sell them at the least cost. The classifications of the print era with their relatively sharp differentiations between news, drama, documentary, and so on, do not apply as much to television. Heavy viewers watch more of everything. Different time and program segments complement and reinforce each other as they present aspects of the same symbolic world.

There is little age, regional, or even ethnic separation of the symbolic materials that socialize members of an otherwise heterogeneous community into a common culture. Most children control their own (if not their whole family's) sets and watch mostly adult programs and problems depicting this common culture. Minority groups see their own image shaped by the dominant interests of the larger "common" culture.

Television is today's central agency of the established order—the common culture—and as such serves primarily to maintain, stabilize, and reinforce—not subvert—conventional values, beliefs, and behaviors. All societies have ways of explaining the world to themselves and to their children. Socially constructed "reality" gives a coherent picture of what exists, what is important, how things are related, and what is right. The constant cultivation of such "realities" is the task of rituals and mythologies. They legitimize actions along lines that are conventionally acceptable and functional. Television today serves that function in its nearly universal use as a demonstration of social reality.

Cyclical and Repetitive Programming

Most regular viewers of television are immersed in a vivid and illuminating world which has certain repetitive and pervasive patterns. At the center of this coherently constructed world is network drama. Drama is where the bulk of audience viewing time is. Drama is where total human problems and situations, rather than abstracted topics and fragments, are illuminated.

The stories of the dramatic world of television need not present credible accounts of what things *are* to perform the more critical function of demonstrating how things really *work*. The illumination of the invisible relationships of characters and dynamics of life has always been the principal function of drama and fiction. The function is best performed when the "facts" can be invented so as to lend themselves to compelling demonstrations of the inner meaning and order of things. Television has invented characters and actions, especially violent actions, which demonstrate by their consistency the essential order of things. In the following two sections we will describe these characters and violent actions using results reported in some of our previous publications (Gerbner & Gross, 1976; Gerbner, Gross, Jackson-Beeck, Jeffries-Fox, & Signorielli, 1978; Gerbner, Gross, Morgan, & Signorielli, 1980; Gerbner, Gross, Signorielli, Morgan, & Jackson-Beeck, 1979; Gross, 1979) and using the results of new analyses of data from our archives.

Characters. In one week the typical evening (8–11 P.M.) viewer of a single network station will encounter about 300 dramatic characters playing speaking roles. This figure is for drama alone, not counting commercials, news, game or talk shows, documentaries, or, of course, other viewing times. Of these 300 characters, 217 are males, 80 are females, and 3 are animals or robots of no clear gender. The racial composition of this typical slice of the world of primetime dramatic television is 262 whites, 35 members of other races, and 3 whose race is hard to tell. The children of the typical family will meet an additional 137 dramatic characters in speaking parts during weekend daytime hours. Gender and race in weekend daytime programs (clearly identifiable for only two-thirds of these—mostly cartoon—characters) are about the same as in prime-time. Overall, the world of television is three-fourths American, three-fourths between ages 30–60 (compared to one-third of the real population), and three-fourths male.

Clearly the world of television is not like the real world. Looking at it through the prism of age reveals a population curve that, unlike the real world but much like the curve of consumer spending, bulges in the middle years of life. That makes children and the elderly relatively neglected, old people virtually invisible, and the portrayals of these and other minorities, as well as of women, as sensitive barometers of the dramatic equities—or inequities—of life.

Types of activity—paid and unpaid—also reflect dramatic and social purposes. Six in ten characters are engaged in discernible occupational activity and can be roughly divided into three groups. The first group represents the world of legitimate business, industry, agriculture, finance, and so on. The second group is engaged in activity related to art, science, religion, health, education and welfare, as professionals, amateurs, housewives, patients, students, or clients. The third makes up the forces of official or semiofficial authority and the army of criminals, outlaws, spies, and other enemies arrayed against them. One in every four leading characters fits into this last category as he—or occasionally she—acts out a drama of some sort of transgression and its suppression at home and abroad.

Approximately five in ten characters (or five of the six engaged in any occupational activity) can be unambiguously identified as gainfully employed. Of these, three are proprietors, managers, and professionals. The fourth comes from the ranks of labor—including all those employed in factories, farms, offices, shops, stores, mining, transportation, service stations, restaurants, and households, and working in unskilled, skilled, clerical, sales, and domestic service capacities. The fifth serves to enforce the law or preserve the peace on behalf of public or private clients.

Violent Action. In this world where men outnumber women four to one, it is not surprising that much of the action revolves around questions of power: how to manage and maintain the social order. Violence, which we have defined as the overt expression of physical force compelling action against one's will on pain of being hurt or killed or actually hurting or killing, is the key to the rule of power. It is the cheapest and quickest dramatic demonstration of who can and who cannot get away with what against whom. It is an exercise in norm-setting and social typing. It occupies about one-third of all male major characters (but very few women) in depicting violations and enforcement of the rules of society.

Violence is thus a scenario of social relationships. Its calculus of opportunities and risks demonstrates one's odds upon entering the arena. In the world of television, four-fifths of all primetime and weekend daytime programs contain violence, and two-thirds of all major characters get involved. The exercise of power through violence is clearly a central feature of that world. In weekend daytime children's programs the rate of involvement is even greater—80%. Men are more likely to encounter it than are women, and adults are more involved than are children, although about half of all women and children still get involved in violence. The question is who comes out of it and how. A character's chances to be a violent or a victim (or both) suggest degrees of vulnerability and probable fate.

Therefore, violence as a scenario of power has a built-in index of risk: It is the numerical relationship of violents to victims within each social group compared to other groups. That index, called the risk ratio, shows the chances of men and women, blacks and whites, young and old, and so on, to come out of a violent encounter on top instead of on the bottom.

In the world of dramatic television, 46% of all major characters commit violence and 55% suffer it (with many being both violents and victims). Thus, the overall risk ratio is − 1.2; meaning that there are 12 victims for each 10 violents. The ratio for women is 13 victims, for nonwhite women 18 victims, and for old women 33 victims for every 10 violents. So, if and when involved, women, nonwhite women, and older women characters bear a higher burden of relative risk and danger than do the majority types.

Of course, not all violence is alike. A blow by the oppressed against unbearable odds or by the exploited against the exploiter may be a message of liberation rather than of established power. Even if the violent hero perishes (and thus counts as a victim in the risk ratio), the tragedy exposes inequity and injustice instead of perpetrating them. But considering that the average output of violent episodes in the massive flow of entertainment programming is 5 episodes per primetime and 18 per weekend daytime hour, such tragic scenes are very rare.

Causes of Cycles and Repetition. Our annual monitoring of network television drama since 1967–1968 shows a remarkably consistent pattern despite changes in program titles, formats, and styles. Many times a day, 7 days a week, the dramatic pattern defines situations and cultivates premises about society, people, and issues. What is the root cause of this unity and coherence of the universal curriculum of the world of television? It is called "cost per thousand," the price advertisers pay television for assembling and delivering a thousand viewers of commercials. It is computed by dividing the number of thousands of viewers (as measured by Nielsen, Arbitron, or whatever) by the price charged for assembling them in front of the set, including the cost of the program. But since most viewers will watch whatever is on, the size of the audience (and the price paid for delivering it) depends mainly on the time of day rather than on the program. As any Nielsen will show, network differences in audience size tend to be small compared to day-part differences, despite the competitive hue and cry. The best policy is, therefore, the cheapest and least offensive programming, and any program policy that does not strive for competitive audience ratings at the least cost is beyond the scope of serious consideration. This places a premium on the most broadly acceptable, conventional fare. Other types of programs do not sell so well and do not have the same chance of becoming significant parts of the common symbolic environment.

Concerns about Violence

The televised stories that generate the most concern—despite the fact that they are still heavily viewed—seem to be those that contain scenes of violence. Why should this be? First, it is because, even when committed in the name of law and order, acts of physical aggression are suspected of inciting impressionable viewers to commit similar acts. This is an invariable reaction of "established classes" (adults in this case) when members of "subservient classes" (children, here) are exposed to mass-mediated stories.

A second reason for concern about television violence is the frequency of aggressive acts depicted in television drama, particularly in programs aimed specifically at children. It has often been noted that by the time the average American child graduates from high school, he or she will have seen more than 13,000 violent deaths on television. Given the sheer amount of children's potential exposure to televised violence, we worry that children will become jaded, desensitized, and inured to violence not only on television, but in real life as well.

It appears to be a justifiable fear that viewing televised violence will make people, children in particular, somewhat more likely to commit acts of violence themselves (see Chapters 8, 9, and 11, this volume for reviews of the evidence). Our own research (Gerbner et al., 1978) also has found that young viewers who watch a lot of television are more likely to agree that it is "almost always all right" to hit someone "if you are mad at them for a good reason."

Yet, if the most consistent effect of viewing television violence were that it incited real acts of violence, we would not need elaborate research studies. The average sibling, parent, and teacher would be reeling from the blows of television-stimulated aggression. Clearly this is not the case. Imitative aggression among children may be frequent, but it is relatively low-level. Widely publicized cases of serious violence which seem to be influenced by television programs or movies are rare. At any rate, spectacular cases of individual violence threatening the social order (unlike those enforcing it) have always been "blamed" on some corrupter of youth—from Socrates through pulps, comics, and movies, to television. Are there no other grounds for concern?

Yes! Violence plays an important role in communicating the social order. It provides a calculus of life chances in conflict and shows the rules by which the game is played. It demonstrates the relative distributions of power and of the fear of power. The few incidents of real-life violence it incites may only serve to reinforce that fear. The scenario needs both violents and victims; both roles are there to be learned by viewers. The patterns show the power of dominant types to come out on top. They tend to cultivate acquiescence to and dependence on their rule. If at times (though very rarely) television also incites violence by the ruled against the rulers, that may be the price paid for the tranquilization of the vast majority.

To reduce that tranquilization, it is not enough to decrease the number of violent incidents; the patterns of power and risk would have to give way to those which are more diversified and equitable. But entertainment—the most informative and educational force of any culture—is inherently pleasing precisely because it does not challenge conventional beliefs of right and might. It demands happy endings which prove fate and society to be just, as well as strong. The least offensive programming at the lowest cost and best "cost per thousand," as well as the institutional interests of established society, require the cultivation of conventional morality and the stroking of conventional egos. Television violence is by and large a cheap industrial ingredient whose patterns tend to support rather than to subvert the established order. In generating among the many a fear of the power of the few, television violence may achieve its greatest effect.

Teaching the Social Order

We have addressed this hypothesis in the Cultural Indicators project by determining the extent to which exposure to the *symbolic* world of television cultivates conceptions about the *real* world among viewers. This question about broad enculturation is different from the usual research question about individual messages, campaigns, programs, or genres. Traditional procedures of media effects research must be reconceptualized and modified for television.

Research Procedures

First, we cannot presume consequences, as the conventional research paradigm tends to do, without the prior investigation of content. Nor can the content be limited to isolated elements (e.g., news, commercials, specific programs) taken out of the total context or to individual viewer selections. Only system-wide analysis of television messages can reveal the symbolic world which structures common assumptions and definitions for the generations born into it and provides bases for interaction (though not necessarily of agreement) among large and heterogeneous communities.

Another conventional research assumption is that the experiment is the most powerful method and that change is the most significant outcome. When the treatment is television, however, we must turn this paradigm around: Stability (or even resistance to change) may be the significant outcome. We cannot look for change as the most significant accomplishment of the chief arm of established culture if its main social function is to maintain, reinforce, and exploit rather than to undermine or subvert prevalent conceptions, beliefs, and behaviors. The relative ineffectiveness of many isolated campaigns may itself be testimony to the power of mainstream communications.

Much of the research on media violence has focused on the observation and measurement of behavior which occurs after a viewer has seen a particular program or even isolated scenes from programs. All such studies, no matter how clean the design and clear the results, are of limited value because they ignore a fundamental fact: The world of television drama consists of a complex and integrated system of characters, events, actions, and relationships. It is a total symbol system composed largely of stories whose effects cannot be measured with regard to any single element or program seen in isolation.

Neither can we assume that television cultivates conceptions easily distinguishable from those of other major entertainment media. We assume, instead, that television's historically novel standardizing and legitimizing influence comes largely from its ability to streamline, amplify, ritualize, and spread into hitherto isolated or protected subcultures, homes, nooks, and crannies of the land the conventional capsules of mass-produced information and entertainment. The effects of television are most likely to be those of the centralization and efficient organization and popularization of those elements of mainstream culture that best support the medium's institutional mission.

Therefore, in contrast to the more usual statement of the problem, we do not believe that the only critical correlate of television violence is to be found in the stimulation of occasional individual aggression. The consequences of living in a symbolic world ruled largely by violence may be much more far-reaching. Television violence is a dramatic demonstration of power which communicates much about social norms and relationships, about goals and means, about winners and losers, about the risks of life, and about the price for transgressions of society's rules. "Real-world" victims as well as violents may have to learn their roles. Fear—that historic instrument of social control—may be an even more critical residue of a show of violence than is aggression. Expectation of violence or passivity in the face of injustice may be a consequence of even greater social concern.

The Findings of Research

To find out what viewers in fact learn from television we search for those assumptions about "facts" of life and society that television tends to cultivate among its more faithful viewers. That search requires two different but related methods of research. The first is the periodic analysis of large and representative aggregates of television output (rather than individual segments) as the system of messages to which total communities are exposed. The purpose of message system analysis is to establish the composition and structure of the symbolic world. The second step is to determine what, if anything, viewers absorb from living in that world. Here the findings of message system analysis are turned into questions about social reality. To each of these questions there is a "television answer" that is like the way things appear in the world of television, and there is another answer which is closer to the way things are in the observable world.

We have asked these questions of samples of adults, adolescents, and children. All responses were related to television exposure, other media habits, and demographic characteristics. We then compared the responses of light and heavy viewers controlling for sex, age, education, and other characteristics. The margin of heavy viewers over light viewers giving the "television answers" within and across groups is the "cultivation differential" indicating conceptions about social reality that viewing tends to cultivate. The independent contribution of television to the cultivation of assumptions can best be seen in those areas where television presents a pattern different from or more extreme than other sources. One such area is violence.

The results of our previous adult and child surveys (Gerbner & Gross 1976; Gerbner et al., 1978, 1980) showed consistent learning and children's particular vulnerability. They confirmed that violence-laden television not only cultivates aggressive tendencies in a minority but, perhaps more importantly, also generates a pervasive and exaggerated sense of danger and mistrust. Heavy viewers revealed a significantly higher sense of personal risk and suspicion than did light viewers in the same demographic groups who were exposed to the same real risks of life. They more often responded in terms more characteristic of the television world than of the real world when asked about their chances of being involved in some kind of violence, the percentage of men employed in law enforcement and crime detection, and the percentage of crimes that are violent. They were more likely to believe that most people just look out for themselves, take advantage of others, and cannot be trusted.

The analysis showed a significant tendency for heavy viewers to overestimate the prevalence of violence and its concomitants compared to the estimates of the light viewers. The analysis also demonstrated that these presumed effects of television cannot be accounted for in terms of the major demographic variables of age, sex, education, or even, in the case of our children's sample, IQ. The effects were consistent and robust for both children and adults across a range of undoubtedly powerful control comparisons.

Surveys of adolescents extended these findings in important new directions (Gerbner *et al.*, 1979). Analyses were based on data collected from two samples of adolescents, one of seventh and eighth graders from a public school in suburban/rural New Jersey (N=447) and one of fifth through twelfth graders from a New York City private school (N=140). Students filled out questionnaires which offered two answers to each question, one answer based on facts or statistics and one answer based on the "facts" as depicted on television. Information on viewing habits and demographic variables was also requested. It indicated that the samples were roughly equivalent except that the parents of the New York City children were better educated and that the New York City children watched fewer hours of television per day. Results in four areas—chances of involvement in violence, fear of walking alone at night, perceived activities of police, and mistrust—were examined.

Heavy viewers in both the New York and New Jersey schools were more likely than were light viewers to overestimate the number of people involved in violence and the proportion of people who commit serious crimes. In the New York sample, the finding was especially strong for boys—those of lower socioeconomic status (SES), those who had not been victims of either personal or family-directed violence, and those with middle or low achievement scores. In the New Jersey sample, the relationship was stronger among girls, frequent newspaper readers, and heavy television news viewers, as well as among those whose fathers had not attended college. Despite these variations, the association remained consistently positive for each comparison group: Heavy viewers in every case were more likely than were light viewers to believe that a greater number of people are regularly involved in violence. Similarly, heavy viewers in the New Jersey sample were generally more likely to overestimate how many people commit serious crimes. The relationship was the strongest among females and occasional newspaper readers.

Most of the New Jersey students (about 80%) felt that it was dangerous to walk alone in a city at night. Yet within every comparison group, heavy viewers were more likely than were light viewers to express this opinion. This pattern was most evident among girls, occasional newspaper readers, and infrequent viewers of network news. Although most considered it dangerous, there was a fair degree of variation in who was afraid to walk alone in a city at night. The New Jersey students were more afraid than were the New York students; in both samples and again, especially in New Jersey, the females were considerably more afraid. Within every group, however, heavy viewers were more likely than were light viewers to express this fear. This pattern was not as consistent in the New York sample, although it persisted notably for females, those of lower SES, low achievers, and those who had not been victims of crime. Responses to a question about one's willingness to walk alone at night in one's own neighborhood showed a strong and consistent relationship between the amount of viewing and being afraid. Females and young students were more afraid overall. These two groups also showed the strongest relationship between the amount of television viewing and the fear of walking alone at night in one's own neighborhood.

Television viewing also seems to contribute to adolescents' images and assumptions about law enforcement procedures and activities. Among the New Jersey students, more heavy than light viewers in every subgroup believed that police must often use force and violence at a scene of violence. Among the New York students, there was a consistent, positive relationship between amount of viewing and the perception of how many times a day a policeman pulls out a gun. Adolescents in New Jersey showed a positive relationship across the board between amount of viewing and the tendency to believe that police who shoot at running persons actually hit them.

Finally, adolescent heavy viewers also tended to express mistrust in people and to express the belief that people are selfish. Although the differences were not as pronounced as they were for violence- and fear-related questions, the patterns were stable across most groups. Those who watched more television remained more likely to say that people "are mostly just looking out for themselves" (rather than trying to be helpful) and that one "can't be too careful in dealing with people" (rather than that they can be trusted).

These findings provide considerable support for the conclusion that heavy television viewers perceive social reality differently from light television viewers, even when other factors are held constant. There was considerable variation between groups in the scope and magnitude of these patterns: The extent of television's contribution is mediated, enhanced, or diminished by powerful personal, social, and cultural variables, as well as by other information sources. Yet the relationships remained positive in almost every case. The amount of viewing made a consistent difference in the responses of these adolescents, even the "more sophisticated," "less impressionable" New Yorkers.

Results which parallel and therefore strengthen these have also been found for a slightly younger age group. In a survey of 2200 7- to 11-year-old children and their parents conducted by the Foundation for Child Development, a significant relationship was found between amount of television viewing and violence-related fears, even with controls for age, sex, ethnic background, vocabulary, and the child's own reports of victimization (Zill, 1979). We may conclude, then, that viewers' expressions of fear and interpersonal mistrust, assumptions about the chances of encountering violence, and images of police activities can be traced in part to television portrayals.

Coping with Power

Given these findings that heavy television viewing cultivates a pervasive fear of violence, as well as its occasional perpetration, why is the most vocal concern about television-incited violence? The answer rests in the complex nature of the social scenario called violence and its multiple functions. As action, violence hurts, kills, and scares. The last is its most important social function because that is what maintains power and compels acquiescence to power. Therefore, it is important who scares whom and who is "trained" to be the victim.

The privileges of power most jealously guarded are those of violence and sex. In the public realm it is government that claims the legal prerogatives to commit violence (in defense of law, order, and national security) and to regulate the commission and depiction of sexual acts (in defense of "decency"). In the private realm, parents assert the same prerogatives over their children—the power to determine the range of permissible and forbidden behavior. It would stand to reason, therefore, that the representatives of established order would be more worried about television violence as a threat to their monopoly over physical coercion, however limited that threat might be, than about insecurities that drive people to seek protection and to accept control.

The violence scenario thus serves a double function. By demonstrating the realities of social power, it generates insecurity and dependence and serves as an instrument of social control. This objective is achieved at a great human price. The price is the inciting of a few to destructive violence, the cultivating of aggressive tendencies among some children and adults, and the generating of a sense of danger and risk in a mean and selfish world.

There is no scientific way to determine what "price is right" for the maintenance of a society's structure of power. But the increasing number of citizens who have a feeling that the price may be too high should recognize that the mechanism for extracting it is rooted deeply in the structure of television as a social institution. Despite all the hue and cry, the frequency of violence has not even changed more than 10% from the norm of 10 years. To alter it and to provide a freer, fairer, and more equitable experience for child and adult viewers alike, far-reaching measures will be necessary.

First, the education of creative resources and critical viewing skills will have to become a primary task of schooling. Liberal education was always designed to liberate the growing person from unwitting dependence on the immediate cultural environment. That is why the "great" art, science, history, and literature of an age was the heart of a liberal education. But that has always involved only a small minority. Today's fresh approach to the liberal arts demands liberation from unwitting dependence on the mass-produced cultural environment that involves everyone every day. We need education for the age of television.

Second, the imperatives of television as a social institution will have to give way to a freer market in television production. The iron censorship of "cost per thousand" viewers makes violence the cheapest—as well as an otherwise attractive—industrial ingredient in the present system of dramatic mass production. The resource base for television will have to be broadened to liberate the institution from total dependence on advertising monies and purposes. The potential riches of television and the willingness to pay for a more diversified fare through cable and other means show that consumers and citizens want a television system more responsive to their needs.

Third, a high-level national commission is needed to examine the ways in which democratic countries around the world manage their television systems in the interest of children and minorities, as well as in the interest of the big middle-consumer majority. The commission should recommend a mechanism that will finance a freer and more democratic system, one that can present a fairer and more democratic world on television. That is the only way to reduce violence and its fallout to what is artistically sound, socially desirable, and humanly defensible. For example, one thing that would reduce violence and restore some sense of equity to the world of television would be the casting of more women. But the few producers who have tried that report that nonconventional casting and dramatic patterns, injected into the present context, suffer in ratings and sales appeal. Therefore, financial resources and the appropriate context are needed to create a freer pattern of representation and cultivation.

Finally, television service should become at least as much a part of the process of self-government, overcoming its present policy insulation from the citizenry, as is energy, education, or health. A broad advisory group composed of prominent citizens representing the major civic organizations concerned with culture, education, and health will have to come into being to offset the pressures of private interest groups and to protect the freedom of creative professionals from both governmental and corporate dictation. Only then will television's professionals be free to produce the diversified and equitable fare they know how to produce but cannot produce under existing constraints and controls.

Our review of research on the violent face of television and its lessons has led us into a deeper examination of the institution of television, its role in society, and the conditions for altering that role as the prerequisite for dealing with violence. There is obviously no simple or easy way to transform the mass-produced dreams that hurt our children into the dreams that would heal them.

References

Gerbner, G., & Gross, L. Living with television: The violence profile. *Journal of Communication*, 1976, *26*(2), 173–199.

Gerbner, G., Gross L., Jackson-Beeck, M., Jeffries-Fox, S., & Signorielli, N. Cultural indicators: Violence profile no. 9. *Journal of Communication*, 1978, *28*(3), 176–207.

Gerbner, G., Gross, L., Morgan, M., and Signorielli, N. The mainstreaming of America. *Journal of Communication*, 1980, *30*(3), 12–29.

Gerbner, G., Gross, L., Signorielli, N., Morgan, M., & Jackson-Beeck, M. The demonstration of power: Violence profile no. 10. *Journal of Communication*, 1979, *29*(3), 177–196.

Gross, L. Television and violence. In K. Moody & B. Logan (Eds.), *Television awareness training* (2nd ed.). Nashville: Parthenon, 1979.

Concomitants of Television Violence Viewing in Children[1]

MONROE M. LEFKOWITZ
L. ROWELL HUESMANN

Most of the empirical findings summarized in the Surgeon General's report (1972) have been confirmed by more recent research, and a clear consensus has emerged among researchers that television violence and behavior are related. Yet the controversy regarding the explanation of these findings has not subsided. Perhaps too much emphasis has been placed on the collection of empirical data and too little, on the organization of these data into a coherent framework. Therefore, in the second part of this chapter we will attempt to arrange the available evidence about the psychological processes through which television violence influences behavior. Such a framework should provide the means for a clearer resolution of the major questions about how television violence affects behavior.

To some extent, the topic of television violence has stimulated a search for possible effects other than violence or aggression. Insofar as we could marshall the pertinent data, we will report in the first part of this chapter on all the concomitants of violence viewing. Thus, in addition to aggression, other areas of behavior which have been related to television

[1] The preparation of this chapter was supported in part by NIMH Grant MH29788 to the senior author and Grants MH28280 and MH31886 to the junior author.

violence will be reviewed. Such an accounting necessarily builds on the invaluable effort rendered by Comstock and his colleagues (Comstock, 1975; Comstock & Fisher, 1975; Comstock & Lindsey, 1975) in assembling, categorizing, and abstracting the relevant research on this topic up through the mid-1970s. We found that the work they summarized and more recent work as it relates to children could be sorted into four categories, each representing a major concomitant. Not necessarily mutually exclusive, these concomitants are: (a) aggression; (b) socialization and values; (c) physiological responses; and (d) mood. Ordered by the volume of research for each concomitant, studies on aggression were by far preponderant.

Concomitants of Viewing Violence

Aggression

On the basis of commissioned studies and other earlier work, the Surgeon General's Scientific Advisory Committee (1972) concluded that there was "a preliminary and tentative indication of a causal relation between viewing violence on television and aggressive behavior [p. 11]." However, it also temporized that there was an indication that any such causal relation operates only on some children (who are predisposed to be aggressive). The more recent studies and analyses strongly support the Committee's major conclusion but provide little support for this latter restriction.

Modeling has been implicated as a link between violence viewing and aggressive behavior in two laboratory studies published since the Surgeon General's report. In the first (Kniveton, 1973), children were either exposed or not exposed to a film portraying aggressive behavior. Those viewing the aggressive film exhibited a broader range of modeled aggressive acts and more overall aggression than did the control group. In the second study (Kniveton & Stephenson, 1973), the authors found that the propensity of children to imitate aggressive models was an enduring characteristic. However, in contrast to the general consensus among researchers, Kniveton (1974) concludes that the relationship between violence viewing and aggression is mediated by intellectual deprivation: Children with few interests are simply more susceptible to imitating television models.

Driving behavior as a dependent measure was studied by Greenberg and Wotring (1974) in a simulated context to determine whether exposure to televised violence increases aggressive driving in a postviewing situation. Separated into three groups, the high school students watched a violent television show, a nonviolent show, or no show at all. There were no important between-group differences in the postviewing driving situation. However, the violent show did not contain scenes of aggressive driving. Furthermore, adolescents rather than young children were studied. The authors suggest that perhaps a significant effect would have occurred if the violence viewing had consisted of aggressive car chase scenes like those presented in many television police dramas.

A number of field studies have been conducted since the Surgeon General's report and, like the laboratory studies, most have provided unequivocal evidence of a positive relation between violence viewing and aggression. A 5-year longitudinal study by McCarthy, Langner, Gersten, Eisenberg, and Orzeck (1975) in which data from 732 children were obtained clearly supports the hypothesis that television violence viewing is related to aggression. All obtained data on children's aggression—conflict with parents, fighting, and delinquency—were positively correlated with the weighted television violence score. Uniquely, the violence score in this study also encompassed the amount of television viewed. Unfortunately, since television viewing data were not collected in the first wave of the study, no causal analyses could be undertaken. However, the children's quantity of television viewing and amount of violence viewing were clearly related to the absence of desirable life events during the preceding 5 years. Similarly, earlier psychopathology and lowered intellectual functioning were predictive of amount of television viewing 5 years later. Also new was the finding that amount of television viewed was positively related to aggression. While older studies (Robinson & Bachman, 1972) had found no relation between total amount of viewing and aggression, some more recent field studies in addition to McCarthy et al. (1975) also have found positive relations (Eron & Huesmann, in press; Huesmann, Fischer, Eron, Mermelstein, Kaplan-Shain, & Morikawa, 1978; Lagerspetz, 1979).

A unique cross-cultural, longitudinal study of the impact of television, particularly television violence, on a previously unexposed community in the remote Canadian north was reported by Granzberg and Steinbring (1980). Three communities, two comprised of Manitoba Cree Indians and the third of Euro-Canadians, were involved. Data on three measures of aggression were obtained prior to and after introduction of television to the experimental Cree community. These data were subsequently compared to similar data obtained from the two controls: The unexposed Cree community and the 20-year-exposed Euro-Canadian community. The major hypothesis was that viewers' levels of aggression would increase most for the experimental group between testings because they were the only children whose television viewing time had substantially increased. No pre-post differences in levels of aggression between the experimental and control communities, taken as a whole, occurred. But, when children were classified by amount of daily exposure to television, significant differences in aggressive attitude were found. In the experimental community, high exposed children increased in aggressive attitude while low exposed children decreased in aggressive attitude. Thus, introduction of television into a community resulted in greater aggression of children with high exposure to television as compared to their low-exposure peers in that community and also as compared to children in the Euro-Canadian community. In this study, in a similar one by Williams (1978), and in the one by McCarthy et al. (1975), amount of television viewed proved to be the critical potentiating variable in elucidating the relationship between violent television and aggressive behavior.

In a study of Finnish children in first and third grades, Lagerspetz (1979) and Eron and Huesmann (in press) found a significant correlation for boys between television violence viewing and aggression when the television model was male. When the model was female no significant relationship occurred. For the girls in this study, there were significant correlations between television violence and aggressive behavior irrespective of the gender of the television model. When comparable data had been collected on 748 children in first through fourth grades in urban and suburban schools in the Chicago area (Eron & Huesmann, in press; Huesmann et al., 1978), a positive correlation between television violence viewing at home and aggressive behavior in school was found for the entire sample. The correlations were significant for both sexes irrespective of the sex of the television model. However, the correlation between violence viewing and aggression was larger for both boys and girls when the television model was male. These correlations are of the same order of magnitude ($r = .15-.20$) as occurred in most of the prior field studies. In a discussion of these findings, Eron and Huesmann (in press) note that it may not be the sex of the model which influences behavior of the viewers, but rather the behaviors the model is performing. Consequently, "if masculine activities are intrinsically more appealing to subjects of either sex, then they would be more likely to imitate those activities regardless of the sex of the model [p. 13]."

Although the relationships between television violence viewing and aggressive behavior were positive for both boys and girls, cross-sectional analyses of the data showed the correlation between these two variables to increase from first to third grades for boys, but to decrease through these grades for girls. It is thought that girls are less likely to be influenced by aggressive models as they proceed through the primary grades, whereas boys are more likely to be influenced by such models during this period. These contrasting results are attributed to differential socialization of the sexes.

An important aspect of the Chicago and Finnish studies is their investigation of the fantasy-catharsis hypothesis. The prototypical argument proferred by Feshbach and Singer (1971) was that the expression of fantasy, for example on television, reduces aggressive drives and consequently reduces aggressive behavior. More recently, Feshbach (1976) found that the depiction of fantasy aggression on television tended to lower or leave unaffected a child's acting out of aggressive tendencies. But, the depiction of real aggression, particularly when it was reinforced, tended to facilitate aggressive behavior. Analysis of this topic on the 748 children in the Chicago area sample (Rosenfeld, Maloney, Huesmann, Eron, Fischer, Musonis, & Washington, 1978) illustrated that, when a child viewed television as realistic, television violence viewing, particularly in girls, was positively related to aggression. In part, these findings agree with those of Feshbach (1976) but, as Eron & Huesmann (in press) note, there is no evidence in their data that fantasy has any cathartic effect. On the contrary, children who fantasize about aggressive acts tend to act aggressively. Ominous, therefore, are the implications of those forms of psychotherapy which encourage aggressive fantasy in the hope of reducing aggressive acts.

Two other field studies have provided support for the television violence–aggression relation. In a study of adolescents in the United States, Hartnagel, Teevan, and McIntyre (1975) found a significant though low correlation between violence viewing and aggressive behavior. Furthermore, those subjects who perceived television programming as violent or perceived the violence as an effective means to a goal engaged in more violent behavior than did those who did not perceive their favorite show to be violent. Finally, Greenberg (1975) found correlations between violence viewing and aggression in a sample of London school children, correlations that were remarkably similar to those reported for American children. In the main, therefore, contemporary laboratory studies and field studies both in the United States and in other western countries have continued to find a significant relationship between violence viewing and aggression. The few studies capable of testing causal theories clearly suggest that the most plausible direction is from violence viewing to aggression.

Socialization and Values

Our concern here is with the child's recognition of a link between behavior and consequences. The child becomes aware that if the consequences are deleterious, the behavior should not be emitted, and, therefore, behavior whose consequences are positive, or at least not negative, to others or to oneself becomes positively valued. Germane to this feature of socialization are those studies relating television violence viewing to the disinhibition of aggressive behavior or to an increase in the tolerance for such behavior.

One such study (Drabman & Thomas, 1974a) examined the hypothesis that exposure to televised violence increases children's tolerance of real-life aggression. Immediately after viewing a film, a child was placed in charge of two younger children and told to notify the experimenter if there were any trouble. As compared to children who saw a nonviolent film, those who saw an aggressive film took longer to seek adult help. Furthermore, these children were much more likely to tolerate all but violent physical aggression before they sought such help. Using a more contemporary aggressive film, Drabman and Thomas (1974b) replicated these results while controlling for arousal effects. In a further study of the same topic, Thomas and Drabman (1975) again found that children shown the violent film were slower to get adult help in an aggressive situation. Moreover, first graders were significantly slower than third graders. Drabman and Thomas (1976) suggest that apathy to real-life violence is produced by fictional violence on television because television violence teaches children "that aggression is a way of American life and therefore not to be taken seriously [p. 331]." Moreover, since media violence is much more vicious than that which children normally experience, real-life aggression appears bland by comparison. This group of studies illustrates how television violence can adversely affect the socialization of children by inculcating such negative values as the tolerance of aggressive behavior.

Collins (1973) tested an interesting developmental hypothesis concerning the temporal separation between motivation for an aggressive act, the act itself, and the consequences. Four minutes each of commercials were placed between the portrayal of an actor's motive and his aggressive behavior and between his aggression and the consequences. It was found that third graders but not older children had difficulty relating motives, aggression, and consequences when the commercials were interspersed. A later study (Collins, Berndt, & Hess, 1974) tested these same abilities to link motives, aggression, and consequences using a violent television program exactly as it had been broadcast. A higher proportion of kindergartners and second graders, as compared to older subjects, associated aggression only with consequences. Older children recalled primary and secondary motives for the aggressive act as well as consequences. Because younger children are not able to draw the relationship between motives and aggression, exposure to violent television may prove even more deleterious for very young children inasmuch as the retardation of socialization might begin at an earlier age with longer lasting and more dire consequences.

Socialization of children has been shown to be affected by the realism of aggression portrayed by television actors (Noble, 1973). When children were exposed to scenes of realistic violence, they played significantly less constructively afterward. On the other hand, constructive play occurred when aggression was stylistic and consequences to the victim could not be seen. Although these findings antedate those of Feshbach (1976) and Rosenfeld et al. (1978) described earlier, they are all in general accord.

In a study of children's values of helping or hurting (Collins & Getz, 1976), children who had seen models of constructive coping demonstrated a greater frequency of prosocial responding than did those exposed to the aggressive resolution of an interpersonal conflict. Vividly illustrated by this study is the fact that children will imitate prosocial behavior. That children are, however, primarily instructed in a system of antisocial values by viewing television violence is dramatically illustrated in Cline's (1976) description of explicit, documented instances of crimes committed as a direct result of television violence viewing. He concludes that there is a great deal of scientific evidence which suggests that children from average home environments exposed to television violence accept aggression as a normal mode of behavior. In effect, violence succeeds, and children are socialized to interpret aggressive behavior as a positive means for goal attainment. Television teaches children how to be aggressive much more often than it provides lessons in positive values (Liebert, 1974), and this has wide ranging implications for the socialization of children in the acceptance of violence as an integral feature of, to paraphrase Margaret Mead (1971), coming of age in America.

Physiological Responses

Certain physiological responses have been documented to be concomitants of television violence viewing. In one study (Silverman, 1973), children were aggressively aroused by being frustrated and insulted by an experimenter and were then allowed to give shocks to this person. A parallel experiment was conducted with adults. It was found that children were significantly more aggressive than adults, that blood pressure was lowest for all subjects while watching television, and that diastolic blood pressure of children, but not adults, was significantly higher while they were giving shocks than while viewing television. The findings support the catalyst position that observing aggression generates both a predisposition to aggressive behavior, as indicated by the diastolic blood pressure rise, and the actual manifestation of aggression.

In another study (Surbeck, 1973), heart rate was measured while children viewed three televised film episodes—one concerned with human violence, another with cartoon violence, and the third designated as a control. During the violent episodes the heart rates of all subjects decreased, but they returned to baseline levels for the nonviolent scenes. Human violence or cartoon violence did not produce differences in heart rate response, but the heart rate of younger subjects decreased more than did that of older subjects in response to the violent episodes.

Pulse amplitude was used as a measure of arousal in a study of desensitization of children to television violence (Cline, Croft, & Courrier, 1973). Among children shown violent and control films, the low television viewers showed greater changes in arousal than did the high viewers. Similar results were found in experiments with children and college students who were shown either a violent police story or an exciting volleyball game (Thomas, Horton, Lippincott, & Drabman, 1977). Subsequently, the children were shown a film of children fighting, the college students were shown a film of the riots at the 1968 Democratic National Convention, and emotionality in both groups was measured by changes in skin resistance. Except for the college-age females, those who previously had viewed the aggressive film were less aroused by the filmed scenes of real-life aggression than were those who viewed the control film. Moreover, an inverse relationship was found between the amount of television violence normally viewed and responsivity during the viewing of aggression. These findings suggest that the excessive display of violence on television may be desensitizing the population and producing youngsters who respond to real-life violence in a jaded manner.

Mood

Mood as a concomitant of television violence viewing in children is just being explored. Only three studies which refer to mood changes related to television violence viewing were found. In the first of these studies (Biblow, 1973), a shift of mood from anger to shame to sadness occurred after children viewed an aggressive film. After viewing a nonaggressive film, mood shifted from anger to elation. These findings support the theory that fantasy helps to create mood change. Children accustomed to fantasy may respond to a fantasy situation such as television violence viewing with a wide range of affect. To our knowledge, this is the first study to show that sadness or perhaps depression might be a concomitant of television violence viewing.

In the longitudinal study cited earlier (McCarthy et al., 1975), mothers were asked about changes in their children's moods as a result of television viewing. Longer viewing was significantly related to the measure of depression. But more important for this section on mood as a concomitant was the finding that the weighted violence score, comprised of violence and hours watched, was significantly correlated with mothers' ratings of children's depression.

In the third study (Lefkowitz, 1978), a significant correlation was discovered between children's self-ratings of depression and two independent measures of television violence viewing. The findings, more consistent for girls than for boys, were interpreted within the learned helplessness model of depression (Abramson, Seligman, & Teasdale, 1978). Direct expression of aggression by males can effect an outcome in real life, but such overt aggression is not approved behavior for females. Therefore, when females witness the success of mostly male violent models on television in controlling outcomes but cannot themselves emulate such behavior in reality, they tend to feel helpless. The helplessness is personal rather than universal, because females are able to compare themselves to males who are able to effect a response–consequence contingency. The manifestations of such helplessness in females are depressed affect and, because the helplessness is viewed as personal, lowered self-esteem.

The Processing of Observed Violence

As we have seen from the foregoing data, there are consistent, well-established relations between television violence viewing and children's behavior. Not so clear are the directions of the relations and the mechanisms through which they are formed. Various researchers have postulated at least five types of processes: (a) the observational learning of behaviors appearing on television; (b) the reduction by catharsis of viewers' drives to perform certain behaviors as a result of observing others perform them; (c) attitude changes generated by violent material presented on television; (d) changes in emotional and physiological responsiveness brought about by television violence viewing; and (e) the reinforcement of viewing behaviors as a result of the viewers' attainment of vicarious rewards.

By far the most widely discussed of the processes have been observational learning and catharsis, which are usually presented as competing explanations for the occurrence of aggressive behavior. For most children, however, the catharsis hypothesis is difficult to consider seriously because of the accumulation of other explanatory evidence in recent years. Longitudinal observational studies of 10 years' duration (Lefkowitz, Eron, Walder, & Huesmann, 1977), 3 years' duration (Huesmann *et al.*, 1978), and 1 year duration (Singer & Singer, 1978) have yielded no evidence that violence viewing can reduce the likelihood of aggressive behaviors. The results of cross-lagged correlations and regression analyses emanating from these studies make it implausible that an "aggressive drive" could be stimulating violence viewing. While it seems that violence perceived as unreal is less likely to be imitated (Feshbach, 1976), there is little convincing evidence that such portrayals decrease a viewer's aggressiveness. Therefore, our discussion will concentrate on observational learning rather than on catharsis.

Observational Learning

Observational learning has been advanced primarily as an explanation for the relation between children's television violence viewing and aggressiveness; however, it could also be implicated in the formation of

the relation between television viewing and other behaviors. Theoreti-
cally, children imitate the behavior of people they see on television just as
they learn cognitive and social skills by imitating parents, siblings, and
peers. Since the original laboratory experiments (Bandura, Ross, & Ross,
1961, 1963b), a large number of experiments and observational field
studies have further elucidated the process of observational learning.

It has become clear that the extent to which a child imitates an actor
is greatly influenced by the reinforcements received by the actor. If the actor is seen being rewarded for aggressive behavior, the child is more likely
to imitate the behavior (Bandura, 1965; Bandura, Ross, & Ross, 1963a;
Walters, Leat, & Mezei, 1963). If the actor is punished for a behavior, the
behavior is less likely to be modeled (Bandura, 1965; Walters & Parke,
1964). This appears to be true for prosocial as well as for antisocial
behavior (Morris, Marshall, & Miller, 1973).

While such vicarious reinforcements influence the probability of the
child emitting the actor's behaviors, the persistence of the behavior seems
to depend on the reinforcements the child receives. Interestingly, actual
reinforcement does not seem to affect modeled behaviors any differently
than it affects behaviors acquired in other ways. Bandura (1965) found
that offering a reward for an aggressive act had no greater effect on
children who had recently watched the act performed than on control
children. Hicks (1968) discovered that adults' comments about an aggressive scene influenced the likelihood that a preschooler would imitate
the scene only so long as the adult was present, though Grusec (1973)
found that adults' comments had more lasting influence with older
children.

One of the problems with such studies is that the reinforcing properties of aggression are difficult to manipulate. For some children aggressive
behavior may often produce inherently reinforcing consequences. Hayes,
Rincover, and Volosin (in press) have recently shown that even the reflex-
ive movement of objects of aggression can be reinforcing to children.
These authors also found purely additive effects for imitation and reinforcement on aggression. Such results are in accord with longitudinal
findings of Lefkowitz et al. (1977). Besides the well-publicized 10-year effect of television violence viewing on aggression, they discovered a less
significant curvilinear effect for parental punishment. Very low and very
high punishing parents were found to have the most aggressive children.
Again, no interaction between reinforcement and television violence was
apparent.

Another factor frequently hypothesized to be implicated in observational learning is the viewer's identification with the actor or actress being modeled. Within the existing literature, however, the evidence is ambiguous on the role that identification plays in observational learning.
Bandura et al. (1963a, 1963b) found that both boys and girls more readily

imitated male rather than female models. In the 3-year longitudinal study with first- and third-grade children, Huesmann *et al.* (1978) found that regardless of the child's sex there were higher correlations of the child's aggressiveness with the child's viewing of male actors' violence than with the child's viewing of female actors' violence. Still, the correlations with female actors' violence were slightly higher for girls than for boys, and in a parallel study in Finland (Lagerspetz, 1979) the correlations with female performers' violence were much higher for girls than for boys. One of the problems with using gender as a measure of identification with a television model is that aggression is highly correlated with a male sex-role orientation (Huesmann *et al.*, 1978; Lefkowitz *et al.*, 1977). Girls who are aggressive may in fact identify more with male actors than with most female actors.

Studies measuring other types of identification have also yielded ambiguous results. In studies comparing the race of the actor and viewer, black children have sometimes been found to imitate white models more than black (e.g., Neely, Heckle, & Leichtman, 1973), and in some cases children have been found to imitate adults more than peers (Nicholas, McCarter, & Heckle, 1971) at least at a time long after viewing (Hicks, 1965). Even with two peer actors differing greatly in likability, no difference has been found in the propensity of the viewer to imitate either of the actors (Howitt & Cumberbatch, 1972). On the other hand, when subjects are asked to mentally assume the role of an actor who is aggressive, they do behave more aggressively (Turner & Berkowitz, 1972). While perceived similarity of interest between the model and child can enhance the likelihood of imitation (Rosekrans, 1967), the above findings suggest that a simplistic view of identification will not aid much in the understanding of observational learning. Rather, it appears that a child is most likely to imitate a model perceived to possess valued characteristics.

Along these lines, a few researchers (e.g., Huesmann *et al.*, 1978; Rosenfeld *et al.*, 1978; Turner & Fenn, 1978) have recently attempted to tie the repeated emission of observationally learned behavior more closely to theorizing in cognitive psychology. One recent idea about human memory—Tulving and Thomson's (1973) concept of encoding specificity—seems particularly relevant. They have argued that the likelihood of an item being recalled depends on the specific encoding context (acquisition context) being reproduced, including even apparently irrelevant aspects. The idea that many forms of aggressive behavior are elicited by the presence of specific cues is not new (Berkowitz, 1974), and there is evidence for the importance of specific cues from a violent film during testing (Geen & Berkowitz, 1966; Turner & Fenn, 1978; Turner & Layton, 1976). More recently, Rosenfeld *et al.* (1978) have argued that the rehearsal of specific aggressive acts observed on television through daydreaming or imaginative play could increase the probability that the aggressive acts will be performed. Indeed, in their data Rosenfeld *et al.* (1978) have found aggressive fantasies are positively correlated with aggressive behavior and in some cases with television violence viewing. This cognitive, information-processing interpretation of observational learning could also explain why violent scenes perceived as unreal are not modeled as readily (Feshbach, 1976). The observer stores for later retrieval and rehearsal those scenes that have subjective utility as solutions to likely social problems. Acts perceived as unreal would not be likely to fulfill this requirement and hence would not be stored.

The foregoing approach has important implications for the controversy over whether television violence disinhibits general aggressive behavior or teaches observers specific aggressive acts. The research on observational learning and cognitive processes suggests that the observed relations between violence viewing and aggressiveness do not require a disinhibition theory. Children who observe large numbers of aggressive behaviors on television can store and subsequently retrieve and perform those behaviors when the appropriate cues are present. Even seemingly irrelevant aspects of the scene (e.g., color) could serve as triggering cues. The recall of an aggressive behavior which provides a solution to a problem a child faces may lead to the emission of the behavior. While reinforcement of the behavior will increase the likelihood that the child will emit that behavior again, it is not a prerequisite for the behavior. Furthermore, it may be that the child forms an aggressive concept on the basis of his or her observation of numerous aggressive behaviors. If the aggressive concept becomes associated with successful social problem solving, new aggressive behaviors may emerge that are unrelated to the original, observed behaviors. Of course, one might wish to call this process "disinhibition of aggression." However, what seems more important than arguing over the terminology is understanding the process.

Attitude Change

Another way in which television violence exerts its influence on children is through the molding of children's attitudes. The more television a child watches the more accepting is the child's attitude toward aggressive behavior (Dominick & Greenberg, 1972). Equally important, the more a person watches television, the more suspicious a person is and the greater the person's expectancy of being involved in real violence (Gerbner & Gross, 1974; see also Chapter 10 in this volume). Why? Again, from an information processing standpoint, attitudes are rules and explanations induced from observations of behavior. They serve as heuristics for future behavior. If a child's, or for that matter adult's, major exposure to social interaction occurs through television, the conception of social reality will quite naturally be based on such observations. The attitudes toward aggression of heavy television viewers are more positive because they perceive aggressive behavior to be the norm. While a fair amount of violence viewing might be required to affect an adult's attitudes, experiments by Drabman and Thomas (Drabman & Thomas, 1974a, 1974b, 1976; Thomas & Drabman, 1975) have revealed, as described earlier, that young children's willingness to accept aggressive behavior in other children can be increased by even brief exposures to violent film scenes. Such accepting attitudes, in turn, make it more likely that the child may behave aggressively and perhaps make it more likely that the child will model aggressive acts. Meyer (1972) has reported that whenever a subject observes violent acts perceived as justified, the probability increases that the subject will act aggressively. If one wishes to use the term "disinhibition," here is where it seems appropriate. An attitude of acceptance toward aggression and violence can increase the likelihood of aggression and violence being displayed.

Emotional and Physiological Responsiveness

One might designate the changes in attitudes brought about by frequent violence viewing as a cognitive desensitization to violence. Similarly, there is significant evidence to indicate that a real emotional and physiological desensitization can occur. In the quasi-experimental field study described earlier (Cline et al., 1973), boys who regularly watched a heavy diet of television violence displayed less physiological arousal in response to new scenes of violence than did control subjects. While these results have apparently been difficult to replicate in the field, Thomas et al. (1977) have discovered similar short-term effects in laboratory studies of the Galvanic Skin Response to violence. It should not be surprising that emotional and physiological responsiveness to scenes of violence habituates as other responses do.

It is more difficult to make the case that such habituation would influence the future probability of aggressive behavior. On the one hand, one could argue that arousal heightens the propensity of the person to behave aggressively. Studies by Geen and O'Neal (1969) and Zillmann (1971) demonstrate that increasing a subject's general arousal increases the probability of aggressive behavior. While more recent experiments (Baron, 1977) have placed limits on these results, it might follow that children who watched the least violence previously would be the most aroused by violence and the most likely to act aggressively afterward. On the other hand, one could argue that the arousal fostered by television and film violence is an unpleasant consequence that serves as a negative reinforcer. In this case, the desensitized heavy violence viewers would be expected to behave more aggressively than those not desensitized. Still a third alternative is suggested by the recent research of Hayes et al. (in press) on the self-reinforcing properties of aggression. If we adopt the viewpoint that there is an optimal level of arousal which each individual finds most satisfying, then it follows that aggressive behavior might be used to generate appropriate levels of self-arousal. Since aggressive behavior of necessity produces heightened arousal, the desensitized violence viewer might behave more aggressively to achieve the desired level of arousal. Such a model provides a role for arousal both as a precursor of aggression and as a consequence of aggression.

Reinforcement of Viewing Behavior

The final process to be discussed is one too often neglected in the psychological literature. Viewing of television violence can be inherently reinforcing. Not only can the stimulation of the observed action provide desirable levels of arousal, but also vicarious gratification can be obtained from observing actors obtaining rewards desirable to the child. If viewing is a pleasurable experience, it is certainly natural that the various cognitive and social behaviors associated with viewing will become more prominent, whereas competing responses would be extinguished.

What cognitive and social behaviors are concomitants of viewing? Certainly social isolation is one, and data from Lefkowitz et al. (1977) and Huesmann et al. (1978) indicate that lowered popularity is correlated with greater amounts of television viewing. From a cognitive side, though, the empirical research available is sparse. Claims that the child is anesthetized by television violence (Winn, 1977) have not yet been substantiated by rigorous research. While lowered intellectual functioning is associated with greater television viewing (Huesmann et al., 1978; Lefkowitz et al., 1977), longitudinal analyses suggest that the deficit in intellectual functioning is a precursor to television viewing. The same is true of the relation between popularity and television watching. The more plausible process model would seem to be that children try to obtain vicarious rewards and stimulation from television after they encounter difficulties in obtaining these rewards in other ways. Additional research may well reveal that the cognitive behaviors promoted by excessive viewing of television violence do indeed interfere with the development of normal cognitive processes.

Summary and Conclusions

The causal relationship between television violence viewing and aggressive behavior has been confirmed by research subsequent to the publication of the Surgeon General's report. Nevertheless, no significant diminution in television violence can be documented. Violence, endemic in American society, has reached epidemic proportions particularly among male youths, and the problems of prevention are a concern not only of agencies of law enforcement but also of those of public health. Television violence has contributed to this epidemic as evinced in the findings of the Surgeon General's report and in the subsequent empirical and observational studies cited in this chapter.

Additionally, we have cited evidence in this chapter suggesting that television violence viewing is implicated in emotional arousal. Since continued arousal is habituating, prudent emotional responsivity to real-life violence could be blunted. Furthermore, television violence has been shown to be associated with impaired socialization and dysphoric mood. Recent research suggests that excessive television viewing, independent of content, is also associated with aggressive behavior and may be related to other kinds of psychopathology in children.

Finally, the medical profession has begun to raise its voice against the overwhelming, noxious effects on children of viewing television violence. This increasing concern and involvement are demonstrated by the increasing frequency of articles in medical journals dealing with the problems of television violence (Somers, 1976a, 1976b). Rothenberg (1975) pointed to the data from 146 articles on the effects of television violence, involving some 10,000 children from a wide array of backgrounds. Having demonstrated that violence viewing produces increased aggressive behavior in children, these studies, according to Rothenberg, suggested the need for immediate remedial action with respect to television programming. He stated, "The time is long past due for a major, organized cry of protest from the medical profession in relation to what, in political terms, I consider a national scandal [p. 1043]."

But cries of protest, even accompanied by rigorous data, have had little influence on the television industry in the past. Regulation in some form is necessary, and at least one of three basic actions is ineluctable: (a) systematic and methodical regulation by parents of children's exposure to television; (b) self-regulation with respect to the portrayal of violence by the television industry; or (c) government regulation of this feature of television programming. The latter action has its analogue in the intervention by the United States Public Health Service when the threat of disease reaches epidemic proportions.

Acknowledgment

The authors wish to thank Kathleen Sutton for her invaluable assistance in the production of this manuscript.

References

Abramson, L. Y., Seligman, M. E. P., & Teasdale, J. D. Learned helplessness in humans: Critique and reformulation. *Journal of Abnormal Psychology*, 1978, 87(1), 49–74.

Bandura, A. Influence of models' reinforcement contingencies on the acquisition of imitative responses. *Journal of Personality and Social Psychology*, 1965, 1, 589–595.

Bandura, A., Ross, D., & Ross, S. A. Transmission of aggression through imitation of aggressive models. *Journal of Abnormal and Social Psychology*, 1961, 63, 575–582.

Bandura, A., Ross, D., & Ross, S. A. Imitation of film-mediated aggressive models. *Journal of Abnormal and Social Psychology*, 1963, 66, 3–11. (a)

Bandura, A., Ross, D., & Ross, S. A. Vicarious reinforcement and imitative learning. *Journal of Abnormal and Social Psychology*, 1963, 67, 601–607. (b)

Baron, R. A. *Human aggression*. New York: Plenum, 1977.

Berkowitz, L. Some determinants of impulsive aggression: The role of mediated associations with reinforcements for aggression. *Psychological Review*, 1974, 81, 165–176.

Biblow, E. Imaginative play and the control of aggressive behavior. In J. L. Singer (Ed.), *The child's world of make-believe: Experimental studies of imaginative play*. New York: Academic Press, 1973.

Cline, V. B. The child before the TV. *The Police Chief*, 1976, 43(6), pp. 22; 26; 28–29.

Cline, V. B., Croft, R. G., & Courrier, S. Desensitization of children to television violence. *Journal of Personality and Social Psychology*, 1973, 27, 360–365.

Collins, W. A. Effect of temporal separation between motivation, aggression, and consequences: A developmental study. *Developmental Psychology*, 1973, 8, 215–221.

Collins, W. A., Berndt, T. J., & Hess, V. L. Observational learning of motives and consequences for television aggression: A developmental study. *Child Development*, 1974, 45, 799–802.

Collins, W. A., & Getz, S. K. Children's social responses following modeled reactions to provocation: Prosocial effects of a television drama. *Journal of Personality*, 1976, 44, 488–500.

Comstock, G. *Television and human behavior: The key studies*. Santa Monica, California: Rand, 1975.

Comstock, G., & Fisher, M. *Television and human behavior: A guide to the pertinent scientific literature*. Santa Monica, California: Rand, 1975.

Comstock, G., & Lindsey, G. *Television and human behavior: The research horizon, future and present*. Santa Monica, California: Rand, 1975.

Dominick, J. R., & Greenberg, B. S. Attitudes toward violence: The interaction of television exposure, family attitudes, and social class. In G. A. Comstock & E. A. Rubinstein (Eds.), *Television and social behavior* (Vol. 3). *Television and adolescent aggressiveness*. Washington, D.C.: United States Government Printing Office, 1972.

Drabman, R. S., & Thomas, M. H. Does media violence increase children's toleration of real-life aggression? *Developmental Psychology*, 1974, 10, 418–421. (a)

Drabman, R. S., & Thomas, M. H. Exposure to filmed violence and children's tolerance of real life aggression. *Personality and Social Psychology Bulletin*, 1974, 1, 198–199. (b)

Drabman, R. S., & Thomas, M. H. Does watching violence on television cause apathy? *Pediatrics*, 1976, 57, 329–331.

Eron, L. D., & Huesmann, L. R. Adolescent aggression and television. *Annals of the New York Academy of Sciences*, in press.

Feshbach, S. The role of fantasy in the response to television. *Journal of Social Issues*, 1976, 32(4), 71–85.

Feshbach, S., & Singer, R. D. *Television and aggression*. San Francisco: Jossey-Bass, 1971.

Geen, R. G., & Berkowitz, L. Name-mediated aggressive cue properties. *Journal of Personality,* 1966, *34,* 456–465.

Geen, R. G., & O'Neal, E. C. Activation of cue-elicited aggression by general arousal. *Journal of Personality and Social Psychology,* 1969, *11,* 289–292.

Gerbner, G., & Gross, L. P. *Violence profile no. 6: Trends in network television drama and viewer conceptions of social reality: 1967–1973.* Unpublished manuscript, Annenberg School of Communications, Univ. of Pennsylvania, 1974.

Granzberg, G., & Steinbring, J. *Television and the Canadian Indian.* Technical Report, Department of Anthropology, University of Winnepeg, Manitoba, Canada, 1980.

Greenberg, B. S. British children and televised violence. *Public Opinion Quarterly,* 1975, *38,* 531–547.

Greenberg, B. S., & Wotring, C. E. Television violence and its potential for aggressive driving behavior. *Journal of Broadcasting,* 1974, *18,* 473–480.

Grusec, J. E. Effects of co-observer evaluations on imitation: A developmental study. *Developmental Psychology,* 1973, *8,* 141.

Hartnagel, T. F., Teevan, J. J., Jr., & McIntyre, J. J. Television violence and violent behavior. *Social Forces,* 1975, *54,* 341–351.

Hayes, S. C., Rincover, A., & Volosin, D. Variables influencing the acquisition and maintenance of aggressive behavior: Modeling versus sensory reinforcement. *Journal of Abnormal Psychology,* in press.

Hicks, D. J. Imitation and retention of film-mediated aggressive peer and adult models. *Journal of Personality and Social Psychology,* 1965, *2,* 97–100.

Hicks, D. J. Effects of co-observer's sanctions and adult presence on imitative aggression. *Child Development,* 1968, *38,* 303–309.

Howitt, D., & Cumberbatch, G. Affective feeling for a film character and evaluation of an anti-social act. *British Journal of Social and Clinical Psychology,* 1972, *2,* 102–108.

Huesmann, L. R., Fischer, P. F., Eron, L. D., Mermelstein, R., Kaplan-Shain, E., & Morikawa, S. *Children's sex-role preference, sex of television model, and imitation of aggressive behaviors.* Paper presented at the meeting of the International Society for Research on Aggression, Washington, D.C., September, 1978.

Kniveton, B. H. The effect of rehearsal delay on long-term imitation of filmed aggression. *British Journal of Psychology,* 1973, *64,* 259–265.

Kniveton, B. H. The very young and television violence. *Journal of Psychosomatic Research,* 1974, *18,* 233–237.

Kniveton, B. H., & Stephenson, G. M. An examination of individual susceptibility to the influence of aggressive film models. *British Journal of Psychiatry,* 1973, *122,* 53–56.

Lefkowitz, M. M. *Violent television preference and depression.* Paper presented at the meeting of the International Society for Research on Aggression, Washington, D.C., September, 1978.

Lefkowitz, M. M., Eron, L. D., Walder, L. O., & Huesmann, L. R. *Growing up to be violent: A longitudinal study of the development of aggression.* New York: Pergamon, 1977.

Liebert, R. M. Television and children's aggressive behavior: Another look. *American Journal of Psychoanalysis,* 1974, *34*(2), 99–107.

McCarthy, E. D., Langner, T. S., Gersten, J. C., Eisenberg, J. G., & Orzeck, L. Violence and behavior disorders. *Journal of Communication,* 1975, *25*(4), 71–85.

Mead, M. *Coming of age in Samoa.* Magnolia, Massachusetts: Peter Smith, 1971.

Meyer, T. P. Effects of viewing justified and unjustified real film violence on aggressive behavior. *Journal of Personality and Social Psychology,* 1972, *23,* 21–29.

Morris, W. N., Marshall, H. M., & Miller, R. S. The effect of vicarious punishment on prosocial behavior in children. *Journal of Experimental Child Psychology,* 1973, *15,* 222–236.

Neely, J. J., Heckel, R. V., & Leichtman, H. M. The effect of race of model and response consequences to the model on imitation in children. *Journal of Social Psychology*, 1973, *89*, 225–231.

Nicholas, K. B., McCarter, R. E., & Heckel, R. V. Imitation of adult and peer television models by white and Negro children. *Journal of Social Psychology*, 1971, *85*, 317–318.

Noble, G. Effects of different forms of filmed aggression on children's constructive and destructive play. *Journal of Personality and Social Psychology*, 1973, *26*, 54–59.

Robinson, J. P., & Bachman, J. G. Television viewing habits and aggression. In G. A. Comstock & E. A. Rubinstein (Eds.), *Television and social behavior* (Vol. 3). *Television and adolescent aggressiveness*. Washington, D.C.: United States Government Printing Office, 1972.

Rosenfeld, E., Maloney, S., Huesmann, L. R., Eron, L. D., Fischer, P. F., Musonis, V., & Washington, A. *The effect of fantasy behaviors and fantasy-reality discriminations upon the observational learning of aggression*. Paper presented at the meeting of the International Society for Research on Aggression, Washington, D.C., September, 1978.

Rosekrans, M. A. Imitation in children as a function of perceived similarities to a social model of vicarious reinforcement. *Journal of Personality and Social Psychology*, 1967, *7*, 307–315.

Rothenberg, M. B. Effects of television violence on children and youth. *Journal of the American Medical Association*, 1975, *234*, 1043–1046.

Silverman, R. E. Short term effects of television viewing on aggressive and psychophysiological behavior of adults and children (Doctoral dissertation, State Univ. of New York, Buffalo, 1972). *Dissertation Abstracts International*, 1973, *33*, 3922B–3923B. (Univ. Microfilms No. 73–5174, 116)

Singer, J. L., & Singer, D. G. *Associations between hours television-viewing, aggression and imaginative play in preschoolers*. Paper presented at meeting of the International Society for Research on Aggression, Washington, D.C., September, 1978.

Somers, A. R. Health policy 1976: Violence, television, and American youth. *Annals of Internal Medicine*, 1976, *84*, 743–745. (a)

Somers, A. R. Violence, television and the health of American youth. *New England Journal of Medicine*, 1976, *294*, 811–817. (b)

Surbeck, E. Young children's emotional reactions to TV violence: The effects on children's perceptions of reality (Doctoral dissertation, Univ. of Georgia, 1973). *Dissertation Abstracts International*, 1973, *33*. (Univ. Microfilms No. 75–2659, 69).

Surgeon General's Scientific Advisory Committee on Television and Social Behavior. *Television and growing up: The impact of televised violence*. Report to the Surgeon General, United States Public Health Service. Washington, D.C.: United States Government Printing Office, 1972.

Thomas, M. H., & Drabman, R. S. Toleration of real life aggression as a function of exposure to televised violence and age of subject. *Merrill-Palmer Quarterly*, 1975, *21*, 227–232.

Thomas, M. H., Horton, R. W., Lippincott, E. C., & Drabman, R. S. Desensitization to portrayals of real-life aggression as a function of exposure to television violence. *Journal of Personality and Social Psychology*, 1977, *35*, 450–458.

Tulving, E., & Thomson, D. M. Encoding specificity and retrieval processes in episodic memory. *Psychological Review*, 1973, *80*, 352–373.

Turner, C. W., & Berkowitz, L. Identification with film aggressor (covert role taking) and reactions to film violence. *Journal of Personality and Social Psychology*, 1972, *21*, 256–264.

Turner, C. W., & Fenn, M. R. *Effects of white noise and memory cues on verbal aggression*. Paper presented at the meeting of the International Society for Research on Aggression, Washington, D.C., September, 1978.

Turner, C. W., & Layton, J. F. Verbal imagery and connotation as memory-induced mediators of aggressive behavior. *Journal of Personality and Social Psychology*, 1976, *33*, 755–763.

Walters, R. H., Leat, M., & Mezei, L. Inhibition and disinhibition of responses through empathetic learning. *Canadian Journal of Psychology*, 1963, *17*, 235–243.

Walters, R. H., & Parke, R. D. Influence of response consequences to a social model on resistance to deviation. *Journal of Experimental Child Psychology*, 1964, *1*, 269–280.

Williams, T. M. *Differential impacts of TV on children: A natural experiment in communities with and without TV*. Paper presented at the meeting of the International Society for Research on Aggression, Washington, D.C., September, 1978.

Winn, M. *The plug-in drug*. New York: Viking, 1977.

Zillmann, D. Excitation transfer in communication-mediated aggressive behavior. *Journal of Experimental Social Psychology*, 1971, *7*, 419–434.

12

Some of the People Some of the Time—But Which People? Televised Violence and Its Effects

AIMEE DORR
PETER KOVARIC

[When] fear of the authority leads to strong temptation to violate conventional rules against hurting others, conventional subjects (Stage 5) will comply.

—Kohlberg, 1969, p. 396.

Blondes have more fun.

—Television commercial.

The stage at which one reasons about moral issues and one's hair color both represent criteria that some have used to explain the different things people have done or are doing, to anticipate and prepare for the different things they will do, and to provide some of them with special treatment. Criteria that actually helped us to do any of these things would clearly be something to know about. With them we could cope better with the facts that the same stimulus may have different effects on different people and that different stimuli may produce the same effect on different people. We will seek such criteria in this chapter for the area of television violence viewing and aggression. We will begin with considerations of the kinds of effects and dependent measures one might examine and the

CHILDREN AND THE FACES OF TELEVISION:
Teaching, Violence, Selling

methods for doing so, move to a presentation of the available evidence for a variety of individual difference variables, and conclude with an evaluation of this evidence and its significance for practice and policy.

Kinds of Effects and Measures and Their Import

Suppose we knew that certain segments of our population were more likely than were others to increase their aggression when their viewing of television violence increased. If we thought this were undesirable, we could try to ameliorate it through any number of actions (e.g., limit viewing, provide training to better withstand the effects of viewing, or plan for the consequences of aggressive acts). If the segments were numerically large or if their aggression were particularly devastating to our society, then we might even want changes in federal policy.

Although demonstrated individual differences in susceptibility to the influence of televised violence probably have the clearest import for practice and policy, there are two other areas in which individual differences might be important. The first is aggressiveness. Suppose viewing television violence increases aggression for those segments of our population whose aggressiveness is of particular concern already. We may then conclude that something needs to be done about television violence or about these segments of the population and television violence, because their aggressiveness is harmful enough that it needs to be reduced by all possible means. The second is the viewing of televised violence. Suppose certain identifiable segments of the population do more such viewing. Given that this might then increase their aggressiveness, we might choose to adopt practices or policies to diminish their exposure or its effects.

Thus, one might be interested in individual difference variables which predict differences in susceptibility to the effects of exposure to televised violence, in usual aggressiveness, or in viewing of televised violence. Clear findings in any of these areas would be interesting from a purely scientific point of view and might be the basis for revisions of our practices or policies so as to decrease the overall level of aggression expressed by a group. This approach does not imply that we believe that television violence is the only, or even the major, cause of aggression and violence in our society. But it is a factor whose contribution we may be able to diminish.

Methods for Studying Individual Differences

The preceding considerations have direct implications for the kinds of research designs and data analyses one employs. These are straightforward for individual differences in viewing patterns and in aggressiveness.

They are not so straightforward for differences in susceptibility to the effects of exposure to television violence. Let us illustrate the problem using the area of sex differences as an example. Some studies expose boys and girls to either aggressive or nonaggressive stimuli, measure aggressive behavior afterward, and then run two by two (sex by stimuli) analyses. If a main effect for sex is found, it is most often that boys are higher than girls, which is frequently described as boys being more affected than girls. Unfortunately, however, this result may only reflect the fact that boys are generally more aggressive than girls. To show that boys are more *affected by exposure* than are girls, one would need either to find a significant and appropriate interaction, not just a main effect for sex, in post-viewing measures, or to measure behavior prior to exposure and then find a main effect for sex differences in change scores. Without belaboring these difficulties in design and interpretation further, let us simply note that there are far fewer studies which truly address the issue of differences in susceptibility to effects than there are studies which researchers and reviewers have claimed do this.

No matter what designs or analyses were utilized in studies included in this chapter, all of those which involved two or more groups exemplify a common problem in research into individual differences. That is, the stimuli, measures, and general procedures to which the different groups were exposed were the same. So as not to cast stones when our house is also glass, we'll illustrate the problem with this approach using work done by the senior author (i.e., Leifer & Roberts, 1972). In this work, if *Rocket Robin Hood* was considered to be an aggressive program for kindergartners, it was also that for sixth graders. If kicking was aggressive behavior for girls, it was also that for boys. And so on. This has the admirable quality of allowing the unambiguous, face-valid conclusion that the only variable which could account for obtained group differences was age or sex. Imagine the problems if we had found differences between kindergartners who had seen only *Rocket Robin Hood* and sixth graders who had seen only *Felony Squad*. We wouldn't have known whether to attribute these differences to age, to program viewed, or to some ineffable combination of these.

On the other hand, this research strategy of treating all groups the same has, at the least, a logical problem in it. First, we assume that the groups will react differently to a violent program which they have seen. Then we also assume, rather illogically, that they will not differ in anything else including the sense they make of the program and the meaning they attribute to the dependent measures. Suppose, for instance, that we found that *Rocket Robin Hood* increased kindergartners' aggression but not that of sixth graders. We would most often conclude then that television violence does not affect sixth graders. Alternatively—and this is the problem—perhaps we should conclude that *Rocket Robin Hood* isn't an example of television violence for sixth graders.

Obviously, we should not continue in this vein. We sink further into a morass of relativity—a Gordian knot which no one has yet successfully untangled. The issue had to be raised, however, because it applies to nearly every study we reviewed. The unanimous choice of researchers for resolving it was to assume that the stimuli, measures, and procedures meant the same to all groups. We are inclined to agree, but we cannot be certain.

Individual Difference Variables

In this chapter we have confined ourselves to those individual difference variables for which there is at least some research literature and for which one can make reasonable arguments as to the utility of studying them. Furthermore, we have chosen to utilize only that literature which deals with "normal" viewers of television, with viewers who are college-age or younger, with responses to viewing violence portrayed live or on film, videotape, or television, and with viewing patterns and preferences. All studies are available in English, most were conducted in the United States, and nearly all have been published. These constraints still leave us many studies to summarize. In doing so we will look at differences in aggression, in television violence viewing, and in the effects of such viewing based on: age, cognitive ability, sex, ethnicity, social class, personality characteristics, and propensity for aggression.

Age

Of those studies which examined the differential impact of television violence on viewers of differing ages, six found no differential impact (Collins & Getz, 1976; Leifer & Roberts, 1972; Liebert & Baron, 1972; Milgram & Shotland, 1973; Thomas & Drabman, 1978; Walters & Thomas, 1963), and three found differential impact (Furu, 1971; Grusec, 1973; Thomas & Drabman, 1975).

There are no immediately obvious explanations for why one study would show differential impact and another would fail to show it. All but one of the studies (Furu, 1971) was an experiment involving at least two different age groups and at least two different levels of televised violence. Moreover, except for Milgram and Shotland (1973), experimental studies were essentially laboratory rather than field experiments, even if some testing was done in schools. Finally, the age groups compared and the stimuli used were approximately the same for those studies which show differential impact and for those which do not, except for Milgram and Shotland (1973) which compared 16- to 19-year-olds with adults.

The only plausible explanation seems to be differences in the dependent measures. Among studies which do not show a differential impact, the dependent measures include opinions about how common violence is (Thomas & Drabman, 1978), intended responses to hypothetical interpersonal conflict situations (Leifer & Roberts, 1972), actual occurrences of thievery (Milgram & Shotland, 1973), the Buss aggression machine (Walters & Thomas, 1963), and the child version of it (Collins & Getz, 1976; Liebert & Baron, 1972). Among the studies which show differential impact, the dependent measures were reported conflict with parents (Furu, 1971), aggressive behavior when playing with toys (Grusec, 1973), and time taken to stop an apparent fight between two children (Thomas & Drabman, 1975). Measures which are more clearly behavioral, aggressive, and likely to be reasonably frequent in daily life seem to be more common in studies which found a differential impact.

Assuming that the three studies which reported differential impact are not reporting spurious findings, what can we conclude? We find that third graders are more affected than are first graders in the latency of intervening in an apparent fight (Thomas & Drabman, 1975), that 10-year-olds are more affected than are 5-year-olds in the aggressiveness of their toy play (Grusec, 1973), and that tenth graders are more affected than are fourth and seventh graders in their reported conflicts with parents (Furu, 1971). In addition, the Leifer and Roberts (1972) article, although reporting no significant differential impact, does include trends which suggest greater impact on children in the later elementary grades than on either younger or older children. One might conclude, therefore, that middle-aged children are more likely to be affected in their actual aggressive behavior than are either older or younger children, though the results of the Furu (1971) study make this conclusion quite tentative.

All studies which examined the differential impact of televised violence also examined simple age differences in the dependent measure, and there are many other studies which employed only one age group in studying the effects of exposure to televised violence (for summaries see Chapters 9 and 11; Leifer, Gordon, & Graves, 1974; Liebert, Neale, & Davidson, 1973; Stein & Friedrich, 1975; and Surgeon General's Scientific Advisory Committee, 1972). Taken altogether, they generally support the notion that exposure to televised violence can and sometimes does influence any and each age group. No particular age seems to be immune. Likewise, no particular age seems to be more or less aggressive than another. The majority of the studies reviewed here did not find significant age differences per se (Furu, 1971; Grusec, 1973; Liebert & Baron, 1972; Milgram & Shotland, 1973; Thomas & Drabman, 1975; Walters & Thomas, 1963), nor does the literature on developmental differences in aggressive behavior give us good data to support such differences (see Feshbach, 1970). Thus, we find all age groups capable of being affected by exposure to televised violence, but no age group which seems to be more clearly aggressive than are others.

Like our conclusion about aggressive behavior, our conclusion about age differences in exposure to televised violence is ambiguous. We have some evidence that preadolescent and early adolescent youth are likely to view more violence than are late adolescent youth, with the division being roughly between junior and senior high school (Chaffee & McLeod, 1972; Greenberg, 1974–1975) and some evidence which directly contradicts this (Lyle & Hoffman, 1972a). Differences among preschool and elementary school age children have not been studied in a similar way.

Indeed, these ages present problems for such a study, since younger children like and watch cartoons, which are likely to be their major source of televised aggression, while older children like and watch action/adventure and crime drama programs (Lyle & Hoffman, 1972a, 1972b; Schramm, Lyle, & Parker, 1961). Content analyses suggest that cartoons are more violent than any other genre on television except movies and that weekend morning children's programs (which are more likely to be viewed by younger rather than older elementary school children) are the most violent of all (Gerbner, Gross, Jackson-Beeck, Jeffries-Fox, & Signorielli, 1978). Yet much of the violence in weekend morning and cartoon fare is likely to occur in a humorous context. Given these differences in the kinds of violence and the frequencies of them to which younger and older children are likely to be exposed, who is to say who watches more violence?

Cognitive Ability

Many researchers believe that any age differences which one may find in television's effects are at least partially due to differences in cognitive ability—ability to understand a plot, to remember it, to classify it as just entertainment, and the like. In this sense, all the preceding studies of age differences are also studies of cognitive ability differences. Since, however, they confound changes in cognitive ability with all the other things which may change with age, they are not good tests for the importance of cognitive ability per se. Unfortunately, we found only one partially relevant study (Thomas, 1972). Even it tended to confound age with cognitive ability in that *younger* elementary-school-aged children whose cognitive abilities were more rather than less differentiated, organized, and articulated were less likely to be affected by exposure to televised violence than were their opposites. Both groups were, however, affected by exposure to televised violence, and apparently neither group showed more aggression overall than the other.

Two studies related cognitive ability to violence viewing and/or preferences and found that more intelligent youth watched less violence on television (Chaffee & McLeod, 1972; Stein & Friedrich, 1972). This was true for preschool boys and girls and for junior and senior high school boys and girls. As one might expect, however, the magnitudes of the relationships were small, with correlations never greater than about − .30.

Sex

Looking first at the question of whether one sex is more likely to be affected by exposure to televised violence, we found 12 relevant articles. Eight reported no such differences between the sexes (Collins & Getz, 1976; Dominick & Greenberg, 1972; Drabman & Thomas, 1974; Hicks, 1965; Leifer & Roberts, 1972; Milgram & Shotland, 1973; Rabinovitch, McLean, Markham, & Talbott, 1972; Thomas & Drabman, 1975), one reported a difference (Grusec, 1973), and three reported a difference for one measure or study but not for another (Hapkiewicz & Roden, 1971; Liebert & Baron, 1972; Thomas, Horton, Lippincott, & Drabman, 1977).

With the possible exception of one study (Thomas *et al.,* 1977), we found no clear explanations for why some studies did and others did not show differential impact on the two sexes. Both groups of studies generally used the same ages of children, the same kinds of stimuli, and the same kinds of measures. Therefore, we tentatively conclude that neither sex is more susceptible to the effects of televised violence. This should not imply, however, that they are not both influenced by such exposure. All the research we reviewed here and other studies which worked with only one sex (usually boys) indicate that both boys and girls can be and sometimes are affected by such exposure.

Even if both sexes can be affected by exposure and seem to be about equally likely to be affected, we can still ask if one of them is likely to show overall higher levels of aggression to which exposure might contribute. We found nine published studies of television violence which measured aggressive behavior, some close facsimile of it, or both, in boys and girls. Of these, five of the six which measured direct aggressive behavior found boys overall to be more aggressive than girls (Bandura, Ross, & Ross, 1963; Hapkiewicz & Roden, 1971; Hicks, 1965; Liebert & Baron, 1972; and Siegel, 1956, versus Grusec, 1973), neither of the two which used the child Buss aggression machine found any overall sex differences (Collins & Getz, 1976; Liebert & Baron, 1972), and the one which used aggressive resolutions for hypothetical conflict situations found a difference (Leifer & Roberts, 1972). In all cases in which differences were found, boys were more aggressive than were girls. Other work also suggests that boys may be more directly aggressive in their behavior (cf., Maccoby & Jacklin, 1974). Thus, there is the suggestion that boys—at least those in preschool and in the elementary grades which were studied here—may be somewhat more likely than girls to behave aggressively in their interactions with toys and peers. The question for a concerned adult would then become whether exposure to television violence ought to be controlled so as to decrease somewhat the aggressiveness which younger boys may display.

An adult may think even more about this upon learning that research suggests that American boys watch more television violence and prefer it more than do American girls. This has been found for preschoolers, when cartoons are included as violent (Lyle & Hoffman, 1972b; Stein & Friedrich, 1972), for first, sixth, and tenth graders (Lyle & Hoffman, 1972a), for junior and senior high school students (Chaffee & McLeod, 1972), for 9-, 12-, and 15-year-olds (Greenberg, 1974–75), and for fourth, sixth, and eighth graders (Atkin, Greenberg, Korzenny, & McDermott, 1979). Only two studies report no sex differences, one from subsidiary analyses (Lyle & Hoffman, 1972a) and one from a study of British teenagers (Howitt, 1972). We conclude, therefore, that boys are likely to be exposed to more televised violence than are girls and also to like it better.

Ethnicity

We were unable to find studies of ethnic differences in the effects of exposure to televised violence. A recent review suggests that, should the literature exist, we would not find such differences but would find that all ethnic groups could be influenced by exposure to televised violence (Dorr, 1978a). Of course, without the studies we cannot be certain—and sometimes even with them. This is the case for ethnic differences in aggressiveness per se: The available data are flawed and contradictory. For viewing patterns and preferences, we find the suggestion that among older children (9-, 12-, and 15-year-olds) nonwhites may watch more television violence than do whites (Greenberg, 1974-75), although an earlier study failed to find ethnic differences among sixth and tenth grade Anglos, Blacks, and Mexican-Americans (Lyle & Hoffman, 1972a). Among younger children, violent cartoons may be more popular with Anglos and Mexican-Americans than they are with Blacks (Lyle & Hoffman, 1972b). Obviously, we need more work in this area too before we can say anything definite.

Social Class

In three articles reporting studies of the differential impact of exposure to televised violence on children of the lower and of the middle classes, one found differential impact (Noble, 1970) and two found a difference in some measures or study but not in others (Feshbach & Singer, 1971; Wotring & Greenberg, 1973). Clearly, one cannot easily arrive at some conclusion. The number of studies is few, all but Noble (1970) were limited to boys, the results are far too mixed, and the Noble (1970) and Feshbach and Singer (1971) studies have been subjected to serious criticism (Dorr, 1978b; Liebert, Davidson, & Sobol, 1972; Liebert, Sobol, & Davidson, 1972).

So far as one can tell from these studies, and their manner of reporting does not make it easy, both lower and middle class viewers can be and sometimes are affected by exposure to televised violence. Whether or not one class is more aggressive than the other—and we might, therefore, be more concerned about its exposure to televised violence—cannot be determined largely because pertinent data are not reported. Unfortunately, other research on simple class differences in aggression also does not help much for a variety of methodological, philosophical, and political reasons which are more properly explored elsewhere (see Feshbach, 1970, and Hess, 1970, for reviews).

Similar problems in obtaining or interpreting data do not occur, however, when one examines social class differences in exposure to televised violence. Here, the evidence with youth ranging from preschool through high school is reasonably clear. Lower class youth are likely to report—or their mothers to report for them—that they watch more televised violence than do middle class youth (Chaffee & McLeod, 1972; Foulkes, Belvedere, & Brubaker, 1972; Greenberg, 1974–75; Howitt, 1972; Stein & Friedrich, 1972). Lyle and Hoffman (1972a) are the only researchers to report a lack of clear social class differences in data from sixth and tenth graders. What evidence there is, then, suggests that lower class youth are heavier viewers of televised violence than are middle class youth but that the differential impact (if any) of viewing violence is uncertain.

Personality Characteristics

Only three studies can be included here. Two are classic experiments which found that emotionally disturbed and nondisturbed 7- to 13-year-old and adolescent boys generally reacted similarly to exposure to televised aggression (Heller & Polsky, 1976; Walters & Willows, 1968), although on some measures Heller and Polsky reported greater susceptibility in the nondisturbed boys. The third study showed that 5-year-old boys were consistent in their tendency to imitate an aggressive film model over testings with two different films presented four months apart (Kniveton & Stephenson, 1973). While this study does not really test differential impact, we have included it because it seems such a small step to conclude that those who were higher imitators (apparently a relatively consistent characteristic) would show greater sensitivity to televised violence. None of these studies suggests that either group was not influenced by exposure to televised violence, and none examined differences in viewing patterns or preferences. Heller and Polsky (1976) found that emotionally disturbed boys were generally more aggressive than were homeless boys, but Walters and Willows (1968) found no such difference. Obviously, one cannot say much more about individual differences in personality with only three studies, of somewhat different characteristics, available.

Propensity for Aggression

Aggressiveness is one personality characteristic which may be a particularly important individual difference variable, since three experimental studies have found that more aggressive youth were more likely than were less aggressive youth to be impacted by exposure to televised or film violence. This was true for preschool boys and girls who watched *Batman* and *Superman* in nursery school and whose behavior was measured during free play there (Stein & Friedrich, 1972); for adolescent, delinquent boys who watched a specially made film of a fight during a basketball game and whose behavior was measured using the Buss aggression machine (Hartmann, 1969); and for adolescent, delinquent boys who viewed aggressive films in their cottages and whose behavior was measured during regular daily activities (Leyens, Camino, Parke, & Berkowitz, 1975).

The only exception to this trend is a study by Collins (reported in Leifer & Roberts, 1972) in which more aggressive third, sixth, and tenth graders increased their aggression less after viewing a violent television program than did less aggressive youth. However, problems in comparing this study to the preceding three arise both because the dependent measure here was stated intentions to behave aggressively rather than actual aggressive behavior and because the aggressive program was edited so that all aggression occurred for bad reasons and had bad consequences. This is unique television fare which is incomparable to that in the other three studies in which crime may not have paid but violence by the good guys certainly did. We believe one can conclude that those who are more aggressive in their daily activities are also more likely to increase their aggressiveness after exposure to typical televised violence.

These studies also obviously support the conclusion that more aggressive youth are affected by exposure to televised violence. This conclusion is strengthened by a study in which adolescent boys in a minimum security prison who saw an aggressive movie were found to be more aggressive later than were similar boys shown a nonaggressive movie (Sebastian, Parke, Berkowitz, & West, 1978). Since we have numerous studies which demonstrate similar effects of exposure to televised violence for the "normal" population, we can conclude that exposure to television violence affects both the more and less aggressive segments of society. Finally, simply by virtue of the way in which these two groups are selected, we know that the more aggressive or delinquent group is more aggressive. Thus, one might be concerned about the amount of televised violence they view, since such viewing correlates with aggressive behavior.

Like others, we have interpreted the positive correlation between violence viewing and aggression to mean that exposure leads to increased aggression (see Chapters 9 and 11, this volume; Chaffee, 1972; Comstock, Chaffee, Katzman, McCombs, & Roberts, 1978; Leifer *et al.*, 1974; Liebert *et al.*, 1973; and Stein & Friedrich, 1975, for reviews). The opposite interpretation, that more aggressive people watch more violence on television, is also possible (Halloran, Brown, & Chaney, 1970; Smith, 1969). It may be that the reality is a cycle of viewing, increased aggression, and increased viewing, with a modest relationship between the two—a relationship that received some support from Belson (1978), who found that adolescent boys who reported watching more violent television also reported involvement in more serious crimes, while the reverse relationship was not as strong. Probably the best we can do at this time is to point to the evidence for both relationships and to suggest that either one implies a need to be concerned about violence viewing by more aggressive youth.

Evaluation of Studies of Individual Differences

We have reviewed research about seven individual differences. For most, the amount of research is small enough and/or the results are mixed enough that conclusions cannot be very firmly drawn. In examining the differential impact of exposure, we must eschew conclusions for individual differences based on cognitive ability, social class, ethnicity, and personality characteristics; in examining the extent to which exposure to televised violence can affect a group, we must eschew conclusions for cognitive ability; in examining differences in usual levels of aggression, we must eschew conclusions for age, cognitive ability, social class, ethnicity, and personality characteristics; and, finally, in examining differences in viewing behavior and preferences, we must eschew conclusions for age, cognitive ability, ethnicity, personality characteristics, and propensity for aggression.

What then are we left with? First, we conclude that television violence seems to be capable of affecting viewers of both sexes and varying ages, social classes, ethnicities, personality characteristics, and levels of usual aggressiveness. Second, we conclude that males and females are equally likely to be influenced by exposure but that within each sex those who are more aggressive are more likely to be influenced. We will also advance the tentative conclusion that "middle-aged" children, those between the ages of about 8 and 12, are somewhat more likely to be affected than are either younger or older youth. Third, we conclude that in actual behavior boys are more likely to be aggressive than are girls, and, by definition, delinquents and others who are measured as more aggressive in their daily behavior are more aggressive than are their obvious comparison groups. Fourth, we conclude that in terms of actual viewing of and preference for televised violence, boys are likely to exceed girls and members of the working class are likely to exceed those of the middle class.

Long ago, in pioneering American work on children and television, Schramm, Lyle, and Parker (1961) asserted that "there are spectacular differences in the children who go to television. . . . What they select from television, and what they do with it, will invariably reflect these differences [p. 143]." Similarly, the Surgeon General's Scientific Advisory Committee (1972) alluded to individual differences in its summary: "Thus, the two sets of findings converge in three respects: a preliminary and tentative indication of a causal relation between viewing violence on television and aggressive behavior; an indication that any such causal relation operates only on some children . . . [p. 11]." Our attempt here has been to elucidate the characteristics which define those "some of the people who some of the time" will be affected. With one major and one minor exception, such characteristics have not been generally acknowledged by policymakers, television industry members, nor the public—whether or not research evidence suggests they should be.

The major exception to this generalization is young children. They are quite likely to be singled out as being more susceptible, and they are the one group for which the public, academics, policymakers, and the television industry itself are most likely to agree about susceptibility. Members of the television industry are understandably reluctant to admit that television violence may affect anyone—even young children—and most of them manage to avoid such an admission; however, their codes at least acknowledge the special status of child viewers (e.g., Gerbner, 1972; NAB Television Code, 1978). The Federal Communications Commission (1974) apparently feels similarly, although it has no specific regulations about the content of programming which children may view or which is broadcast specially for them.

Some television industry members have also singled out another susceptible group. This minor exception to our generalization has been variously identified as those who are already aggressive, as the criminal element, and as the lunatic fringe. Sometimes one of these people does something she or he has seen on television—hijack an airplane, douse a woman with gasoline and set her afire, or rape a girl with a bottle—but it is argued that this individual would have carried out this act or another equally violent one without ever watching television and that television certainly didn't contribute to the overall level of violence or criminality expressed by this individual. Such an argument obviously leads to the conclusion that in our practices and policies we need not do anything special about televised violence, but is that the conclusion we should reach?

Implications for Practice and Policy

When we began this chapter, we suggested that finding individual differences in aggressiveness, exposure to televised violence, or its impact could have implications for our practices and policies. Even without the additional research needed for many variables, we believe one can identify some groups who would probably profit from some special treatment with regard to televised violence. These groups were described in the preceding section. Exactly what special treatment would be most efficacious for any or all of them cannot yet be specified with assurance. One can, however, consider a number of alternatives:

1. Controlling television viewing at home
2. Controlling the content which can be broadcast over television
3. Controlling the day-part in which certain content can be broadcast
4. Teaching group members to alter their viewing patterns
5. Altering or adding to television content so that it would be less impactful (e.g., adding a disclaimer that all events are fantasy)
6. Teaching group members to be less susceptible to the effects of exposure to televised violence
7. Teaching group members to be less aggressive overall
8. Changing group members' environments such that their opportunities and instigations to aggress are lessened

These alternatives obviously differ in their cost, in the extent to which they rely on the decisions and actions of individual citizens, and in the extent to which they require changes in—and probably changed regulations for—the television industry. When an alternative is inexpensive, voluntary, and unlikely to require much from the television industry or from regulatory agencies, it is easy to suggest its employment even if our evidence of need and efficacy is limited. For other alternatives it becomes desirable to have a stronger evidential base from which to argue.

Assuming that our practice and policy decisions were to be made in a logical, evidence-based way, we certainly could not argue at this time for many large-scale changes. Only for delinquents and others who would be rated as above the norm in aggressiveness might one argue that serious changes in practice or policy could be considered. Yet, even here we lack information on what proportion of these individuals' aggressiveness is attributable to exposure to televised violence, on methods (other than decreasing exposure) for decreasing their susceptibility to such content, and on other strategies for decreasing their aggressiveness or for lessening its undesirable consequences. In addition, there are the more nearly ineffable considerations about some "chilling effect" on First Amendment rights should television content be further regulated as a means of decreasing exposure to televised violence.

This is obviously not the place to begin—or end—a discussion about practice and policy vis-à-vis televised violence. Neither practice nor policy is easy to justify, institute, or change, nor is either ever a fully rational activity. If rationality and evidence are to be part of decision making about practice and policy, we believe that the material reviewed here could contribute. At the level of making decisions about major changes in practices or policies it can help only a little. When the changes being considered are not so major, it can help more. In particular, we would recommend consideration of actions to change viewing, susceptibility, and/or aggressiveness perhaps for middle-aged children and almost certainly for boys, members of the working class, and those who are already considered to be more aggressive in their daily activities.

References

Atkin, C., Greenberg, B., Korzenny, F., & McDermott, S. Selective exposure to televised violence. *Journal of Broadcasting*, 1979, *23*, 5–13.

Bandura, A., Ross, D., & Ross, S. A. Imitation of film-mediated aggressive models. *Journal of Abnormal and Social Psychology*, 1963, *66*, 3–11.

Belson, W. A. *Television violence and the adolescent boy.* Westmead, Farnborough, Hampshire, England: Saxon House, 1978.

Chaffee, S. H. Television and adolescent aggressiveness (overview). In G. A. Comstock & E. A. Rubinstein (Eds.), *Television and social behavior* (Vol. 3). *Television and adolescent aggressiveness.* Washington, D.C.: United States Government Printing Office, 1972.

Chaffee, S. H., & McLeod, J. M. Adolescent television use in the family context. In G. A. Comstock & E. A. Rubinstein (Eds.), *Television and social behavior* (Vol. 3). *Television and adolescent aggressiveness.* Washington, D.C.: United States Government Printing Office, 1972.

Collins, W. A., & Getz, S. K. Children's social responses following modeled reactions to provocation. *Journal of Personality*, 1976, *44*, 488–500.

Comstock, G., Chaffee, S., Katzman, N., McCombs, M., & Roberts, D. *Television and human behavior.* New York: Columbia Univ. Press, 1978.

Dominick, J. R., & Greenberg, B. S. Attitudes toward violence: The interaction of television exposure, family attitudes, and social class. In G. A. Comstock & E. A. Rubinstein (Eds.), *Television and social behavior* (Vol. 3). *Television and adolescent aggressiveness.* Washington, D.C.: United States Government Printing Office, 1972.

Dorr, A. *Television and the socialization of the minority child.* Paper prepared for a conference on Television and the Socialization of the Minority Child, Univ. of California, Los Angeles, April, 1978. (a)

Dorr, A. The uses and abuses of watching television. (Review of *The plug-in drug* by M. Winn and *Children in front of the small screen* by G. Noble). *Contemporary Psychology*, 1978, *23*, 28–29. (b)

Drabman, R. S., & Thomas, M. H. Does media violence increase children's toleration of real-life aggression? *Developmental Psychology*, 1974, *10*, 418–421.

Federal Communications Commission. Children's television programs—report and policy statement. *Federal Register*, 1974, *39* (215), 39396–39409.

Feshbach, S. Aggression. In P. H. Mussen (Ed.), *Carmichael's manual of child psychology* (Vol. 2). New York: Wiley, 1970.

Feshbach, S., & Singer, R. D. *Television and aggression*. San Francisco: Jossey-Bass, 1971.

Foulkes, D., Belvedere, E., & Brubaker, T. Televised violence and dream content. In G. A. Comstock, E. A. Rubinstein, & J. P. Murray (Eds.), *Television and social behavior* (Vol. 5). *Television's effects: Further explorations*. Washington, D.C.: United States Government Printing Office, 1972.

Furu, T. *The function of television for children and adolescents*. Tokyo: Sophia Univ., 1971.

Gerbner, G. The structure and process of television program content regulation in the United States. In G. A. Comstock & E. A. Rubinstein (Eds.), *Television and social behavior* (Vol. 1). *Media content and control*. Washington, D.C.: United States Government Printing Office, 1972.

Gerbner, G., Gross, L., Jackson-Beeck, M., Jeffries-Fox, S., & Signorielli, N. Cultural indicators: Violence Profile No. 9. *Journal of Communication*, 1978, *28* (3), 176–207.

Greenberg, B. British children and televised violence. *Public Opinion Quarterly*, 1974–75, *38*, 531–547.

Grusec, J. E. Effects of co-observer evaluations on imitation: A developmental study. *Developmental Psychology*, 1973, *8*, 141.

Halloran, J. D., Brown, R. L., & Chaney, D. C. *Television and delinquency*. (Television Research Committee Working Paper No. 3). Leicester: Leicester Univ. Press, 1970.

Hapkiewicz, W. G., & Roden, A. H. The effect of aggressive cartoons on children's interpersonal play. *Child Development*, 1971, *42*, 1583–1585.

Hartmann, D. P. Influence of symbolically modeled instrumental aggression and pain cues on aggressive behavior. *Journal of Personality and Social Psychology*, 1969, *11*, 280–288.

Heller, M. S., & Polsky, S. *Studies in violence and television*. New York: American Broadcasting Company, 1976.

Hess, R. D. Social class and ethnic influences on socialization. In P. H. Mussen (Ed.), *Carmichael's manual of child psychology* (Vol. 2). New York: Wiley, 1970.

Hicks, D. J. Imitation and retention of film-mediated aggressive peer and adult models. *Journal of Personality and Social Psychology*, 1965, *2*, 97–100.

Howitt, D. Attitudes towards violence and mass media exposure. *Gazette*, 1972, *18*, 208–234.

Kniveton, B. H., & Stephenson, G. M. An examination of individual susceptibility to the influence of aggressive film models. *British Journal of Psychiatry*, 1973, *122*, 53–56.

Kohlberg, L. Stage and sequence: The cognitive–developmental approach to socialization. In D. A. Goslin (Ed.), *Handbook of socialization theory and research*. Chicago: Rand McNally, 1969.

Leifer, A. D., Gordon, N. J., & Graves, S. B. Children's television: More than mere entertainment. *Harvard Educational Review*, 1974, *44*, 213–245.

Leifer, A. D., & Roberts, D. F. Children's responses to television violence. In J. P. Murray, E. A. Rubinstein, & G. A. Comstock (Eds.), *Television and social behavior* (Vol. 2). *Television and social learning*. Washington, D.C.: United States Government Printing Office, 1972.

Leyens, J. P., Camino, L., Parke, R. D., & Berkowitz, L. Effects of movie violence on aggression in a field setting as a function of group dominance and cohesion. *Journal of Personality and Social Psychology*, 1975, *32*, 346–360.

Liebert, R. M., & Baron, R. A. Short-term effects of televised aggression on children's aggressive behavior. In J. P. Murray, E. A. Rubinstein, & G. A. Comstock (Eds.), *Television and social behavior* (Vol. 2). *Television and social learning*. Washington, D.C.: United States Government Printing Office, 1972.

Liebert, R. M., Davidson, E. S., & Sobol, M. P. Catharsis of aggression among institutionalized boys: Further discussion. In G. A. Comstock, E. A. Rubinstein, & J. P. Murray

(Eds.), *Television and social behavior* (Vol. 5). *Television's effects: Further explorations.* Washington, D.C.: United States Government Printing Office, 1972.

Liebert, R. M., Neale, J. M., & Davidson, E. S. *The early window.* New York: Pergamon, 1973.

Liebert, R. M., Sobol. M. D., & Davidson, E. S. Catharsis of aggression among institutionalized boys: Fact or artifact? In G. A. Comstock, E. A. Rubinstein, & J. P. Murray (Eds.), *Television and social behavior* (Vol. 5). *Television's effects: Further explorations.* Washington, D.C.: United States Government Printing Office, 1972.

Lyle, J., & Hoffman, H. R. Children's use of television and other media. In G. A. Comstock, E. A. Rubinstein, & J. P. Murray (Eds.), *Television and social behavior* (Vol. 4). *Television in day-to-day life: Patterns of use.* Washington, D.C.: United States Government Printing Office, 1972. (a)

Lyle, J., & Hoffman, H. R. Explorations in patterns of television viewing by preschool-age children. In E. A. Rubinstein, G. A. Comstock, & J. P. Murray (Eds.), *Television and social behavior* (Vol. 4). *Television in day-to-day life: Patterns of use.* Washington, D.C.: United States Government Printing Office, 1972. (b)

Maccoby, E. E., & Jacklin, C. N. *The psychology of sex differences.* Stanford: Stanford Univ. Press, 1974.

Milgram, S., & Shotland, R. L. *Television and antisocial behavior.* New York: Academic Press, 1973.

National Association of Broadcasters. NAB television code. In *Broadcasting yearbook 1978.* New York: Broadcasting Publications, 1978.

Noble, G. Film-mediated aggressive and creative play. *British Journal of Social and Clinical Psychology,* 1970, 9(1), 1–7.

Rabinovitch, M. S., McLean, M. S., Markham, J. W., & Talbott, A. D. Children's violence perception as a function of television violence. In G. A. Comstock, E. A. Rubinstein, & J. P. Murray (Eds.), *Television and social behavior* (Vol. 5). *Television's effects: Further explorations.* Washington, D.C.: United States Government Printing Office, 1972.

Schramm, W., Lyle, J., & Parker, E. B. *Television in the lives of our children.* Stanford: Stanford Univ. Press, 1961.

Sebastian, R. J., Parke, R. D., Berkowitz, L., & West, S. G. Film violence and verbal aggression: A naturalistic study. *Journal of Communication,* 1978, 28(3), 164–171.

Siegel, A. E. Film-mediated fantasy aggression and strength of aggressive drive. *Child Development,* 1956, 27, 365–378.

Smith, J. R. Television violence and driving behavior. *Educational Broadcasting Review,* 1969, 3, 23–28.

Stein, A. H., & Friedrich, L. K. Television content and young children's behavior. In J. P. Murray, E. A. Rubinstein, & G. A. Comstock (Eds.), *Television and social behavior* (Vol. 2). *Television and social learning.* Washington, D.C.: United States Government Printing Office, 1972.

Stein, A. H., & Friedrich, L. K. Impact of television on children and youth. In E. M. Hetherington, J. W. Hagen, R. Kron, & A. H. Stein (Eds.), *Review of child development research* (Vol. 5). Chicago: Univ. of Chicago Press, 1975.

Surgeon General's Scientific Advisory Committee. *Television and growing up: The impact of televised violence.* Report to the Surgeon General, United States Public Health Service. Washington, D.C.: United States Government Printing Office, 1972.

Thomas, S. A. Violent content in television: The effect of cognitive style and age in mediating children's aggressive responses. *Proceedings of the 80th annual convention of the American Psychological Association,* 1972, 7, 97–98.

Thomas, M. H., & Drabman, R. S. Toleration of real life aggression as a function of exposure to televised violence and age of subject. *Merrill-Palmer Quarterly,* 1975, 21, 227–232.

Thomas, M. H., & Drabman, R. S. Effect of television violence on expectation of other's aggression. *Personality and Social Psychology Bulletin,* 1978, 4, 73–76.

Thomas, M. H., Horton, R. W., Lippincott, E. C., & Drabman, R. S. Desensitization to portrayals of real life aggression as a function of exposure to television violence. *Journal of Personality and Social Psychology*, 1977, *35*, 450–458.

Walters, R. H., & Thomas, E. L. Enhancement of punitiveness by visual and audiovisual displays. *Canadian Journal of Psychology*, 1963, *17*, 244–255.

Walters, R. H., & Willows, D. C. Imitative behavior of disturbed and nondisturbed children following exposure to aggressive and non-aggressive models. *Child Development*, 1968, *39*, 79–89.

Wotring, C. E., & Greenberg, B. S. Experiments in televised violence and verbal aggression. Two exploratory studies. *Journal of Communication*, 1973, *23*(4), 446–460.

13

The Political Environment for Change[1]

PERCY H. TANNENBAUM
WENDY A. GIBSON

As this volume and other recent publications attest, children's television currently exists in an atmosphere for change and reform.[2] At the least, there is enough restlessness among the natives so that the various actors and agencies in the communication policy arena—the branches of government, different facets of the television industry, public advocacy groups, and even social scientists—are getting into the fray in earnest. Just what changes can, should, or will be made; through what mechanisms; under whose impetus and control; and with what consequences (intended or otherwise) is, of course, less clear. This chapter attempts to sketch (with limited detail commensurate with the restricted space) the existing environment for change and the various political, economic, organizational, and social considerations that must be addressed in any mapping of the terrain for intervention. Although much of the concern has been precipi-

---

[1] The preparation of this paper was supported in part by a grant from the Markle Foundation to the senior author which, although directed at information systems for the elderly, actually shares much in common with the issues addressed in this chapter.

[2] Although the concern is shared in many countries, we will confine our treatment to the United States and its particular broadcasting structure. Given the common interest in the problem but considerably different broadcasting systems and existing policies, one rather obvious direction for systematic inquiry is the different or similar consequences that result from varying kinds of systems.

CHILDREN AND THE FACES OF TELEVISION:
Teaching, Violence, Selling

tated by the so-called violence issue, we will adopt a broader perspective rather than confining our discussion to this one area.

Background and Setting

Current concern over children's television is neither novel nor unique. The control and improvement of child-directed media are causes that have a short history but a long past. Furthermore, they are intimately linked with other trends and features of the American political scene, several of which deserve mention here since they constitute major influences on the existing environment for possible intervention.

Children as a Special Audience

Most societies have had to face the fact that members of the human species are helpless at birth and cannot be left to their own devices for physical, emotional, and intellectual development. Compared to other species, the human young spend an inordinate proportion of the life span learning to cope with their environment and becoming socialized—processes necessary for survival, let alone cultural evolution. In most societies, the family serves as the primary protector, controller, and socializer, with other more centralized institutions (e.g., education and religion) developing and extending their domains to assume responsibility for part of the developmental functions.

Just where the responsibilities and rights of the parent and family end and where those of society begin varies among societies. The American situation is as ambiguous as any in this regard, perhaps more so because of its pluralistic nature and strong legalistic tradition. Some transition from individualized, family-centered to more centralized control is apparent when parents are increasingly regarded as a major source of their children's current and later problems and when state intervention is introduced to "compensate for" inadequate or undesirable parental influence. Some have even entertained the notion of adults suing their parents for an "improper" upbringing. The readiness of the society to shift some of its more critical problems into the children's arena—for example, the school busing issue (Glazer, 1976)—is further evidence of public sector interventions. Just how effective such mechanisms will prove to be is another matter, but a climate for more public intervention in the "interests" of children clearly exists.

Risklessness as a Social Goal

Another factor contributing to the atmosphere surrounding the children's television issue is a general trend toward the reduction, if not the total elimination, of risk. Again, this is not a new phenomenon, but it has been increasing at an accelerating pace of late and is reaching into areas of private as well as public life. In the marketplace the burden of proof for a new product has shifted from the consumer to the laboratory, and demonstration of total product safety prior to release is becoming mandatory. New regulations abound and, with them, new bureaucracies to monitor and "insure" product and service performance as promised or advertised.

The efforts are probably well intended—after all, it is all in the good name of consumer protection—but the skeptic remains to be convinced that governmental intervention will really improve our quality, let alone our way of life. Skepticism converts into cynicism as private preferences are transformed into public mandates toward the proposed end of protecting individuals from themselves (e.g., the required presence but not the use of seat belts).

Television as a Special Risk. Viewed in this context, the issue of protecting children from media influence is no more compelling than are many other issues based on children's perceived vulnerability. The available media have always been seen as a potential source of influence—for good or for evil—and subject to some control. Long before the era of mass communication, Plato voiced concern over possible deleterious effects on children of an uncensored delivery of information. More recently and closer to home, comic books, radio, and films were each selected as targets for reform before television entered the scene, and there are still periodic reports of removing certain books from the shelves of school and public libraries.

It can be argued, however, that a new dimension was added to this old concern with the advent and subsequent development of television. For the first time, children too young to read or explore beyond their immediate home environments gained ready access to (though probably not the full understanding of) a wide range of vivid, vicarious experiences which far surpass their immature physical and cognitive capacities. Given television's ubiquity and obvious popularity with children, this access to vicarious experiences led to the claim that the parental–family monopoly on children's information had been broken (Jones & Gerard, 1967; Roberts, 1973), and that a new and potentially powerful force for socialization and training had emerged.

To be sure, parents have not been left totally impotent in controlling this new and invasive medium. But either because of indifference, their own inclinations to use the set as a source of entertainment and information, or truly inherent difficulties in monitoring exposure to this all-too-readily available medium, the control has been spotty at best. Summarizing the available evidence, Comstock, Chaffee, Katzman, McCombs, and Roberts (1978) conclude that while direct parental control is evident in some cases it is not a dominant factor in children's viewing habits in the United States.

As a result—and with the implicit support of the above-mentioned trends—agencies external to the family have gotten into the act. Eager beavers in various governmental regulatory agencies, do-gooder public advocates, and card-carrying social scientists clamor for more protection for the helpless and unrepresented child. Networks and stations are seen as guilty of both sins of omission and commission—not enough good programs with prosocial themes and too many bad ones with too much violence. In addition, it is claimed that children are being abused by opportunistic advertisers who promote worthless, even potentially harmful products, using seductive appeals and sophisticated selling strategies beyond the young consumers' comprehension and defense.

Again, there is little reason to question the motives and intentions of the various reform advocates, although some are bound to be more genuine and others, more self-serving in their contentions that American television is polluting the air and the minds of our youth. But there are babies—literally—in that figurative bath water. By bringing the issue into the social policy arena, reformists have inevitably brought in politics, with its own sets of rules, of costs considered along with benefits, of compromises, trade-offs, and so on. One cannot help but wonder if our children will in fact be the beneficiaries of productive change or whether the proposed cures may be as bad as or worse than the alleged disease. There is, after all, enough evidence of misguided if well-intended efforts, unforeseen side effects, and unanticipated consequences to give the skeptics among us as much cause for concern as those urging reform see in their cause.

The New Entrepreneurs. Among the factors contributing to the general trend of risk reduction has been the emergence of quasi-professional change agents. Operating first on the fringes of but increasingly from within the established structures, these individuals have acquired the requisite backing and political skill to bring certain risk issues onto the public calendar and to raise the position of others in the hierarchy of the political agenda. Special interest groups have always been part of our political system, but rarely have they been represented by such entrepreneurs of reform.

Since the children's cause, generally, and the television issue, particularly, are seen as justifying protective intervention, the new entrepreneurship is found in this area as well, some individuals specializing, others free-lancing. The medium itself (Mander, 1978; Winn, 1977) but more so its programs and commercial content are seen as too risky a proposition, especially for the more naive and innocent. Hence it must be legislated or otherwise persuaded into a low-risk position. As with other such causes, big business is among the proposed culprits, and the fact that the broadcast industry has adopted a defensive posture on this and related issues while amassing very substantial profits makes this particular cause all the more attractive.

Social Research Support. Any would-be reformers (or defenders, for that matter) should be expected to use whatever support and ammunition they can muster, and in this case they have found considerable and willing support from the social science research community. Partly because "the cause is right" (after all, who other than W. C. Fields can be against children), partly because of a desire to be "relevant" (the policymaking process is "where the action is"), but mostly because the research findings genuinely tend to testify to some adverse effects of television exposure, numerous academics have worked with and testified for various action and governmental groups on one or another of the children's television controversies. While we have some personal reservations as to just what the available evidence has actually proven—indeed, whether contemporary social research can actually "prove" most proposed effects—for our purposes here we accept these findings as pointing to a proper cause for social concern.

A key problem in evaluating the existing data from a policy as well as a scientific standpoint is whether a statistically significant finding is also socially significant. For example, a researcher may quite acceptably report in a professional journal a zero-order correlation of .14 or a fourth-order partial correlation of .13, accepting these findings as significant enough to warrant a conclusion that "children's beliefs have been affected by television." But it is hard to convince a doubting member of Congress that anything accounting for just 2% of the variance can be important enough to invite restrictive action.[3]

Similarly, most studies indicate that only a minority of any sample of subjects—usually less then 10%, rarely over 25%—shows any adverse effect. It is bad science to deny a majority effect and concentrate solely on a minority one, although it may be an acceptable basis for public policy. Indeed, many policies are concerned solely with minority segments of the population considered to be in special need.

Policy judgments involve much more than knowledge of the magnitude and nature of a particular effect. Political and social values, not statistical ones, are dominant in addressing issues concerned with the qualities and behaviors which are to be nurtured in children, what kinds of harm they should be protected from, and at whose expense (Wald, 1976). The critical questions concern what kind of an effect a society accepts as justifying attempts at ameliorative action and what price it is willing to pay for the change. In the absence of quantitative standards, the tendency is to ad hoc it from situation to situation. Either way, such policy matters

---

[3] The critical factor here may be one of expectation. One of us (PHT) had occasion some years ago to testify before a congressional subcommittee to the effect that television exposure, as such, probably accounted for no more than 5–8% of the variance in antisocial behavior. To one congressman, fearful that the effect might be over 50%, this result was too trivial to worry about further. To another, originally skeptical that the effect could be over 2%, the testimony was more ominous.

are essentially political decisions to be made through constitutionally vested political institutions. It is obviously desirable for such decisions to be informed as much as possible by the findings of research but it is just as obvious that other considerations must operate as well.

The researcher entering this process ought to know what she or he is getting into and be prepared to pay the entry and membership fees. Despite the current zeal for "policy-relevant" research, the academic scholar will find it very difficult to have it both ways—to be the independent scientist while pursuing a partisan cause—for very long. Either role is apt to suffer, probably both. At the very least, when the research is nonpartisan to start with, one should expect (otherwise be disappointed) to have one's findings and testimony distorted, used selectively, and even misrepresented by adversaries championing their side of a controversial issue. When the research is initially motivated to serve a particular side of the question, it invites even more political manipulation since that is in keeping with the rules of the game.

Content as the Specific Focus

The reform movement has adopted a number of targets for change, ranging from overhauling the structure of broadcasting to changing the specific wording in selected 30-second commercials. But, as Branscomb and Savage (1978) remind us, "genuine reform of program content . . . is the bottom line" for most of these efforts. We will accordingly restrict our discussion to this far from simple area. This is not to deny that, regardless of what the medium does or does not present, a most critical issue in children's television is that there is simply too much of it available, that children use it to an excessive degree, and that, as a result, they do not do enough of the other usual things such as playing outdoors or reading books. One delightful BBC program of recent years sought to meet this problem head-on by suggesting a variety of other activities children could engage in instead of watching television, but that was a rare bird indeed. It may well be that the best solution for whatever problems the medium may evoke in American society—in adults as well as in children—is the sheer reduction in the amount that is available.

The content issue, as we have already noted, arises in both the general programming and advertising domains, and this fact introduces some concern, let alone confusion, as to the specific locus of the problem. In the former area, the main criticism has been that children and society are poorly served by the plethora of aggressive, unreal, antisocial, distorted material. It is charged that children selectively learn undesirable lessons (e.g., to aggress) from such content because they lack the adult's sophistication to distinguish reality from fiction or to get the implicit message (e.g., that "crime doesn't pay"). But it does imply a substantial degree of comprehension, enough apparently to influence their subsequent judgments and behavior.

A somewhat different emphasis is often introduced in arguments against both the content and format of commercial material. As exemplified in the recent proposal to ban all commercials for programs where the majority of the audience is under 8 years of age (Federal Trade Commission, 1978), one argument is that the very young simply cannot understand the implicit selling intent of such messages and respond solely to authoritative exhortations to buy the product (they do not do the buying, of course, but apparently can nag and dun their parents to do so).

We are thus left with the somewhat uncomfortable claim that television has a negative influence on children because they understand it and because they do not—at least, with a highly selective type of understanding. Such a seeming contradiction may well be more apparent than real—for example, some research clearly demonstrates that incomplete or faulty comprehension can lead to the learning of unintended lessons (Bandura, 1977) or to limited cognitive defenses against persuasion (Roberts, 1978)—but the problem merits more detailed consideration than it has received to date. Just what children can and do comprehend and the consequences of that selective comprehension have to be accounted for better than hitherto. Compounding the comprehension issue further is the fact that much (perhaps 80%) of children's viewing time is devoted to programming aimed for adults.

Just what to make of—let alone do about—such a state of affairs is not clear. It is a fact of nature that children are different from adults and that they process the world about them differently. To some, this is seen as a distinct disadvantage and produces the belief that children should either be isolated or protected from that other confusing world. To others, it is seen as an advantage in that a child's world is relatively free of those very complications and fine-tuned distinctions that make adult living such a chore and a bore so much of the time. Again, it remains that television may prematurely expand the environment to which children are exposed. Since we do not completely isolate our children in most other matters of our daily living, doing so distinctively for television is difficult to justify and to accomplish without enforced restraints.

The Existing System as a Condition

Some advocates of reform believe that without a complete restructuring of the existing broadcasting system, especially the removal of advertising as the main if not the sole form of financial support, any changes are apt to fall considerably short of their goals. Our analysis here excludes the consideration of any such revolutionary change for the simple reason that we regard it as unrealistic.

It is no accident that the American broadcasting structure exists in its present form. In most nations, communication policy is derivative in the sense that it reflects the dominant economic and political—and, in some cases, cultural—institutional structures. Broadcasting developed here in the spirit of a profit-making free enterprise operation and, because of that, advertising support was a "natural" development. As McLuhan, among others, has noted, for the first part of this century a dominant American motto may well have been "business is our culture," and it did not take much for broadcasting to convert it to "culture is our business" (personal communication).

In any event, the present television system is rooted in other existing legal, institutional, and economic traditions and structures, and to change it radically means equally radical alterations in other spheres. The effects will be deep and far-reaching, and for this reason alone major changes, except possibly those along the existing lines of development, are too unrealistic to merit serious consideration. But between the impossibility of total revolutionary reform and the seeming inevitability of some change, if only symbolic, there is a range of alternatives which does deserve reasoned analysis.

Points of Intervention

These options are best addressed in terms of specific loci of treatment. We will consider the possible interventions along a scale of increasing degree of activity required for any change to occur—first in terms of the receivers, then the senders, then the governmental apparatus—on the grounds that the alternatives requiring the least change (although even that change may be difficult to realize) are in principle the likeliest to succeed.

In examining the various options, we will be governed by considerations of feasibility. One such criterion, sheer degree of change required, has already been mentioned. Others include economic feasibility—basically how much it will cost, in terms of both lost and newly-required funding, and who will pay for it; legal feasibility—both on constitutional grounds and for existing and required legislation; political feasibility—whether the necessary political support is available or realistic to expect; and organizational feasibility—whether the change can be effectively implemented and carried out through existing institutions and personnel or, if not, what the expectations are for new, institutionalized structures to be developed. These criteria will not be treated in check-list fashion, but they did contribute to our overall assessments.

The Home

In matters of children's television usage it would no doubt be optimal if discretion, along with charity, could be learned at home. Unfortunately, this is rarely the case. Children can hardly be expected to possess the maturity to limit their viewing time and to restrict themselves to programs which will "optimize" their socialization. Such a possibility of self-regulation—rare enough in any other area of human development—seems especially remote when one considers the difficulty mature adults experience in moderating their own viewing (witness the television hangovers of late-movie fans and the apparent futility of carrying on an interesting conversation while a television set is playing within view). If anything, television appears to have an opposite, almost mesmerizing attraction for most children—something akin to the lure of sugar-sweetened candies.

Nor are adults highly effective as selectors of children's television diets. As many parents have discovered, it is far from simple to restrict either the hours or the content of children's viewing unless they are willing to forego a set in the house, and even then, children have access to other sets. While some alarmists decry the tendency of many parents to "use television as a babysitter," it is understandable for even conscientious parents not to deny themselves some quiet weekday afternoons or an extra hour of shut-eye on Saturday mornings.

The essential point is not that adult monitoring cannot be effective, but that it does not come easily. In some homes, viewing hours, total time, and certain types of programs are often restricted to some degree. It is even possible to install control devices which limit set usage to a single channel or to the hours specified on a preset timer. To discourage "backsliders" in the campaign against indiscriminate viewing, television reformers have produced stickers and placards to be attached to home sets, although this is apt to have the same limited effect as cigarette package statements. At least one network is now broadcasting public service messages urging parents to watch television with their children and to talk with them about what they have seen.

All of these tactics may help mediate some of the effects for some of the children some of the time. They are relatively low in financial (although high in psychic) cost, and they place no demands on the television industry or on government regulatory structures. Unfortunately, they are probably least effective for precisely those children in precisely those homes where television is most likely to be a problem. Advocates of reform cannot afford to ignore evidence that the problems, whatever they may be, are less apt to be evenly distributed among all young viewers than to be concentrated in certain population groups. How to identify these particularly susceptible subpopulations remains a dilemma because the problems are still individual rather than aggregate. The available evidence suggests that the particular subpopulations are a relatively small minority of viewers and that their susceptibility is linked to such factors as poverty, educational limitations, or psychological disturbances within the family—just where it is unrealistic to expect self-regulation to occur or to be effective.

Even if the higher-risk children could be identified within the television audience, there is still the important question of a selective rather than a mass intervention to avoid an unacceptable "tyranny of the minority." Just as a ban on all children's consumption of ice cream because some youngsters are diabetic would be regarded as "unfair," so too for most across-the-board control bans in television. Some advocates suggest, however, that the issue of children's television is different in that the vast majority of children is apt to experience some undesirable consequence (as if all children were incipient diabetics). That, in effect, is what is suggested in the case of the proposed ban on advertising sugar-coated cereals. Just as in the case of banning saccharine because it may be carcinogenic even though it helps diabetics and others function more easily, there are important social trade-offs involved here, not the least of which is tolerance of a dominant, governmental "big brother" approach in an individualistic society such as ours.

The Industry

Whatever reform may be initiated, it will likely be ultimately manifest and implemented through the television industry. Like many large industries, it is a rather complex enterprise, involving different sets of actors and institutions, each with its own goals and incentives. The three main networks constitute the hub of the industry, but individual affiliated stations, independent local stations, the production complex, and the advertisers all play critical roles in determining the available fare for children.

The entire process is fueled by the rating system and its attendant link to advertising rates, revenues, profits, and stock market values. When a 1 point, prime-time rating gap can mean a difference of $30 million in income, one might expect a rigorously controlled rating system, backed up by a battery of indicators. Actually, the present system is not all that sophisticated but persists, warts and all, because all parties participating in the exchange have agreed to accept it as the main currency, and it is apt to continue that way for some time.

Children's television—particularly the Saturday morning kidvid scene—is a money-maker for all three networks and is thus subject to all the stresses and strains of a highly competitive business where the main goal is to expand one's share of the market. The present limited range of offerings, repeats, and redundant, animated action shows is the result. The industry has done relatively little to deviate from established formulas, and there is little reason to expect it to change dramatically on its own.

The Broadcasters. The networks are the central brokers of the industry, bartering the air time and audience of their affiliates (although each owns and operates its own outlets in the major urban markets) for advertising income. They bear the major responsibility for programming but also have to be responsive to the desires of the affiliated stations operating in local markets. If in other countries considerations of culture and education enter into programming decisions, they play a decidedly lesser role in the United States because it is viewed here essentially as a business, of both national and local proportions, which is run by business people rather than by arbiters of cultural tastes.

A certain amount of social consciousness is, of course, affordable and may even make for good public relations. Accordingly, there have been some excellent special programs for children, and there are some signs of more such activity of late. In addition, possibly in response to pressure both within and outside the federal regulatory structure, the networks have begun a campaign of public service announcements addressing the child and parent audiences. It is possible for such efforts to have some appreciable impact, but that still remains to be seen. While the networks and local stations cannot be expected to do much on their own, they are obviously not totally immune from national and local pressures and inducements.

The Producers. At the production level, demands for novelty or change place a real strain on existing creative and technical capacities. Successful writers, producers, and actors are no less self-serving and defensive than are members of any other profession and may thus be expected to defend the status quo that has served them so well (e.g., a substantially shared belief that tension and conflict are essential to fiction plots). Perhaps more important is the fact that skills and formats, along with a sophisticated technology, have been developed to turn out action-packed programs featuring car chases, shootouts, and other forms of mayhem relatively quickly and cheaply. On the other hand, sophisticated dialogue requires the kind of writing, directing, and acting skills that have not been as developed and nurtured to date.

Where show business criteria predominate, those who can deliver a reliable, entertaining product are apt to be more rewarded than are those concerned with child development or pedagogy. Few of the individuals involved in children's programming are deliberate, evil exploiters of child-

ren—most in fact, are decent enough family people and parents—but they
exist in an intensely competitive environment where the stakes for success
or failure are fairly large. Many claim their desire to do more innovative
programs with prosocial themes is thwarted by network and local programmers, but the latter deplore the paucity of imaginative scripts that
would attract appreciable enough audiences. The upshot is that all parties
on the scene are reluctant to assume the risks and burdens of change. The
motivation to break the logjam is lacking, the competitive market provides all too few incentives, and there is still the lingering question of
whether the available talent and training are sufficient to develop new
formats sensitive to the developmental needs of the specialized children
audience. Exceptions do exist but they are unlikely to become the rule.

The Advertisers. Advertisers may have tarnished halos, but in our
system they are the angels of most television programming, including that
for children. Motives and tactics aside, they pay the bills and are not at all
devious about why they do so—to buy audiences in order to sell products.
To them, the value of a television program is its effectiveness in carrying a
commercial message to a maximum number of potential consumers.

Not suprisingly, that which makes advertisers the kingpins of the
system also makes them the most potent locus for change. While they
have little intrinsic interest in the aesthetic or social values of the programs their sponsorship makes possible, advertisers are vulnerable to
consumer behavior. Thus, whether to curry favor of some groups and/or
to help deflect the complaints of others, certain advertisers have recently
changed their pattern of ad placement to avoid programs labeled as
highly violent, and others have undertaken direct sponsorship of particular "worthwhile" public and commercial television offerings.

But that, of course, can lead to the advertiser having a more direct
say in determining program content. It is ironic that those who cam-
paigned in the past to remove the payer of the piper from calling the tune
now find that same constituency to be the major potential contributor to
desirable change. Clearly, this is not the most comfortable of situations,
and some appropriate modus vivendi will have to be worked out if this
avenue is to be more fully pursued.

When it comes to their own offerings, the enticing commercials themselves, the advertisers are far from being innocent bystanders. Also operating in the competitive marketplace, they can be expected to employ
every means allowed to induce the consumer to buy more of their products and brands. As noted before, there are those who believe the child
audience has been particularly exploited in this regard, and there have
been particularly aggressive efforts to induce changes, including banning
the advertising of certain products and even totally removing commercials in certain cases. Again, the outcome of such efforts is uncertain, but
clearly this does represent a more plausible, if limited, avenue for change.

The Government

When all else fails, turn to the government. While not exactly in the American tradition, in recent times we have seen more resort to government intervention on a variety of fronts. Children's television has been no exception, since the potential for control is directly available through existing legislative, regulatory, and licensing power. But the control is far from absolute. There are built-in constraints and political considerations that render the process less than fully satisfactory to all sides of a controversial issue. As a result, the most important aspect of governmental reform rests in its potential deterrent effect by which the possibility of interference can induce the networks, stations, and advertisers to generate activities of their own to defuse a problem.

The Judicial Branch. If it is true, as Winston Churchill supposedly said, that democracy is the worst form of government except for all the others, a constitutional republic may well be the worst form of democracy except for the other varieties. The U.S. Constitution has been a powerful contributor to the kind of government we enjoy, but it is often a source of frustration to those who would use government clout as an instrument of reform. In particular, the First Amendment to the Bill of Rights, guaranteeing freedom of the press among other things, has been a barrier to any attempts to control the content of our public media, including television.

While the First Amendment is subject to interpretation in specific cases, the Supreme Court has been consistent in barring any attempts at governmental interference with content except in certain specified areas (e.g., libel and treason) and even then with some ambiguity. It has handled the problem of pornography circumspectly and has generally preferred to pass the buck rather than to face the touchy issue in an absolute manner. In championing the First Amendment, the Court has also reinforced the authority of those who control access to the various mass media, but that is part of the price we pay for the system we evidently prefer.

The Court has also specifically recognized that broadcasting is a business enterprise in a number of rulings, not least in upholding the contentions of Norman Lear and representatives of television writers and producers that the industry-imposed "Family Hour"—allegedly designed to reduce violent and sexual content at hours when children are more apt to be viewing—constituted a constraint of trade (*Writers Guild of America versus FCC,* 1976). While not dealing directly with advertising content, in a recent ruling sanctioning advertising by the legal profession, it made reference to the intent of the First Amendment to apply to "commercial information." Just how far this principle will be extended remains to be seen if and when subsequent cases are brought before the courts, but it may be a deterrent to regulation for the present.

On the other hand, the Supreme Court has assumed an activist role in introducing policy changes, especially in decisions involving children's education, and it may not be that large a leap to extend the concept of governmental intervention to the children's television arena. In a time of shifting values, the future of judicial rule-making is apt to remain somewhat clouded. It will depend on just which cases are brought before the Court, whether it wishes to recognize that a fundamental constitutional issue is involved, and perhaps on the composition of the Court at the given time. For the present, the salience of the provisions of the First Amendment remains a most significant inhibitor to any attempts at enforcing standards for program content. It is somewhat less so for advertising content (as witnessed by the current efforts at the FTC to introduce reform), although the Federal Communications Commission (FCC) recently refused a request to require the broadcasting of public service announcements for children on the grounds it would be violating the First Amendment by "putting words in the mouths" of broadcasters (*Council on Children, Media and Merchandising,* 1977).

The Legislative Branch. The virtual collapse of efforts by the Van Derlin subcommittee to rewrite the Communication Act of 1934 is adequate testimony to the difficulties of gaining political support for legislative reform. The only parts of that effort apt to survive are those dealing with common-carrier rather than broadcast communication, and it was precisely on the latter that the opposition was greatest. Perhaps not so curiously, the objections came from both sides but for different reasons—the public advocate reformists argued that the proposed changes either did not go far enough or would make for an even more commercial, less public interest system, and the broadcasters objected to licensing changes and a proposed levy on profits.

Nevertheless, some impetus has been given to some reform in an admittedly outdated system, and it is quite possible it will be heard from in the future, especially as new technologies force new regulations. Perhaps unfortunate from the reform standpoint, most signs in recent activities from the Court, the executive branch, and the Congress point to deregulation being the pattern for the immediate future. This does not mean that those reforms aimed at children's television are doomed to failure, only that an atmosphere of deregulation is hardly conducive to increasing regulatory or legislative control.

The Executive Branch. The President proposes, Congress disposes, and the bureaucracy composes regulations and paperwork in applying new and old mandates. Recent administrations have flirted with some reform in the communication field, but partly because of a more demanding agenda, interconstituency conflicts and the lack of congressional support, they have generally adopted a passive approach. The Carter administration has put some muscle into the general movement by forming a relatively strong National Telecommunication and Information Agency in the Department of Commerce and by its appointments to the FTC and FCC, the two federal agencies most directly involved with the broadcast industry.

As already noted, the FCC has generally tended to its knitting and stayed away from program standards in most areas. By and large, it has been a defender of the present broadcast industry structure, even in the face of new technologies such as cable television. Even when it adopted what most would identify as a public interest stance in requiring cable systems to set aside channels for local access and government use, the Court ruled it had overstepped its jurisdictional boundaries. In the face of such actions and recent trends toward less regulation on the general Washington scene, one might not expect the FCC to be particularly bold on the children's television front. But, with both internal staff and external political pressure, it did make some forays into the area in the mid-1970s—for example, successfully negotiating a scaling down of the amount of advertising on children's programs and issuing a set of guidelines calling for more children's programming, better distributed over the week, with more balance between "entertainment" and "educational" content. A more recent FCC task force found compliance with such guidelines to be wanting and, at the time of this writing, the Commission has given the industry until mid-1980 to respond while it entertains five options in this area. Just what will happen is anyone's guess, our own being that it will continue its favorite tactic of getting the industry to mend its own fences while avoiding direct intervention—a tricky operation under the best of circumstances and somewhat hazardous in the present atmosphere of deregulation.

Just how hazardous this can be is shown on the FTC front when that agency adopted a more activist stance, particularly on children's program advertising. This was in part due to advertising content being more accepted as "fair game" for regulation and to several Commission appointments which President Carter sought to satisfy his political constituency of consumer advocates. Emboldened by certain established precedents— for example, that deceptive or misleading advertising is objectionable and that counteradvertising is acceptable—the FTC has assumed a leading role in the field. It has sponsored more research, supplied funding for public advocacy groups to prepare their case (a new wrinkle in the U.S. political adversary process), and held hearings on major proposed changes. At the time of this writing, the status of those changes is still uncertain, but the network activity noted above is largely a consequence of the FTC initiatives.

There are clearly multiple avenues for reform available through government, but a good deal of political skill is required and there are real constraints as to how much can be achieved. And always there is the question of whether the net outcome will represent a real improvement. For example, if the proposal to ban commercials on programs aimed at the very young is adopted, the likely consequences are no programming at all in that time slot (perhaps the biggest blessing), or some banal sitcom repeated in its stead, or even the probable dropping of other desirable programs (e.g., *Captain Kangaroo*) which will inadvertently be caught in the regulatory web. It will not be the first or last time that the consequences were not as anticipated by well-meaning advocates of change.

Some Remaining Thoughts

It is clear that we do not see many simple or easy answers to the questions involved. Since we regard children's television as a special case at the intersection of several other more general social phenomena, a lot will depend on what happens in those related arenas. Even then, we have some lingering doubts which deserve more detailed discussion than we can offer here:

1. One of the few certainties, along with death and taxes, is that there is no such thing as a free lunch. Too many suggestions for reform fail to consider the costs of new production and possibly some form of reparation for lost revenues. Good television programming costs money. If it will not be supported from advertising, it has to come from some place, and just pointing to general government support is no guarantee that it will be there or that the product will be excellent.

2. The critical policy question, here or elsewhere in broadcasting, is who makes the content selection. A somewhat less critical question is by what criteria. If it is not programmers responding to their vision of the marketplace, who then—a tribunal of government officials, public advocates, social scientists, all of the above, or none of the above? The answers, again, are more complicated than meet the eye.

3. What will the new programming be like? We can glibly talk about prosocial television, but achieving some consensus on what it should be and making it manifest is another matter. If fewer children will watch it, they will turn to other programming that may be worse yet. The better it is, and the more there is of it, the greater the likelihood of an even more undesirable result—more children spending still more time in front of their sets instead of engaging in other activities. How to achieve the optimal balance in quality and quantity is no easy matter.

4. Not least, this entire discussion—indeed, this entire book—may be purely academic, in both senses of the term. We are told that we are on the brink of a major communication revolution when the technology will make broadcast television, as we know it now, an historical relic within a

generation's time, to be replaced by a more consumer-based system. Some of that is already upon us, and clearly more is on the way. Even if it does not supplant network television entirely, the new gadgetry will reinforce the market system with all its apparent faults for children. Control will be back in the home, the apparent gap between children of different social and economic groups is apt to widen, the family information monopoly may be reinstated, and we may well be back at square one.

References

Bandura, A. *Social learning theory.* Englewood Cliffs, New Jersey: Prentice Hall, 1977.

Branscomb, A. W., & Savage, M. The broadcast reform movement. *Journal of Communication,* 1978, *28*(4), 225–234.

Comstock, G., Chaffee, S., Katzman, N., McCombs, M., & Roberts, D. *Television and human behavior.* New York: Columbia Univ. Press, 1978.

Council on Children, Media and Merchandising. FCC 2nd, 1977, 65, 421.

Federal Trade Commission Advisory Staff. *FTC staff report on television advertising to children.* Washington, D.C.: Federal Trade Commission, 1978.

Glazer, N. *Affirmative discrimination.* New York: Basic Books, 1976.

Jones, E. E., & Gerard, H. B. *Foundations of social psychology.* New York: Wiley, 1967.

Mander, J. *Four arguments for the elimination of television.* New York: Morrow Quill, 1978.

Roberts, D. F. Communications and children: A developmental approach. In I. de Sola Pool & W. Schramm (Eds.), *Handbook of communication.* Chicago: Rand McNally, 1973.

Roberts, D. F. *Children's information processes: Perceptions of and cognitions about TV commercials and supplementary information.* Testimony submitted to FTC Hearing on Television Advertising to Children, 1978.

Wald, M. Legal policies affecting children: A lawyer's request for ideas. *Child Development,* 1976, *47,* 1–5.

Winn, M. *The plug-in drug.* New York: Viking, 1977.

Writers Guild of America vs. FCC. Fed. Supplement, 1976, *423,* 1064.

14

Research Findings and
Social Policy

ALBERTA E. SIEGEL

No longer do we think of a child's life as shaped almost entirely by family, home, neighborhood, and local school. For many years, when asked to discuss a child's opportunities to develop well, psychologists raised questions like: Is this child wanted? Will experiences in infancy create a lasting emotional bond between mother and child? Will there be intellectually nurturing experiences as the child's cognitive potential unfolds? Are the parents effective disciplinarians? Is the child abused or neglected? Do significant people develop the child's positive feelings of self-worth and self-esteem? Are there role models of sex-appropriate behavior? Will school teachers be friendly and sympathetic as well as informed and competent? Now we recognize that the answers to these questions are not sufficient to describe the child's life space.

Increasingly, we recognize that a child's life is shaped by larger social forces. Is the nation at war or peace? Is the child growing up in the welfare class, the working class, the educated and professionalized middle class, or among the affluent? Does the economy's agricultural system afford an opportunity to be decently nourished? Are public health measures undertaken to keep the water pure and the air breatheable? Will there be inoculations against polio and other cripplers? Does the family live in a

CHILDREN AND THE FACES OF TELEVISION:
Teaching, Violence, Selling

crowded, noisy, and disintegrating slum neighborhood or in a community with safe streets, clean housing, and private spaces? Is suitable medical and hospital care available to the mother and to the child? All of these issues arise when we ask even such a simple question as whether the child will survive to maturity. They become more pointed when the question is not simply whether the child will remain alive but whether she or he will arrive at adulthood in robust health. And they are critical if the question bears not only on the child's survival in good health into adulthood but also on his or her emergence as a productive and decent citizen and a good parent.

Research and Its Utilization

Those of us who study the child's development have a long tradition of seeking utilization of research findings for the child's welfare (Sears, 1975). We have not retreated from social pressures into an ivory tower or a sophisticated laboratory but instead have sought to conduct research which will be useful to those who share our concern for the child's well-being. Today's developmental psychologist, like those in the past, is socialized in an environment which assumes that research findings will find application, being readily translated into action in the lives of children.

Traditional Users of Developmental Psychology Research

There are very few developmental psychologists in America, perhaps fewer than 2000 with a doctoral degree, and there are hundreds and thousands of people who are eager for knowledge about child development to apply in their professional or lay work with infants and children. Such knowledge has been transmitted to the medical practitioner and to the teacher not only through formal teaching in professional schools but also through collegial interaction at professional meetings and at work in the solution of the problems of clinic and school. Social workers and students of home economics are also schooled in the research findings of developmental psychologists—their textbooks draw on our research. Lay persons, too, are an interested audience. Finally, the parent education movement has been allied with developmental psychology in America throughout the twentieth century, and the professionalization of nursery school educators has drawn more heavily on developmental psychology than on any other discipline.

Journalists regularly turn to developmental psychologists for information, knowing of their readers' interest in new research findings. Our best newspapers and magazines offer reports of research in some of our leading laboratories. We may cavil at the accuracy or completeness of these reports, but we cannot deny the frequency and enthusiasm with which journalistic reports of research are transmitted.

As developmental psychologists have come increasingly to appreciate the larger social forces directly shaping a child's life, we have sought discourse with lawyers, public health specialists, economists, and anthropologists. Some of the best current discussions of social policy and child development draw on those fields as well as on those with which we have long had intellectual links—psychiatry, education, pediatrics, social work, and psychology (Keniston, 1977; National Research Council, 1976).

Use of Research about Children and Television

Developmental psychologists who entered the field in the 1950s and 1960s were the beneficiaries of a legacy of positive relations with the professions and the public which had been built by our predecessors in the 1920s and 1930s. We enjoyed the support of parents, teachers, and health professionals, because our professors and their professors had worked to gain acceptance for developmental psychology. Our own efforts were centered on generating new research findings, on conveying these research findings to undergraduate and graduate students, and on educating graduate students in the research methods which were proving productive of dependable knowledge.

Research on the effects of television on children was launched almost as soon as commercial television became important in America, in the late 1940s and early 1950s. Research findings began to appear in the scholarly journals in those years, and more appeared in the 1960s after Bandura devised ways to apply experimental methods productively to the question of television's effects.

Because of the intellectually benign and supportive environment in which postwar developmental psychologists have been nurtured, we have been slow to recognize the response which research on television and children has engendered and even slower to deal contructively with that response. We have tended to assume that the motivations of the consumers of this knowledge would be similar to the motivations of the consumers of our research knowledge in such areas as childrearing, children's learning, cognitive development during infancy and the preschool years, and the development of intelligence. Specifically, we have tended to take for granted that others share our concern for the well-being of children and for their healthy development. As well, we have tended to assume some familiarity with the research enterprise and respect for research findings.

These assumptions have not been entirely erroneous. In fact, research findings alerting us to the hazards of television violence for children's healthy development have evoked concern among educated parents and have found an organized outlet in the Parent Teacher Association, in Action for Children's Television, and in other lay groups. And the research findings have mobilized the medical and teaching professions. The organized response of the American Medical Association, hardly a bunch of activists, has been noteworthy.

The availability of support for research is another index of the professional world's response to our findings. The National Institute of Mental Health has financed research on children and television, despite arguments from some that the topic is tangential to their primary mission. Research support has come as well from the National Institute of Education and from the Office of Child Development. And there has been support for research and promulgation of research findings from the private foundations, with several foundations devoting major portions of their resources to this topic.

The response from government and foundations has included extensive support for alternatives to commercial television for children, including most of the programs that have drawn praise from developmental psychologists and from such child development professionals as educators, psychiatrists, pediatricians, and social workers. Without heavy financial support from the federal government and from private foundations, we would not have *Sesame Street, Misterogers Neighborhood,* or any of the other programs especially produced for children on public television.

So our research findings about television and children have elicited appropriate responses from the research audiences with whom we have long been allied: educated parents, teachers, physicians, government agencies, and private sources of funding for programs benefiting children.

What has dismayed us has been the response from the community of commercial television producers, performers, and purveyors. Here the primary response to our research findings has been indifference, compounded by ignorance.

Causes for Television Industry Responses to Research

As social scientists, we should have been better prepared for commercial television's negative response to our research. We ought to have recognized the institutional and structural forces which create the setting for it. There is no requirement or expectation that people in the world of commercial television will have met any educational requirements. They are not like the teachers, doctors, nursery school teachers, and educated parents with whom we have long been linked. The entertainment world has not yet participated in the trend of ever-rising expectations or requirements for educational achievement.

A history of the United States could be written around the theme of the ever-increasing educational level of our population. Each generation of Americans has included a higher proportion who finished grade school, more who attended high school, more with a high school diploma, more who went to college, and more with postgraduate education. Schooling has been increasingly available to women, immigrants, and blacks, as it has long been available to white males. It is a rare American family whose children do not have more years of schooling than their parents. Even more anomalous is a family whose children are less schooled than their grandparents.

With the rising level of general education in the population we have seen the professionalization of more and more occupations. For professions that have long been numbered among the educated in America, the educational standards have climbed dramatically in the twentieth century. Emphasis on the continuing education of professional persons is growing in importance, too. This has always been a feature of the life of a scientist, and now it characterizes the life of applied scientists, especially physicians and engineers, and of teachers as well.

The teaching profession illustrates all these trends well. Grade school teachers and high school teachers have more years of schooling today than they did a generation or two ago and much more than they had in the nineteenth century. Continuing education of teachers is the norm, with summer school courses, weekend conferences on teaching, journals of professional practice, and the rest. And teaching is increasingly molded by research findings. The teacher training institution has educational and developmental psychologists, sociologists, historians, and applied statisticians on its faculty, facilitating the translation of research knowledge into educational practice.

Lack of Relevant Formal Education

Nothing of the sort holds true in the world of commercial television. It is not to be assumed that a television writer, performer, or producer, or the president of a television network, or the manager of a local station has graduated from a university where research is conducted on child development. If he or she did chance to attend such an institution, it is not to be assumed that his or her own pattern of courses would include any in which children were discussed nor indeed any in which any behavioral science research was covered. More likely, the person now working in commercial television took courses in accounting, organizational management, and the like, or perhaps courses in theatre, performing arts, and

0

maybe journalism. Even more likely, the employee now in the television world never had any formal education in any research-oriented institution.

No Continuing Education

There is no expectation of continuing education for the employee in the world of commercial television. "Keeping up" in that world means watching other people's shows, maintaining surveillance of the other networks' offerings, reading the trade journals, reading magazines for the public such as *TV Guide,* and reading newspapers. "Keeping up" does not expose the employee to research findings any more than his or her original education did.

No Tradition of Respect for New Knowledge

Finally, there is no tradition of respect for new knowledge in the world of the television employee. Whatever a doctor's private opinion might be of the merits of applications of research in clinical medicine to the daily practice of medicine, she or he works in an environment of shared expectations of respect for science. That respect is notably absent in the television world. Instead, respect and admiration go to the big earners and to the daring innovators who manage to make their innovations pay.

Probably the research scientist is perceived by television people according to various derogatory and mocking stereotypes, including the Mad Scientist, The Absent-Minded Professor, The Do-Gooder, The Repressed Prude, and The Censorious Critic. Even more likely, the psychologist is thought of as a clinician whose professional opinions are shaped by what he or she hears from neurotic patients.

If the television employee has any awareness at all of social science research, most likely the model is the public opinion poll. The approach of seeking out a sample of persons and asking them their opinions on stated questions is familiar. Like many college sophomores when they first enroll in an introductory course, the television employee is likely to think of survey research as the standard approach in the behavioral sciences and to regard percentages as our highest form of statistical sophistication.

No Use of Published Reports of Research

Research scientists publish their findings in scholarly journals. They are not widely read. The lay public hardly knows of their existence. It would be surprising to meet any employee working in the television business, other than those in the social science research offices, who is aware that scholarly journals exist, much less to meet an employee who has read a scientific article about television's effects on children. If the employee should chance upon such an article, he or she would probably not be equipped with the education needed to read it with understanding.

Scholars increasingly rely on scholarly review articles. These are written by specialists in the field and are reviewed by other specialists for their exhaustiveness and objectivity before they are published in scholarly books. Over the past 20 years, review articles have summarized our knowledge about television and children (e.g., Rubinstein, 1978; Stein & Friedrich, 1975). My guess is that toilers in the vineyards of commercial television are as unaware of the existence of such scholarly reviews as they are of the research reports covered by them.

Our students rely on textbooks, which are at yet another level of remove from the original research. One must wonder whether anyone in the commercial world of television has ever read a textbook in child development. I doubt it. Our current textbooks contain summaries of our research knowledge about children and television. College sophomores are better informed on this knowledge than are employees of the networks.

Still farther away from research publications are books written for the public, including books for parents. Such books, even today, tend to be based more on the authority of the writer than on research. If their rhetoric makes any appeal other than to authority, it is to the reader's own experience and common sense. Rarely do books for the public on the topic of child development contain descriptions of research or appeals to the reader's knowledge of research. When such books do appear (e.g., the series of separately authored paperbacks edited by Bruner, Cole, & Lloyd [1977] addressed to "parents, educators, child-care professionals, students of developmental psychology, and all others concerned with childhood"), they seem to reach the professionals in their intended audience more effectively than the lay public. These remarks apply to popular books about television and its effects as well as to popular books about childrearing, the education of children, and children's health. We professionals have not mastered the art of writing about research findings in ways that appeal to a wide audience. Some of our colleagues have tried (e.g., Liebert, Neale, & Davidson, 1973), and my own feeling is that such efforts are so badly needed that these pioneers deserve special commendation.

My guess is that people in the commercial world of American television are aware of "trade" books written about children for the lay public, however unaware they may be of journal articles, scholarly reviews, and textbooks. To the extent that such books can be based on empirical research findings, they serve our purposes in seeking to bridge the chasm between research and social policy.

Isolation of Social Scientists in
the Organizational Structure

These remarks about the scientific illiteracy of the employees of the television networks—the producers, writers, executives, and station managers—do not apply to the social scientists who are employed by the networks to monitor research and to conduct research studies. But these individuals, who typically hold doctorates in sociology, communications, or social psychology, seem to be located in their organizations in ways that keep them thoroughly insulated from the day-to-day work of planning and producing. My own impression is that they serve as buffers rather than as communicators in the wide gap between the world of research and the world of broadcasting.

In some lines of work, the rank and file employee is uneducated and uninformed about advances in knowledge, but he or she works under leadership from the educated and informed. The teacher's aide is supervised by a qualified teacher. The practical nurse is supervised by a registered nurse and by physicians. The clerk in the drugstore is supervised by a licensed pharmacist. The job sets the uneducated and uninformed employee in a context in which work is monitored, observed, and supervised.

In the world of the employee in television, on the other hand, direct superiors and workers in contiguous fields are likely to be as uneducated as is the employee. Advertising people need not meet any educational requirements and are not expected to display any knowledge of social science research. The same may be said for movie people and for the television critics who write for newspapers and magazines.

Television Reform

My purpose has been to show that in no sense does commercial television conform to the model of professionalism. We entrust our health to physicians and the education of our children to teachers, because we know that they are professionals, educated in the accumulated knowledge in their fields and keeping up with the new knowledge which research is generating. The child's television teachers were not educated for their jobs, nor do they keep up with the research knowledge about what they are doing. Nor is the field paraprofessional. It differs from, say, practical nursing in which the practitioners take their leadership and direction from professional people, with the latter taking responsibility for their work. Television in the United States today is strictly a commercial enterprise and an exceedingly profitable one. Given this, how best can we reform it?

Governmental Regulation and
the First Amendment

Governmental regulation is the usual approach to protecting the public's health against commercial depredation. We rely on licensing, inspection, and detailed rules and regulations to keep our food free of adulterants, to keep our drugs pure, to maintain sanitary standards in barber shops, and to protect the health of those who work with dangerous chemicals. Although the process is not perfect, in general it works to give us safe food and drugs even though those products come from straight commercial, profit-making enterprises. Are licensing and inspection the way to go in dealing with commercial television in America?

Academics have not urged governmental regulation of television. It is not an approach with which we have much familiarity. Where we have dealt with it, for example in the licensing of clinical psychologists by states, we have not been impressed by its efficiency or efficacy. More important to us, the television industry is part of the publishing and communications world, which includes newspapers, plays, films, scholarly books and journals, magazines, and trade books as well as television. We prize freedom of communication for this entire network of businesses.

Research workers and other academics cherish freedom of speech not only because it is a dearly valued personal liberty but also because it is essential to our work. Research and scholarship flourish in a climate of free expression. Rarely do scientific and creative advances in knowledge occur under totalitarian and bureaucratic regimentation. One can think of many marvelous operas and symphonies which have been composed in totalitarian eras and of beautiful paintings and sculptures wrought by artists under conditions of political tyranny and abuse. But when one thinks of advances in scientific understanding one is struck that they occur usually in nations with freedom of expression. This is so because, while often the artist's work can be solitary or in a small group, science is much more a communal venture, with many scientists in diverse laboratories contributing tiles to the mosaic of new knowledge. Advances occur with free communication among these persons.

Indeed, we hold freedom of speech so dear we sometimes cringe to hear it praised by network apologists upholding their right to beam endless hours of mindless violence to their audience of children. We wince as we hear the First Amendment lauded by the purveyors of children's cartoons and the hucksters of plastic dolls. We wish that money were available to protect the academic freedom of our colleagues here and abroad in amounts like those that are spent so freely to defend the broadcasters' right to sell soap.

Somewhat wistfully, then, we turn away from governmental regulation as an approach for bringing social responsibility to television. Some consumerists have been less fastidious. Efforts to improve television broadcasting through the Federal Trade Commission and the Federal Communications Commission are detailed elsewhere in this volume. My remarks may help to explain why it is consumer activists and not research scientists who have been leaders in these.

In any event, I doubt that efforts to bring government into a regulatory role with commercial television will have major successes. Television is deeply imbedded in America's political processes today, and rightly or not, many federal legislators believe they were elected and will be re-elected because they play ball with the networks. It seems unlikely that they will choose to impose unwanted constraints on their fellow players in the political game.

Self-Regulation

It is the considerations sketched above, rather than any demonstrated successes of self-regulation, which bring social scientists with a concern for children to favor self-regulation within the television industry. To date, it has not been successful. What might a successful self-regulatory effort look like?

First, it would involve continuing discussion of the meaning of terms like *aggressive, violent,* and *children.* All of us are weary of the haggling and nit-picking, which often serves as a delaying tactic, but in fact my conversations with people in the industry do suggest that there are no shared definitions and this is one source of lack of communication. This is so not simply because these persons are "psychopaths who are morally blind," however accurate the substantive description behind the hyperbole may be in particular instances. When we talk about "children," we are still thought to be speaking of youngsters in school, about age 10. "Aggression" is still merged with competitiveness and with energetic assertiveness. Some consensus needs to be sought through the usual methods of dialogue and discussion, perhaps aided by consultation with concerned outsiders like parents, the clergy, social critics, and social scientists.

Second, a publication is needed within the television industry which presents the results of research. This "house organ" should be widely distributed to executives, producers, writers, board members, and others and should offer straightforward and unvarnished accounts of research efforts and their findings. The sarcasm, cynicism, and sniping which pervade some trade journals' discussions of research would have no place in this honest effort at industry self-regulation. Some investigators would be invited to speak to the industry in their own words in its pages. Those researchers who are employed within the industry would have their work presented on an equal footing with the presentations of research by academics.

Third, it would involve discussions with writers and producers which center on particular examples of their work. Terms like *sex stereotyping* and *role models* can gain meaning for practitioners if discussed in terms of their own creations. Elizabeth Roberts and the Project on Human Sexual Development have pioneered this approach to the creative people in television, with promising results.

Fourth, there would be awards and recognition for excellence. Television productions which are thought by critics, communications researchers, child development professionals, and others to be models of achievement would be singled out for public praise and awards, for renewed presentations to wider audiences at primetime, and the like. Within-industry efforts to recognize excellence can be bogged down in petty self-congratulation and back-slapping mediocrity; the involvement of the wider public and of independent critics would be essential to elevate these awards to prestige and significance.

Fifth, the networks should employ competent social scientists to conduct in-house research which is independent and well-respected. These individuals should be encouraged to publish their results in the usual scholarly journals, to attend the usual professional meetings, and generally to engage in the typical interchanges among professionals. This would greatly enhance exchange of information between the academic world and the television industry world, especially if those researchers employed by the industry are from the fields now making the liveliest contributions to the literature. The ethical drug industry provides one model for employment in business of scholars who are in the same field as are their colleagues in university medical schools. There are models in engineering as well.

Sixth, travel fellowships are needed to enable television writers and producers to study abroad. Programming for children in other nations is more successful than it is in the United States. Our industry people should be supported to observe first-hand how countries like Canada, England, Sweden, Norway, Denmark, Israel, and others have succeeded in attracting child audiences without saturating them with repetitive and senseless violence. The television industry might collaborate with private foundations on a matching basis both to pay for these fellowships and to choose the recipients.

The modesty of these proposals, each of which would be a real change from today's reality, is an index of how absurd the situation is now. The fact that such inexpensive and moderate measures have not been adopted by a highly profitable industry with an incomparably large exposure to the public should dampen our hopes for rapid change.

Support for Public Television

At the same time that we urge industry self-regulation, we need vastly increased support for public television. Those in public television, with the support of private foundations, are likely to turn their energies to creative and constructive programs for children. Many who work in commercial television are mimics and faddists. As the public television shows attract child audiences, they will be imitated by commercial producers, and a chain of change will have been forged whose links include the industry's mimicry and faddism.

Monitoring Televised Violence

We continue to need an independent monitoring agency to provide regular reports on the levels of violence in television entertainment. Professor Gerbner's periodic reports meet this need in part, but they deserve wider and more systematic distribution, and their survival should not rest on the energies and resources of a single university's faculty. Linked to periodic "smog" bulletins alerting the public to the level of violent pollution currently being emitted by their home television receivers, we need to have information on who is paying for the violent programming and how those sponsors may be reached in protest. Here I am reiterating a suggestion advanced by Professor Bandura and later urged by me (Siegel, 1972) at Senator Pastore's hearings.

Social Change and Satisfaction

As in so many fields in America today, the pace of technological change is dizzyingly rapid and the pace of social change is discouragingly slow. The progress we have been able to achieve (Siegel, 1975) is modest and would be a source of greater satisfaction if the challenges were not so enormous. My hope is that this book will constitute another step toward finding ways to meet those challenges.

References

Bruner, J., Cole, M., & Lloyd, B. (Eds.) The developing child. Cambridge, Massachusetts: Harvard Univ. Press, 1977.

Keniston, K., & The Carnegie Council on Children. All our children: The American family under pressure. New York: Harcourt Brace Jovanovich, 1977.

Liebert, R. M., Neale, J. M., & Davidson, E. S. The early window: Effects of television on children and youth. New York: Pergamon, 1973.

National Research Council, Advisory Committee on Child Development. Toward a national policy for children and families. Washington, D.C.: National Academy of Sciences, 1976.

Rubinstein, E. A. Television and the young viewer. *American Scientist*, 1978, *66*, 685–693.

Sears, R. R. Your ancients revisited: A history of child development. In E. M. Hetherington, J. W. Hagen, R. Kron, & A. H. Stein (Eds.), *Review of child development research* (Vol. 5). Chicago: Univ. of Chicago Press, 1975.

Siegel, A. E. Testimony before Hearings of the Subcommittee on Communications of the Committee on Commerce, United States Senate, by the Surgeon General's Scientific Advisory Committee on Television and Social Behavior. March, 1972.

Siegel, A. E. Communicating with the next generation. *Journal of Communication*, 1975, *25* (4), 14–24.

Stein, A. H., & Friedrich, L. K. Impact of television on children and youth. In E. M. Hetherington, J. W. Hagen, R. Kron, & A. H. Stein (Eds.), *Review of child development research* (Vol. 5). Chicago: Univ. of Chicago Press, 1975.

Part III

THE SELLING FACE
OF TELEVISION

A child experiences selling. A child learns. At first glance, the selling face of television seems to have all the family features of the teaching face—planned "curricula" and intentional teaching. Yet, on closer scrutiny, one sees that the advance planning is not specifically directed to the child's learning needs nor is it completely oriented toward cognitive readiness to assimilate given content. The primary goal is to "close the sale"—delivering the child audience to a given product or product line. Questions of fostering a child's growth, health, or well-being can be peripheral to this delivery process. The child has come face-to-face with our nation's private enterprise system and, as the chapters will indicate, the encounter raises such issues as what age, what techniques, and what products are appropriate for this early encounter.

Adler's three-part introduction to these issues historically traces the evolution of children's programming and advertising, the development of the children's television advertising issue, and the emergence of research in the field. He creates the picture of television, the newborn, whose future as a privately owned, profit-making enterprise had been planned long before its birth. He outlines the events which led from the broadcasting of children's programming on a sustaining basis to its use to generate income through the sale of advertising time. Concern with this targeting of commercials to children is followed in the development of consumer groups, early interactions between government and industry, and a mid-1970s progress report. Research, the latecomer, is then reviewed in relation to the reform movement and the recent *Federal Trade Commission Staff Report on policy options of advertising to children*.

Rossiter brings a current complexion to the selling face. He sets out to identify and "critically examine policy issues in the controversial area of television advertising directed to children [p. 251]." he operationally defines a children's television policy issue and uses the definitional framework to structure his review of current policy actions. His framework has facts/values and means/ends distinctions which translate into the four categories of false advertising, misleading advertising, unfair means, and unfair ends. For each policy issue within this system, he assesses the contribution of research to policy. He ends with some personal observations on policy issues and policymaking.

Barcus focuses on the content of children's television advertising. He chronologically traces changes in the commercial-to-program time ratio, noting percentage differences between network affiliates and independent stations. Looking at the types of products advertised, he finds the children's advertising world to be one of toys, cereals, candies, and fast foods. He next examines selling techniques, including the presentation method, attention-getting devices, qualifiers or disclaimers, and types of appeal, finding many to be implicitly oriented toward psychological states and such intangibles as fun and popularity. Finally, he comments on the value lessons to be learned from spokespersons who generally are white males pursuing leisure-time activities and discusses what he considers to be four basic, ethical questions about advertising to children.

Atkin reviews 10 years of social science research evidence in each of four effects areas. He first assesses direct impact on product preferences as measured by desire for the advertised product and rate of consumption, evaluates the relationship between amount of television viewing and number of product requests, and looks at impact on desire for products of the same type as that advertised. Moving to more general effects, he examines basic nutritional attitudes and beliefs and then moves on to unintended effects on parent–child conflict and feelings of sadness, anger, or aggression. In prosocial public service messages, he finds a promising potential for constructive change.

Wartella's chapter centers upon children's individual differences—particularly by age—in attention to, comprehension of, and use of television advertising in product decision-making. In the area of children's attention, she specifically considers research relating to attention level, production factors, and program/commercial separation. For comprehension, she assesses to what extent the child understands the purpose of advertising, the conditions which foster a child's recall of advertising information, and the level of critical skill a child uses in evaluating advertising messages. The decision-making area covers product requests and a child's desire for advertised products.

Choate speaks as an informed participant in the change process. He sketches in the essential political background and outlines the development of the citizen action group movement. He further develops the arena as an interactive one involving federal regulatory agencies and the academic and business communities. In the concluding portion of the chapter, one participates first-hand in a current scene within the political drama—experiencing the tension, the complexity, and the fragility within the change process.

As her chapter title suggests, Griffin develops the basic premise that "children's television, including children's television advertising, can and should be made better [p. 339]." She follows this premise with the corollary that future change will occur only if those who care about the television medium and children are willing to be constructively critical of its past in order to constructively guide its future. Looking initially at its past, she makes a distinction between quantitative and qualitative change—limiting some content versus improving quality. She discusses the influence advertising can have on programming as a funding source and a source of new ideas and methods, and she addresses the question of "how advertising itself might develop in the future as a positive element in children's television [p. 343]."

15

Children's Television Advertising: History of the Issue

RICHARD P. ADLER

Concern over the effects of television advertising on children is not new. It can be traced back at least to 1961, when the National Association of Broadcasters adopted guidelines regulating toy advertising on television to children. However, only within the past few years has children's television advertising emerged as a major national policy issue.

Today, the principle that children are a special television audience deserving special protection in terms of advertising has been widely accepted by both industry and government policymakers. This chapter will examine how this came about, largely as the result of efforts by consumer groups such as Action for Children's Television and the Council on Children, Media and Merchandising, with assistance from the accumulated body of research evidence on the effects of television advertising on children. We will look first at the evolution of television programming and advertising intended for children, then at the emergence of concern about the possible negative effects of the advertising, and finally at the increasingly important role played by empirical research in documenting the actual effects of advertising on children.

CHILDREN AND THE FACES OF TELEVISION:
Teaching, Violence, Selling

The Evolution of Children's
Programming and Advertising

Long before television became available to the public, there was little doubt that the medium would be developed as a profit-making enterprise controlled by private (though government regulated) interests whose revenues would come from advertising. Writing nearly 20 years before the general introduction of television service, Felix (1931) recognized that the battle over the control of broadcasting had already been fought and decided

> The precedents established by sound broadcasting apply so logically to television that it will be next to impossible to establish the newer field on a different basis. . . . Television will find a complete structure ready to commercialize it. Broadcasting stations have organized personnel and established contacts in the advertising field, the advertising agencies have specialists in handling radio problems for their clients, and the advertiser is already accustomed to radio as a medium of approach to the public. Advertising will be ready for the visual medium long before the visual medium is ready for advertising [p. 116].

And so it was. When television arrived after World War II, the only major question of concern to government regulators (and it proved a difficult one) was how to allocate scarce television licenses among the competing private applicants. Noncommercial interests were recognized when the Federal Communications Commission reserved a portion of channel allocations for "educational" broadcasting in 1952. Essentially, however, there was no effective opposition—or alternative—to the commercialization of the new medium.

Certainly, the general public was happy with what it was offered. As soon as television service became available, Americans began buying television sets at a remarkable rate. While less than one household out of a hundred had a set in 1947, just under one out of ten had one by 1950. By 1960 nine out of ten homes were equipped with television, and by 1970 television ownership was virtually universal, with many homes having two or more sets.

The growth of television's advertising revenues paralleled the growth of the television audience. In 1950 the industry as a whole had revenues just over $100 million. By 1960 revenues had reached $1.2 billion. In 1976 the television industry showed a profit of $1.2 billion on total revenues of $5.2 billion (Sterling & Haight, 1978).

The development of children's programming and advertising represents but one chapter in the story of American television. Although this is a story which has yet to be told in detail, it is possible to trace the general outlines of its evolution—an evolution linked closely to the overall economic development of the medium. As we shall see, one reason that advertising to children did not emerge as an issue until relatively recently is that for many years, broadcasters did not consider their audience of child viewers as a particularly valuable market for advertisers.

In the very beginning of commercial television, children's programming was given a greater prominence than it would ever have again. In the late 1940s the primary purpose of programs was not to provide an audience for advertising but to help promote the sale of television sets. Not until the number of sets in use began to increase rapidly in the mid-1950s was there a meaningful national television audience for commercials. As a result, these early years were "probably the only time in the history of commercial television when the primary concern of the industry was with programming that would appeal to viewers rather than attract advertising sponsors [Melody, 1973, p. 36]." Programs for children were a significant part of this strategy. For parents, children's programming provided a powerful inducement (or a useful excuse) to invest in a television set.

Almost all the early network children's programs were either live action (e.g., *Captain Video; Hopalong Cassidy; Mr. I. Magination*) or featured puppets (e.g., *Howdy Doody; Kukla, Fran and Ollie*); many were carried during the early evening hours when the child audience was largest (e.g., *Howdy Doody* was broadcast at 5:30 P.M.; *Kukla, Fran and Ollie* at 7:00 P.M.). Some of the programs were sponsored, in many cases, by cereal manufacturers who simply switched their child-directed advertising from radio to television. However, approximately half of all children's programming in 1949 was offered by the networks on a "sustaining" basis—with no commercial sponsorship.

As the size of the viewing audience began to expand in the early 1950s, the economic importance of advertising also grew. Sponsors began to take control of programming, and advertisers were unwilling to pay as much for reaching children as they were for reaching adults. As a result, children's programs began to lose their places in the prime-time schedule and were shifted to the less valuable morning and early afternoon hours.

This trend was checked temporarily in 1954, when ABC scored an unexpected success with a new prime-time program called *Disneyland*. Since most households contained only one television set, programs which appealed to children as well as to adults were seen as a way of attracting entire families. Thus, much of the advertising which supported this sort of children's programming was for adult-oriented products. Programs intended solely for specialized audiences continued to be perceived as uneconomical. Melody (1973) notes that "with sponsors shifting to prime-time family programming [in the mid-1950s], such network children's favorites as *Mickey Mouse Club, Howdy Doody,* and *Kukla, Fran and Ollie* became network casualties [p. 44]." In fact, the networks entirely abandoned the 4:00–7:00 P.M. period, returning it to the local stations. After a period of experimentation, many of these stations found a profitable formula for the late afternoon hours by offering old movies and theatrical cartoons introduced by a local "host" who helped sell products to the child audience.

By the 1960s prime-time advertising was reaching the saturation point, as was television set ownership. The networks realized that if they were to continue to increase their earnings, they would have to find new sources of income. The experience of local stations had demonstrated that children's programming could be profitable. Saturday morning, "once regarded as time for do-good programs to please the women's groups [Barnouw, 1975, p. 348]," was a period when few adults were willing to watch television, but which was capable of drawing a large child audience. The "kidvid ghetto" was born.

Although advertising rates for children continued to be lower than rates for adults, the networks discovered ways of keeping down the costs of children's programming: Cartoons made expressly for television using cost-saving, "limited animation" techniques became a Saturday morning staple, and further savings were realized by repeating each new episode many times, compared to a single rerun for most prime-time programming. In addition, broadcasters allowed themselves, through the National Association of Broadcasters' *Television Code* (1965), to see twice as much advertising time during children's programming as was permitted during prime-time.

The formula proved successful, and toy, cereal, and candy makers quickly found that Saturday morning advertising was an effective way to sell their products to a national audience of children. Thus, "by 1967 the three networks were engaged in an increasingly intense competition for the attention of the weekend television-viewing child, which had developed into a multimillion dollar market in network television alone [Melody, 1973, p. 51]." By 1970 combined revenue for the three networks from their weekend children's programming was $66.8 million (Pearce, 1974). In terms of the competition for ratings, the use of programming and counterprogramming strategies, and the close links between the needs of sponsors and programming decisions, Saturday morning had become virtually a carbon copy of prime-time except that the target audience for both programs and commercials was not adults but children between the ages of 2 and 12.

Development of the Children's Television Advertising Issue

As we noted, advertising to children did not emerge as a significant issue until the 1970s. Before the 1970s complaints about broadcast advertising were limited almost completely to irritation with adult-oriented advertising. Thus, a survey of audience attitudes about radio during its heyday reported that listeners disliked commercials which used "hard sell" techniques, commercials which were "boring and repetitious," and the fact that commercials interrupted programs (Lazarsfeld & Kendall, 1948). The possible adverse effect of radio advertising on children was not mentioned as an issue at all. In fact, nowhere in this survey are children mentioned as a subject of special concern in terms of radio listening.

In contrast, when television arrived, the possible effects of the new medium on children quickly became an issue—probably because children soon were spending much more time watching television than they had spent listening to radio. However, the first major study of American children and television makes only passing mention of advertising. The authors stated that Lazarsfeld and Kendall's "observations on attitudes toward radio (advertising) . . . might be repeated verbatim today with reference to television [Schramm, Lyle, & Parker, 1961, p. 56]."

A later survey, one of those conducted periodically since 1959 for the television industry by the Roper Organization, indicates that the level of adult dissatisfaction with television advertising has remained relatively constant over more than a decade. In 1963, 39% of adult respondents stated that they disliked "practically all" or "most" commercials on television, while 55% considered most commercials to be "perfectly all right" or even enjoyable. In 1974 the responses to the same question were 40% negative and 58% positive (Roper Organization, 1975). It is interesting to note that the first time any question concerning attitudes about *children's* television advertising appeared in the Roper survey was in 1971. What had happened, after more than 20 years of television, to make children's advertising finally a sufficiently important issue that it was recognized by broadcasters?

In retrospect, the emergence of children's television advertising as an issue can be seen as a logical, probably inevitable, reaction to the identification of children as a special target audience by sponsors and broadcasters in the mid-1960s. However, the issue did not begin to attract wide attention until a group of mothers in Massachusetts began organizing and protesting. What turned out to be the founding meeting of Action for Children's Television (ACT) took place in January, 1968 when a group of mothers—including Peggy Charren, Evelyn Sarson, Lillian Ambrosino, and Judith Chalfen—met in Newton, a suburb of Boston, to discuss what they considered the poor quality of television being offered to their young children. Although they began with programming, their focus soon shifted to the role of advertising (Cole & Oettinger, 1978:

> "When we first talked, we were most concerned with violence," Judy Chalfen recalls, "but we got off that. Violence is so hard to define and really, it's just part of the whole picture of poor quality—something we were all aware of." Charren adds, "We knew that if we got into violence alone, we would be treading into the area of censor-

ship. That's not what we wanted. But after almost a year of discussion and argument, we could all agree that we didn't want our children to be dismissed by the medium simply as a market—a group of naive little consumers." Evelyn Sarson notes, "The only point of television programs, as we saw them, was to sell things to kids. But it wasn't enough for us to say that. We decided we needed statistics to back us up. So the first thing we did was to sit and watch hours of television [p. 248–249]."

At first, the group members concentrated on local television. After monitoring *Romper Room* in the spring of 1969, the mothers circulated a petition protesting the show's practice of having the host sell products, including a line of "Romper Room Toys," directly to the audience.

Before long, the group was turning its attention to the national level. In late 1969 ACT members asked to meet with officials of the three networks to discuss their concerns and urge them to adopt a "code of ethics" that would, among other things, clearly separate programs from commercials. Officials at ABC and NBC refused outright to meet with the group. CBS was more hospitable but indicated little inclination to make any unilateral changes which would put it at an economic disadvantage to its competitors. By early 1970 ACT was looking to the federal government for help.

In February of that year, ACT met for the first time with members of the Federal Communications Commission (FCC) and presented a petition asking the FCC to adopt the following rules:

1. There shall be no sponsorship and no commercials on children's programs.
2. No performer shall be permitted to use or mention products, services, or stores by brand name during children's programs, nor shall such names be included in any way during children's programs.
3. As part of its public service requirement, each station shall provide daily programming for children and in no case shall this be less than 14 hours a week.

At the time that ACT presented its petition, "the Commission didn't have what could be called a policy toward children's programming [Cole & Oettinger, 1978, p. 248]." Nonetheless, several FCC commissioners, including then-Chairman Dean Burch, were sympathetic to ACT's concerns. Within a week, the FCC had published ACT's proposals and asked for comments on them. Not surprisingly, the responses from sponsors and broadcasters were uniformly and vehemently negative. However, ACT's leaders were able to use the controversy to generate considerable publicity about their organization and the issues they were raising. Articles about ACT's campaign began appearing in magazines and newspapers across the country. In October 1970, ACT attracted additional attention when it held what turned out to be the first annual Symposium on Children and Television.

Psychologists, lawyers, consumer advocates, and government officials made presentations to the conference; these presentations were soon issued in paperback (*Action for Children's Television*, 1971).

At about the same time, a second front against advertising to children was being opened, this one—the Council on Children, Media and Merchandising (CCMM)—aimed primarily at the food products being sold to children via television commercials. Robert Choate had been a staff member of the 1969 White House Conference on Food, Nutrition, and Health. In July, 1970, in testimony before a Senate committee, he criticized children's breakfast cereals as providing what he characterized as "empty calories." In later testimony, Choate (1975) stated, "Eighteen months later, 36 of 40 children's cereals I criticized had been reformulated. Vitamins and minerals were added, but the sugar content still remained high. The Council on Children, Media and Merchandising was then born [p. 55]." Choate and the CCMM pressed for the reform of children's advertising by petitioning the FCC and FTC, testifying before a variety of congressional committees, and encouraging research on the effects of television advertising on children.

As 1971 began, the pace of activity quickened. In January the FCC issued a formal notice of inquiry and proposed rulemaking "looking toward the elimination of sponsorship and commercial content in children's programming and the establishment of a weekly 14-hour quota" as called for by ACT (Federal Communications Commission, 1971). The following month, FCC Chairman Burch (1971), in a speech to the American Advertising Federation, endorsed the principle that children should be regarded as a special and especially vulnerable audience in terms of advertising:

> I believe that in the case of advertising directed to children, the standards of what is false and deceptive must be judged in light of the crucial fact that the audience is so unsophisticated, so young and trusting. It is, I submit, intolerable to seek to bilk the innocent with shoddy advertising appeals. As some person aptly put it, that is akin to statutory rape.

One by-product of the FCC's inquiry was some impressive evidence that concern about the impact of television and television advertising on children had apparently become widespread. Cole and Oettinger (1978) report that by July 1971, "roughly 80,000 letters in support of the ACT proposal had been sent to the Commission." In September of that year, Chairman Burch announced creation of a "permanent children's unit" within the FCC.

Despite these encouraging developments, ACT decided not to rely solely on the FCC for relief and turned its attention to the agency charged with the regulation of advertising, the Federal Trade Commission (FTC). Up to that point, the FTC had acted from time to time against specific children's commercials it considered to be deceptive or misleading, but it had never developed any general rules regulating children's advertising. In the 5-month period from December 1971 through April 1972, ACT petitioned the FTC to prohibit all televised advertising for toys to children, to prohibit the selling of all food products to children on television, and to prohibit the advertising of vitamins directly to children by three major drug manufacturers.

By this time, pressure was building rapidly for sponsors and broadcasters to do something about advertising to children. In the summer of 1972 the reform movement gained its first substantive victory: Three months after ACT filed its petition against vitamin advertising to children, the three drug companies named in the petition agreed voluntarily to withdraw all their commercials intended for children. Then in January 1973 the National Association of Broadcasters (NAB) announced changes in the *Television Code* to prohibit the practice of host selling in children's programs and to reduce the allowable advertising time in children's programming from 16 minutes to 12 minutes per hour. (The following year, the NAB further cut the maximum allowable advertising time on weekend children's programming to 10 minutes per hour by the end of 1974 and to 9.5 minutes by 1975. In January 1979 ABC announced that it was unilaterally reducing the commercial time on its weekend children's programs to 7.5 minutes by January 1980.) In March 1974 the Council of Better Business Bureaus established a Children's Advertising Review Unit within its National Advertising Division. The new unit, which developed its own set of *Children's Advertising Guidelines* and reviewed commercials about which it received complaints, represented a second self-regulatory mechanism, supplementing the NAB's Code Authority.

There were other signs that the legitimacy of concern about children's television advertising was becoming increasingly recognized. In a speech to the Young Lawyer's Section of the American Bar Association, then-Chairman of the FTC, Lewis Engman, announced his agency's interest in children's advertising. Citing legal precedents for providing special protection for children, Engman (1973) declared that:

> The time has come for action on children's television advertising. . . . If television advertising deceives our children, if it frustrates them through false or misleading promises, if it promotes the sale of dangerous toys or other products, if it fosters dietary habits which endanger their health—if it does these things, I think television advertising will soon find itself circumscribed by legal restrictions and requirements.

Engman concluded by announcing the formation of a committee composed of advertising, broadcasting, and consumer representatives whose task, under FTC sponsorship, would be to devise a voluntary code for children's television advertising acceptable to all parties.

All these actions and statements suggested that the issue of children's television advertising had grown rapidly since it first emerged in 1969.

However, proponents of reform were about to discover that while small victories were possible, any truly major changes in children's advertising would be difficult to achieve. Thus, the FTC's committee met several times but made little progress. After a series of proposals submitted by the consumer representatives was rejected by industry members in early 1974, the effort reached an impasse and was abandoned. In November 1974 the Federal Communications Commission finally issued a report on the children's programming inquiry it had begun in 1971. Noting that "broadcasters have a special responsibility to children," the Commission concluded that "special safeguards may be required" to protect children against possible advertising abuses (Federal Communications Commission, 1974, p. 39,399). However, the Commission did not adopt any of ACT's proposed rules and, in fact, decided against requiring any specific changes in children's programming or advertising practices. The Commission clearly indicated its preference for industry self-regulation over government action.

Thus, by the mid-1970s, the reform groups had brought about few significant changes in children's advertising but had succeeded in generating wide awareness of the issues and had identified a number of questionable practices. A later review (Adler, Friedlander, Lesser, Meringoff, Robertson, Rossiter, & Ward, 1977) noted that all the various issues were based on four fundamental concerns:

1. That children were being exposed to advertising for products or categories of products (e.g., drugs and heavily sugared foods) which might be hazardous or unhealthy if misused
2. That specific techniques used in television advertising (e.g., host selling, use of premium offers) may be deceptive or misleading to children who lack the skills to evaluate them properly
3. That any advertising directed to children is de facto bad because it exploits their vulnerabilities
4. That long-term cumulative exposure to television advertising may have adverse consequences on the development of children's values, attitudes, and behaviors

During the remainder of the 1970s, each of these concerns would continue to receive attention.

The Emergence of Research on Children's Television Advertising

One reason—though certainly not the only nor even the most important reason—for the lack of more vigorous regulatory action during the early 1970s was the absence of research documenting the actual effects of advertising on children. In the absence of such research, the allegations of the reform groups were simply that—allegations. Virtually all the research on children's advertising before 1970 had been conducted by advertising agencies or by private research firms working under contract to sponsors. Most of this research was concerned with testing the effectiveness of individual commercials; almost all of it was proprietary.

Even after children's advertising became a controversial policy issue in the 1970s, academic research in this area continued to lag. First to appear were content analyses of commercials directed to children (e.g., Barcus, 1971; Winick, Williamson, Chuzmir, & Winick, 1973). These studies helped document the amount and nature of advertising to which children were actually being exposed. Thus, Barcus (1971), in a study sponsored by ACT, provided data on the kinds of appeals and production techniques used in children's commercials, as well as the proportion of advertising for various product categories (e.g., toys, cereals, candies, and snack foods). Because advertising practices change over time, periodic content analyses of this kind have played a useful role in keeping information up to date on the actual content of commercials.

A second important strand of nonbehavioral research in this area has consisted of economic studies of children's television. Pearce (1972, 1974), in studies prepared for the FCC's Children's Television Inquiry, ascertained the financial contribution of children's advertising to overall network revenues and argued that the amount of commercial time in children's programs could be substantially reduced "with minimal overall financial hardship." Melody (1973), in another study sponsored by ACT, argued that broadcasters were financially capable of offering good quality children's programming with no commercial sponsorship.

The first major behavioral research on children's advertising appeared in 1972 as part of the report of the Surgeon General's Scientific Advisory Committee on Television and Social Behavior. Although that report focused on the issue of televised violence and children, the accompanying technical papers contained a series of related studies by Ward and his colleagues on the effects of television advertising on children and adolescents (see Ward, 1972, for a summary of this work). Included in this research were observational studies of children watching television commercials, interviews with children about their attitudes toward and understanding of advertising, and a survey of mothers concerning their children's purchase influence attempts and the mothers' responses to them. Among other results, Ward reported that young (kindergarten age) children were confused "about the relationships between commercials and reality" and "exhibited no understanding of the purpose of commercials [Ward, 1972, p. 440]."

Additional studies on various aspects of children's advertising appeared over the next several years, but a 1974 review of research in the field still found a relatively small amount of work (Sheikh, Prasad, & Rao, 1974). The authors suggested three reasons for the apparent lack of interest among researchers: (a) compared to the effect of televised violence, political socialization through television, and the instructional uses of television, this field is not considered sufficiently respectable in academic circles; (b) many researchers share the belief that research would have little impact; and (c) research findings might be used poorly by policymakers (Sheikh *et al.*, 1974, p. 133).

Although this diagnosis was accurate historically, signs began to appear in the mid-1970s that policymakers were beginning to recognize the need for empirical research. In the speech cited above, for example, FTC Chairman Engman (1973) observed that "there is really no definitive pool of information on the specific impact of television advertising on children. This remains a field which should be subject to more extensive research [unpaginated]." Even more important, research findings began to play a real if modest role in the formulation of policy. For example, in deciding against banning the use of premium offers in children's television advertising, the FTC made explicit reference to research which found that such offers did not, as had been alleged by critics of the practice, tend to distract children from other attributes of the products being advertised (Federal Trade Commission, 1977). The Federal Trade Commission also used empirical evidence in considering the alleged deceptiveness of nutritional claims made in commercials to children for several food products (FTC, 1975).

From the mid-1970s on, the quantity and diversity of research in the area increased markedly. A 1977 review of available research (Adler *et al.*), while stating that "scientific inquiry into the effects of television advertising on children is still in its infancy [p. 151]" also noted that more than three-quarters of all studies included in the review had appeared after 1974. What was perhaps most noteworthy about this report was that, for the first time, a review of research results in the area was organized around outstanding policy issues. On the basis of statements from government, industry, and consumer groups and a survey of representatives of these groups, Adler *et al.* derived a list of 10 major policy issues, then reviewed the current state of knowledge relevant to each issue (see Chapter 16 for more information). The authors concluded that "the current state of knowledge is still inadequate in some areas, but is sufficient in others to provide meaningful guidance to policymakers [p. i]." Specifically, the authors found that "the variable that emerges most clearly across numerous studies as a strong determinant of children's perceptions of television advertising is the child's age. Existing research clearly establishes that . . . to treat all children from 2 to 12 as a homogeneous group masks important, perhaps crucial differences [Adler *et al.*, 1977, p. i]."

The publication of the Federal Trade Commission *Staff Report on Television Advertising to Children* (1978b) represents a final milestone in the utilization of research in the development of regulatory actions. Thus, in calling for the banning of all commercials directed to children too young to understand their selling intent, the staff report cited empirical evidence regarding age-related differences in comprehending and responding to advertising. The FTC's subsequent notice of proposed rule making (Federal Trade Commission, 1978a) and the voluminous testimony submitted to the FTC's hearings on these proposals have further emphasized the role of empirical research.

Of course, research results, no matter how unequivocal, are unlikely to prove decisive in formulating regulatory policies; legal, economic, and, particularly, political forces will continue to operate in policymaking.[1] But however this current rule making is resolved, children's television advertising will continue to attract the attention of researchers and policymakers for some time to come.

References

Action for children's television. New York: Discus Books, 1971.

Adler, R. P., Friedlander, B. Z., Lesser, G. S., Meringoff, L., Robertson, T. S., Rossiter, J. R., & Ward, S. *Research on the effects of television advertising on children.* Washington, D.C.: United States Government Printing Office, 1977. (Revised ed., Lexington, Massachusetts: Lexington Books, 1980).

Barcus, E. *Saturday children's television: A report of television programming and advertising on Boston commercial television.* Newtonville, Massachusetts: Action for Children's Television, 1971.

Barnouw, E. *Tube of plenty.* New York and London: Oxford Univ. Press, 1975.

Burch, D. Speech to the American Advertising Federation. Washington, D.C., February 2, 1971.

Choate, R. Statement before the Subcommittee on Communications of the Committee on Interstate and Foreign Commerce, United States House of Representatives, July 14, 1975.

Cole, B., & Oettinger, M. *Reluctant regulators.* Reading, Massachusetts: Addison-Wesley, 1978.

Engman, L. Speech to the Young Lawyers' Section of the American Bar Association, Washington, D.C., August 6, 1973.

Federal Communications Commission. Notice of inquiry and notice of proposed rulemaking. Docket number 19142. *Federal Register*, 1971, *36*(20), 1429–1430.

Federal Communications Commission. Children's television programs: Report and policy statement. *Federal Register*, 1974, *39*(215), 396–409.

Federal Trade Commission. In the Matter of General Foods Corporation Complaint; Decision and Order (Docket C-2733), 1975.

Federal Trade Commission. Statement of reasons for rejecting the proposed guide on television advertising of premiums to children. *Federal Register*, 1977, *42*, 15069.

Federal Trade Commission. Children's advertising: Proposed trade regulation rulemaking and public hearing. *Federal Register*, 1978, *43*(82), 17967–17972. (a)

---

[1] The action taken by Congress to curb the FTC's power in general, and the children's television advertising rule-making in particular, is a graphic demonstration of this fact.

Federal Trade Commission. *Staff report on television advertising to children.* Washington, D.C.: United States Government Printing Office, 1978. (b)

Felix, E. *Television: Its methods and uses.* New York: McGraw-Hill, 1931.

Lazarsfeld, P. F., & Kendall, P. *Radio listening in America.* New York: Prentice-Hall, 1948.

Melody, W. *Children's television.* New Haven: Yale Univ. Press, 1973.

National Association of Broadcasters. *The television code.* (10th ed.), August, 1965.

Pearce, A. *The economics of network children's television programming.* Unpublished manuscript, Federal Communications Commission, 1972.

Pearce, A. *The economics of children's television: An assessment of the impact of a reduction in the amount of advertising.* Unpublished manuscript, Federal Communications Commission, 1974.

Roper Organization, Incorporated. *Trends in public attitudes toward television and other mass media, 1959–1974.* New York: Television Information Office, 1975.

Schramm, W., Lyle, J., & Parker, E. B. *Television in the lives of our children.* Stanford: Stanford Univ. Press, 1961.

Sheikh, A. A., Prasad, V. K., & Rao, T. R. Children's TV commercials: A review of research. *Journal of Communication,* 1974, *24*(4), 126–136.

Sterling, C. H., & Haight, T. R. *The mass media: Aspen Institute guide to communication industry trends.* New York: Praeger, 1978.

Ward, S. Effects of television advertising on children and adolescents. In E. A. Rubinstein, G. A. Comstock, & J. P. Murray (Eds.), *Television and social behavior* (Vol. 4). Washington, D.C.: United States Government Printing Office, 1972.

Winick, C. L., Williamson, L. G., Chuzmir, S. F., & Winick, M. P. *Children's television commercials: A content analysis.* New York: Praeger, 1973.

16

Children and Television Advertising: Policy Issues, Perspectives, and the Status of Research

JOHN R. ROSSITER

This chapter delineates and critically examines policy issues in the controversial area of television advertising directed to children. The chapter has four sections. The first section presents a unique endeavor to define the concept of a policy issue and then provides an analytical framework for classifying policy issues in children's television advertising. The second section utilizes the definition and analytical framework to evaluate major statements about children's television advertising policy that have appeared to date. The third section focuses on the contributions and the limitations of children's television advertising research as an input to policy decisions and describes the likely role of research in the ultimate determination of policy. The fourth section presents a summary and brief outlook on the "selling face" of children's television and the future direction of policy in this area.

The Nature of Policy Issues

Everyone seems to have an implicit understanding of what a policy issue is. Yet the concept has nowhere, to my knowledge, been explicitly

CHILDREN AND THE FACES OF TELEVISION:
Teaching, Violence, Selling

defined. Here I will first offer an operational definition applicable to policy issues in children's television advertising. I will then expand on this definition to provide an analytical framework which will serve as a basis for policy issue evaluation in the remainder of the chapter.

Policy Issues: A Definition

Policy issues in children's television advertising arise when (a) a specific advertising practice; or (b) an entire category of advertising is perceived; as (c) utilizing means; or (d) resulting in ends; which are (e) contrary to the ethical values; (f) held by some publicly significant party. Although the concept of a policy issue is defined here in the context of children's television advertising, it may be noted that a policy issue *in general* arises when some action is perceived by some publicly significant party as utilizing means or resulting in ends which are contrary to the ethical values held by that party. The term *ethical values* here refers to beliefs that given modes of conduct are right versus wrong or good versus bad.

The utility of this six-component definition of policy issues in children's television advertising will, I hope, become evident as the chapter proceeds. We will see, for example, that some publicly significant parties [component (f) in the definition], notably industry groups who have assumed self-regulatory responsibility, focus mainly on specific advertising practices (a); whereas others, notably consumer advocacy groups and federal regulatory agencies, tend to focus on entire categories of advertising (b). Similarly, some statements of policy identify only the means underlying certain practices or categories of advertising (c); others identify only ends (d); and still others, though infrequently, identify both the means and the ends. Inextricably woven through every policy issue in children's television advertising are the ethical values (e) and consequent value judgments of the publicly significant parties with whom the issues originate.

An Analytical Framework

The preceding definition can be expanded to provide an analytical framework for classifying policy issues in children's television advertising (see Rossiter, 1977, for an earlier version). The analytical framework postulates that policy issues can be regarded as propositions or statements, the subjects of which are either particular advertising practices or else entire categories of advertising, and the predicates of which (a) are either empirically verifiable (facts) or not empirically verifiable (values); and (b) refer to either alleged causes (means) or to alleged effects (ends). The framework is shown schematically in Table 16.1. As can be seen

Table 16.1
An Analytical Framework for Classifying Policy Issues in Children's Television Advertising

	Proposition refers to		FTC Act concepts
	Means	Ends	
Facts (empirically verifiable proposition)	False advertising	Misleading advertising	Deception
Values (nonverifiable proposition)	Unfair means	Unfair ends	Unfairness

from the table, the two dimensions lead to a fourfold typology of policy issues. Why are these two dimensions important?

The first dimension, that of empirical verifiability, bears critically on the potential contribution of research as an input to policy. The notion of empirical verifiability derives most directly from the philosophical arguments of A. J. Ayer (1936; 1960). Some propositions express matters of fact; that is, they can, at least in principle, be proven true or false. For example, the proposition "television advertising leads to parent–child conflict" can be subjected to empirical investigation and the extent of its truth or falsehood established to some criterion of certainty. Other propositions, in contrast, express matters of value; that is, they cannot be proven true or false but only agreed with or disagreed with in an attitudinal or emotional sense. For example, the proposition "parent–child conflict is bad" expresses a value, an ethical judgement of rightness or wrongness, not something that is capable of empirical proof through research. Sometimes, policy issues are stated in a more complex form which includes a factual and a value proposition, but we shall see that such complex statements are reducible to simpler, unitary propositions.

The principle of ethics which applies universally in children's television advertising policy is Durkheim's (1915) "social approbative theory" which holds that "X is good or right" = "society approves of X." More precisely, according to the earlier definition of policy issues, the ethical principle in children's television advertising policy might be called "party approbative theory" in that some publicly significant party, such as the Federal Trade Commission (FTC), consumer advocacy groups, the general public, or industry representatives, is doing the approving. Empirical research obviously has no role in value propositions incorporated in policy issues, except in the minor sense that research methodology may be used to poll the value judgments of relevant parties.

The second dimension, that of whether the proposition entailed in the policy issue refers to the means involved in or to the ends resulting from an advertising practice or category of advertising, is equally important. The importance of the means–ends distinction is dramatically illustrated in the current policy controversy (discussed more extensively later in this chapter). Consumer advocacy groups and the FTC have alleged that it is "inherently deceptive and unfair" to advertise to children who cannot understand the selling purpose of advertising. This is a *means* proposition—no effects or ends are specified. Industry representatives have demanded to know what (harmful) effects have resulted from advertising to such children. That is, they are calling for an *ends* proposition. The FTC has recently responded to this demand in a very interesting way, as we shall see in the next section of the chapter.

Together, the two dimensions produce four categories of policy issues as shown in Table 16.1. These categories refer to specific advertising practices or to entire categories of advertising that are false, misleading, employ unfair means, or result in unfair ends. These categories are illustrated briefly below and then are used in the policy analyses that follow.

False advertising is represented by propositions that are empirically verifiable (factual) but that focus only on advertising inputs (means) and not on advertising effects. It is a commonly held ethical value that the advertiser should not lie, deliberately or inadvertently, even if the falsehood has no effect on the consumer. For example, advertisements promoting mystical or occult services are prohibited on television because such services are regarded as being empirically false, regardless of whether consumers personally believe in the truth or falsehood of these phenomena. Interestingly, the FTC occasionally makes exception to this principle and allows "white lies." A classic case is the legally permissible substitution of shaving cream for real cream or ice cream in food advertising, where the lighting may melt the real product during filming. Generally, however, both self-regulatory and federal regulatory policies prohibit the use of objectively false claims or techniques regardless of any associated consequences or ends that might result.

Misleading advertising is represented by propositions that are empirically verifiable (factual) but that focus only on the effects of advertising (ends). The distinction between this and false advertising—both of which come under the FTC Act's concept of "deception"—is evident when one realizes that an advertising practice or category of advertising may be factually true yet result in consumer beliefs that are factually false (see Gardner, 1975; Jacoby & Small, 1975). For example, an orange juice beverage advertised to children might claim to be the "best there is." This claim might be objectively true, with the product consisting of the highest percentage and highest quality orange juice on the market. However, it may mislead children to believe that the product is uniquely superior to other orange juice beverages, which may not be a factually true belief (other orange juice beverages could have equally good ingredients and also be the "best there is"). Of course, advertising can also be false *and* misleading, but note that policy issues regard either case as sufficient to prohibit the offending practice or category.

Unfair means represent propositions that are not empirically verifiable (values) and that focus only on advertising inputs (means) without regard to effects. For example, the policy statements of both the self-regulatory codes and the FTC regard it as unfair to allow children's program characters to serve as product presenters in advertising within or adjacent to the character's own program. No evidence has ever been submitted showing that this "host selling" practice results in any particular consequences for children (Adler, Lesser, Meringoff, Robertson, Rossiter, & Ward, 1980). The practice is simply regarded as per se unfair; that is, it is regarded as contrary to the ethical values of both the self-regulatory parties and the FTC.

Unfair ends represent propositions that are not empirically verifiable (values) and that focus only on the effects (ends) of a given advertising practice or category of advertising. An excellent example is provided by the category of proprietary or over-the-counter drug advertising, which is prevented by self-regulatory codes from being directed to children or aired during children's programs. It is not that this advertising is false or misleading nor that it involves unfair means in its presentation. It is that one of the alleged effects of such advertising would be that children developed "excessive" beliefs in the efficacy of these products and were "overly predisposed" toward requesting them or, when older, taking them when illness symptoms occurred (Robertson, Rossiter, & Gleason, 1979). It is the "excessive" and "overly predisposed" which are judged the unfair ends. In such policy issues it is the end results of the advertising that are considered to be unfair. One cannot prove fairness empirically; one simply agrees or disagrees depending on one's ethical values.

An Analysis of Policy Issues to Date

There have been five major statements of policy issues in children's television advertising to date: those of the self-regulatory codes, the Federal Communications Commission (FCC) in 1974, the National Science Foundation-sponsored review in 1977, the FTC Advisory Staff proposal in 1978, and the FTC Presiding Officer's recommendations of July, 1979. These statements can be readily classified into the four categories of false advertising, misleading advertising, unfair means, or unfair ends that I have just described, and they will be reviewed here in terms of this analytical framework.

Self-Regulatory Codes

Television advertising directed to children or aired during children's programs (i.e., children's television advertising as I have used the term here) has been and is at present governed directly by the self-regulatory codes of the National Association of Broadcasters (1975; periodically issued) and the National Advertising Division of the Council of Better Business Bureaus (1977). The two codes are quite similar in their identification of policy issues and share two characteristics which are crucial to the present analysis:

1. The codes identify as policy issues only *specific advertising practices and certain subcategories* of advertising. They do not question the general legitimacy of television advertising directed to children.
2. The codes focus primarily on *means* issues, that is, deceptive means (false advertising) and unfair means. They usually do not specify effects or end results that may be deceptive or unfair.

The first characteristic reflects the broad value judgment of those who prepared the codes (manufacturers, advertisers, and academic advisers) that, in general, advertising directed to children is a legitimate personal, social, and economic activity. Other publicly significant parties, notably Action for Children's Television (ACT), the Council on Children, Media and Merchandising (CCMM), and also the FTC, do not share the value judgment that television advertising directed to children is a legitimate activity. A major source of policy dispute, therefore, is whether only specific advertising practices should be regulated, whether advertising for certain products should be regulated, or whether children's television advertising in general should be regulated. As the FTC has recently brought this dispute more clearly into focus, I will consider the grounds for it in the sections dealing with the FTC's policy position.

The second characteristic, the codes' focus on means issues rather than effects or ends issues, is a subtle one. It is true that the self-regulatory codes identify various effects which children's television advertising should either avoid, since they are negatively valued, or aim for, since they are positively valued. The National Advertising Division (NAD) code is the more explicit in this respect, referring to such negative effects as unreasonable expectations of product quality and behaviors that can affect the child's health and well-being and to such positive effects as friendship, kindness, and constructive parent–child relationships. The subtlety, however, is that many of the prohibited practices specified in the codes *are not tied to these effects.*

Basically, the prohibitions, like that on advertising medications to children, reflect a value judgment about the types of products and the types of advertising practices that are "appropriate" for child audiences. They are not based on demonstrated negative effects from such advertising. Thus, manufacturer and advertiser acceptance of these "no effects specified" prohibitions is paradoxical in the context of their strong criticism of proposed FTC rules that do not identify effects. Proponents of self-regulatory codes, which themselves rely primarily on a means definition of policy issues, are demanding that the FTC adopt not a means definition but a means-and-ends definition of policy issues. Paradox aside, the important point here is that both these major parties to the controversy have primarily adopted a means approach to policy issues, with no clear effects specified.

Although the self-regulatory codes' policy statements themselves rarely specify effects, it is noteworthy that the NAD's executive decisions based on its code do, in fact, rely quite heavily on allegations of an effect —misleading advertising. Most of the cases heard by the Children's Advertising Review Unit of NAD have involved advertisements that are alleged to result in beliefs about the product that are untrue (National Advertising Division, 1979). Rarely have the advertisements themselves been false. Most notably, the NAD rulings have avoided the other two categories of policy issues—unfair means and unfair ends. It is in these categories of value judgments rather than empirical verifiability that the self-regulatory codes are meeting their greatest challenge from consumer advocacy groups and from the FTC.

The 1974 Federal Communications Commission Policy Statement

The FCC's role in formulating children's television advertising policy has been a relatively minor one. Its 1974 report and policy statement (Federal Communications Commission, 1974) contained just two relevant points: (a) that the amount of advertising allowable during children's programs should be reduced; and (b) that commercials during children's programs should be more clearly separated from programs. In terms of our definition of policy issues, both points refer to the entire category of children's television advertising rather than to subcategories or to specific advertising practices. This is consistent with the FCC's self-designated role (Steinberg, 1974) of concern with program content and the relationship of commercials to programs (the volume and separation issues above) rather than the content of commercials. Incredibly, the FCC's policy proposal to reduce advertising volume on children's programs has received an indirect snub from an unexpected quarter. The U.S. Department of Justice in 1979 filed suit against the National Association of Broadcasters (NAB) seeking to remove self-regulatory limits on the number of commercials that can be broadcast per hour, charging that such limits may drive advertising prices up and restrict competition.

The interesting aspect of these two policy issues from the standpoint of our analytical framework is that neither the FCC in making these policy statements nor the NAB in enacting them gave concrete reasons for reducing children's advertising volume or for trying to separate commercials more clearly from programs. The two policy issues are, therefore, based merely on value judgments about what is "proper" conduct (unfair means). It is equally surprising that neither action has been challenged in serious fashion by advertisers or broadcasters demanding to know what harmful *effects* result from advertising volume or lack of clear separation from programs.

The 1977 National Science Foundation Report

The NSF Report, as it has come to be known, reviewed policy-related statements from federal, industry, and consumer group sources and arrived at a summary list of 10 policy issues (Adler, Friedlander, Lesser, Meringoff, Robertson, Rossiter, & Ward, 1977). It may be noted, in connection with the definition of policy issues earlier, that the first five issues concern specific advertising practices; the next two concern large subcategories of advertising; and the last three concern children's television advertising in general (see Table 16.2). In what follows I will describe these issues, placing them in the analytical framework I have developed.

Program-Commercial Separation. The issue of program–commercial separation originated with the FCC and was adopted as a self-regulatory issue by the NAB. Recently, mainly through FTC action, this issue has expanded from its original focus on children's ability to distinguish advertising material from nonadvertising material to the more complex issue of whether, or at what age, children can not only recognize commercials but also understand their ostensible intentionality, that is, advertising's persuasive or selling intent. The FTC, as we shall see below, has recently advanced a complex argument linking this issue to others. As it stands, however, the program–commercial separation issue is basically one of alleged *unfair means*. In other words, according to the FCC, NAB, and FTC, children "should" be able to understand the difference between programs and commercials and, in the FTC's view, also understand that a persuasive attempt is being made. While the question of whether, or at what age, children can reliably exhibit these types of understanding is an empirically researchable one, note that the central proposition of the issue is not. The proposition, essentially, is that children should not be persuaded "without their awareness"—a value judgment about unfair means.

Format and Audiovisual Techniques. The basic concern underlying this issue is that various particular advertising formats and audiovisual techniques may mislead children. For example, particular wording in product claims, special sound effects, or special angles in photography may lead children to develop beliefs about the appearance, performance, or associated characteristics of the product that are factually untrue. Many

Table 16.2
Policy Issues Identified in the 1977 NSF Report and Their Status Relative to the FTC Presiding Officer's Recommendations

NSF report: issue and scope of issue	Policy category	FTC presiding officer's recommendations
A. Specific advertising practices		
1. Program–commercial separation	Unfair means	Subsumed in Issue 1 (selling intent)
2. Format and audiovisual techniques	Misleading	
3. Source effects and self-concept appeals	Unfair means; misleading	Subsumed in Issue 2 (ability to defend against specific techniques)
4. Premium offers	Unfair ends	
5. Violence and unsafe acts	Unfair ends	
B. Subcategories of advertising		
6. Proprietary drug advertising	Misleading; unfair ends	Judged a nonissue because not "children's advertising"
7. Food advertising	Misleading; unfair ends	Partially subsumed in Issue 3 (effects of sugared food advertising)
C. Advertising in general		
8. Volume and repetition	Unfair ends	Not directly addressed but would be affected by ban(s)
9. Consumer socialization	Unfair ends	Judged a nonissue because effects too tenuous
10. Parent–child relations	Unfair ends	Judged a nonissue because effects too mild

such instances of false beliefs have been empirically verified in NAD hearings and in FTC actions against individual advertisers. Obviously it is not feasible to conduct empirical tests in every particular instance, so policymakers, in this case the NAB and the NAD, have tried to identify classes of advertising techniques that are likely to produce misleading effects. Misleading children, intentionally or otherwise, is universally held to be unfair, so unfairness becomes an assumed characteristic. The correctness of their identification is, however, disputable and open to empirical verification that the techniques do mislead. The issue is therefore placed in the policy category of *misleading* advertising.

Source Effects and Self-Concept Appeals. Two related policy issues are actually subsumed here, as noted in the NSF report. The first is that certain types of product presenters and characters, such as celebrities or authority figures, are restricted from appearing in children's commercials because they presumably represent means of trying to persuade children that are "too powerful" or that are not based on the intrinsic merits of the product. The prohibition against these spokespersons clearly centers on *unfair means*—a value judgment. The second issue concerns appeals to children's self-concepts, for example, that by having the product they can emulate the skills of the presenter or otherwise derive personal benefits. These claims or suggestions may not be empirically valid and so the child may be misled. Accordingly, self-concept appeals can be placed in the policy category of *misleading* advertising.

Premium Offers. The critical policy dispute over the use of premium offers in children's television advertising is that they may lead children to want products for the "wrong" reason. It is not that children are led to believe anything false or different about the product. The crux of the issue is that children are making "poor" choices, not "false" ones. This is, obviously, a value judgment, and the premium issue is best categorized as involving *unfair ends.*

Violence and Unsafe Acts. Policy prohibiting violent portrayals or the depiction of unsafe behavior in children's commercials at first appears to require the empirical demonstration that violent portrayals cause aggressive behavior and that unsafe act depictions cause unsafe imitative behavior. However, no deception is involved and empirical tests are generally precluded by the value judgment that one cannot ethically test for (presumed) effects which include dangerous behaviors. Consequently, policymakers have made a value judgment about the *risk* of effects that does not depend on empirical proof and therefore reduces to a value judgment about *unfair ends.*

Proprietary Drug Advertising. Proprietary drug advertising is the first of two policy areas in which entire product categories, rather than particular advertising practices, are at issue. Analysis of the charges that led to prohibition of proprietary drug advertising directed to children or broadcast during children's programs reveals that there are two types of alleged effects: (a) that proprietary drug advertising may foster in children unrealistic beliefs about the efficacy of common medicines; and (b) that proprietary drugs are not products about which children should be making usage decisions including influencing their parents' decisions. In the first instance, the factual nature of beliefs brings the issue into the policy category of *misleading* advertising. In the second instance—since the products or their conditions of use are not themselves illegal—this policy issue can be viewed as centering on *unfair ends,* as well as involving to some extent the alleged misleading aspect just outlined.

Food Advertising. Food advertising (including beverages and snacks) is the second policy issue that pertains to an entire subcategory of children's television advertising. It has been alleged by consumer advocacy groups such as ACT and CCMM that the types of food products advertised to children represent only a limited range of "suitable" foods and that, due to the effectiveness of the advertising, children's dietary and nutritional values and behaviors are being biased toward these foods.

This allegation falls into the policy category of *misleading* advertising in that children are being led to falsely believe, according to medical evidence, that these foods alone constitute an appropriate dietary and nutritional intake. The proposition here is clearly empirical in nature and depends on factual evidence.

There is a related allegation that pertains to "heavily sugared" foods, a subdivision of the subcategory "food advertising." Here the policy emphasis shifts to *unfair ends*. It is alleged, by the FTC as well as consumer advocacy groups, that consumption of heavily sugared foods is per se undesirable because of the risk of dental and other problems and that advertising, even if it is not false, misleading, or unfair in its presentation, should not be allowed to contribute to this undesirable behavior. The food advertising issue is a major part of the FTC's current policy position, and I shall return to this issue in the next two sections.

Volume and Repetition. This and the next two policy issues apply to children's television advertising in general rather than to specific advertising practices or subcategories of advertising. There has been a long-standing contention, by consumer advocacy groups in particular, that there is "too much" advertising directed to children and that the commercials are repeated "too often." These value judgments have been acted on by the FCC and the NAB in that both the amount of commercial time per hour and the number of times an individual commercial can be shown per hour during children's programs have been reduced over the past several years. The ABC television network has instituted a further voluntary reduction in children's advertising time. Concerns about too much volume and too much repetition place this issue in the *unfair ends* category. The fear seems to be that children will become "too persuasible." While this is an empirically testable proposition, no deception or misleading effects have been alleged, nor have policymakers such as the FCC and the NAB taken the empirical evidence on volume, repetition, and persuasibility into account (Rossiter, 1979). The restrictions on volume and repetition are simply value judgments.

Consumer Socialization. A frequent charge against children's television advertising in general is that it fosters undesirable values in children, with materialism most often cited as an example. Defenders of children's advertising, in contrast, claim that positive socialization effects occur, such as the development of knowledge about the economic marketplace. They also suggest that children's experimentation with minor purchases based on advertising may even provide valuable inoculation against the real-world vicissitudes of sales transactions. Whichever position is true—and both, of course, may be—the debate centers on the appropriateness of these values for children. Accordingly, the consumer socialization issue is most clearly categorized as involving *unfair ends*.

Parent–Child Relations. This, the last of the major policy issues, also pertains to children's television advertising in general. In formal terms, this issue is identical to the previous two: That is, an empirical effect is alleged, but it is not an effect that can be categorized as true or false, so the misleading category does not apply. Rather, the effect is considered to be undesirable, so that the applicable category is *unfair ends*. In this instance the unfair ends consist of conflict between parents and children which may result when children ask for products they have seen advertised on television.

The 1978 FTC Staff Proposals

In 1978 an advisory staff of the Federal Trade Commission prepared three proposed regulations for children's television advertising policy. These proposals were launched under the expanded authority given the Commission by the Magnuson–Moss Act of 1975, which legally allows it to regulate entire industries, such as children's television advertising, instead of proceeding on a case-by-case basis with individual companies. The source for these proposals was petitions to the FTC, filed in 1977 by two consumer advocacy groups, Action for Children's Television and the Center for Science in the Public Interest. In response to these petitions, the FTC Advisory Staff proposed the following items of policy:

1. A total ban on television advertising directed to children "too young to understand the selling purpose of, or otherwise comprehend or evaluate" commercials [Federal Trade Commission Advisory Staff, 1978, p. 10], tentatively identified as referring to children below 8 years of age.
2. An additional ban on television advertising for "sugared products, the consumption of which poses the most serious dental health risks [Federal Trade Commission Advisory Staff, 1978, p. 11]," directed to older children, tentatively identified as being ages 8–11.
3. A requirement that television advertising directed to older children for sugared products not included above (proposal 2) be "balanced by nutritional and/or health disclosures funded by advertisers [Federal Trade Commission Advisory Staff, 1978, p. 11]."

The first policy proposal is an extension of the program–commercial separation issue. The underlying proposition is that it is unfair to advertise to children who are not cognitively aware of what an advertisement is nor of its purpose. As noted, this is an *unfair means* issue. The second policy proposal is the same as the second aspect of the food advertising issue. The alleged effects of such advertising are to encourage consumption of heavily sugared foods which in turn will lead to dental health problems. As noted, this is an *unfair ends* issue. The third policy proposal is related to the first aspect of the food advertising issue. The proposition here is that required disclosures about nutritional and health considerations in consuming sugared foods would help to offset children's purportedly false beliefs about these foods. This issue is therefore a proposed "remedy" for an implicit allegation of *misleading* advertising on the part of sugared food manufacturers.

The FTC Advisory Staff's broad proposals, which not surprisingly generated much controversy among the publicly significant parties in the children's television advertising arena, formed the basis for public hearings held early in 1979. The FTC Presiding Officer, Judge Morton Needelman, after reviewing extremely detailed testimony on these and other matters by representatives of the various parties, recently issued recommendations concerning, in his view, disputed issues and non-disputed issues in the controversy. As we shall see, the FTC's proposals are modified in the presiding officer's recommendations.

The FTC Presiding Officer's Recommendations

From the point of view of the probable course of policy determination, *if* the FTC's authority is not weakened by the threat of congressional veto (a proposal to allow Congress veto power over the FTC is currently before the U.S. Senate) nor removed by passage of the bill, the FTC presiding officer's recommendations are the most important policy-relevant statements yet to emerge. Even more important, of course, will be his final recommendations based on the response to the hearings and the FTC Commissioners' findings, which are not expected until the early 1980s. However, the present recommendations are likely to determine what will be pursued as policy issues by the FTC and what will not, and so it is worthwhile to examine both sets of issues here.

Issues That Will Be Pursued. The FTC presiding officer took the first two policy proposals of the FTC Advisory Staff and transformed them into three related issues. Those issues are stated, verbatim, here [Federal Trade Commission, 1979, pp. 6–7, emphasis added]:

1. To what extent can children between the ages of 2 and 11 distinguish between children's commercials and children's programs to the point that they *comprehend the selling purpose* of television advertising aimed at children?
2. To what extent can children between the ages of 2 and 11 *defend against persuasive techniques* used in these commercials, such as fantasy or cartoon presenters, premiums, limited information, and various associative appeals?
3. What *health effects,* actual or potential, attach to any proven lack of understanding or inability to defend against persuasive techniques?

The three issues are related because, according to the presiding officer's supporting arguments, they form a hierarchy. My interpretation of this hierarchy is shown in Table 16.3. The first two issues are called "cognitive issues" by the presiding officer. One reason for this, as shown on the right-hand side of the table, is that they may be deemed sufficient to justify regulation *even if they do not have any behavioral consequences*. Note that "psychological consequences" are not considered. These two issues rest simply on value judgments about *unfair means* of advertising to children. Note, further, the potential enormity of the scope of these two cognitive issues because of the hierarchical argument. This argument says, in effect, "If lack of understanding of selling intent is not a sufficient reason to warrant an unfair means ruling, let's try the stiffer criterion of inability to defend against persuasive techniques." These unfair means tests, especially the latter, could eliminate television advertising to nearly all children up to age 11, depending on how "inability," "defenses," and so on are defined.

If unfair means are not judged later by the presiding officer nor by the FTC commissioners to alone be sufficient to justify regulation, then the third issue states that effects or ends may be examined. The "effects

Table 16.3

The Author's Interpretations of the Policy Implications of the FTC Presiding Officer's Recommendations

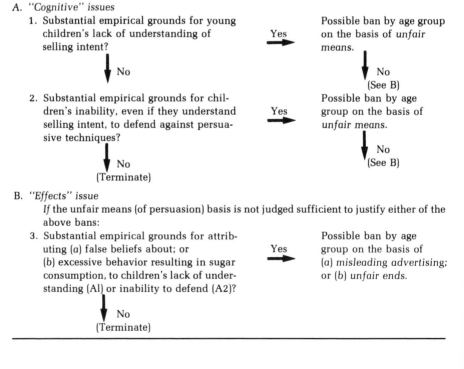

A. "*Cognitive*" issues
1. Substantial empirical grounds for young children's lack of understanding of selling intent?   **Yes** →   Possible ban by age group on the basis of *unfair means*.

No ↓   No ↓ (See B)

2. Substantial empirical grounds for children's inability, even if they understand selling intent, to defend against persuasive techniques?   **Yes** →   Possible ban by age group on the basis of *unfair means*.

No ↓ (Terminate)   No ↓ (See B)

B. "*Effects*" issue
If the unfair means (of persuasion) basis is not judged sufficient to justify either of the above bans:
3. Substantial empirical grounds for attributing (a) false beliefs about; or (b) excessive behavior resulting in sugar consumption, to children's lack of understanding (Al) or inability to defend (A2)?   **Yes** →   Possible ban by age group on the basis of (a) *misleading advertising*; or (b) *unfair ends*.

No ↓ (Terminate)

issue" as the presiding officer calls it, does not refer to all children's television advertising as the first two do, but only to sugared food advertising. Note that it does not make the tenuous distinction between "heavily sugared" foods and "other sugared" foods as the FTC Advisory Staff proposal did. Rather, the onus is shifted entirely to effects. Note, secondly, that it refers to *potential or actual* physical harm. The concept of potential harm includes "beliefs about sugared food consumption . . . that are contrary to . . . generally accepted professional, medical, and dental opinion . . . [Federal Trade Commission, 1979, p. 9]." These would be, ostensibly, false beliefs, and so this part of the issue can be categorized as concerned with *misleading* advertising. Actual harm, on the other hand, as exemplified by dental cavities, can be placed in the *unfair ends* category.

Issues That Will Be Pursued Further. The FTC Presiding Officer's recommendations are informative in identifying (in his opinion) not only disputed issues for further research and debate but also issues not in dispute and therefore not worth further pursuit by the FTC. These undisputed issues range from narrow to broad in scope, and only a selective list of (in my opinion) the five major ones is presented below. All quotations are from the FTC Presiding Officer's recommendations (Federal Trade Commission, 1979):

1. That television advertising that is not specifically designed for or directed to children is not at issue (cf., the proprietary drug advertising issue, where children are exposed to adult-oriented proprietary medicine advertising).
2. That television advertising directed to children "does what it is intended to do. It persuades children to ask for the products advertised [p. 18]." (Note that this conclusion is relevant only to the "effects" issue and that it does not cover the issue of whether false beliefs are among the effects.)
3. That some parent–child conflict does result from children's television advertising but that this conflict is "generally not especially severe nor longlasting [p. 19]."
4. That "overconsumption" of sugar contributes to the formation of dental caries and to obesity but not, at least according to the present weight of evidence, to coronary heart disease, diabetes, cancer, or hypertension.
5. That it has not been established that children's television advertising results in "significant psychological harm, unrealistic materialistic notions, or overstimulation of desires [p. 20]."

Because of the previous emphasis placed on the issues identified in the NSF Report and because these issues may continue as a basis for self-regulatory policy should the FTC's current endeavors be blocked or voluntarily terminated, it is useful to summarize their status vis-à-vis the FTC presiding officer's recommendations. As indicated in Table 16.2, Issues 6,

9, and 10 from the NSF Report were judged to be nonissues while Issue 8 was not directly addressed in the presiding officer's comments. The remaining six issues are subsumed in the three disputed issues identified by Judge Needelman; specifically, NSF Issue 1 is subsumed under "comprehending the selling purpose," NSF Issues 2–5 are subsumed under "defending against persuasive techniques," and NSF Issue 7 is partially subsumed under "health effects."

The Status of Research

It should be apparent that most of the policy issues described in the second part of this chapter involve complex combinations of empirical research evidence and purely ethical value judgments. The analytical framework which identified the four policy categories of false advertising, misleading advertising, unfair means, and unfair ends merely shows the locus of the major policy decision in each case. As a prelude to this section which discusses the contributions and limitations of research as an input to policy decisions, it may be instructive to consider the complexity in this respect of the FTC Presiding Officer's third issue (Table 16.4). Even if research evidence were forthcoming on all of the hypothesized linkages in the causal chain needed to support this issue *empirically,* it should be clear that a final policy decision will depend on an even more intricate set of value judgments. Obviously, research makes a necessary contribution here, but research alone cannot decide policy.

Contributions of Research

Empirical research can contribute to each of the four policy categories I have included in the analytical framework (see Table 16.1). First, it can establish or refute matters of fact, although value judgments are still needed. Second, it can reduce some of the arbitrariness in value judgments, but it cannot replace them. In the next four sections I will illustrate these two principles for the four categories.

False Advertising. Research can help in false advertising determination by providing evidence against the allegedly false practice. This is usually "laboratory" research, for example, to investigate a claim that a battery in a child's toy will last for 100 hours of use. It may, however, sometimes involve consumer research, for example, to investigate a claim that a new toothpaste will reduce cavities in childhood to a significantly greater extent than presently available toothpaste.

Misleading Advertising. Research is instrumental in supporting or refuting allegations of misleading advertising. Such advertising does not necessarily involve false claims, and often it is unintentional on the part of the advertiser. Most of the cases that come before the self-regulatory

Table 16.4

Illustration of the Roles of Research Evidence and Value Judgments in the FTC's Presiding Officer's Food Advertising "Effects" Issue

---

Empirical causal chain

	A1: Lack of understanding of selling intent	B1: False beliefs about sugared foods	C1: Dental caries

Children's food advertising → or → or → or

A2: Inability to defend against persuasive techniques

B2: Overconsumption of sugared foods

C2: Obesity

Research evidence needed on causal relationship between:

1. A1 and B1
2. A1 and B2
3. A2 and B1
4. A2 and B2
5. B1 and C1
6. B1 and C2
7. B2 and C1
8. B2 and C2
9. A factors as mediating causes between advertising and B factors
10. B factors as mediating causes between A factors and C factors.

Value judgments required

A1: 1. Definition and measure of "understanding of selling intent"
2. Judgment of "substantial proportion" of children who reveal lack of understanding

A2: 3. Definition and measure of "ability to defend against persuasive techniques"
4. Similar to 2

B1: 5. Selection and measures of beliefs about sugared foods
6. Judgment about how deviant beliefs must be from fact to be considered mistaken or false

B2: 7. Measure of sugar consumption
8. Judgment about what level of consumption constitutes "overconsumption"

C1: 9. Measure of dental caries

C2: 10. Definition and measure of "obesity"

General: Selection of appropriate sampling design, tests, and significance levels for establishing causal relationships specified in 1–10 at left.

Children's Advertising Review Unit of NAD are of this nature, as are many FTC-initiated cases. Often, research evidence is submitted by the advertiser to show that the advertising is not misleading to children. Occasionally, though, the advertiser's research findings are used to support the regulatory allegation or else the regulatory agency will conduct its own research to investigate the issue.

Unfair Means. This is the policy category where reseach is least relevant in a direct sense because nothing has to be demonstrated other than the fact that the advertiser (or category of advertising) is using the means in question. Research can, however, be relevant *indirectly* by reducing some of the arbitrariness in the value judgments about unfair means (principle 2, above). For example, the NAB and the NAD, both of whose codes prohibit "host selling," presumably surveyed or polled their executive board members' opinions in deciding on this prohibition. This "research" procedure could become more formal by conducting a similar survey of other publicly significant parties such as psychologists and parents. This in itself reflects the value judgment that value judgments should be more democratic.

Unfair Ends. Research is involved in the determination of unfair ends in that it has to be proven that advertising is indeed a cause of the effects. The proprietary drug advertising and food advertising issues are cases in point. The primary locus of the policy decision, however, is on the value judgments concerning the effects themselves, for example, whether or not it is desirable for children to be making decisions about proprietary drugs, whether sugar consumption and its physiological consequences are bad, and so on. Here too, though, research can be employed in its indirect role for polling the value judgments of publicly significant parties.

Limitations of Research

In attempting to define the concept of a policy issue at the outset of this chapter, I commented that value judgments are intrinsic to every policy issue—even those which seem to depend on "hard facts." Herein lies the essential limitation of empirical research. Research is itself a value-laden activity. This point will be illustrated briefly below in conjunction with the four policy categories.

False Advertising. Sometimes falsehoods are permitted in advertising because they are evaluated as justifiable. An example is the use of shaving cream in food advertising as cited earlier. Research is irrelevant to this type of false advertising issue. Another example is nonabsolute claims alleged to be false, for example, that a children's cereal contains "significantly more vitamins" than other brands. The word "significant" has to be interpreted, and this is a value judgment which research cannot provide.

Misleading Advertising. The limitations of research are even more apparent in the second of the "factual" categories, that of misleading advertising. Arbitrary judgments have to be made about the extent of untruth that constitutes "misleading," either in terms of degree of falsehood, number or proportion of children misled, or both. Also, in some instances children (and adults) may even, in some people's view, be "benevolently misled." It is well known, for example, that many common medicines work, for many people, largely through a placebo effect based on the subjective belief that the medicine will work (Bishop, 1977). Still another form of misleading advertising that is tolerated as not being unfair is "puffery." Thus, in policy, there are fair untruths and unfair untruths, where our two dimensions of facts and values coalesce.

Unfair Means. As noted above, research faces its greatest limitations in the policy category of unfair means. Research, for example, cannot decide whether it is a good or bad thing for children to be exposed to various selling techniques or for children to be persuaded or to want various advertised products. The limitations of research are especially apparent when the unfair means allegation is not tied to any alleged unfair *consequences.* Prime examples are the FTC presiding officer's "cognitive" issues, which simply state that children *should* be aware of selling intent and *should* be able to defend against persuasive techniques, even if no "harm" can be shown to result from lack of these factors. One could ask, as many industry representatives have, whether the unfair means concept (without unfair ends) is itself a fair basis for regulating children's television advertising.

Unfair Ends. Jacoby and Small (1975) have presented a sophisticated analysis of the value judgments involved in unfair ends policy issues. The critical considerations are (a) what is the probability of occurrence of the effect; and (b) how serious or harmful is the effect? Overall "risk" or potential unfairness might then be calculated as a function of (a) x (b), though even the appropriateness of this formula is a value judgment. Unfair ends policy issues, as exemplified by the FTC Presiding Officer's "effects" issue pertaining to sugared food advertising, utilize research but depend in the ultimate sense on value judgments.

Summary and Outlook

In this chapter I have tried to get at what a policy issue really is and to analyze the bases for policy issues in children's television advertising. I have stressed, with many examples, the fact that policy determination depends vitally on the ethical values of publicly significant parties. With this in mind, I would like to conclude with some personal observations about this system and about the future directions that I think children's television advertising policy should take. These observations are threefold: (a) because children's television advertising policy depends so heavily on ethical values, these values should be more ethically—or I should say democratically—decided on; (b) the "unfair means" category of policy issues should be eliminated unless "unfair ends" are proven to result; (c) we should be as willing to dismantle policy as to add to it. Research plays a role in each of these observations as, inevitably, do values.

The Meta-Value: Who Shall Decide?

A number of publicly significant parties are involved in children's television advertising policy determination: Children, parents, child development experts, advertisers, consumer advocates, and federal officials. However, the major short-run decisions are in the hands of federal officials, notably the FTC. The meta-value judgment I would like to apply here is that values should be represented more democratically. For the present and the immediate future, in my view, the FTC's values are not appropriately representative. I would like to see systematic research into the relevant value systems of the various parties and an adult public referendum taken about whose values should receive what weight in the overall decisionmaking regarding children's television advertising policy.

Unfair Means Alone Should Not Be a Basis for Policy

The unfair means category, in the absence of unfair ends, has always seemed to me to be an indefensible basis for imposing policy. My own inclination is toward Bertrand Russell's (1954) ethical principle that nothing should be censored unless it can be demonstrated to have consequences that are harmful to others. This viewpoint would make it incumbent on the FTC and on self-regulatory agencies to demonstrate that children's lack of understanding of advertising or inability to defend against persuasive techniques has empirical consequences that we can measure and evaluate. In the absence of these consequences, censorship—in the form of restrictions, bans or whatever—seems pointless. Note that I am proposing a critical task for research, to demonstrate that given means cause given ends, and for value judgments, to decide the ethical status of the ends. The paramount value judgment, however, is whether means should be considered if they cannot be demonstrated to have consequences.

Policy Should Be Reduced and Not Just Added To

There are policies currently in force in children's television advertising which appear to have very little evidentiary justification. This is especially true if we eliminate the vacuous unfair means category from policy and concentrate on false advertising, misleading advertising, and advertising shown to produce effects which publicly significant parties deem unfair. To cite a few examples (others can be found in the Adler et al., 1980 review) in which research so far has produced no supporting evidence: The helpfulness of program–commercial separation devices (see also a recent study by Palmer & McDowell, 1979); the effectiveness of host versus nonhost selling; the extent to which premium offers mislead children; the deleterious effects on children of proprietary drug advertising; and the relationship between the ability to understand selling intent and persuasibility. Of course, one might argue that it is impossible to prove null hypotheses and that research someday might find these alleged effects. This "potential" risk argument is in itself a major value judgment. My point is that if we are going to look to research to confirm our fears about what television advertising is doing to children we should also look to research to dispel these fears. So far we have not done this. We have added to policy but rarely dismantled it.

Children's television advertising policy remains a complex area which leaves few people satisfied. By examining more closely what each policy issue entails, we may arrive at policy decisions on a more reasonable and hopefully more satisfactory basis. I have tried to illustrate this process, using recently past and current policymaking and research as the basis for the analysis.

References

Adler, R. P., Friedlander, B. Z., Lesser, G. S., Meringoff, L., Robertson, T. S., Rossiter, J. R., & Ward, S. Research on the effects of television advertising on children. Washington, D.C.: United States Government Printing Office, 1977.

Adler, R. P., Lesser, G. S., Meringoff, L. K., Robertson, T. S., Rossiter, J. R., & Ward, S. The effects of television advertising on children. New York: Lexington, 1980.

Ayer, A. J. Language, truth and logic (2nd ed.). London, United Kingdom: Gollancz, 1936, 1960.

Bishop, J. E. Placebos are harmless, but they work, posing problems for medicine. The Wall Street Journal, 1977, 140, 1, 33.

Durkheim, E. The elementary forms of religious life. New York: Macmillan, 1915.

Federal Communications Commission. Children's television programs—report and policy statement. Federal Register, 1974, 39, 25505–25510.

Federal Trade Commission Advisory Staff. FTC staff report on television advertising to children. Washington, D.C.: Federal Trade Commission, 1978.

Federal Trade Commission. Presiding officer's order no. 78: Certification to the commission of recommended disputed issues of fact. Washington, D.C.: Federal Trade Commission, 1979.

Gardner, D. M. Deception in advertising: A conceptual approach. Journal of Marketing, 1975, 39, 40–46.

Jacoby, J., & Small, C. The FDA approach to defining misleading advertising. Journal of Marketing, 1975, 39, 65–73.

National Association of Broadcasters. Children's TV advertising. Washington, D.C.: NAB Code Authority, periodically issued.

National Association of Broadcasters. The television code (18th ed.). Washington, D.C.: NAB Code Authority, 1975.

National Advertising Division, Council of Better Business Bureaus, Incorporated., Children's Advertising Review Unit. Children's advertising guidelines (Rev. ed.). New York: Council of Better Business Bureaus, Incorporated., 1977.

National Advertising Division, Council of Better Business Bureaus, Incorporated, A four year review of the Children's Advertising Review Unit: June 1974 through June 1978. New York: Council of Better Business Bureaus, Incorporated, 1979.

Palmer, E. L., & McDowell, C. N. Program/commercial separators in children's television programming. *Journal of Communication.* 1979, *29*(3), 197–201.

Robertson, T. S., Rossiter, J. R., & Gleason, T. C. *Televised medicine advertising and children.* New York: Praeger, 1979.

Rossiter, J. R. *Facts and values in children's advertising regulation.* Paper presented at the Fifth Annual Telecommunications Policy Research Conference, Airlie, Virginia, 1977.

Rossiter, J. R. Does TV advertising affect children? *Journal of Advertising Research,* 1979, *19*(1), 49–53.

Russell, B. *Human society in ethics and politics.* London: George Allen & Unwin, 1954.

Steinberg, M. S. The FCC as fairy godmother: Improving children's television. *UCLA Law Review,* 1974, *21*, 1290–1338.

17

The Nature of Television Advertising to Children

F. EARLE BARCUS

In the current debate over the control of television advertising to children, a necessary step is to look at the nature of the sales messages themselves. One needs to understand the extent of such advertising, the kinds of products most frequently advertised, the techniques utilized to induce sales, and the psychological and value appeals being utilized. This chapter is devoted to the task of summarizing what we know about the ways in which advertisers appeal to children through the sales messages presented during children's programs. By "children's programs" I will mean those programs specifically addressed to children and with predominantly child audiences. They are broadcast primarily on Saturday and Sunday mornings and during the after-school weekday hours from 3:00 to 6:00 P.M.

Since 1971, as public concern about and attention to television fare for children has been increasing, several studies have been conducted on the contents of programming and advertising.[1] Although there have been

[1] Many of the figures cited in the following pages were compiled from content analysis studies I have conducted as research consultant to Action for Children's Television. Many of them involved programming and advertising broadcast in the Boston area, while some were national in focus. Specific references are cited in the text.

some changes in the manner in which such advertising is presented and the total amount broadcast, many of the basic features of the ads have remained the same.

The Amount of Time Devoted to Advertising

Due to pressures by citizens' groups such as Action for Children's Television (ACT) and to the investigation into children's television by the FCC between 1971 and 1974, the total allowable time for advertising to children has been reduced by the National Association of Broadcasters (NAB) Code Authority in progressive steps over the past several years (see Chapter 15 for more detail). These restrictions have been relatively effective for network-affiliated and code member stations. However, up to this time they have had little or no effect on independent stations which were given special consideration (presumably for economic reasons) in the code regulations (National Association of Broadcasters, 1976). Many of these stations broadcast children's programs in the early morning and late afternoon hours, and the 1976 code time standards permitted up to 16 minutes per hour in this non-prime-time.

In June of 1971 the first major content analysis of children's television revealed that nearly 20% of program time on Saturday mornings was devoted to commercial material on the average (Barcus, 1971). Some stations utilized more than 25% of the broadcast hour for such material. Children were being exposed to an average of nearly 26 commercial messages per hour. In November of that same year, during the pre-Christmas season, nearly 25% of time was devoted to advertising and an average of more than 30 announcements was broadcast each hour (Barcus, 1972).

By April of 1975 about 15% of total time on network affiliated stations was devoted to advertising to children (about 20 announcements per hour); and by October, 1977 this was reduced to about 14% and 18 announcements per hour (Barcus, 1975b, 1978a). This is about where things stand today. This historic pattern reflects progress in the struggle to reduce the amount of advertising to children—at least on stations regulated by the NAB code.

Largely speaking, however, the independent television stations have been forgotten until recently.[2] In fact, a national sampling of 10 independent television stations broadcasting weekdays in the after-school hours (3:00–6:00 P.M.) actually showed an increase between 1975 and 1977 from 20% to 22% of total time devoted to commercial messages—and from 21 to 25 such messages per hour (Barcus, 1975b, 1978a).

---

[2] Action for Children's Television submitted a petition to the FCC in 1979 stating that NAB self-regulation of nonprogram time has not been successful and requesting that independent stations be subject to the same time standards as are network-affiliated code television stations.

In any event, commercial advertising directed toward children still consumes a significant portion of the child's viewing time. Latest figures in a study of 33 hours of programming in Boston indicate that on the average the child is exposed to 15 commercial messages, five program promotional announcements, and two public service announcements per viewing hour (Barcus, 1978c).

The Types of Products Advertised to Children

The staples of children's advertising consist of four product categories—toys, cereals, candies, and fast-food restaurants. These four categories account for at least 80% of all ads broadcast on children's television with one exception—the independent station after-school broadcasts in which a large number of record offers and advertisements for local products, services, and the like are aired.

The most recent figures available are from a study of 33 hours of children's programming on weekends and weekdays in Boston, which includes three network affiliated VHF stations and three independent UHF stations. The patterns show that cereal and candy manufacturers more often utilize network affiliated stations, whereas toy manufacturers and makers of other products utilize the independent UHF stations. Figures for all product types are given in Table 17.1.

Toy commercials may comprise 50% or more of child-directed ads in the October–November pre-Christmas season. On one New York independent station studied in November, 1975, there were 80 commercial an-

Table 17.1
Commercial Announcements on Network-Affiliated and Independent Television Stations, by Product Type[a]

Product type	Network affiliated stations (%)	Independent stations (%)
Toys	12	49
Cereals	34	13
Candies/sweets	29	13
Snack foods	3	—
Other foods	1	(b)
Eating places	15	9
Household products	—	1
Personal care products	(b)	(b)
Other (records, etc.)	6	15
	100	100
	(250)	(245)

[a] Source: Barcus, 1978c.
[b] Less than .5%.

nouncements broadcast on one day between 3:00 and 6:00 P.M., 67 of
which were for toys (Barcus, 1976).

In June, 1978 food commercials comprised about 60% of all ads
broadcast during one week's sample of children's television (82% on network affiliates and 35% on independent stations). Of all ads 24% were
for cereals, 21% for candies, and 12% for fast-food restaurants such as
Burger King and McDonald's. Of all food ads, about seven out of ten are
for highly sugared products such as sugared cereals, candy, cakes, and
cookies. Only a few food commercials aimed at children advertise more
nutritious food products such as meats, bread, dairy products, fruits, or
vegetables (see Table 17.1).

Selling Techniques in Children's Advertising

Basic techniques in selling to children will be discussed here under
three headings: (a) product presentation; (b) attention-getting devices; and
(c) qualifiers, disclaimers, and disclosures.

Product Presentation Methods

Different product types vary in the basic presentation formats used.
For example, nearly all toy commercials are nonanimated, using "live"
action scenes to demonstrate the product. Advertisements for most other
types of products depend heavily on animation techniques. About 80% of
cereal ads use animation, often in conjunction with nonanimated scenes
(Barcus, 1978a; Doolittle & Pepper, 1975). A familiar example is Tony the
Tiger at the breakfast table talking with real children.

The off-stage announcer as the chief selling agent is most frequently
used in toy commercials (in about nine out of ten). Cereals and snack food
ads, on the other hand, most often present their products by short dramatic skits, with the main character in the skit giving the sales message.
Another presentation format frequently used is the musical jingle. At least
one-half of child-directed ads utilize musical jingles to create identification with the product (Barcus, 1978c).

Although the same techniques are available, children's television ads
are structured differently than are ads aimed at adults. Much less frequent are testimonials for the product and straight sales messages by announcers or onstage performers. For example, of 133 children's ads for
food products studied in 1978, only 4% used onstage announcers and 5%
used testimonials by real or representational figures (Barcus, 1978c).

In the 1970s there was a decrease in the use of program personalities,
cartoon characters, or other celebrities either giving testimonials or direct
endorsements of the products advertised. This was due primarily to continuing pressures on the advertisers, as reflected in NAB code guidelines,

to discontinue this practice because of young children's vulnerability and the trust they may place in such authority figures. At one time, so-called host selling was an important issue in children's television advertising. This no longer seems to be the case. Another non-issue is the use of comparative claims, often used in advertising to adults, and now prohibited by the NAB Code for advertising to children.

Children's television ads seldom urge children to pressure their parents into buying certain products with such phrases as "ask Mom to get one for you" (Atkin & Heald, 1977). This does not mean that such pressures do not exist, however, for the very nature of the child as consumer impels children to pressure parents to buy. This often creates parent–child conflict (Sheikh & Moleski, 1977).

The use of premium offers as extra inducement to buy is a fairly common practice, which showed an increase between 1971 and 1975 and a decline after 1975. A selling device utilized primarily by cereal commercials, premiums were offered in 28% of cereal ads in 1971, 47% in 1975, and 25% in 1977 (see Barcus, 1971, 1975b, 1978a). The use of premiums as sales devices has been criticized as irrelevant to the product message and tending to confuse the young child. The FTC has questioned such techniques in a proposed trade regulation issued in 1974, stating that the premium "must inevitably increase the likelihood of confusion and of the purchase of an inferior product [Federal Trade Commission, 1974]."

Attention-Getting Devices

A number of techniques are employed in children's advertising primarily to attract attention rather than to relate specifically to a sales message or product information. Those most frequently employed are repetition, unusual sound or visual effects, animation effects, and the use of violent activity, magic, and fantasy.

The average number of repetitions of the product name in a 1978 sample of food commercials was 3.9 verbal and 4.3 visual repetitions per 30-second commercial (Barcus, 1978c). Extremes showed 10 or more repetitions in the form of quick cuts from one scene to another of children using the product or in jingles in which the product name was repeated in the lyrics a dozen times. An example is the Kellogg's Apple Jacks commercial in which children sing the jingle: "Apple Jacks, Apple Jacks, cinnamon toasted Apple Jacks. . . ."

Unusual sound effects employed include the use of echo chambers, speeded up or slowed down sound track, and other mechanical and electronic sound techniques. Visual effects frequently shown are animated figures interacting with "live" children, speeded up camera action, and "camera magic" that transforms objects, causes mysterious flight of people and objects, and makes things seem to disappear magically.

Violent activity is also present in a significant number of children's commercials. Although often presented in a humorous manner, it is not unusual to find characters crashing through walls, getting hit on the head, or being attacked by wild animals.

Fantasy situations and settings are probably the most frequently employed devices for attracting the child's attention. More than one-half of all food, and almost nine out of ten cereal, commercials studied in 1978 utilized fantasy techniques (Barcus, 1978c). Fantasy settings include such places as the inside of cereal boxes where children play, strange planets, and fantasy kingdoms. Fantasy situations include talking with lepre-chauns, elves, animals, and outer-space beings. There are serious questions as to whether young children have the capacity to distinguish fantasy and reality, and this may account for the heavy use of fantasy in children's television ads. Witnesses in recent FTC hearings testified that such techniques were intentionally used to appeal to the special vulner-abilities of children (Action for Children's Television and the Center for Science in the Public Interest, 1979).

Qualifiers, Disclaimers, and Product Disclosures

Generally speaking, television advertisers include verbal qualifiers in their ads only under pressures from the NAB Code Authority and the Code of the Toy Manufacturers Association. These code rules were instituted as a reaction to complaints by consumers and citizens' groups. Conse-quently toy ads frequently utilize qualifiers such as "assembly required," "batteries not included," or "items sold separately." In a study of 536 toy commercials, about two-thirds utilized some form of qualifier and about 90% of them were of the three types just described (Barcus, 1978a). For products other than toys, statements such as "artificially flavored' (can-dies), "in specially marked boxes" (cereal premiums), or "not sold in stores" (records) are fairly common qualifiers. Qualifiers are most likely to be given only auditorily, even though it has been recommended that they be presented both visually and auditorily.

Another public criticism was made when, in 1971, the nutritional value of cereal products was analyzed and found to be low in many cases. Not only did cereal companies immediately add vitamin and mineral for-tification to most cereal products, but also code regulations were written requiring cereal advertisers to include a statement to the effect that the cereals were "part of a balanced breakfast."

Although most current toy and cereal ads include required dis-claimers or disclosures, there is a question as to their effect. Such quali-fiers are usually very brief, intermixed with the sales message, and worded in ways which may prevent full understanding. For example, for toys the wording "some assembly required" is more difficult to under-stand than "you have to put it together" (Liebert, Sprafkin, Liebert, & Rubinstein, 1977). For cereals, the idea that they are "part of a balanced breakfast" may create an impression in the child that one *needs* the cereal product as a *necessary part* of a balanced breakfast.

There may be need for other disclaimers or disclosures that are sel-dom currently included in children's ads. Examples of warnings about possible consequences from "unwise" use of a product include electrical shock hazards and dental caries. Useful disclosures for parents would be age-labeling of toy products and the percent of required nutrients and caloric values of food products.

Appeals in Children's Television Advertising

As in all television advertising, many types of appeals are built into children's television ads to motivate the consumer. There is very limited use of rational appeals through presentation of product information. The bulk are instead indirect appeals to psychological states, associations with established values, or unsupported assertions about the qualities of the products.

In studies covering both network and independent station advertis-ing, the basic "themes" of commercials were coded (Barcus, 1975a, 1975b, 1977). "Hard" product information such as price/economy, the quality of manufacturing, or information on the materials or ingredients was given infrequently. It was often difficult or impossible to determine whether a toy was made of plastic, metal, or cardboard; how much it cost; the age level for which it was intended; or its performance qualities. In-stead the toy ads emphasized themes of "appearance," "action," and the "fun nature" of the product. In the pre-Christmas season, they also util-ized the "newness" theme (e.g., "new from Mattel").

In a similar manner, cereal ads focused primarily on taste and tex-ture, with little information on ingredients aside from the common state-ment that it was "fortified with essential vitamins." The sweet or sugary nature of the product was often mentioned as well. In many cases, unless included as part of the name (e.g., "corn flakes"), one could not discern even the major cereal grain in the product.

Verbal Appeals

The basic appeals in children's television advertising are presented both verbally and visually. The verbal messages in the ads are relatively easy to analyze utilizing four basic categories, which constitute the verbal buying rationale: (a) assertions; (b) attributed qualities; (c) product properties; and (d) product composition.

1. *Assertions* are statements made in the ad about the potential benefits of the product to the user. Examples are, it "will save you money," "is fun," and "is convenient."
2. *Attributed qualities* are statements that represent someone's (usually the advertiser's) opinions about the qualities of the product. Examples are "tastes great," "it's unique," "the best," and "country fresh." These statements are subject to debate and are difficult if not impossible to verify.
3. *Product properties* include descriptions of the physical properties of the product which are amenable to demonstration. Statements might refer to texture, size, shape, color, or sturdiness.
4. *Product composition* refers to statements about the physical nature of the materials or ingredients. They include information on materials used in toys, for example, or compounds and generic foodstuffs as food ingredients.

These categories were utilized in the analysis of 133 separate food commercials broadcast in June, 1978 (Barcus, 1978c). Only about three out of ten made any kind of *assertion* of how the product might benefit the user. When they did, however, it was generally that it would provide fun or pleasure to the user and sometimes that it was convenient or easy to use. Almost nine out of ten *attributed qualities* to the food product about which we may or may not agree. According to the food advertisers, the most important quality of their products was the taste (attributions in eight of ten food ads), with "newness" or "uniqueness" attributed in about one of ten ads. Other qualities such as aroma, appearance, freshness, or quality were seldom attributed.

Seven of ten food commercials described some basic *product properties* which might appeal to the child audience. The major properties emphasized by four out of ten food commercials (and six of ten cereal ads) were the texture of the product (e.g., crunchy, chewy), size or quantity, and the shape or form of the product. Almost nine of ten cereal ads gave some indication of *product composition*. About four in ten gave some indication, either in the verbal message or in the product name, of the grain used to make the cereal. Most frequently, however, cereal ads mentioned the vitamin/mineral content, followed in frequency by mentions of grains, flavors, sugar or honey, and chocolate.

The overall picture from this analysis is that of a lack of attention by advertisers to product information that the intelligent consumer may need and a concentration instead on more vague attributions and product properties that may appeal to the child audience.

Visual Appeals

A buying rationale may also be presented visually. It is possible to think of "visual assertions" about the fun nature of a product when it is presented with children laughing and playing. Its qualities, properties, and composition may also be visually depicted—for example, chocolate pouring over nougat in processing a candy bar. Often, however, the visual message, as compared to the verbal message, is more diffuse and difficult to classify in these specific terms. I have therefore developed a coding system for associational "themes" that are often conveyed through the series of images and actions in children's commercials.

Some themes, although avoided in direct verbal statements, are often conveyed visually. In my study (Barcus, 1978c) of food commercials, for example, it was never stated verbally that the products would provide energy. Yet one-fourth of such ads visually portrayed vigorous physical activities closely associated with the consumption of the food. Similarly, advertisers are extremely cautious about verbally asserting their product will make one more popular. Visually, however, this association is made in about one out of ten commercials (Barcus, 1978c).

The overwhelming visual appeal in advertising to children, however, is to "fun." This hedonistic message is conveyed in at least 70% of the children's food commercials I studied (Barcus, 1978c), and most probably in a high percentage of toys and other product ads. Other less common associations are with adventure, nature, and family activities. There is little doubt that such associations are resonant with children's desires, fantasies, and often their lifestyles. This is what makes them effective. The continuous reinforcement of such appeals to hedonism may lead to undesirable effects on children's values and behavior; particularly undesirable when one thinks about such other possible appeals as work activities, education, business, or parent–child relationships.

Value Lessons in Children's Advertising

The visual associations just discussed provide one key to values reinforced and promoted in children's television advertising. Other messages may well be conveyed by the nature of the characters who provide sales messages (spokespersons), the nature of other characters depicted in the ads, the activities in which the characters engage, and the basic settings of the commercials.

The chief spokesperson for products is an authority figure in the commercial and may suggest to children who is important or credible in our society. Spokespersons for products are male in about nine out of ten commercials overall. More female spokespersons appear in adver-

ients for certain classes of products, such as foods, restaurants, and household products. Even here, however, males constitute seven or more out of every ten spokespersons. In addition to being male, spokespersons are also predominantly adult and white. For example, in both weekend and weekday samples of children's television in 1977, whites constituted 97% in one sample and 99% in the other (Barcus, 1978a).

The distribution of all characters in commercials reveals the same sort of bias—if not as extreme. In four separate samples of children's television in 1975 and 1977, several thousand characters were counted in the commercials (Barcus, 1975a, 1975b, 1978a). Between 60% and 70% of all characters were male, and 90% to 95% were white. By age group, in contrast to adults as spokespersons, children constitute about 60% of all characters. Teenage characters are the forgotten group, constituting only about 5% of the total.

The activities of the characters may also provide clues for imitative or modeling behavior of children viewing them. In a 1978 study of 133 food commercials (Barcus, 1978c), nearly one-half showed children in leisure activity, another one-fourth in daily living activities, and about one in ten in adventurous activity. Fewer than one in twenty depicted characters engaged in work activities. Fantasy settings were basic to about two out of ten of the food ads. The remainder were more related to "real-life" settings at home, in public places, or in natural surroundings. Again, only 2 of the 133 food ads studied took place in the work setting.

Ethical and Other Issues in Children's Television Advertising

There are obviously more than ethical considerations in the problems of control and regulation of children's advertising on television. It is well known that millions of dollars of revenues are involved annually. Toy, cereal, and candy manufacturers are exerting powerful political pressures on the Congress and regulatory commissions. The ethical dimension, however, underlies all other considerations in the area.

Recently I have outlined four major ethical questions to be answered with respect to children's advertising (Barcus, 1978b):

1. Should we advertise to children at all?
2. If so, how much advertising should we allow?
3. What should we (or should we not) permit to be advertised?
4. How should we advertise? (What techniques are fair?)

These questions have been addressed by industry, regulatory agencies, and citizens' groups with varying intensity and outcomes. Since much of this activity is reviewed in Chapters 15 and 16, I will be brief in my own discussion of the ways in which these questions have been answered.

Over the past decade, much attention has been devoted to the fourth question. This is reflected in a large number of guidelines written by trade associations prohibiting the use of certain production techniques as potentially misleading to the child. There are also provisions prohibiting messages that cajole the child to ask a parent to buy a product, imply that the product will improve the child's peer status, contain antisocial and violent behavior, or violate safety standards. Moreover, celebrities are enjoined from endorsing products, and certain audio and visual disclosures are required (for full codes, see National Advertising Division, 1977; National Association of Broadcasters, 1976).

The first question, whether to advertise to children at all, was raised in 1971 by the ACT petition to the FCC. One of the chief arguments for eliminating television advertising to children is that they do not understand the purpose of advertising and have no defenses against it. A second argument is that since children have little or no purchasing power as independent consumers, the only purpose of such advertising is to use them as surrogate salesmen urging their parents to purchase.

After 3 years of deliberation the ACT petition was denied, and the FCC left the burden for deciding the amount and methods of advertising to the industry (Federal Communications Commission, 1974). Recently the FTC reopened the issue with a staff report recommending the banning of all commercials addressed to young children, the banning of advertising addressed to older children for certain highly sugared foods, and requiring the industry to broadcast nutrition public service announcements.

Although not yet successful in banning advertising to children, citizens' groups have been able to accomplish a reduction in the amount of advertising (question 2). As early as 1974 Westinghouse Broadcasting Company limited commercial time to half that allowed by industry guidelines (Committee on Interstate and Foreign Commerce, 1975). Recently, ABC–TV Network President James E. Duffy announced plans to reduce network commercial time by 2 minutes by 1981 (ABC–TV Network, 1979).

There are certain types of products, such as cigarettes, liquor, and firearms, that have long been prohibited from advertising on the air (question 3). In children's programming, advertising for vitamins and drug products has been removed, since the products have been deemed potentially hazardous to young children. The recent FTC hearings have been concerned with the elimination of other potentially dangerous food products—those high in sugar content.

Many of the issues raised in the FTC hearings are still subject to some dispute. Although the hearings have been addressed primarily to matters of scientific proof rather than to ethical arguments, they have been quite useful in clarifying some basic issues related primarily to theories of child development and mental capacities. As such they are age-related issues. They are presented in Chapter 16 in some detail, and the interested reader can turn to it for more specific information.

Summary

As the next chapter by Atkin makes clear, there is little dispute that television advertising to young children may have a variety of effects, some of which are not in the best interests of the child. There is evidence that the child does develop brand preferences and that he or she also pressures parents to buy. The total amount of such advertising is necessarily related to the extent of the effect. But other content characteristics must also shape advertising's effects.

The content characteristics of children's ads discussed here—at least some of which may affect children—include the types of products advertised, the manner in which they are presented, attention-getting devices, and the types of verbal disclosures. They often include complex appeals to psychological states through verbal buying rationales and visual messages which reinforce certain values. These characteristics of television advertising to children constitute messages about the world beyond the home and may be important illustrations of that world for the child viewer.

References

ABC–TV Network. *ABC will reduce the amount of network commercial time by two minutes in Saturday and Sunday morning children's programs over two year period.* Press release, January 22, 1979.

Action for Children's Television and the Center for Science in the Public Interest. *Proposed disputed issues of fact.* Submission to the Federal Trade Commission, June 1, 1979.

Atkin, C., & Heald, G. The content of children's toy and food commercials. *Journal of Communication,* 1977, *27*(1), 107–114.

Barcus, F. E. *Saturday children's television: A report of TV programming and advertising on Boston commercial television.* Newtonville, Massachusetts: Action for Children's Television, 1971.

Barcus, F. E. *Network programming and advertising in the Saturday children's hours: A June and November comparison.* Newtonville, Massachusetts: Action for Children's Television, 1972.

Barcus, F. E. *Television in the after-school hours.* Newtonville, Massachusetts: Action for Children's Television, 1975. (a)

Barcus, F. E. *Weekend children's television.* Newtonville, Massachusetts: Action for Children's Television, 1975. (b)

Barcus, F. E. *Pre-Christmas advertising to children: A comparison of the advertising content of children's programs broadcast in April and November of 1975.* Newtonville, Massachusetts: Action for Children's Television, 1976.

Barcus, F. E. (with R. Wolkin). *Children's television: An analysis of programming and advertising.* New York: Praeger, 1977.

Barcus, F. E. *Commercial children's television on weekends and weekday afternoons.* Newtonville, Massachusetts: Action for Children's Television, 1978. (a)

Barcus, F. E. Ethical problems in television advertising to children. In B. Rubin (Ed.), *Questioning media ethics.* New York: Praeger, 1978. (b)

Barcus, F. E. (with L. McLaughlin). *Food advertising on children's television: An analysis of appeals and nutritional content.* Newtonville, Massachusetts: Action for Children's Television, 1978. (c)

Committee on Interstate and Foreign Commerce. *Broadcast advertising and children.* Hearings, House of Representatives, 94th Congress, 1st Session, July, 1975.

Doolittle, J., & Pepper, R. Children's TV ad content: 1974. *Journal of Broadcasting,* 1975, *19*(2), 131–141.

Federal Communications Commission. Children's television programs—report and policy statement. *Federal Register,* 1974, *39,* 39396–39409.

Federal Trade Commission. Food advertising: Proposed trade regulations rule and staff statement. *Federal Register,* 1974, *39,* 39842–39862.

Liebert, D. E., Sprafkin, J. N., Liebert, R. M., & Rubinstein, E. A. Effects of television commercial disclaimers on the product expectations of children. *Journal of Communication,* 1977, *27* (1), 118–124.

National Advertising Division, Council of Better Business Bureaus, Incorporated, Children's Advertising Review Unit. *Children's advertising guidelines* (Rev. ed.). New York: Council of Better Business Bureaus, Incorporated, 1977.

National Association of Broadcasters. *The television code* (19th ed.). Washington, D.C.: NAB Code Authority, 1976.

Sheikh, A., & Moleski, L. M. Conflict in the family over commercials. *Journal of Comunication,* 1977, *27*(1), 152–157.

Effects of Television Advertising on Children

CHARLES K. ATKIN

This chapter examines the consequences of children's exposure to thousands of television commercials, especially those Saturday morning ads that are targeted to young audiences. The first section assesses the degree of direct impact on product preferences, which is the major goal of child-oriented advertising. Since most ads promote food products, the next section describes children's learning about nutrition and other food attributes featured in commercials. The following section discusses some of the unintended side effects of advertising, including parent–child conflict and child unhappiness. A final section briefly surveys children's responses to nonproduct messages such as public service announcements and political ads.

The bulk of the chapter is devoted to a review of the social science research evidence on each topic. A rapidly increasing volume of surveys and experiments has been conducted throughout this decade, beginning with the seminal work of Scott Ward in 1970 and concluding with research studies commissioned for the 1979 Federal Trade Commission (FTC) hearings. Before describing these empirical findings, some general effects theories will be briefly outlined, followed by an overview of children's perceptions of television ads.

CHILDREN AND THE FACES OF TELEVISION:
Teaching, Violence, Selling

Several theoretical perspectives apply to the question of advertising impact on children. Conventional persuasion paradigms suggest that viewers will learn about product attributes, form positive images, and consume advertised brands (Bogart, 1973; Krugman, 1965; Ramond, 1976). Social learning theory indicates that modeled behaviors such as food eating or toy playing portrayed in commercial messages will lead to higher levels of viewer consumption of corresponding products (Bandura, 1971). This impact should be generic rather than brand specific, since disinhibition or response facilitation processes explain responses to a broad category of products rather than to the distinctive brands within a category (Atkin, 1976). Finally cognitive developmental theory predicts that children have an increasingly sophisticated capacity to understand the advertising process, learn information, and resist persuasion (Ward, Wackman, & Wartella, 1977).

Inferences regarding children's acceptance of advertising claims depend, however, on the measurement procedure employed. When given a dichotomous forced-choice question asking whether ads are true or untrue, the proportion of children who exhibit generalized distrust rises from about one-fourth of the pre-8-year-olds to three-fourths of those over 10 years old (Atkin, 1975c, 1975d; Robertson & Rossiter, 1974; Rossiter, 1977; Ward, 1972; Ward et al., 1977). However, rejection of specific advertisements and persuasive claims is not as prevalent as the generalized measures would indicate. Although children are skeptical about assertions in commercials for familiar toys, they readily accept technical claims of a medical or nutritional nature (Atkin, 1975c, 1975d; Haefner, Leckenby, & Goldman, 1975). Heavy viewers of commercials are more likely to believe ads than are light viewers (Atkin, 1975c; Atkin, Reeves, & Gibson, 1979).

Comprehension of disclaimer jargon (e.g., "partial assembly required") is very limited, especially for children under 8 years of age (Atkin, 1975a; Barry, 1978; Liebert, Sprafkin, Liebert, & Rubinstein, 1977; Stern & Resnik, 1977). Younger children generally like to watch individual Saturday morning commercials more than do older children who express more ambivalent feelings (Atkin, 1975c; Robertson & Rossiter, 1974; Rossiter, 1977; Ward, 1972). Children report that they especially enjoy humor and other entertaining qualities of television ads (Atkin, 1975c; Ward, 1972). Such enjoyment of "irrelevant" aspects of an ad may contribute to acceptance of its messages.

Impact of Advertising on Product Preferences

The intended effects of advertising can be assessed along three interrelated dimensions: product desires, parental purchase requests, and consumption patterns. The degree of advertising impact on each of these responses will be examined here as will one influential component of child-oriented advertising: premium appeals.

Impact on Desire for Advertised Products

Many research projects have sought to determine the role of television advertising in the development of children's awareness of and preference for toy and food products. One method is simply to ask children or parents where they learn about desired products. Donohue (1975) asked black elementary school children to name their favorite toy and tell where they first found out about it; television watching was most often mentioned, followed by seeing it in the store, and by friends having it. Caron and Ward (1975) told children to list Christmas gift wishes in a letter to Santa and to indicate where they got the idea for each item. Four sources were prevalent: television, friends, stores, and catalogs. According to mothers of young children interviewed by Barry and Sheikh (1977), television ranked first as learning source for products in general, followed by friends and catalogs. Both mothers and children studied by Howard, Hulbert, and Lehmann (1977) cited television as the most important information source for cereal and toy products.

Children have also been asked to report about the impact of ads on desires. Responding to the question, "Would you like to have most things they show on television commercials?", two-thirds of kindergartners and half of third and sixth graders interviewed said "yes" (Ward et al., 1977). In a correlational survey study, Atkin et al. (1979) measured preferences for various food brands in a sample of 5- to 12-year-olds. There was a strong positive relationship between viewing television commercials and liking the 12 frequently advertised foods ($r = +.59$). On the average, 66% of the heavy viewers said they liked each advertised product, compared to 46% of the light viewers.

Experimental studies that contrast children exposed and not exposed to a product commercial also provide information about the impact of the ads on desires. Atkin and Gibson (1978) found that nine-tenths of the young children exposed to a Pebbles cereal commercial wanted to eat that cereal, compared to two-thirds of the control group. A parallel experiment with Honeycombs cereal showed no significant impact on desire, perhaps due to less effective ad execution. Goldberg and Gorn (1978) found that exposed children were considerably more likely both to want to play with an advertised toy than with their friends and also to want to play with a not-so-nice child who owned the toy then with a nice one without that toy. In an experiment with low-income boys between 8 and 10 years old, those who saw an ad for an unfamiliar toy were more likely to have a positive attitude toward it and to work on a task to obtain it than were those who didn't see the ad (Gorn & Goldberg, 1977). In a more extreme experimental test, Resnik and Stern (1977) created a bland ad for an unfamiliar potato chip brand, with no useful information, appealing models, or elaborate production techniques—the message simply communicated the product's existence. When offered a choice between two unknown brands, exposed children were much more likely to choose the advertised potato chips. Finally, Atkin (1975b) tested an acne cream commercial with pre-adolescents. Half of the exposed subjects liked the product compared to one-third of the nonviewers, and more than four-fifths said they might buy that product if needed, compared to less than two-thirds of the control group.

Impact on Requests for Advertised Products

Since children do not have the means to buy most of the products advertised on television, most preferences are expressed in terms of requests to parents. Of course, children tend to ask parents to buy a large number of products; the issue concerns the extent to which advertising stimulates these requests.

One method of assessing this is the self-report of impact. Atkin (1975c) asked, "Many of the TV commercials are for toys—things like games and dolls and racing cars. After you see these toys on TV, how much do you ask your mother to buy them for you?" Across the 3- to 12-year-old sample, 28% said "a lot" and 55% said "sometimes." The same question was repeated for breakfast cereals; 33% reported asking "a lot" and 45% replied "sometimes." In another survey of fourth to seventh graders, one-fifth reported that they asked "a lot" for cereals after viewing these products on television (Atkin, 1975d). When mothers in the first study (Atkin, 1975c) were asked to report on requests received, responses almost identical to those of the children were obtained.

Four separate self-report studies indicate that heavier viewers are more likely than lighter viewers to report impact. In one, children who watched the most Saturday morning commercials asked much more often for toys and cereals, with about twice as many heavy viewers as light viewers falling in the "a lot" category (Atkin, 1975c). In another, heavy viewers of cereal advertising made more requests, by a two-to-one margin over lightly exposed children. Furthermore, almost half of those who watched television heavily often asked to go to highly advertised fast food restaurants, compared to one-fourth of light viewers (Atkin, 1975d). In the third study, children who viewed the most Saturday commercials asked most often for advertised foods ($r = +.47$). Summing across nine food products, heavy viewers reported making almost twice as many requests as light viewers (Atkin et al., 1979). Finally, in a study using reports by mothers of 8- to 13-year-olds, there was a positive relationship between Saturday morning viewing and frequency of food requests (Clancy-Hepburn, Hickey, & Nevill, 1974).

A second method of assessing impact on requests is behavioral observation. Galst and White (1976) assessed the extent to which 3- to 11-year-olds attended to commercials in a laboratory setting and subsequently observed them in a trip to the supermarket. Children engaged in an average of 15 purchase influence attempts per shopping expedition; those paying relatively greater attention to ads made far more requests. Request frequency was also moderately related to amount of home viewing of commercial programming, but it was unrelated to viewing of public television programming.

A third assessment method is the projective technique. Sheikh and Moleski (1977) told children to complete a story which began with a hypothetical child seeing several ads for toy, food, or clothing items. When asked if they thought the child felt like requesting the item, nine-tenths replied affirmatively. However, only three-fifths said the child would actually make the request, indicating that children use some discretion in expressing desires to parents.

Impact on Rate of Consumption of Advertised Products

Once an edible product is available in the home, the actual consumption rate becomes an important outcome. In a survey with fourth to seventh grade students (Atkin, 1975d), those who watched the most cereal advertising ate advertised cereals much more frequently; for example, 25% of the heavy viewers reported eating Sugar Smacks "a lot" compared to 13% of the light viewers. The relationship between candy advertising exposure and the frequency of eating candy was also moderately strong; for example, 49% of heavy viewers and 32% of light viewers ate Hershey Bars "a lot." Indeed, general television viewing was positively related to consumption of general snack and processed foods (e.g., potato chips, soda pop, hot dogs). Other studies have also reported positive relationships between reported viewing and consumption of candy (Atkin et al., 1979), of heavily advertised foods (Sharaga, 1974), and of heavily sugared cereal, candy, snack food, and empty calorie food (Dussere, 1976). A positive correlation has also been found between exposure and between-meal eating (Dussere, 1976).

Turning now to usage of personal hygiene products and medicines rather than foods, Atkin (1975d) found a moderately strong relationship between viewing ads for deodorants, mouthwash, and acne cream and the frequency of using these products; heavy viewers were almost twice as likely as light viewers to say they used mouthwash and acne cream "a lot." The relationship for cold and stomach ache remedies was only slightly positive.

Impact of Advertising on Generic Preferences

Aside from the direct effects on preferences for advertised brands, television commercials may also stimulate greater consumption of other brands within the generic product class. The theoretical basis for this outcome is social learning theory (Bandura, 1971), which predicts that those who view a behavioral sequence (such as consuming a product) may vicariously acquire new patterns of behavior, strengthen or weaken inhibitions governing the expression of previously learned responses, and be reminded to perform already learned responses. This occurs through processes of attention, retention, motivation, and generalization generated by exposure to symbolic modeling stimuli, such as television advertising portrayals. The impact should not necessarily be tied to the particular brands featured in the ads; the key factor is the modeled actions, such as eating a certain kind of food.

This can most clearly be illustrated in the case of cereal consumption. Most children have established habitual patterns of behavior regarding cereal eating and have experienced enjoyment and approval for these actions. In such a case, advertising can serve as a cue that instigates the previously learned eating response through a reminder function. Such response facilitation is made more likely by the depicted enjoyment of the models in the cereal commercials. The response might be expected to "generalize" to unadvertised brands for two reasons: The brand-unique cues in a given ad might be perceived as peripheral to the more central, modeled sequence of preparing and eating a bowl of cereal, and the overall message environment of numerous competing cereal brands may produce a cumulative impression of "eating cereal" rather than learning substantive and symbolic distinctions between various brands. From a visual modeling perspective, the basic theme conveyed is consumption behavior, since there are often no unique features of specific brands that observers can act out.

To determine whether advertising exposure produces brand-specific or generalized reactions, Atkin (1975c) measured consumption of heavily and lightly advertised cereal brands in a survey of fourth to seventh graders. Exposure was indexed by attention to specific cereal brand ads and attention to that general category of ads, weighted by the amount of Saturday morning television viewing time. The correlation between viewing and eating eight highly advertised cereals was strong (+.41). The association was also positive but less strong for eating five less advertised brands (+.27). Thus, advertising does have a clear impact on brand consumption; in addition, the influence appears to diffuse to other brands to some extent.

A different process, disinhibition, seems most applicable to candy eating. Saturday morning commercials repeatedly portray models happily consuming a variety of candies, occasionally with the additional reinforcement of tacit adult approval. Candy consumption is, however, considered by children to be a partially proscribed behavior. Parental communication and primitive judgment typically serve to restrain candy intake through creation of mild inhibitions. Extensive exposure to candy ad modeling stimuli may suggest to the child that excessive eating is acceptable behavior, thereby reducing personal guilt or fear of social disapproval. This effect should be reflected in greater amounts of candy bars eaten by the child; since inhibitions probably don't pertain to particular brands, the impact should be generalized to all brands regardless of advertising weight. The above-mentioned survey of fourth to seventh graders found that candy exposure and consumption correlated $+.29$ for heavily promoted brands and $+.30$ for lightly advertised brands. A later, similar survey showed correlations of $+.27$ for heavily advertised candies and $+.23$ for lightly advertised brands (Atkin et al., 1979). This provides compelling evidence that television ads do influence candy consumption in a generic manner.

Impact of Premium Appeals

Although there is considerable research dealing with the overall influence of advertising on preferences, less attention has been given to the specific message factors that maximize effectiveness. The type of appeal that has come under closest study, and the one which I'll review here, is the premium offer that is often featured in cereal commercials.

In the mother–child study by Atkin (1975c), mothers who reported that their children asked for cereals were asked, "When your child asks for a specific cereal, what does he/she usually say . . . what reasons does he/she give for wanting it?" Forty-five percent said that the premium featured with the cereal was a reason given by the child, and an additional 36% cited premiums in response to a follow-up query specifically asking about this as a reason. Mothers mentioned the premium factor far more often than any other motive. Moreover, according to mothers, 70% of the children who view an hour or less of Saturday morning television ask for cereal because of premiums, compared to 86% of those watching 2 hours and 90% of those watching 3 hours or more. Similar findings have been reported in a more recent study in which, among 5- to 12-year-olds, heavy viewers were more than twice as likely as were light viewers to cite premiums as an important reason for cereal preferences (Atkin et al., 1979). Further support for the importance of premiums comes from Reilly (1973), who asked children, "When you see a television commercial for a product, would you like the product more if . . ." followed by pairs of alternatives. More than half of the 6- to 10-year-olds chose the premium attribute over nutrition, compared to one-third of those 11–15 years old.

Observational and experimental methods also demonstrate the power of premiums. Observation of parent–child interactions at the cereal shelf of the supermarket showed that one-tenth of the children explicitly identified the premium as the primary reason for wanting a particular brand (Atkin, 1978b). Another one-fourth were judged to be making their decision primarily on the basis of the premium, although this motivation was not overtly expressed. In addition, one-tenth of the children mentioned the premium, although it was not judged to be a more salient motive than desire for the cereal product. Thus, almost half of the children appeared to take account of the premium in choosing a cereal.

An experimental test of a Kellogg's Poptarts commercial with or without a premium offer also yielded evidence of its effectiveness (Atkin, 1975a). When asked after viewing to indicate why kids like to get Poptarts, relatively few of the children referred to the premium but almost all of those who did were in the condition in which they had viewed the premium version of the commercial. Children in this condition also showed a greater desire for Poptarts, as 83% compared to 72% of the nonpremium viewers said they wanted to eat it "a lot." However, this interest was not translated into any greater intention to ask for Poptarts in the supermarket, as 77% of each group intended to request it.

Conclusions

There is ample evidence that television advertising plays a dominant role in shaping children's product preferences. Both children and mothers cite commercials as the leading source of awareness of preferred toys and foods. Both experiments and surveys show how exposure to advertising increases desire for, requests for, and consumption of advertised products. Heavier viewers of television advertising are far more likely than are lighter viewers to request that parents buy food and toy products for them. Furthermore, the evidence indicates that advertising stimulates higher usage levels for those consumable products available in the home. There is some tendency for this impact to generalize to other brands in the heavily advertised product category, thus producing generic consumption as well as brand preferences. Among the message components that may maximize effects, premium offers have been shown to be highly influential.

Nutrition Learning from Food Advertising

Not only does food advertising influence food preferences, but it also can shape the basic nutritional beliefs and attitudes of the child. Content analysis research indicates that although commercials tend to promote the non-nutritional aspects of a limited array of predominantly sweetened cereal, candy, and snack products (e.g., Atkin & Heald, 1977; Barcus, 1978) they also often refer to the importance of a balanced breakfast in cereal ads and they occasionally describe vitamin attributes. Thus, there is the potential for certain effects on nutrition learning. Since nutritional aspects of foods are not emphasized, youngsters may make food choices based on non-nutritional criteria and/or nutrition may not even be a salient dimension for evaluating products. In addition, young viewers may develop incorrect beliefs about presweetened products and/or may learn about balanced breakfasts.

Salience of Nutrition to Children

Research studies have examined the extent to which children consider nutritional aspects of foods when making a request. For example, Atkin (1975c) interviewed mothers of 4- to 12-year-olds about the main factors affecting children's cereal selection. Just 3% said that their children typically expressed nutrition-related reasons in requesting cereals (as reported above, 45% said the premium was the most central reason). A follow-up question specifically asked if the child ever mentioned the nutritional value of a cereal; 16% replied affirmatively. There was a slight positive correlation between Saturday morning advertising exposure and citing nutrition when asking for cereals. In another study, children's degree of food commercial viewing was moderately related to their rated importance of "fun of eating" cereal and candy, the premium contained in cereal boxes, and the chewiness and lastingness of candy. The sweetness dimension was slightly more salient for heavy viewers, while viewing was not related to nutrition salience (Atkin et al., 1979). In a third study, Atkin and Gibson (1978) showed 4- to 7-year-olds an ad for Cocoa Pebbles cereal, where Fred Flintstone and Barney Rubble claimed that it was "chocolaty enough to make you smile." Among the reasons for wanting to eat Pebbles, two-thirds cited the "chocolaty" taste, three-fifths wanted it because it would make them smile, and more than half desired the cereal because Fred and Barney liked it.

Children's Perceptions of Food Advertising

Children do not seem to apply critical evaluation in processing food advertising. Young children tended to accept claims made in four ads identified by the FTC as possibly deceptive (Haefner et al., 1975). Furthermore, viewing a Post Grape Nuts cereal commercial depicting the edibility of wild vegetation led 5- to 12-year-olds to rate similar-appearing toxic plants as edible (Poulos, 1975). Finally, almost two-thirds of a group of 4-to 7-year-olds who saw an ad featuring a circus strongman lifting a playhouse and eating a cereal thought that the cereal would contribute to their own strength, including one-third who said that the cereal would make them strong enough to lift a really heavy object. Those who frequently viewed Saturday morning cereal advertising at home were much more likely to express the strength beliefs than were those who were infrequently exposed (Atkin & Gibson, 1978).

By promoting the strength or energy benefits of foods, advertising may lead children to believe that these products have more nutritional value. Sharaga (1974) found that the heaviest television viewers had less correct perceptions of the validity of nutrition claims in food commercials and had lower nutrition knowledge. Atkin et al. (1979) found that heavy viewers of food ads were twice as likely as light viewers to say that sugared cereals and candies are highly nutritious. Since these ads typically omit references to the cavity-producing qualities of sugared foods, children may not realize that these products pose dental risks. Indeed, the study of 4- to 7-year-old children (Atkin & Gibson, 1978) showed that less than half realized that presweetened cereal was more cariogenic than nonsweetened cereal and that none thought presweetened cereal was riskier than cake (even though the sugar content by weight is greater in each case). In the study of 5- to 12-year-olds (Atkin et al., 1979), three-fifths believed that presweetened cereals are cariogenic, but heavy viewers were somewhat less likely to hold this view.

Advertising claims which may lead to the kinds of knowledge (and lack of it) reported here are often presented by attractive characters who are identified with the product. Children find them to be credible sources of nutrition information. For instance, one-third of a sample of 4- to 7-year-olds thought that Fred Flintstone and Barney Rubble knew "very much" about which cereals children should eat. Heavy cereal ad viewers were far more likely than light viewers to attribute credibility to the animated figures (Atkin & Gibson, 1978). Similarly, in a sample of 5- to 12-year-olds, one-third of the heavy viewers compared to one-tenth of the light viewers thought that Cookie Jarvis was a knowledgeable source of cereal information.

Children's Understanding of the Balanced Breakfast Concept

Many Saturday morning commercials cite the importance of eating a nutritious, well-balanced breakfast that includes cereal, milk, orange juice, and toast. In a survey of 10- to 14-year-olds, Atkin (1975d) found that those who reported paying close attention to this portion of cereal commercials were significantly more likely to say it's "very important to start your day with a nutritious and balanced breakfast." Close attentiveness was also related positively to beliefs that toast and juice are "good for you."

Atkin and Gibson (1978) examined 4- to 7-year-old children's understanding of the balanced breakfast concept. In the laboratory, they were shown a cereal ad containing the balanced breakfast disclosure. When asked to recall which foods were portrayed with the cereal, two-thirds could remember nothing. Furthermore, two-thirds had no idea what the term "balanced breakfast" means. A follow-up item inquired whether a bowl of cereal alone would constitute a balanced breakfast. Two-thirds of the preschool subgroup thought that it would be sufficient to provide a balanced breakfast while few of the 7-year-olds agreed. Frequent viewing of television commercials at home apparently contributes little to understanding, since the heavily exposed youth knew less than light viewers.

Conclusions

Among the factors that children weigh in selecting cereals, nutritional value does not seem to be an important dimension. There is some evidence that children are persuaded to want the cereals for nonsubstantive reasons—character endorsements, toy premiums, and chewiness—which are the types of appeals featured most prominently in advertising. Some findings suggest that children's beliefs about the nutritional value of various foods and sugar are shaped by advertising, that they are not critical evaluators of advertising claims, and that they attribute competence to cartoon product presenters. The balanced breakfast concept, which is mentioned in most cereal ads, is not well understood by younger children. Rather than informing young viewers about the need for other foods at breakfast, this "disclaimer" may actually give the impression that cereal alone is sufficient. In addition, these ads do not seem to provide adequate awareness of the sugar levels in presweetened cereals or of the cariogenic risk associated with the consumption of sugared cereals.

Side Effects of Children's Advertising

Several types of behavioral and emotional responses of a negative or antisocial nature may be associated with television advertising. Among the undesirable outcomes that have been studied are parent–child conflict and child unhappiness.

Impact of Advertising on Parent–Child Conflict

The previous section demonstrated how television advertising caused higher levels of child requests for parental product purchases. When such demands are not satisfied, it may result in arguments and verbal aggression between parent and child.

The most direct approach to measuring this outcome is to ask each party about the incidence of conflict, as done in the Atkin (1975c) survey of preschool and elementary children and their mothers. Children were asked, "When your mother says you cannot have a toy/cereal that you ask for, how much do you argue with her?" For toys, 17% reported "a lot" of arguing and 34% said "sometimes." For cereals, there was 13% "a lot" and 31% "sometimes." Among mothers who denied cereal requests, 44% said that arguments followed at least occasionally; arguments developed most frequently after premium-based requests. After denials of toy requests, 53% of the mothers said that at least some arguing occurred. A survey of fourth to seventh graders by Atkin (1975d) asked the same question for cereal arguing; 17% reported that conflict happened "a lot" and 34% said it occurred "sometimes." In Atkin's (1978b) supermarket observation study, 65% of all parental denials were accompanied by manifestations of parent–child conflict, usually in the form of brief and mild arguments by the child. Finally, Ward and Wackman (1972) found a mild positive correlation between child product requests and the level of general parent–child conflict.

An experiment by Goldberg and Gorn (1978) is relevant to this issue. Four- and five-year-old children either saw advertising for a new toy or were in a nonexposed control condition. The children were then asked a projective question about how a hypothetical child would react if his parent denied a request for that particular toy; about three-fifths of the exposed subjects said the child would express rejection rather than positive affect toward the parent, compared to two-fifths of the control group. In a projective study, young children were asked what would happen if a hypothetical child's request for an advertised product were denied; 23% of them too said the child would express hostility toward the parent and 16% said the child would persist in demanding the desired item (Sheikh & Moleski, 1977).

Of course, none of this necessarily proves that advertising is responsible for the conflict. To examine that question, the amount of exposure to ads needs to be related to the degree of arguing. Children heavily exposed to Saturday morning commercials in the Atkin (1975c) study were clearly more likely to experience frequent conflict: In averaging reactions to cereal and toy denials, it was found that 21% of the heavily exposed children compared to 9% of the lightly exposed children argued "a lot." This effect is apparently due to the higher rate of requests generated by advertising exposure, which in turn produced more denials. In the Atkin (1975d) study, heavy viewers got into more arguments than light viewers, by a 20% to 14% margin in the "a lot" category. All of which suggests that advertising is at least partially responsible for the conflict.

Impact of Advertising on Child Unhappiness

There are several ways that commercials may contribute to unhappy feelings among young viewers: (a) when advertising-induced requests are denied or unobtainable, children may become angry and upset; (b) when the child's own social or psychological condition is less satisfactory than life situations portrayed in the commercial, dissatisfaction may result; and (c) when ads create high expectations regarding the performance of products, actual experience with the product that falls short of anticipation may engender disappointment.

Two investigations used projective techniques and one used observation to determine how children feel after denial of requests. Goldberg and Gorn (1978), in the experiment described above, asked young children how a hypothetical child would respond to a parental rejection of a toy request. A feeling of sadness was projected by 60% of those exposed to advertising for the toy and by 35% of the control group. The Sheikh and Moleski (1977) study described previously also asked young children how a hypothetical child would respond to a product denial; 33% estimated that the child would cry or display some other negative feeling. Supermarket observation of child responses to cereal-request rejections also showed child unhappiness, judged to occur 48% of the time (Atkin, 1978b).

Four surveys asked children directly how they responded to unattained desires. Two weeks after Christmas, Robertson and Rossiter (1976) found that 35% of the children indicated disappointment after gifts were not received; the rate was higher for heavy television viewers. Atkin and Reinhold (1972) asked children, "How often does it make you feel bad when you see things in television commercials that you know your parents won't buy for you?" Negative feelings were experienced "a lot" by 13% of the children, "sometimes" by 38% and "never" by 49%. A sample of preadolescents was asked, "When your mother says that you cannot have a cereal that you ask for, how much do you get mad at her?" One-fifth got mad "a lot" and one fourth "sometimes" got mad; 24% of the heavy advertising viewers and 15% of the light viewers fell in the "a lot" category (Atkin, 1975d). An identical question posed to preschool and elementary students yielded almost identical results, as 24% of the heavy viewers and 11% of the light viewers got mad "a lot" (Atkin, 1975c). These younger children were also asked about toy denial responses; one-fifth got mad "a lot" and two-fifths "sometimes," and 26% of heavy viewers compared to 18% of light viewers reported "a lot." In the same study, 5% of mothers said their children got angry and 21% reported disappointment or pouting, with greater unhappiness among children who asked for a cereal to obtain the premium. When toy requests were denied, angry reactions were reported by 10% of the mothers and disappointment or pouting by 29%. Child unhappiness over both toy and cereal denials was substantially higher for those watching more television advertising.

Two surveys deal with emotional dissatisfaction aroused during exposure to commercials portraying an idealized lifestyle. Donohue, Meyer, and Henke (1978) showed young black and white children a fast-food commercial depicting a happy middle-class family enjoying lunch at the restaurant. Three-fourths of the low-income blacks perceived that the commercial family was happier than their own family, compared to 4% of the middle-income white youngsters. Atkin (1975d) showed preadolescents pictures from lively soft drink ads portraying teenagers having fun in various happy social situations. They were asked, "When you are sitting around the house, bored and sad, do these commercials make you feel better or worse?" Increased negative feelings were reported by 22%, positive change by 25%, and the rest said they were not affected.

There is limited data showing that ads contribute to product dissatisfaction. In a survey of children's disappointment with Christmas presents, 24% of the heavy television viewers as compared to 8% of the light viewers were dissatisfied with the products they received (Robertson & Rossiter, 1975). Ward et al. (1977) discovered that three-fifths of their elementary school sample had seen a product on television that "wasn't as good as you thought it would be" when they got it. The disappointment rate increased substantially with age. In interviews with mothers, Atkin (1975c) found that two-thirds of their children had been disappointed with a cereal product; however, this was not correlated with television exposure.

Several studies suggest that advertising disruption of the ongoing pleasure of program viewing is a significant irritant. In a survey of fourth to seventh graders, Atkin (1975d) asked, "How much does it bother you when they stop the program to show commercials?" 79% said "a lot" and 18% said "sometimes." Moreover, those who felt that ads should be removed from Saturday morning television most often cited program interruption rather than advertising content as the reason. Another survey posed this same question to a sample of 4- to 12-year-old children (Atkin, 1975c); 56% reported being bothered "a lot" and 23% "sometimes," with the highest irritation in the late elementary school age range studied in the first survey. On the other hand, a parallel survey of mothers of the 4- to 12-year-old sample found that they did not perceive that the disruption was a concern in the case of their children; 23% reported that it was a bothersome problem.

Anger and even aggression may, however, result from unfulfilled expectations, according to an experiment by Atkin (1975a). In a play situation, 3- to 10-year-olds' attempts to build impressive structures with blocks were generally unsuccessful. Those who had previously seen an "exaggerated claim" commercial in which a complex block structure was built were somewhat more likely to display anger, verbal aggression, and isolated incidents of physical aggression than were those who had seen an ad with a modest block structure (28% compared with 18%).

Finally, advertising may directly teach or arouse child aggressiveness. A content analysis study by Schuetz and Sprafkin (1979) showed that aggression incidents, most involving nonhuman characters, occurred 113 times in the 242 commercials studied, with three times as much aggression per minute of advertising as per minute of programming. An earlier study of children's non-toy ads indicated that one-seventh of the commercials contained violence, usually committed by fantasy villains (Winick, Williamson, Chuzmir, & Winick, 1973). While there is some chance that young viewers may imitate specific actions or be instigated to behave antisocially, Adler et al. (1977) point out that the likelihood is slight because most acts are short-lived and many are nonimitable fantasy violence. Although the effect may be slight, it may be enhanced by the fact that ads tend to feature fast-paced action with a high rate of camera shot changes and an exciting soundtrack. Regular programs characterized by these audiovisual formats tend to arouse antisocial acts in young viewers (e.g., Tannenbaum & Zillmann, 1975).

Conclusions

The evidence indicates that television commercials have an effect on intrafamily conflict and child unhappiness. First, parents reject approximately one-third to one-half of child requests for products; toys and candies are denied more often than cereals. This leads to generally mild and infrequent parent–child conflict in about half of all families. Children who see the most advertising have considerably more conflict. Age differences are not significant. Second, about one-third to one-half of the children become unhappy, angry, or disappointed after denials of food and toy requests; again, the rate is considerably higher among those seeing the most advertising. In addition, some children become emotionally dissatisfied when they compare their own situation with the idealized lifestyles portrayed in upbeat commercials for food and drinks or when actual products fall short of the advertised image. Third, advertising interruptions of program enjoyment produce irritation in many viewers. Aggressive responses may also result when exaggerated depictions in commercials are not satisfied in actual product use, when aggressive acts portrayed in ads are imitated, or when fast-paced and exciting commercials emotionally arouse viewers.

Effects of Noncommercial Spot Messages

Aside from commercials for food and toy products, children also have the opportunity to view spot messages of a noncommercial nature. One common type of message is the public service announcement (PSA), which is intended to inform the audience about topics such as health, pollution, and social relations. Periodically, there are also political advertisements promoting various candidates for office.

Public service announcements have been shown to influence children's attitudes and behaviors regarding cooperative play (Liebert, Sprafkin, & Poulos, 1975), nutrition (Atkin, 1975a; Goldberg, Gorn, & Gibson, 1978), littering (Atkin, 1978a), and seat belts (Atkin, 1978a); however, little impact has been demonstrated for drug and smoking PSAs (Atkin, 1978a; Feingold & Knapp, 1977; Morrison, Kline, & Miller, 1976; Smart & Fejer, 1974). Two studies illustrate the success of these informational messages. In an experiment, Atkin (1975a) showed an antilittering PSA to half of a sample of 3- to 12-year-old children. Compared to a nonexposed control group, these children were significantly more likely to dispose properly of the wrapper on a piece of candy they received after the experiment. In a survey with a different sample of 3- to 12-year-olds, there was a slight positive correlation between amount of home exposure to seat belt PSAs and frequency of buckling belts while riding in the car (Atkin, 1978a).

To study the impact of political commercials, Atkin (1977) surveyed 9- to 12-year-old children during the 1976 presidential campaign. The children reported substantial exposure to political ads, and exposure level was moderately correlated with knowledge about and liking for the candidates. Thus, both PSAs and political commercials are influential. In format and style they are similar to product commercials and they succeed for the same reasons—repetitive presentation of simplified, attractively packaged ideas at times when young viewers are before the television set.

Implications of Research Findings
for Advertising Regulation

Although issues of regulating children's advertising are discussed elsewhere in this book, this chapter will conclude with some brief comments linking the research data to regulatory options under consideration by federal agencies. First, the consequences of reducing the amount of advertising allowed during children's viewing periods can be projected by comparing responses of current light and heavy viewers of ads. It appears that less exposure of advertising would lead to a lower likelihood of accepting claims, requesting and consuming advertised products, arguing with parents over purchases, and experiencing unhappiness and dissatisfaction due to ads. In addition, restrictions on specific techniques such as premium appeals and fantasy characters as product presenters may serve to minimize some of the negative outcomes of advertising. Finally, requirement of a greater quantity and quality of PSA-style messages to counterbalance the generic influence of commercials (particularly food ads) seems to offer a promising remedy for certain misleading consequences of advertising.

References

Adler, R. P., Friedlander, B. Z., Lesser, G. S., Meringoff, L., Robertson, T. S., Rossiter, J. R., & Ward, S. *Research on the effects of television advertising on children.* Washington, D.C.: United States Government Printing Office, 1977.

Atkin, C. *Effects of television advertising on children—First year experimental evidence.* Technical report, Michigan State Univ., 1975. (a)

Atkin, C. *Effects of television advertising on children—Second year experimental evidence.* Technical report, Michigan State Univ., 1975. (b)

Atkin, C. *Effects of television advertising on children—Survey of children's and mothers' responses to television commercials.* Technical report, Michigan State Univ., 1975. (c)

Atkin, C. *Effects of television advertising on children—Survey of preadolescents' responses to television commercials.* Technical report, Michigan State Univ., 1975. (d)

Atkin, C. Children's social learning from television advertising: Research evidence on observational modeling of product consumption. *Advances in Consumer Research,* 1976, *3,* 513–519.

Atkin, C. Effects of campaign advertising and newscasts on children. *Journalism Quarterly,* 1977, *54,* 503–508.

Atkin, C. *Effects of public service announcements on young viewers.* Paper presented at the meeting of the Midwest Association for Public Opinion Research, Chicago, 1978. (a)

Atkin, C. Observation of parent–child interaction in supermarket decision making. *Journal of Marketing,* 1978, *42,* 41–45. (b)

Atkin, C., & Gibson, W. *Children's nutrition learning from television advertising.* Unpublished manuscript, Michigan State Univ., 1978.

Atkin, C., & Heald, G. The content of children's toy and food commercials. *Journal of Communication,* 1977, *27* (1), 107–113.

Atkin, C., Reeves, B., & Gibson, W. *Effects of television food advertising on children.* Paper presented at the meeting of the Association for Education in Journalism, Houston, 1979.

Atkin, C., & Reinhold, C. *The impact of television advertising on children.* Paper presented at the meeting of the Association for Education in Journalism, Carbondale, Illinois, August, 1972.

Bandura, A. *Social learning theory.* New York: General Learning Press, 1971.

Barcus, F. C. *Commercial children's television on weekends and weekday afternoons.* Newtonville, Massachusetts: Action for Children's Television, 1978.

Barry, T. *The effect of a modified disclaimer on inner city vs. suburban children.* Paper presented to the meeting of the American Marketing Association, Boston, 1978.

Barry, T., & Sheikh, A. Race as a dimension in children's TV advertising: The need for more research. *Journal of Advertising,* 1977, *6,* 5–10.

Bogart, L. Consumer and advertising research. In I. Pool & W. Schramm (Eds.), *Handbook of communication.* Chicago: Rand-McNally, 1973.

Caron, A., & Ward, S. Gift decisions by kids and parents. *Journal of Advertising*, 1975, 15(4), 12–20.

Clancy-Hepburn, K., Hickey, A., & Nevill, G. Children's behavior responses to TV food advertisements. *Journal of Nutrition Education*, 1974, 6(3), 93–96.

Donohue, T. Effect of commercials on black children. *Journal of Advertising Research*, 1975, 15(6), 41–46.

Donohue, T., Meyer, T., & Henke, L. Black and white children's perceptions of television commercials. *Journal of Marketing*, 1978, 42, 34–40.

Dussere, S. *The effects of television advertising on children's eating habits.* Unpublished doctoral dissertation. Univ. of Massachusetts at Amherst, 1976.

Feingold, P., & Knapp, M. Anti-drug abuse commercials. *Journal of Communication*, 1977, 27(1), 20–28.

Galst, J., & White, M. A. The unhealthy persuader: The reinforcing value of television and children's purchase-influencing attempts at the supermarket. *Child Development*, 1976, 47, 1089–1096.

Goldberg, M., & Gorn, G. Some unintended consequences of TV advertising to children. *Journal of Consumer Research*, 1978, 5, 22–29.

Goldberg, M., Gorn, G., & Gibson, W. TV messages for snack and breakfast foods: Do they influence children's preferences? *Journal of Consumer Research*, 1978, 5, 48–54.

Gorn, G., & Goldberg, M. The impact of television advertising on children from low income families. *Journal of Consumer Research*, 1977, 4, 86–88.

Haefner, J., Leckenby, J., & Goldman, S. *The measurement of advertising impact on children.* Paper presented at the meeting of the American Psychological Association, Chicago, September, 1975.

Howard, J., Hulbert, J., & Lehmann, D. *An exploratory analysis of the effect of television advertising on children.* A working paper described in Adler *et al.*, 1977.

Krugman, H. The impact of television advertising: Learning without involvement. *Public Opinion Quarterly*, 1965, 29, 349–356.

Liebert, D., Sprafkin, J., Liebert, R., & Rubinstein, E. Effects of television commercial disclaimers on the product expectations of children. *Journal of Communication*, 1977, 27(1), 118–124.

Liebert, R., Sprafkin, J., & Poulos, R. Selling cooperation to children. In S. Hald (Ed.), *Proceedings of the 20th Annual Advertising Research Foundation Conference.* New York: Advertising Research Foundation, 1975.

Morrison, A., Kline, F., & Miller, P. Aspects of adolescent information acquisition about drugs and alcohol topics. In R. Ostman (Ed.), *Communication research and drug education.* Beverly Hills, California: Sage Publications, 1976.

Poulos, R. *Unintentional negative effects of food commercials on children: A case study.* Unpublished manuscript, Media Action Research Center, New York, 1975.

Ramond, C. *Advertising research: The state of the art.* New York: Association of National Advertisers, 1976.

Reilly Group, Incorporated. Assumption by the child of the role of consumer. *The Child*, 1973, 1, (entire volume).

Resnik, A., & Stern, B. Children's television advertising and brand choice: A laboratory experiment. *Journal of Advertising*, 1977, 6(3), 11–17.

Robertson, T., & Rossiter, J. Children and commercial persuasion: An attribution theory analysis. *Journal of Consumer Research*, 1974, 1, 13–20.

Robertson, T., & Rossiter, J. *Children's consumer satisfaction.* Unpublished manuscript, Univ. of Pennsylvania, 1975.

Robertson, T., & Rossiter, J. Short-run advertising effects on children: A field study. *Journal of Marketing Research*, 1976, 13, 68–70.

Rossiter, J. Reliability of a short test measuring children's attitudes toward TV commercials. *Journal of Consumer Research*, 1977, 3, 179–184.

Schuetz, S., & Sprafkin, J. Portrayal of prosocial and aggressive behaviors on children's TV commercials. *Journal of Broadcasting*, 1979, 23, 33–40.

Sharaga, S. *The effect of television advertising on children's nutrition attitudes, nutrition knowledge, and eating habits.* Unpublished doctoral dissertation, Cornell Univ., New York, 1974.

Sheikh, A. A., & Moleski, L. M. Conflict in the family over commercials. *Journal of Communication*, 1977, 27(1), 152–157.

Smart, R. G., & Fejer, D. The effects of high and low fear messages about drugs. *Journal of Drug Education*, 1974, 4, 225–235.

Stern, B., & Resnik, A. *Children's understanding of a television commercial disclaimer.* Unpublished manuscript, Portland State Univ., Oregon, 1977.

Tannenbaum, P., & Zillmann, D. Emotional arousal in the facilitation of aggression through communication. In L. Berkowitz (Ed.), *Advances in experimental social psychology* (Vol. 12). New York: Academic Press, 1975.

Ward, S. Children's reactions to commercials. *Journal of Advertising Research*, 1972, 12(2), 37–45.

Ward, S., Wackman, D., & Wartella, E. *How children learn to buy: The development of consumer information processing skills.* Beverly Hills, California: Sage, 1977.

Winick, C., Williamson, L. G., Chuzmir, S. F., & Winick, M. P. *Children's television commercials: A content analysis.* New York: Praeger, 1973.

19

Individual Differences in Children's Responses to Television Advertising

ELLEN WARTELLA

This chapter will examine various aspects of children's responses to advertising, considering individual differences in children's attention to, comprehension of, and use of advertising information in their own consumer activities. It is organized into sections by such measures of how children process television advertising information and use it in various sorts of product decision making. Within each section, the age of the child is the major individual difference variable which will be discussed. Where individual differences in advertising's impact have been examined, most research has been devoted to describing the nature of age-related differences in responsiveness and the ways in which younger and older children differ in processing advertising information. In addition to age differences, consideration will also be given to differential responses to advertising by boys and girls, racial groups, and social classes. Unfortunately, however, very few studies report examination of these latter three individual difference factors, and so my discussion of them is necessarily quite limited.

In the first section of the chapter, consideration will be given to children's attention to television advertising, including patterns of attention to commercials, effects of audiovisual elements on increasing or decreas-

ing attention, and effects of various program/commercial separation
techniques on children's attention patterns. In subsequent sections of the
paper, comprehension and recall of advertising and behavioral outcomes
of exposure to it will be discussed.

Children's Attention to Television Advertising

Attention Level

How much attention do children devote to television advertising?
Most reports of exposure to advertising are estimates based on amount of
exposure to television in general (Adler, Friedlander, Lesser, Meringoff,
Robertson, Rossiter, & Ward, 1977). For instance, the finding that, after
age 2, most children spend about 3–4 hours per day watching television
yields an estimate of about 3 hours of exposure to television advertisements per week (Adler *et al.*, 1977). But are children really watching
the advertisements when they watch television? Observational evidence
of attention patterns to advertisements varies across studies, an important
variant being whether the study was conducted within homes, in school
viewing groups, or in special laboratories.

In one of the few in-home observational studies, Bechtel, Achelpol,
and Akers (1972) reported that commercials accounted for the largest
block of nonwatching behavior in the 30 middle class families studied.
Nearly one-fourth of all nonwatching occurred when commercials were
televised. Furthermore, they found that the 1- to 10-year-old children they
observed watched the commercials only 40% of the time they were on
while the 11- to 19-year-olds watched them 55% of the time they were on.
In a recent observational study of children watching television in their
homes, Winick and Winick (1979) report a similar finding that youngsters
as young as 2 left the room regularly every time a commercial was shown.
They provided no data regarding the frequency with which this occurred,
but they did report that commercials were regarded as relatively unimpor-
tant by the over 300 children observed.

Self-report studies of children's attention patterns while viewing at
home (Atkin, 1975d) indicate that younger children reported heavier exposure to Saturday morning television, and thus perhaps to commercials,
than did older children, and blacks reported more attention than did
whites. Mothers reported that their preschool through third grade children paid close attention over half the time (59% for mothers of preschool
and kindergarten children and 54% for mothers of first and third grade
children). In contrast, only 29% of the mothers of fourth and fifth grade
children reported that their children paid close attention (Atkin, 1978).

Ward, Levinson, and Wackman (1972) and Ward and Wackman (1973) reported data from 65 mothers who observed their 5- to 12-year-old children watching television in the home. Attention was coded as full (eyes on screen), partial, or none. Overall, these children showed slightly higher attention to commercials than found in Bechtel et al., (1972). Children 5–8 years old were at full attention 67% of commercial viewing time, and 9- to 12-year-olds averaged full attention 65% of the viewing time. Several age-related differences in attention were found: The younger children showed higher attention to Saturday morning television and less differentiation in attention to the commercials. For example, they showed a decrease of only 2% in full attention across the block transition from the program to first commercial compared with a 23% decrease for the older children. Furthermore, the younger children showed more stable attention behavior in a variety of other comparisons, including placement of advertisement in show, length of advertisement, time of day of program, and product advertised. In comparison, children in the older age group showed greater differentiation in attention to the advertisements. For these children attention to the commercials increased when they were placed early in the program and when they advertised products presumably for an older consumer such as health and beauty aids. Furthermore, the older children's attention level dropped after the first commercial in a series of commercials and within the longer 60-second commercials.

Two studies in schools found high attention to commercials among school children. In one, Wartella and Ettema (1974) reported that kindergarten and second grade children showed slightly higher overall attention to 12 advertisements inserted into a 30 minute situation comedy program than did nursery school children. Similarly, Atkin (1975a) reported fairly high attention among 500 preschool and grade school children unobtrusively monitored as they watched seven, 30 second commercials embedded into a cartoon program (mean eye contact averaged 25 seconds). Older children (8–10 years) again showed slightly higher mean eye contact than did younger (3–7 years) children by about a 2-second margin.

In contrast with the in-school setting, Zuckerman, Zigler, and Stevenson (1978) videotaped second, third, and fourth grade children watching a program with commercials in a special laboratory viewing room that had toys and other distractors. They reported uniformly *low* attention to both the 15 minute program (either a cartoon or a program about children on a camping trip) and the eight breakfast commercials embedded in it. On the average, only 17% of the children attended to the commercials. In contrast with the Wartella and Ettema (1974) and Atkin (1975a) studies, Zuckerman et al. found attention to the commercials decreased with increasing age of the child.

In general, these findings suggest that where observations or reports of children's viewing have been conducted in more naturalistic environments such as homes or special viewing rooms with distractors present, attention to commercials decreases among older children. Preschool and early elementary school age children show more attention to commercials than do older children. However, in-school studies have found that older children show slightly higher attention to commercials than do younger children. Demand characteristics of the in-school viewing setting may help account for this divergent outcome. None of these observational studies reports sex, racial, or social class differences in attention levels.

Commercial Production Factors
that Affect Attention

Variations in attention due to the specific audiovisual and content characteristics of commercials and to their placement in a program have also been studied. Turning first to audiovisual characteristics, specifically perceptual complexity, we find that Wartella and Ettema (1974) reported that nursery school children showed greater differences in attention to high as compared to low perceptual complexity commercials than did kindergarten and second grade children. The data were derived from in-school observations of 120 upper-middle-class children viewing 12 commercials in a situation comedy program. Atkin (1975a), however, found few differences in the effects of different production factors on younger (ages 3–7) and older (ages 8–10) children, in a sample of about 500 balanced for sex and social class and about 43% black. Children in both age groups showed slightly higher attention to commercials with a video-only disclaimer than with an audiovisual disclaimer.

In terms of content characteristics, Atkin (1975a) found that both older and younger children paid somewhat more attention to commercials where extravagant claims rather than modest ones were made about a product and to commercials featuring white rather than black actors. As compared to younger children, older children did, however, show slightly higher attention to a nonpremium advertisement compared to a premium ad and to a cereal commercial with well-reasoned, "rational" arguments for purchasing compared to one with an emotional appeal format stating that the cereal tasted good and would help them to succeed in sports.

Clustering in commercial blocks does not seem to decrease young children's attention (Atkin, 1975a; Duffy & Rossiter, 1975). In a classroom setting, Duffy and Rossiter (1975) showed groups of first and fourth grade children either a clustered commercial/program format or the traditional dispersed commercial/program format. Classroom observers estimated the percentage of children giving "full attention" to each commercial show. First graders showed slightly higher attention to the clustered commercials while fourth graders were slightly more attentive to the nonclustered commercials. Atkin (1975a) found higher attention to clustered commercials in his study of preschoolers through fifth graders.

Program/Commercial Separation

Children's abilities to distinguish advertising content from other television programming have been the focus of a number of research studies and public policy deliberations in the Federal Communications Commission (FCC) and Federal Trade Commission (FTC), as described in previous chapters. In particular, the FCC in its 1974 report acknowledged the problem young children have in making distinctions between programs and commercials and required all licensees to make a clear separation between programs and commercials. Thus, the issue becomes one for both policy and research.

Shifts in attention patterns at the onset of a commercial provide evidence of one very rudimentary sort of discrimination between programs and commercials. Children as young as 3 or 4 have been found to make such an attentional shift upward at the onset of a commercial (Wartella & Ettema, 1974; Zuckerman et al., 1978). Attention to the screen has been found to decrease over the course of the commercial. Furthermore, when measures have been taken in school situations, as in Wartella and Ettema (1974), there is evidence of shifts to full attention at the onset of the second and third commercial in a sequence. On the other hand, Zuckerman et al. (1978), who reported generally low attention to the television among second, third, and fourth graders, found attention to commercials decreasing at the onset of the second in a series. Correspondingly, when mothers observed their children watching television at home rather than utilizing trained observers in a controlled viewing situation, there was no indication of movement toward higher attention by young children at the onset of commercials (Ward, Levinson, & Wackman, 1972; Ward & Wackman, 1973).

In contrast to children younger than age 8 or 9, older children have been reported to shift attention away from the television set at the onset of commercials (Ward, et al., 1972; Winick & Winick, 1979). Similarly, mothers' observational reports of their children's commercial viewing behavior suggest that older children are more likely to tune out the television commercials (Atkin, 1975a).

In addition to shifts in attention at the onset of commercials, children as young as 4 have shown additional evidence of perceptual awareness of program/commercial differences. Gianinno and Zuckerman (1977) found that about 50% of the 4-year-old children they interviewed could, in eight of ten paired comparisons, correctly pick out a picture of a television commercial character paired with a television program character. On the other hand, nearly all of the 7-year-old children they interviewed could recognize the commercial characters in all ten paired comparisons. When asked to choose the picture of a character who showed products on television, nearly all of both the 4- and 7-year-old subjects demonstrated at least 80% accuracy.

In a recent study, Palmer and McDowell (1979) examined the success of the three networks' attempts to make a clear separation between programming and commercials as required by the FCC in 1974. Sixty kindergarten and first grade children were assigned to one of four viewing groups—a control group which viewed a television program and commercials with no separators and three experimental groups each utilizing a particular network's program/commercial separator format. The videotape was stopped at predetermined points during the commercials and the program, and children were asked whether what they had just seen was part of the show or part of the commercial. Children in the control group were able to distinguish programs from commercials as well as children in any of the experimental groups, correctly identifying commercials in about two-thirds of their response opportunities.

Nevertheless, it is difficult to interpret such perceptual discriminations as evidence of conceptual understanding of the functional differences between programs and commercials. While children may be able to recognize such perceptual features of commercials, it is an inferential leap to assume this is evidence of understanding the purpose of commercials. It is this issue which will be considered in the next section.

Children's Comprehension of Television Advertising

Several aspects of children's comprehension of advertising information have been examined in the literature: ability to understand the purpose of advertising information, memory for commercial and product claims, and belief in commercial claims. Each of these aspects of comprehension will be considered in turn.

Comprehension of the Purpose of Advertising

Research on children's understanding of the purpose of commercials has relied on children's abilities to articulate the persuasive aspect of advertising. Results of the various survey studies seem to indicate that below age 6 (kindergarten) the vast majority of children cannot articulate the selling purpose of advertising (Adler et al., 1977; Bever, Smith, Bengen, & Johnson, 1975; Donohue, Meyer, & Henke, 1978; Meyer, Donohue, & Henke, 1976; Roberts, 1979; Robertson & Rossiter, 1974; Sheikh, Prasad, & Rao, 1974; Ward, Wackman, & Wartella, 1977). Between kindergarten and third grade, that is between the ages of about 5–9 years, the majority of children have usually been shown to be able to articulate the selling intent of advertising. Variations in the different studies in the percentage of children between kindergarten and third grade judged to understand the purpose of commercials appear to be the result of variations in the measurement contexts, question wordings, and scoring systems.

Wackman, Wartella, and Ward (1979) report estimates that range between one-tenth and one-half for the proportion of kindergarten-age children who understand that advertising is trying to sell them products. In a survey study reported in 1977, they interviewed kindergartners in their homes and asked them several different questions about the purpose of advertisements. In response to the question "What is a commercial?", only 10% mentioned the persuasive aspect of advertisements. When asked "What do commercials try to do?", 22% reported that commercials try to get them to buy products. Where kindergartners were shown commercials and then interviewed about the factual information in the commercials, even higher percentages understood selling intent. In response to the question, "What does this commercial for (product X) want you to do?", approximately half of the kindergartners in various viewing conditions (and 62% in one condition) said that the commercial wanted them to buy or try the product.

As children develop beyond early elementary school, a more complete and fuller understanding of persuasive intent and commercial role certainly develops. Several researchers put the demarcation between rudimentary understanding and grasp of persuasive intent at age 8 or older (Atkin, 1979; Roberts, 1979; Robertson & Rossiter, 1974), although the Wackman *et al.* (1979) work might put the dividing line at as young as kindergarten-age. In defining comprehension of persuasive intent, a slightly different criterion than that used by Wackman *et al.* (1979) is offered by Roberts (1979), and perhaps this accounts for the difference in the chosen demarcation points. Roberts argues that just understanding that commercials want someone to buy or try a product is not sufficient evidence that a child understands the purpose and persuasive aspect of advertising. Calling on general cognitive developmental concepts and research on the formation of children's role-taking skills, Roberts (1979) contends that not until age 9 or 10 can children take the advertiser's motivations into account when considering a commercial. In his view, children who lack role-taking skills are unable to recognize that because advertisers are trying to sell them products the presentation of the product information may be biased. Therefore, children below at least 8 years of age cannot be wary consumers of advertising messages. His argument is based on general cognitive development theory and research, but it has not been put to direct empirical test. Donohue, Meyer, & Henke (1978) and Meyer, Donohue, & Henke (1976) found that black children showed lower levels of understanding the purpose of commercials and higher rates of believing television commercials than did white children at all age levels. They used the same verbal measures (e.g., "What's a TV commercial?") as did Ward et al. (1977). No sex differences or social class differences in understanding of advertising have been reported in the literature.

In summary, during the elementary school years children's understanding of advertising proceeds from showing evidence of perceptual discrimination ability and rudimentary conceptual distinctions to an increasingly better articulated grasp of the concept of advertising. Conceptual understanding is articulated verbally by some kindergartners and appears to be well articulated by nearly all children by the time they reach third grade. It is difficult to provide evidence of when children begin to take advertisers' motivations into account when assessing any particular advertisement's claims, although there is reason to argue, as Roberts (1979) does, that this does not occur until after more advanced role-taking skills are acquired.

Memory for Advertising Information

Research on children's memory for advertising information has utilized two types of measurement procedures—measurement of cumulative knowledge about advertising outside of a television viewing situation and recognition or open-ended recall tests immediately after viewing television advertisements. Both measurement procedures have yielded similar results: Children's recognition and recall of advertising messages increase as a function of age. Major increases in memory seem to occur between kindergarten and third grade. Similar patterns are found for both sexes.

Ward (1972) and Ward et al. (1977) studied 5- to 12-year-old children's recall of their "favorite" television commercial. Measures were taken in an interview conducted outside a television viewing situation. The children's responses were content analyzed for the number of commercial elements mentioned, the completeness of the storyline, and mention of brand name and other product features. Both studies found that children's recall for commercials became more complete, coherent, and unified as they grow older. While the kindergarten children tended to recall a single element of the commercial (e.g., there was a girl playing with a doll), the older children tended to recall more product and commercial plot line information. They related the information in a story line sequence and generally gave a more unified multidimensional description of the commercial and product. According to Ward et al. (1977), the major shift in recall from memory for one dimension to multidimensional memory seemed to occur between kindergarten and third grade. The older children recalled more information about the commercial and more different kinds of information—that is, information about the story line, brand name, and product attributes.

Studies of children's memory for commercials they have just been shown tend to support these findings. For instance, Atkin (1975a, 1975b, 1975c, 1975d) reported several studies of children's memory for product elements in several specially produced commercials. In one study, a cereal commercial was produced which claimed that the cereal had four specific vitamins. Immediately after viewing the commercial, 90% of the 8- to 10-year-olds interviewed could recall two or more details from the commercial while about two-thirds of the 4- to 7-year-olds could do so. Moreover, about half of the older age group could name all four of the vitamins mentioned in the commercial as compared to one-seventh of the 4- to 7-year-olds. Similarly, Wackman et al. (1979) report three experimental studies of children's information processing of specially produced television advertisements. Kindergarten and third grade children were shown groups of television commercials for candy or toy products embedded in a half hour cartoon show viewed in their schools. Kindergartners generally performed at levels slightly above chance on recognition measures (accurate recognition of about 40% of the product or commercial storyline elements across recognition measures that offered three choice alternatives). When information was presented about a relatively simple game product in which the kindergartners appeared interested, their performance improved and they answered three-fourths of the recognition measures accurately. Nevertheless, kindergartners' recognition memory overall trailed third graders' recall and recognition memory. Across studies, third graders remembered between two-thirds and three-fourths of the product and commercial elements while kindergartners retained 40%.

One study reported uniformly low recognition memory for commercials (Zuckerman et al., 1978). First through fourth grade children recognized on the average only 19 of 36 segments from cereal advertisements after viewing them in a special laboratory setting. These low estimates of recognition memory are comparable to estimates for the younger children in the Wackman et al. (1979) study.

Despite generally low recognition and recall scores, young children may find certain kinds of information more salient than other kinds. Several studies suggest that children as young as six may be more likely to remember premium information than brand name (Rubin, 1972; Shimp, Dyer, & Divita, 1976). In Rubin's (1972) study, for instance, 72 first, third, and sixth grade children were shown cereal commercials either with or without a premium offer. While children at nearly all grade levels accurately recalled seeing both the product symbol and the premium, relatively few young children could accurately recall brand name (only 16% of first graders compared with 75% of sixth graders in the premium condition).

However, there is evidence that memory for commercial slogans is well established by the time children reach grade school. In a survey of preschool and elementary school children, Atkin (1975d) presented three different slogans with the brand name missing. Almost 50% of the preschool–kindergarten children and 80% of the first to third graders correctly identified the brand referred to in the slogan. Similar findings have also been reported (Burr & Burr, 1977; Hendon, McGann, & Hendon, 1978; Katz & Rose, 1969; Lyle & Hoffman, 1972). Slogan recall generally increases with age as does memory for other commercial information.

Beyond the age dimension, there is very little evidence of individual differences in children's memory for commercials. What sex differences occur appear to be related to memory for sex-linked cues in the commercials. For instance, in a study of children's social learning from advertisements, Atkin and Miller (1975) reported sex differences in grade school children's memory for several specific commercial elements. Compared with their male age mates, fourth and fifth grade girls were more likely to remember seeing a race car commercial which showed girl models. Generally, however, there tend to be few sex differences in recall of advertisements.

Atkin (1975d) reported some modest racial differences in learning from advertisements. Across several studies with 500 preschool and grade school children, he found recall of commercials slightly higher among white children than black children. Across several comparisons there was an average 4% difference between white and black children in brand name recall. However, Atkin acknowledged that black children in his sample were disproportionately from the younger age group (i.e., children below 8). Considering memory for advertisements, age appears to be a more important factor than either sex or race in determining performance.

In addition to age-related increases in children's memory for commercials, understanding commercial claims also appears to increase as a function of age. For instance, several studies of grade school children's comprehension of toy product disclaimers indicated that disclaimer information needed to be presented in simple terms if young children were to understand it (Atkin, 1975b; Barry, 1978; Liebert, Sprafkin, Liebert, & Rubinstein, 1977). In the Liebert et al. (1977) study fewer than half the 5-year-olds understood the wording "partial assembly required" whereas nearly all children could comprehend a disclaimer such as "you have to put it together." Similarly, low understanding among 4- to 7-year-old children has been shown for the concept of "balanced breakfast" which is included in cereal commercials (Atkin & Gibson, 1978). In general, comprehension of a variety of advertising and nutrition information appears to increase as children grow older and have more advanced cognitive skills to interpret the television messages (Atkin, 1979; Wackman et al., 1979; Ward et al., 1977).

Evaluation of the Advertising Message

In addition to studies of children's memory for advertising claims, there has been research on children's acceptance of or belief in advertising. These studies have examined two types of acceptance—willingness to accept the notion that advertising is truthful and willingness to accept advertising claims for specific products.

Trust in commercials generally has shown age, race, and social class differences. When children were asked the general question: "Do commercials tell the truth?" (Atkin, 1975d; Meyer *et al.*, 1976; Robertson & Rossiter, 1974; Rossiter, 1977; Ward *et al.*, 1977), findings indicated that while a minority of 5- to 7-year-old children said "no" to this question, a clear majority of third and sixth grade children said "no." Several studies reported that more than 80% of 10- to 13-year-old children said commercials didn't always tell the truth (Atkin, 1975d; Robertson & Rossiter, 1974; Rossiter, 1977; Ward *et al.*, 1977). The general trend appears to be age-related movement from distrust of advertising based on personal experiences to more global distrust of all advertising (e.g., Bever *et al.*, 1975; Ward *et al.*, 1977; Ward, 1972).

In a series of studies, Atkin (1975a, 1975b, 1975c, 1975d) tested children's acceptance of various advertising claims to determine whether the children believed the product-related claims. Children received question sequences such as "The kids in this commercial look like they are having lots of fun. If you rode a Big Wheel toy, do you think it would be that much fun?" and "The boy in the commercial says the Keds help him play basketball better. Do you think that this is really true?" Approximately 75% of the preschool and kindergarten children accepted these claims compared to less than 50% of the first to third graders and less than 20% of the fourth and fifth graders. In other studies Atkin (1976) compared younger and older children's acceptance of advertising claims about an acne preparation, a cereal, and a prescription drug. Across the various products and advertising claims, he found that children younger than third grade were more accepting of the claim than were older children.

In contrast with most other variables reviewed in this chapter, acceptance of advertising claims and general trust in advertising have both been demonstrated to vary on the basis of social class and race. Black children and children from lower social class backgrounds appear to be more accepting of advertising claims (Atkin, 1979; Donohue *et al.*, 1978; Lewis & Lewis, 1974; Meyer *et al.*, 1976). For instance, in a study of children's perceptions of the intent and value of television commercials, Donohue *et al.* (1978) reported that 70% of the black children they interviewed believed that McDonalds' food was more nutritious than their own food at home. Only 15% of the white children expressed this belief.

The black children also perceived the people in the commercial to be happier than their own families.

Thus, the sort of trust in advertising which is displayed by 5- and 6-year-old children appears to diminish as children grow older and have more experience with products, particularly advertised products (Ward et al., 1977). It also appears to vary by race and social class but not by sex.

Effects of Television Advertising on Product Decision making

Two behavioral outcomes of exposure to advertising will be considered here: (a) children's evaluations of and desire for advertising products; and (b) their product requests.

Desire for Advertised Products

Several studies have examined the impact of television advertising on children's desire for products. Typically, this has been done by asking either parents or children where they have heard about products that the children wish to buy.

Ward et al. (1977) reported that when kindergarten, third, and sixth grade children were asked where they might find out about three kinds of new products (toys, snack foods, and clothing) awareness of television advertising as a source of new product information increased with age. While about one-third of the kindergartners mentioned television commercials as a source of new toy information, over half of the third and sixth graders did so. The younger children were more likely to mention visits to stores and other people as information sources. That young children were most likely to mention stores as a source of toy ideas had been reported earlier by Atkin and Reinhold (1972), although mothers in the same study reported television to be the major source of product information for the children.

In contrast with Ward et al. (1977) and Atkin and Reinhold (1972), several studies have reported that even for kindergartners and first graders television advertising is a major source of product ideas (Caron & Ward, 1975; Frideres, 1973; Howard, Hulbert, & Lehmann, 1977; Robertson & Rossiter, 1977). This finding appears to hold for both sexes and for black as well as white children (Barry & Sheikh, 1977; Donohue, 1975).

Requests for Products

Several studies of children between the ages of 5 to 12 have reported that purchase requests decrease as children grow older. This finding holds both for observational studies of children in supermarkets and stores (e.g., Atkin, 1975c; Galst & White, 1976) and for survey reports by both children and mothers (Caron & Ward, 1975; Clancy-Hepburn, Hickey, & Nevill, 1974; Robertson & Rossiter, 1976; Robertson, Rossiter, & Gleason, 1979; Ward & Faber, 1975; Ward & Wackman, 1972; Ward et al., 1977). For instance, Atkin (1975d) reports several survey studies in which he asked preschool through fifth grade children how often they asked for toys and breakfast cereals after seeing these things on television commercials. While over 50% of the preschool and kindergarten age group reported requesting these products a lot, only 10% of fourth and fifth grade children reported doing so. Two studies, however, found that purchase requests may be curvilinearly related to age, with very young children and older children requesting fewer products than children between third through fifth grades (Galst & White, 1976; Sheikh & Moleski, 1977).

No sex or race differences in the likelihood of requesting products have been reported, and there are mixed findings about social class differences. Some studies have found that middle and upper-middle class children were more likely to request products (Atkin, 1975d; Caron & Ward, 1975; Wells & LoSciuto, 1966). Others, however, have found no link between social class and requesting medicine products (Robertson et al., 1979) and a slight negative relationship between social class and toy requests (Robertson & Rossiter, 1977).

There is some evidence that the short-term impact of advertising on requests for the advertised product or on behavioral compliance to the message of a public service announcement is stronger for younger than older children (Atkin, 1975b; Robertson, 1979; Robertson & Rossiter, 1977). Again, no race, sex, or social class differences in short term effects are noted in the literature.

In summary, children younger than middle childhood appear to be more likely to request products and may be more strongly influenced to desire and request television advertised products after watching commercials. This may be indicative of younger children's weaker cognitive defenses with regard to both the intent of television advertising and the advertisement's claims and messages (Rossiter & Robertson, 1974; Wackman et al., 1979; Wartella, Wackman, Ward, Shamir, & Alexander, 1979).

Summary

Review of the research on children's information processing of television advertising messages and on the impact of these messages on children's own consumer product decision making indicates that *the major individual difference factor which mediates advertising's influence is* age of the viewers. In general, younger children's attention to commercials appears to be more heavily influenced by various production factors. They appear to have lower recall and understanding of advertising claims, and their trust in advertising is higher. Moreover, younger children's pattern of purchase requests and decisions appears to be more heavily influenced by advertising messages.

Relatively few sex, race, or social class differences in television advertising's impact have been noted. It should be pointed out, however, that this is partly due to relatively minimal examination of these other individual difference variables in the literature. Future research could more fruitfully examine the impact of these other factors, particularly racial and social class differences, on children's information processing of television advertising.

References

Adler, R., Friedlander, B., Lesser, G., Meringoff, L., Robertson, T. S., Rossiter, J. R., & Ward, S. *Research on the effects of television advertising on children.* Washington, D.C.: United States Government Printing Office, 1977.

Atkin, C. K. *Effects of television advertising on children—First year experimental evidence.* Technical report, Michigan State Univ., 1975. (a)

Atkin, C. K. *Effects of television advertising on children—Second year experimental evidence.* Technical report, Michigan State Univ., 1975. (b)

Atkin, C. K. *Effects of television advertising on children—Survey of children's and mothers' responses to television commercials.* Technical report, Michigan State Univ., 1975. (c)

Atkin, C. K. *Effects of television advertising on children—Survey of preadolescents responses to television commercials.* Technical report, Michigan State Univ., 1975. (d)

Atkin, C. K. *Children's social learning from television advertising:* Research evidence on observational modeling of product consumption. *Advances in Consumer Research,* 1976, *3,* 513–519.

Atkin, C. K. Observation of parent–child interaction in supermarket decision making. *Journal of Marketing,* 1978, *42,* 41–45.

Atkin, C. K. Testimony before the Federal Trade Commission's rulemaking on children and TV advertising. San Francisco, January, 1979.

Atkin, C. K., & Gibson, W. *Children's nutrition learning from television advertising.* Unpublished manuscript, Michigan State Univ., 1978.

Atkin, C. K., & Miller, M. *The effects of television advertising on children: Experimental evidence.* Paper presented at the meeting of the International Communication Association, Chicago, 1975.

Atkin, C. K., & Reinhold, C. *The impact of television advertising on children.* Paper presented at the meeting of the Association for Education in Journalism, Carbondale, Illinois, 1972.

Barry, T. *The effect of a modified disclaimer on inner city vs. suburban children.* Paper presented at the meeting of the American Marketing Association, Boston, 1978.

Barry, T., & Sheikh, A. Race as a dimension in children's TV advertising: The need for more research. *Journal of Advertising,* 1977, *6,* 5–10.

Bechtel, R. B., Achelpol, C., & Akers, R. Correlates between observed behavior and questionnaire responses on television viewing. In E. A. Rubinstein, G. A. Comstock, & J. P. Murray (Eds.), *Television and social behavior* (Vol. 4). *Television in day-to-day life: Patterns of use.* Washington, D.C.: United States Government Printing Office, 1972.

Bever, T., Smith, M., Bengen, B., & Johnson, T. Young viewers' troubling response to TV ads. *Harvard Business Review*, 1975, *53* (6), 109–120.

Burr, P., & Burr, R. M. Product recognition and premium appeal. *Journal of Communication*, 1977, *27* (1), 115–117.

Caron, A., & Ward, S. Gift decisions by kids and parents. *Journal of Advertising*, 1975, *15* (4), 12–20.

Clancy-Hepburn, K., Hickey, A., & Nevill, G. Children's behavior responses to TV food advertisements. *Journal of Nutrition Education*, 1974, *6* (3), 93–96.

Donohue, T. Effect of commercials on black children. *Journal of Advertising Research*, 1975, *15* (6), 41–46.

Donohue, T. R., Meyer, T. P., & Henke, L. L. *Black and white children's perception of the intent and values in specific adult and child oriented television commercials.* Unpublished manuscript, Univ. of Hartford, 1978.

Duffy, J., & Rossiter, J. *The Hartford experiment: Children's reactions to TV commercials in blocks at the beginning and end of the program.* Paper presented to the Conference on Culture and Communications, Temple Univ., Philadelphia, March, 1975.

Frideres, J. Advertising, buying patterns, and children. *Journal of Advertising Research*, 1973, *13* (1), 34–36.

Galst, J. P., & White, M. A. The unhealthy persuader: The reinforcing value of television and children's purchase-influencing attempts at the supermarket. *Child Development*, 1976, *17*, 1089–1096.

Giannino, L. J., & Zuckerman, P. A. *Measuring children's responses to television advertising.* Paper presented at the meeting of the American Psychological Association, San Francisco, 1977.

Hendon, D., McGann, A., & Hendon, B. Children's age, intelligence and sex variables mediating reactions to TV commercials: Repetition and content complexity implications for advertisers. *Journal of Advertising*, 1978, *7* (3), 4–12.

Howard, J., Hulbert, J., & Lehmann, D. An exploratory analysis of the effects of television advertising on children. Study reported in Adler *et al.*, 1977.

Katz, M., & Rose, J. Is your slogan identifiable? *Journal of Advertising Research*, 1969, 9 (1), 21–25.

Lewis, C. E., & Lewis, M. A. The impact of television commercials on health-related beliefs and behaviors of children. *Pediatrics*, 1974, *3*, 53.

Liebert, D., Sprafkin, J., Liebert, R., & Rubinstein, E. Effects of television commercial disclaimers on the product expectations of children. *Journal of Communication*, 1977, *27* (1), 118–124.

Lyle, J., & Hoffman, H. Explorations in patterns of television viewing by preschool age children. In E. A. Rubinstein, G. A. Comstock, & J. P. Murray (Eds.), *Television and social behavior* (Vol. 4). *Television in day-to-day life: Patterns of use.* Washington, D.C.: United States Government Printing Office, 1972.

Meyer, T., Donohue, T., & Henke, L. *Black children's perceptions of TV advertising: A cognitive developmental study.* Paper presented at the meeting of the Speech Communication Association, San Francisco, December, 1976.

Palmer, E. L., & McDowell, C. N. The program commercial separators in children's television programming. *Journal of Communication*, 1979, *29* (3), 197–201.

Roberts, D. Testimony before the Federal Trade Commission's rulemaking on children and TV advertising. San Francisco, January, 1979.

Robertson, T. S. Parental mediation of television advertising effects. *Journal of Communication*, 1979, *29* (1), 12–25.

Robertson, T., & Rossiter, J. Children and commercial persuasion: An attribution theory analysis. *Journal of Consumer Research*, 1974, *1*, 13–20.

Robertson, T., & Rossiter, J. Short-run advertising effects on children: A field study. *Journal of Marketing Research*, 1976, *13*, 68–70.

Robertson, T. S., & Rossiter, J. R. Children's responsiveness to commercials. *Journal of Communication*, 1977, *27* (1), 101–106.

Robertson, T., Rossiter, J., & Gleason, T. *Televised medicine advertising and children*. New York: Praeger, 1979.

Rossiter, J. Reliability of a short test measuring children's attitudes toward TV commercials. *Journal of Consumer Research*, 1977, *3*, 179–184.

Rossiter, J. R., & Robertson, T. S. Children's TV commercials: Testing the defenses. *Journal of Communication*, 1974, *24* (4), 137–144.

Rubin, R. An exploratory investigation of children's responses to commercial content of television advertising in relation to their stages of cognitive development. Unpublished doctoral dissertation, Univ. of Massachusetts, 1972.

Sheikh, A., & Moleski, L. M. Conflict in the family over commercials. *Journal of Communication*, 1977, *27* (1), 152–157.

Sheikh, A. A., Prasad, V. K., & Rao, T. R. Children's TV commercials: A review of research. *Journal of Communication*, 1974, *24* (4), 126–136.

Shimp, T., Dyer, R., & Divita, S. Advertising of children's premiums on television: An experimental evaluation of the FTC's proposed guide. Unpublished manuscript, George Washington Univ., 1976.

Wackman, D., Wartella, E., & Ward, S. Children's information processing of television advertising. Unpublished manuscript, Univ. of Minnesota, 1979.

Ward, S. Children's reactions to commercials. *Journal of Advertising Research*, 1972, *12* (2), 37–45.

Ward, S., & Faber, R. Validation of mother–child purchase influence frequency reports by the multitrait-multimethod matrix. Unpublished manuscript, Marketing Science Institute, 1975.

Ward, S., Levinson, D., & Wackman, D. Children's attention to television advertising. In E. A. Rubinstein, G. A. Comstock, & J. P. Murray (Eds.), *Television and social behavior* (Vol. 4). *Television in day-to-day life: Patterns of use*. Washington, D.C.: United States Government Printing Office, 1972.

Ward, S., & Wackman, D. Children's purchase influence attempts and parental yielding. *Journal of Marketing Research*, 1972, *9*, 316–319.

Ward, S., & Wackman, D. Children's information processing of television advertising. In P. Clarke (Ed.), *New models for mass communication research*. Beverly Hills, California: Sage, 1973.

Ward, S., Wackman, D., & Wartella, E. *How children learn to buy*. Beverly Hills, California: Sage, 1977.

Wartella, E., & Ettema, J. A cognitive developmental study of children's attention to television commercials. *Communication Research*, 1974, *1*, 69–88.

Wartella, E., Wackman, D., Ward, S., Shamir, J., & Alexander, A. The young child as a consumer. In E. Wartella (Ed.), *Children communicating*. Beverly Hills, California: Sage, 1979.

Wells, W., & LoSciuto, L. Direct observation of purchasing behavior. *Journal of Marketing Research*, 1966, *3*, 227–233.

Winick, M. P., & Winick, C. *The television experience: What children see*. Beverly Hills, California: Sage, 1979.

Zuckerman, P., Zigler, M. E., & Stevenson, H. W. Children's viewing of television and recognition memory of commercials. *Child Development*, 1978, *49*, 96–104.

The Politics of Change

ROBERT B. CHOATE

Long before the spring of 1980, the perennial issue of advertising to young audiences via television had shown an amazing propensity for arousing political interference. The issue's curious regenerative ability has stimulated at least a decade of shrill discussion. As founder and president of the Council on Children, Media and Merchandising, a citizen action group, my commitment has been to constructively change children's television advertising by constantly interacting with the key participants and decision makers. The following historically organized observations of the political process surrounding the issue of television advertising to youth are not born of neutrality; they express my viewpoint.[1]

Development
Citizen Action Groups

Two citizen action groups, Action for Children's Television (ACT) and the Council on Children, Media and Merchandising (CCMM), have figured most prominently in the political agitation surrounding advertis-

[1] The term *children's advertising* connotes a narrow range of messages and products. The Council on Children, Media and Merchandising, however, contends that all advertising intentionally placed before large audiences of children on a regular basis should be subject to special review. Hence we prefer to term this rule-making *children and advertising*.

CHILDREN AND THE FACES OF TELEVISION:
Teaching, Violence, Selling

ing to children. The creation of ACT developed from a concern for the television content that children were watching. CCMM developed from a concern about hunger and nutrition.

Those without enough food or without the right diet became a national cause of the late 1960s. The White House Conference on Food, Nutrition and Health held in December, 1969 drew over 3000 participants and produced some 500 reform suggestions for the new President Nixon. More straightforward food marketing to children and the use of mass media to improve nutrition knowledge were two key topics (White House Conference on Food, Nutrition and Health, 1970). Many of the nation's leading food executives were participants; there was a general promise to take a new look at marketing practices. Some small efforts were initiated; however, by the spring of 1970, the fledgling spirit of food marketing reform seemed to be dying.

Using dry breakfast cereal advertising to children as an example, I appeared before a Senate Commerce Subcommittee to illustrate graphically that the inferior cereals were promoted to children while the nutritionally better cereals were targeted at their parents (Commerce Committee, U.S. Senate, 1970). The testimony received wide news coverage. Middle-class Americans, who had raised their children with utter trust in the food industry, started to analyze what they were feeding them and to question the derivation of their children's food demands. "Empty calories" became a popular term.

Within this atmosphere of public concern and hearings publicity, CCMM was born. Included among its charter members were White House Conference participants, old allies in the hunger battles, and past cohorts familiar with the "War on Poverty." CCMM invited those concerned with hunger to consider the growing power of television to shape U.S. diets (Two guns, 1971).

The Council was in an excellent position to stimulate political interest in children's rights in the marketplace. Its personnel were experienced with Washington scene bureaucracies; its leaders were names familiar to the press; its ability to communicate with both Republicans and Democrats gave it an ear in both houses of Congress. Communication with the business community had always seemed natural to CCMM and thus the Council had contacts in various trade organizations and individual companies.

The Council pattern and strategy was to interact regularly with the Food and Drug Administration (FDA), the Federal Communications Commission (FCC), and the Federal Trade Commission (FTC). Their staffs were exhorted; their Commissioners were solicited. More to the point, the Council maintained pressure on Republicans and Democrats on both sides of Capitol Hill, and they in turn kept the regulatory agencies aware that children did interest the Congress (Cohen, 1974; Congress presses FTC,

1974). Evidence of the Council's strategy and involvement can be seen in various committee reports that emerged from the Hill:

1. On March 8, 1974—during Senate Appropriations Subcommittee hearings—Senator Proxmire asked FCC Chairman Wiley whether there was anything in the FCC budget request and staff allocations "that might be attributable to children's broadcasting." Proxmire then pointed out that there were no apparent allocations for children's issues [Appropriations Committee, U.S. Senate, 1974b, p. 250].

2. Four days later, during House Appropriations Subcommittee hearings, the budget question again surfaced, and when Chairman Wiley's response proved indirect, Congressman Boland expressed the conviction that the FCC should take "another look at the impact of commercials on children" and ought also "to make some inquiry as to whether or not the National Science Foundation is willing to fund a study with respect to . . . the impact of commercials on children, which is getting to be a serious problem [Appropriations Committee, U.S. House of Representatives, 1974b, p. 71]."

3. Two days later, in Commerce Subcommittee hearings, Senator Moss asked FTC Chairman Engman whether the Commission has "undertaken an investigation to determine how much research advertisers and advertising agencies [had] done in order to develop their campaigns directed toward children [Commerce Committee, U.S. Senate, 1974, p. 309]."

4. Nearly 2 weeks later, in Appropriations Subcommittee hearings, FTC Chairman Engman was again reminded of his Commission's responsibilities in this area by Senator McGee who noted that "the Committee has always received inquiries in the form of flak almost universally in reference to the television advertising and its impact on children who watch television" and asked, "What has the Commission been doing in this area [Appropriations Committee, U.S. Senate, 1974a, p. 1190]?"

Such Congressional questioning was not coincidental—the timing was too quick for normal Congressional channels. It did produce a strong Congressional instruction to the FTC:

The Committee received assurances during the hearings that effective regulation of children's television advertising could be achieved under the budget requested. The Committee has accepted those assurances, but if additional funds are required, appropriate actions should be taken to obtain them since the *Committee views this as a high priority topic* [Appropriations Committee, U.S. House of Representatives, 1974a, p. 88, emphasis added].

But the times were not kind to those seeking to reform sponsors, ad agencies, and broadcasters, as well as to alter government agency inaction. The issue of fair market practices to children survived the Nixon years partly by the Council returning with new facts, new statistics, and finally new behavioral evidence. Lawyers on the Hill and in the agencies heard Council analyses on broadcast practices using industry originated statistics converted by the Council into pro-child arguments.

During its ad hoc years, the 16-member Council never said it represented the nation; it only claimed a Washington office. It operated on a shoe-string of donated private money, fighting the business interests that continually opposed it. After becoming a nonprofit corporation in 1976, the Council turned most of its attention to the regulatory agencies.

On another front, Action for Children's Television (ACT) was founded in 1968. It started as a women's movement, not to liberate women, but to reassert the woman's role as mother. Men, generally husbands, were invited to join, but women were and still are the heart of ACT. Evelyn Kaye was ACT's first president. Pensive but persistent, she slowly built ACT into a New England force, then East Coast conscience center. In the early seventies ACT mothers were aroused, but the country was not. In 1972 the presidency of ACT changed. Under Peggy Charren's forceful leadership, the organization grew and developed as a national entity. Through skillful use of media interviews, press releases, and publicity folders, the cause and the organization attained prominent national status. This small group of mothers, meeting in living rooms in Newton, Massachusetts, had now become a strong, nationally based citizen action group. Elected officials knew that children had no vote, but they soon realized that ACT members did. As Senator McGee noted in hearings of the Appropriations Committee, "We are rather literally besieged. . . .Wait until you get the mothers of America on your back because this is where we are getting the static. I think not without reasons [Appropriations Committee, U.S. Senate, 1974a, p. 1192]."

ACT's most apparent strategy for change was the petition—first to the FCC and later to the FTC. One particular legal maneuver enjoined the FCC and ACT in a 4-year struggle (Cole & Oettinger, 1978). In 1970 ACT petitioned the FCC to cut the number of advertisements seen by children on television and to force the broadcasters into better age-specific programming for the young. In short, ACT wanted the broadcasters' revenues to be reduced concomitant with an increase in expenditures for children's television.

Four years later, the FCC issued "Children's Television Programs— Report and Policy Statement." It was, in effect, a gentlemen's agreement to let the broadcast community manage its own reforms (Federal Communications Commission, 1974). The 4 years of apparent indecision allowed the broadcast community to further its commercial solicitation of children; eventually, commercials seen by children on Saturday morning were reduced in time, if not in number.

ACT participated in FCC and FTC hearings; it testified before Congress; it submitted repeated petitions to the FCC and FTC; it wooed and was wooed by the press. It proclaimed that the mothers of the nation were asking for broadcast and advertising reforms. A skeptical nation and a skeptical government, kept unaware of the major industry study which bore out ACT's contention (Gene Reilly Group, 1973), only slowly came to realize that the Newton mothers had a righteous cause.

Established Consumer Organizations

The two longest established consumer groups, Consumers Union and Consumer Federation of America, offered moral support but little leadership on the children's television issue in the early 1970s. Nader launched an examination of food advertising which came to naught. Other than in the Wonder Bread case, children were not a major interest of his organization.

The national PTA awakened to the children's television issue in the mid-1970s. Media literacy, not reform of commercial practices, was their focus. The Boy Scouts and Girl Scouts were silent. Part of the dilemma for these latter three groups is that they have been dependent on the very interests they would need to attack should they become heavily involved in the children's advertising issue. As William Young of the PTA national staff acknowledged to me in a telephone call, many PTAs raise money through sales of candies and cookies. Moreover, publications of these groups, such as the Boy Scouts' *Boys' Life*, need such advertising. This is demonstrated by the promotion obvious in this ad in a 1977 issue of *Advertising Age*:

> This year *Boys' Life* readers will personally spend $435 million for cookies, candy and gum, help out their moms with $609 million in grocery shopping, and directly influence the spending of billions on family grocery products like cereals, soft drinks and desserts. *Boys' Life* reaches 4 million big appetites every month [*Advertising Age*, 1977, p. 47].

The Academic Community

The academic community, with rare exceptions, merely reflected the availability of research money. Many researchers delved into television's impact from the early 1960s on (see Chapters 1 and 8 in this volume), and the advent of *Sesame Street* from the Children's Television Workshop (CTW) brought substance and quality to clinical studies of the impact of short burst TV messages (see Chapter 1 in this volume). CTW's goal was bettering television content through applied communication techniques (see Chapter 21 in this volume). However, it took the Pastore-stimulated Surgeon General's study of television and social behavior (and its $1 million in research funds) to bring established child development specialists to speak to Congress (Cater & Strickland, 1975). Few of these or other academic experts conveyed specific reform ideas to Congress until the mid-1970s. Commercial practices were seldom questioned by the child development experts.

The report to the Surgeon General, *Television and Growing Up: The Impact of Violence,* gave credibility and some stature to the application of child development theories to the television world (Surgeon General's Scientific Advisory Committee, 1972). Part of this credibility spilled over into the child-in-the-marketplace arena, and ACT and CCMM communicated the research findings to federal agencies.

In 1976 the Ford Foundation funded Georgetown University Law Center to host 12 seminars on the subject of television and children. Invited experts, often adversarial in their views, discussed aspects of mass commercial communication to vulnerable audiences before guests drawn from industry, ad agencies, broadcasting, consumer groups, and, most importantly, staffs of Congressional committees and regulatory agencies.

The research funded by corporations who sought to strengthen their sales messages to children was closed to ACT, CCMM, and public officials. No corporations would publicize their child manipulation findings for the public's benefit; "proprietary information" was the response given to those who sought it (Federal Trade Commission, 1979). Some academics of considerable renown earned major consulting fees in such work. They were not among the academic leaders who helped educate the American parent on the impact of television advertising on children.

The Business Community

The knowledge gained from the research on selling techniques was, until recently, entirely "proprietary" and therefore unavailable for the enlightenment of parents, academics, consumer groups, and regulatory agencies. Two prominent examples can be cited.

The first came to light when a nutrition game was to be marketed. In pursuit of this, it was discovered that "motivational research houses" solicited children for corporate testing from schools, Boy Scout groups, and even B'Nai B'rith and Catholic schools. They were asked to participate in focus group sessions while marketing experts observed the children's reactions from behind mirrored windows. This research tested product characteristics and theories regarding product appeal to children. While hundreds of studies thus had been made which could reveal how children respond to shortburst television messages, none had been made public, and the existence of the studies themselves had been concealed. This practice was reported in hearings before the Senate Commerce Subcommittee on Consumer Affairs in July, 1975 (Commerce Committee, U.S. Senate, 1975).

In 1973 the Gene Reilly Group, Incorporated, started producing a research report entitled *The Child* for the nation's major sponsors. Utilizing the expertise of many nationally known behavioral scientists, this report presented information on child/mother consumer attitudes and behavior. The text was designed for and targeted (at $15,000 per edition) to those engaged in selling to and through children. Reilly advocated the use of his services, and of *The Child*, so that:

> marketers can determine the nature and extent of in-family decision making as it affects the kinds of products they produce. Data will be presented on which to base decisions regarding the targeting of advertising and promotion to children or to parents; important information is contained in the report concerning children's responses to advertising, the sources of information they consider important in making purchase and brand decisions, and how children go about trying to influence their parents to buy [Gene Reilly Group, 1973, p. 7].

During the critical years of 1973–1978 the contents of *The Child* were not available to public organizations, to CCMM, ACT, or even to the government. The text was only for the corporate ears of clients such as Burger King Corporation, Campbell Soup Company, CBS Incorporated, General Mills Incorporated, Kellogg Company, and Marx Toys (Tucker Wayne and Company, 1978). (Now, by order of the FTC's Children's Advertising Hearing Officer, dated July 16, 1979, this copyrighted material can be cited.) Among all the advice on when, where, and how to sell to children or their mothers are many observations which unintentionally offered tremendous support for many of the positions held by CCMM and ACT. Consider, for example, these comments from various volumes of *The Child* (Gene Reilly Group):

1. Regarding the most vulnerable audiences: "Six- to seven-year-olds pay a great deal more attention to commercials than 13- to 14-year-olds, and children from lower class homes show a greater tendency to be more attentive to commercials on TV than children from either middle-class or upper-class homes [1974, pp. A–V]."

2. Regarding the child's influence on purchases: "the mother can simply be a 'purchasing agent' for the child. So it is important to know not only what the young child buys, and *why* he buys, but it is also of crucial importance to know what purchases the child influences, *how* he or she influences, and what responses such influence attempts are likely to receive [1973, p. 3]." "Mothers either 'usually' or 'sometimes' bought the child's favorite roughly nine times out of ten with one exception: frozen TV dinners [1973, p. O]."

3. Regarding parent–child interaction on advertising: "The absence of parent–child interaction (on Saturday morning) leaves no opportunity for parents to help their children sort out the plethora of messages received from programs and commercials, and offer them guidance in as-

similating this information into useful behavior, ideas, and attitudes. . . . Mothers express general agreement with the proposition that 'my child likes to watch adult programs on TV as much as children's programs'. . . . The fact that substantial numbers of children in the sample, especially those from age 8 on, are reported to enjoy watching adult programs provides strong evidence [of] the considerable extent to which they are exposed to advertising which may be directed primarily to an adult audience. . . .This kind of repeated exposure to promotional messages for adult products may have important implications for development of brand awareness (and even preferences) among young children, who (it should be stressed) may not actually use such products [1974, p. 34]."

4. Regarding parents' concern about advertising: "When mothers were asked a battery of questions concerning television advertising directed to children, they showed similar attitudes about the need for control. . . .Fifty-four percent maintained that there should be more control over advertising. . . .Fewer mothers (35%) had no opinion, 'didn't care,' 'didn't know,' or had no answer in the advertising area than in the programming discussion (42%). This difference would suggest that children's advertising is an issue which really is on the minds of a great many parents, even more so than the content of television programs . . .[1974, p. 170].

Thus, Reilly told the advertising companies how to penetrate family defenses. He explained children's vulnerabilities and suggested how to use them. However, when testimonies were offered later in FTC proceedings, the industry witnesses revealed none of Reilly's comments indicating parental absence or fairness concerns, but chose to cite his volumes in support of their arguments that advertising, particularly of foods, was regarded benignly by mothers.

Regulatory Agencies

From the beginning, activists have sought effective regulations for television advertising to children, be they "self-regulation" or governmental. CCMM's efforts, like those of others, have been directed at self-regulatory groups like the National Association of Broadcasters (NAB) and the National Advertising Division (NAD) of the Council of Better Business Bureaus and at federal regulatory agencies such as the FTC and FCC.

CCMM at an early date sought an audience before the prestigious Code Board of the National Association of Broadcasters. In May, 1971, acting for CCMM, legal counsel Geoffrey Cowan and I asked the Code Authority for a Code for Advertising Edibles to Children (Choate, 1972). Six months later, the request was denied. This turndown by the key group in the private television sector, on the heels of the White House Conference, set the scene for demands that the government become involved.

William Tankersley, a former CBS executive and long-time adviser to CCMM, came into the presidency of the Council of Better Business Bureaus at about this time. He and Thomas Roeser, soon to be a vice-president of Quaker Oats, discussed with CCMM the question of governmental regulation versus self-regulation. It was generally agreed that the NAB self-regulatory efforts were weak. Roeser and CCMM laid plans for a strong, private regulatory organization. It would have a board of 15 members, with 8 to be drawn from the public. Administration would be open, and its role would be to judge who was right in advertising controversies. Children were to be a rightful concern.

A year later, a coalition of sponsors and advertisers, including Tankersley and his NAD, announced the formation of a National Advertising Review Board (NARB). However, Board membership was set at 50, with only 10 to be members of the public—and even they were to be hand-screened. It quickly became apparent that the NAD and NARB were interested in looking at the special problems of advertising and children only if restricted to the same tight definition used by the broadcasters. The NAB had said its child code governing advertising would be applied when the advertising was "designed primarily for children"—which it defined as "advertising . . . which the advertiser or agency, by [their] media buying patterns or merchandising goals, places in children's programs in order to reach an audience composed primarily of children [children's advertising principles, 1974]." The NARB/NAD said its concern would be with:

> advertising designed to appeal to children eleven years of age and under. This includes children's advertising which is broadcast in children's programs and programs in which audience patterns typically contain more than 50% children. Commercials appearing in shows in which children are a substantial audience segment, but less than 50%, will be regarded as subject to these guidelines only when they are clearly addressed to children eleven and under. Print advertising is subject to these guidelines when it is primarily directed to or primarily read by children [National Advertising Division, 1977, unpaginated].

The Council of Better Business Bureau's National Advertising Division further moved to avert governmental intervention by establishing a Children's Advertising Review Unit (CARU). The NAD invited several of the better known child development specialists to join forces with a nutritional anthropologist and a market researcher to monitor selected children's advertisements. Some CARU members felt somewhat used by the business community, but the Unit did establish a policy of reviewing advertisements seemingly directed to children, including some not aired on Saturday morning. A report (Children's Advertising Review Unit, 1979) of this effort indicates the need for new research to strengthen the hands of those who would write tough guidelines. The report also attests to the staying power of well-intentioned professionals.

While these private efforts did some good, they also served to delay governmental involvement. Both the NAB and the CARU efforts focused primarily on a small portion (perhaps 15%) of the television watched by children (Adler, Friedlander, Lesser, Meringoff, Robertson, Rossiter, & Ward, 1977). Pressures for more major reform were mounting.

The FCC, not known in 1974 for its independence from the broadcaster community, was not a hopeful place for television's critics. However, Nixon's friend Dean Burch, while chairman of the FCC in the early 1970s, repeatedly told the public he thought children deserved better treatment (Cole & Oettinger, 1978). CCMM was skeptical of Burch and the FCC, but ACT—as noted earlier in the chapter—made its major move of the early 1970s with petitions to the FCC. Burch was followed as Chairman by Richard Wiley. Between the two leaders' terms, the FCC delayed any meaningful reform for children's television over 6 years.

The FTC was a different matter, even during Nixon's administration. Nader had criticized the FTC in the late 1960s, and American Bar Association leader Myles Kirkpatrick led the resulting study team. He was then appointed by Nixon to head the FTC. Under his leadership, the FTC in 1971 held hearings on advertising (Hulbert & Howard, 1973). These were first designed to explore children and advertising, but a broadcaster/ ad agency lobby showed its power by quickly converting the hearings into a rather bland forum for ad agency pronouncements. Kirkpatrick listened to parental and ACT complaints regarding vitamin advertising and, stimulated by an 11-year-old girl's personal plea to him for reforms, negotiated a ban on vitamin advertising to children through the agency's Bureau of Consumer Protection. Kirkpatrick's successor, Lewis Engman, brought together sponsors, broadcasters, ad agencies, and consumers for extended negotiations with the hope that they would lead to effective self-regulation on the children's advertising issue. Eventually, a disgusted Engman gave up the effort, declaring in regard to some of the statements of the business community: "You almost have to be impressed with the sophistication of the decadence [Engman, 1974]."

During 1975 the FTC launched a rulemaking designed to put constraints on food advertising. CCMM applied for public funds to supplement its foundation funds so it could support research to show that young children could pick up information on the relative nutritional value of foods through a 5-second exposure to nutrition graphics (Feshbach, Jordan, & Dillman, 1976); CCMM also brought social science evidence and data from industry sources into the hearings (Choate, 1976). The Council's very entry into a food advertising rule-making as an advocate for children caused a stir, but Hearing Officer William Dixon noted that children were "fairly within the bounds of the population affected by the Rule" (Dixon, 1978). Elsewhere in his report he stated that CCMM's "participation was obviously going to be substantial and there can be no question but that the issue of food advertising directed at children was developing into a major consideration" (Dixon, 1978). Thus, at the FTC the children's advertising issue was given respectability, and behavioral evidence was placed on the record vis-à-vis advertising.

The Present

By 1977 it was obvious that the children's television issue had resiliency and growing strength. It was also obvious that private sector reforms were few and far between and generally came only on threats of governmental action. The election of President Carter and a Democratic administration after 8 years of Republican business–White House comraderie suggested there might be changes.

The appointment of Donald Kennedy to direct the FDA reinvigorated that agency, and it offered guidance to CCMM. HEW, its parent organization, through Dr. Julius Richmond, Assistant Secretary for Health, decried television selling to children (Richmond, 1978).

The nomination to the FCC of Charles Ferris, staff leader for Speaker of the House "Tip" O'Neill, was perplexing. He had no communications track record. He certainly was not in the child advocate camp. Three years after his appointment his child concerns are beginning to emerge.

However, at the Federal Trade Commission, the changes were dramatic. Carter nominated Michael Pertschuk as Chairman. He was well known on Capitol Hill and had been the senior staff member of the Senate Commerce Committee when the dry breakfast cereal hearings, the motivational research hearings, and the innumerable oversight and appropriations hearings on the FTC were held. He knew the child-in-the-marketplace issues, and he knew where he stood. He also knew ACT and CCMM.

Pertschuk brought in Albert Kramer as the head of his Bureau of Consumer Protection. Kramer knew the years of toil by ACT and CCMM and had helped in the preparation of some of their position papers. Pertschuk also brought in as Kramer's deputy, Tracy Westen—a long-time advocate of countercommercials, broadcaster reform, and truth-in-advertising. Law professor Westen had been consulted by ACT and CCMM. Carter appointed Robert Pitofsky to an early FTC Commission vacancy. Pitofsky had been staff chief of Kirkpatrick's analysis of FTC failures, and he had engineered the advertising hearings and the disappearance of vitamin advertising from children's programs. He, too, knew ACT and CCMM. With the Chairman's team chosen, the FTC seemed prepared for change.

Pertschuk made no bones about the fact that he thought children deserved better treatment in the marketplace. He spoke out frequently and persuasively (FTC's Pertschuk, 1977). His fellow Commissioners, more cautious but still persuaded, agreed to launch an inquiry into advertising and children. In April, 1978, a staff report was prepared after endless conversations with many of the witnesses and experts which ACT and CCMM had consulted over the previous 5 years.

ACT's primary concern was the commercials seen by young children—those under 7. It advocated that the FTC staff concentrate on this age group—adopting a rule to ban all advertising to those under 7 and heavily constraining sugary commercials to those between 7 and 12. CCMM, on the other hand, urged the FTC staff to recognize that 92% of the television children watched was not Saturday morning, that 85% was unaffected by any NAB Code, and that drug advertising was as dangerous as sugared foods. Most importantly, CCMM wanted the definition of children's advertising to encompass programs heavily watched by children seven days a week, no matter for whom they were originally conceived. CCMM thought a ban impossible to administer if large child audiences were the criterion.

When the FTC staff report emerged, it was the prosecutorial voice of the FTC speaking. There was little judicial restraint and no pro-food-industry arguments. It stressed Saturday morning television; it seemed preoccupied with a ban. The report drew immediate, heated response from the food and toy industries (Don't kill, 1978; General Mills slams, 1978).

CCMM's earlier work in food and drug advertising rulemakings while using public participation funds alerted the business community to the threat of public participation funding. Most of the business trade organizations had opposed a federal Agency for Consumer Affairs when first proposed (Russell, 1975)—suggesting that it was better for each agency to think about consumers without intervention of a super agency. When the FTC experimented with agency-provided consumer funds, industry lawyers and lobbyists made a complete reversal in their previously stated position (Leighton, 1979). The Children's Advertising rulemaking was the first focus.

In 1978 lobbyists sought to cut the public participation funds of ACT and others wanting to submit testimony. In addition, they organized an interindustry lobby to: (a) Cut FTC funds; (b) cut FTC advertising hearing funds; and (c) cut all public participation funds. The *Washington Star's* Bailey Morris gave an insight:

> It is the small group . . . which has succeeded in holding together one of the most powerful coalitions ever formed to fight a specific issue which has become "as emotional as abortion."
>
> This larger coalition includes several huge law firms, the national advertising associations, broadcasters and their associations, the U.S. Chamber of Commerce, the Grocery Manufacturers of America, the sugar associations, the chocolate and candy manufacturers, cereal companies and their associations, and more.
>
> Advertising trade publications have estimated "the war chest" put together by the coalition at between $15 million and $30 million [Morris, 1979a, pp. A–10 and A–13].

The apparent antiregulation mood within the country supported the industry coalition. Despite food scandals, real estate swindles, and nuclear concerns—all of which seemed to warrant stronger regulatory zeal—the major newspapers were making predominantly antiregulation comments (e.g., The FTC as, 1978).

In summary, when the Pertschuk-led FTC launched an investigation of children's advertising, its two major citizen action constituents disagreed on the scope of the issues and the business community charged that Pertschuk was biased, unfair, and in the pocket of the consumer. An industry-mounted legal maneuver temporarily disqualified the FTC Chairman from voting on the issue. A congressional maneuver delayed any decision by the FTC. Commission vacancies led to delayed Commission votes. House and Senate Committees held hearings out of sight of vitally concerned public groups monitoring the children's issue. A Congressional Wives' Task Force belatedly rounded up a lobby of pro-children Congressional spouses to head off the concentrated industry attack.

In November, 1978, the FTC launched its hearings on children and television advertising. Over 200 witnesses appeared, representing the entire spectrum of groups and roles we have discussed. The record was transcribed, reviewed, and contested; the impact of television short-burst communication to children was exhaustively analyzed. There is no comparable record on the subject today.

Although the industry witnesses had made a good case that parts of the Children's Advertising rule-making were ill based, their lawyers feared something more dangerous. The "reasonably prudent" legal rule by which most commercial transactions are judged seemed to be undergoing reassessment as it pertained to advertising to children, since a child, almost by definition, could be deemed imprudent. "Unfairness" seemed a more valid basis to the FTC on which to judge commercial messages to children. Industry lawyers saw this as opening Pandora's box.

Immediately, the broadcasters tried to block any further inquiry (Morris, 1979b); the Grocery Manufacturers of America held that the issue was false and that public participation was a disaster (Leighton, 1979). Cereal companies reduced their sugar content and offered nutrition messages to broadcast stations in an effort to render the issue moot (Edwards, 1979; USDA analyzes, 1979), while the networks increased the number of pro-nutrition public service messages on programs watched by young children. ABC offered to cut the number of its Saturday morning commercials (ABC pares, 1979), and Saturday morning itself became less attractive to advertisers, who took Reilly's hint and turned to family audiences seemingly less vulnerable to self-regulatory and governmental scrutiny (Marketplace forces, 1979).

The Congress itself, in late 1979 and early 1980, went through contortions as industry lobbyists tried to disembowel the FTC. After some 20 committee hearings, reviews, and conferences, a willing and pliant Congress showed the industry forces had won. FTC rule-making was made subject to a Congressional veto without Presidential intervention; "unfairness" as a criterion for weighing advertising viewed by children was dropped from the FTC's powers. Public participation was substantially cut back. Funding for the FTC itself actually lapsed as the Congress argued about teaching all regulatory agencies a lesson. Finally, the House and Senate successfully conferenced; the FTC survived, shaken by its ordeal.

The Children's Advertising rule-making may proceed, but Congress wants to see the proposed rule, this time drafted on the basis of deception only, before any actions are taken. As described to me by FTC's William Baer, assistant general counsel for legislation and congressional liaison, in June 1980:

> While it is too early to predict, it appears the [FTC] Commission is still convinced there is something here worth pursuing; the problem remains a serious one. The Commission views the Congress' action as focussing their activities, but not stopping this inquiry [personal communication, 1980].

Baer acknowledged, however, that a ban on advertising was no longer a feasible option for protecting children.

Despite all the angry words between the two houses of Congress and between consumers and the industry forces, no one seemed to note that CCMM had submitted testimony that anticipated the impossibility of the FTC's banning advertising seen by children. In its statement *"No" is not enough*, CCMM suggested eight amendments to the proposed FTC rule; the amendments would have permitted children and their parents to gain consumer skills needed by any child in the marketplace (Choate, 1978).

ACT and CCMM will remain attentive to the issue, but the handwriting on the wall is clear: Parents must help their children to comprehend the totality of the message in the more than 20,000 commercials per year they view.

References

ABC pares more off Saturday morning ad time. *Broadcasting*, 1979, 96(4), 24.

Adler, R. P., Friedlander, B. Z., Lesser, G. S., Meringoff, L., Robertson, T. S., Rossiter, J. R., & Ward, S. *Research on the effects of television advertising on children.* Washington, D.C.: United States Government Printing Office, 1977.

Advertising Age, 1977, 48(26), 47.

Appropriations Committee, U.S. House of Representatives. Report 93–1120, June 18, 1974. (a)

Appropriations Committee, U.S. House of Representatives, Subcommittee on Housing and Urban Development, Space, Science, Veterans. Federal Communications Commission appropriations hearings. March 12, 1974. (b)

Appropriations Committee, U.S. Senate, Subcommittee on Agriculture. Environmental and consumer protection appropriations hearings. March 26, 1974. (a)

Appropriations Committee, U.S. Senate, Subcommittee on Housing and Urban Development, Space, Science, Veterans. Federal Communications Commission appropriations hearings. March 8, 1974. (b)

Cater, D., & Strickland, S. TV violence and the child: The evolution and fate of the Surgeon General's Report. New York: Sage, 1975.

Children's advertising principles: Questions and answers. Code News, 1974, 7(5), 4.

Children's Advertising Review. Unit, National Advertising Division, Council of Better Business Bureaus, Incorporated. An eye on children's advertising self-regulation. New York: Council of Better Business Bureaus, 1979.

Choate, R. B. A presentation to the National Association of Broadcasters' Television Code Review Board. May 26, 1971. Updated October, 1972.

Choate, R. B. To the Federal Trade Commission in the matter of a trade regulation rule on food/nutrition advertising. Washington, D.C., October, 1976.

Choate, R. B. To the Federal Trade Commission: Part of an inquiry into children and television, " 'No' is not enough." Washington, D.C.: Council on Children, Media and Merchandising, 1978.

Cohen, S. E. Washington beat. Advertising Age, 1974, 45(10), 16.

Cole, B., & Oettinger, M. Reluctant regulators. Reading, Massachusetts: Addison-Wesley, 1978.

Commerce Committee, U.S. Senate. Oversight hearings on Federal Trade Commission. March 14, 1974.

Commerce Committee, U.S. Senate, Subcommittee on Consumer Affairs. Dry cereals hearings. July 23, August 4–5, 1970.

Commerce Committee, U.S. Senate, Subcommittee on Consumer Affairs. Hearings of February 27, 1973, as reprinted in Broadcast Advertising and Children, U.S. House of Representatives, Subcommittee on Communications, Committee on Interstate and Foreign Commerce, July 14–17, 1975.

Congress presses FTC, FCC for action on children's ads. Advertising Age, 1974, 45(11), pp. 2, 78.

Dixon, W. D. Report of the presiding officer, proposed trade regulation rule: Food advertising. Federal Trade Commission, February, 1978.

Don't kill children's ad study (editorial viewpoint). Advertising Age, 1978, 49(19), 12.

Edwards, L. Halfsies, new Quaker cereal lower in sugar, ready to debut. Advertising Age, 1979, 50 (31), 1.

Engman, L. Speech to the American Advertising Federation. June 3, 1974.

Federal Communications Commission. Children's television programs—report and policy statements. Federal Register, 1974, 39(215), 39396–39409.

Federal Trade Commission. Proceedings before the Federal Trade Commission in the matter of over-the-counter antacids, docket no. 215–56, January 19, 1979. Washington, D.C.: Ace Federal Reporters, 1979.

Feshbach, N. D., Jordan, T. S., & Dillman, A. S. The design of a graphic to convey nutritional information to children: Pilot studies. In R. B. Choate (Ed.), To the Federal Trade Commission in the matter of a trade regulation rule on food/nutrition advertising. October, 1976.

The FTC as national nanny. Washington Post, March 2, 1978, p. A-22.

FTC's Pertschuk says children's ads may violate fairness standard. Food Chemical News, 1977, 19(35), 8–10.

General Mills slams claims by FTC. Advertising Age, 1978, 49(40), 86.

Gene Reilly Group. The Child. Darien, Connecticut: The Child, Incorporated, 1973, 1.

Gene Reilly Group. The Child. Darien, Connecticut: The Child, Incorporated, 1974, 3.

Hulbert, J., & Howard, J. Advertising and the public interest. Staff report to the Federal Trade Commission. Washington, D.C., February, 1973.

Leighton, R. Testimony to the Committee on the Judiciary, Subcommittee on Administrative Practice and Procedure, U.S. Senate. July 20, 1979.

Marketplace forces regulation's silent aide: Editorial viewpoint. *Advertising Age*, 1979, *50*(34), 18.

Morris, B. Foes of child ad curbs devised strategy here. *Washington Star*, March 15, 1979, pp. A-10; A-13. (a)

Morris, B. Industry group says it "neutralized" FTC hearings. *Washington Star*, April 18, 1979, p. A-12. (b)

National Advertising Division, Council of Better Business Bureaus, Incorporated, Children's Advertising Review Unit. *Children's advertising guidelines.* New York: Council of Better Business Bureaus, 1977.

Richmond, J. Statement on FTC proposed rulemaking on children's advertising. Washington, D.C., November 24, 1978.

Russell, M. Consumer agency bill clears house. *Washington Post*, November 7, 1975, pp. A-1; A-8.

Surgeon General's Scientific Advisory Committee. *Television and growing up: The impact of televised violence.* Report to the Surgeon General, United States Public Health Service. Washington, D.C.: United States Government Printing Office, 1972.

Tucker Wayne and Company. *Submission to the USDA in response to a request for proposals.* December, 1978.

Two guns take aim at food ads. *Broadcasting*, 1971, *80*(8), 45–46.

USDA analyzes cereals for five food sugars. *CNI Weekly Report*, 1979, *9*(27), 7. *White House Conference on Food, Nutrition, and Health.* Washington, D.C.: United States Government Printing Office, 1970.

21

The Future Is Inevitable: But Can It Be Shaped in the Interest of Children?

EMILIE GRIFFIN

The fundamental assumption of this chapter is that children's television, including children's advertising, can and should be made better. A second and related assumption is that this can only come about if those who care about television as a medium and children as an audience are honestly critical of what has been done up to now—critical, in the sense not only of singling out weaknesses and failures but also of noting successes, particularly those that may have broader application in the development of new television vehicles and may serve as positive models for improved children's telecommunications.

Having said that children's television can and should improve, I am immediately conscious that there is no general and workable agreement in our society about what "good" children's television consists of, and it is probably unrealistic to expect any consensus to develop. In fact, the controversy over children and television often seems to be a matter of people talking entirely at cross purposes. The parties to the issue often hold fundamentally different views of childhood and the role that television does and should occupy in children's lives. From each, different goals arise and often lead in entirely opposite directions.

CHILDREN AND THE FACES OF TELEVISION:
Teaching, Violence, Selling

Quantitative and Qualitative Change

To arrive at any clarity it is necessary at least to understand the fundamental assumptions and the hypotheses and actions which flow from them. At the present time there seem to be two streams in the movement toward improved television, one desiring a quantitative change in children's viewing and the other seeking a fundamentally qualitative change.

The desire for quantitative change springs from a concern about the sheer quantity of television seen by children and from a concern about the dominance it may have in their lives. Many studies about children and television quote viewing figures to show that television has assumed a role (in terms of time spent viewing) that bids fair to replacing the parent, the school, and the church as shapers of ideals, values, and behavior. Educators and parents urge "empty" hours as a necessary experience for children to develop their own creative potential and to participate in play as a natural part of development. A related issue, in children's advertising, is the quantity of commercials directed to children.

Efforts to deal with the children's television phenomenon—in this tradition or stream—often take the form of efforts to limit the amount of children's viewing, to encourage parents and children viewing together, and to limit or eliminate children's exposure to advertising. Many advocates ideally wish for the elimination of advertising directed to children but would compromise on limitation of advertisements to groups 8 years of age and under and on restrictions on advertising of products deemed unacceptable for children. It may be a forced-fit to call this a desire for quantitative change, for in some sense it is qualitative as well.

Desires to limit, ban, or reduce children's exposure to the medium seem to fall within the quantitative area and to flow from an assumption that television viewing is a "passive experience" that is somehow "too much in the lives of children." Critics holding this view feel that such activity, by its very nature, tends to rob children of time and energy to participate in other, more enriching experiences. The benefits of television viewing are judged to be less than the benefits of other real-life experiences which children might have. Perhaps if these critics held a more favorable opinion of what is offered to children through the medium, they would be less likely to think of television as a negative or undesirable experience—one to be restricted and held at bay. But this is only a speculation. It is impossible to say whether those who want less television in the lives of children would feel otherwise if television were developed in a different way.

By contrast, the desire for qualitative change—a second stream in the movement for improved children's television—seems to spring from an underlying view that television has great potential for good, which is not being fully realized. Concerns about negative content such as violence and stereotyping are only part of the issue, for even those who are not specifically concerned about these issues seem to think there is not enough good children's programming available. Regardless of the definition of "good," the common desire is to make children's television better, not by lessening viewing but by changing the content that children see. This may mean increasing the kinds of content which are almost universally admired, or simply increasing the diversity of available content. A pertinent issue then becomes the extent to which advertisers can encourage the development of positive content in television and, indeed, in advertising itself.

Influences of Advertising on Programming

A Funding Source

While advertisers do not directly influence the content of the programs they sponsor, the very nature of the advertising marketplace is such that broadcasters design their programs to attract large audiences of children with a view to attracting major commercial sponsorship. Competition—the very essence of the American marketplace—thus influences networks and stations to seek the most popular formats, the programs which children will like. Very often, it seems, what children "like" is not what educators, parents, and consumer advocates deem "worthwhile." Thus, commercialization itself is seen as the enemy of "good" children's television.

Yet there are many programs which belie this. The ABC network's *Afterschool Special* and *Weekend Special*, recently cited by Action for Children's Television (ACT) as a series of continuing excellence, are cases in point. Even more to the point is the success of a two-part network special, *The Lion, the Witch and the Wardrobe*, based on the highly acclaimed *Chronicles of Narnia* by C. S. Lewis and produced by a group long associated with educational television. Though styled as family fare, the programs were significantly appealing to children and drew large audiences even though they ran opposite *Jesus of Nazareth* and *Battlestar Galactica* on the competing networks. This successful effort may suggest that programming of artistic merit need not be elitist in its appeal, provided that it is handled with understanding of the tastes of a broad audience of American children. It may also provide a model for more such efforts in the future and suggest that the presumed conflict between commercial interests and quality programming is a false one.

There is hope, too, in the recent list of children's television awards given by ACT. Many of the programs which they cited for excellence (though admittedly not the majority) were produced and aired by commercial stations. Also so honored was a Public Broadcasting Service effort, *Once Upon a Classic*, a series of dramatizations of children's literary classics made possible by a grant from a major advertiser, McDonald's. So it may well be that the perceived conflict between commercialization of television and "good" programming is beginning to disappear—if indeed it ever was more than a conflict in the eye of the beholder.

Advertisers have long maintained that advertising itself provides broadcasters with the tremendous sums necessary to innovate. Though this argument was long regarded as laughable by those who thought commercially based programming inadequate, some advocates of better programming for children, as they become more aware of the economics of children's television, are beginning to adopt this argument as well. Some are now supporters of an advertising-based system in the hope that it may generate dollars for better and more innovative programming.

A Source of Ideas and Methods

But the dollars, the technology, the alternative media—these are only means to the goal. The real task that lies ahead of us is to use these means to generate superior television content for children. And it is my hope that, in the development of that superior content, advertising itself will have a meaningful role to play.

It has already done so by example in one resounding children's television success—*Sesame Street*. One of the stated inspirations for that landmark in children's television programming was the proven attention-getting techniques of television advertising that were adapted to the teaching of cognitive skills. To be sure, much of the delight and joy of the *Sesame Street* episodes was in their sheer, unbridled use of the imagination, especially in a humorous vein. And advertising has no corner on either imagination or humor. But it is worth noting that much of the style of *Sesame Street* and its successful communication to preschoolers was influenced by advertising. Its simplicity, its bid for attention, its vernacular style, and even the shortness of the teaching units all were patterned after advertising.

I am not suggesting that better children's programming efforts in all cases should borrow from advertising techniques to communicate with children. Indeed, I am not in favor of any kind of rigid formulas for the development of better children's programming. But I do think that much can be learned about how to communicate successfully with children from the experience of advertising people. If there is one lesson advertisers learn from the marketplace, it is to understand the needs and interests of their audiences as directly and personally as possible and to try out their proposed communications efforts on samples of consumers. Advertisers do not assume, if they are wise, that what they want to communicate is inherently interesting, that simply because what they have to say is "worthwhile" it will therefore be listened to and heard. Instead, advertising messages are shaped by the opinions and reactions of those who will view them.

Such well-shaped advertising often seems to capture the public imagination, to be remembered, to "catch on," to hold attention, and to motivate. Indeed, this is one of the most maddening things about advertising—including advertising to children—to those who oppose it. When advertising catches on (and it does not always do so), it does so, not because advertising people are geniuses or Svengalis, but because they have taken the trouble to develop insights into the needs and interests of their audiences and to develop their messages in ways that speak directly to those needs.

So I think that some progress can possibly be made by those who develop programming for children—and who desire to make "worthwhile" programs attractive to large audiences of children—by using the kind of learning process that advertising people undertake in developing their own messages. It is an attitude that assumes that the public is not simply sitting in front of the set waiting for what a programmer or advertiser has to say—and this humility and a belief in the need to experiment and improve styles of communications are precisely what work toward improving the medium's content.

An even more practical application for the experience of advertising to improve television content for children seems to be in the area of public service announcements—the use of advertising-like messages to inform children and teach them in areas that are particularly relevant to their health, welfare, and emotional growth. A number of experiments by private organizations and by broadcasters themselves have been undertaken in this regard, a good sampling of which are reviewed in Chapter 18 in this book. But little is known about the effects of these messages, not only because they have been produced without much testing of their communications power but also because they have been scheduled randomly rather than in an intensive advertising-like media campaign. A new effort in this area is presently underway, under the sponsorship of the United States Department of Agriculture, which will design a media campaign to encourage children to become more knowledgeable about nutrition. The creative work is being done by an advertising agency known for its effective children's advertising communications. If successful, this effort could prove the model for more child-directed public service campaigns.

The Future of Advertising

But perhaps the most crucial question of all, at least in the perspective of this chapter, is how advertising itself might develop in the future as a positive element in children's television.

At present, the future of advertising directed to children hangs in the balance. But if it survives, it will do so in part because of the firm belief of marketers that advertising serves a constructive purpose in the lives of children. It orients them to the marketplace, making choices available and informing about product availabilities, and gives them, in short, the same access to the marketplace which adults have, but keyed to their specific areas of interest.

There seems to be little doubt that children remember and enjoy commercials and in a great many instances ask for the products that they see advertised. For critics, this fact is in itself enough to make them suggest that there should be no advertising, owing to the vulnerability of children. But many advertisers have long believed that children are equal to the challenge of advertising directed to them, that they are in fact very alert to the content of advertising and to the manner in which children and products are represented. Advertisers have always wanted "better" advertising—but by this, in general, they have meant advertising that communicates effectively the intended message and that conveys product information in an attention-getting way.

Many educators and others who are critical of children's advertising have a different definition of "good" children's advertising. (If we subtract those who cannot see children's advertising as a "good" at all.) They suggest that advertising ought to be sensitive to social and moral content at the same time that it is effectively communicating product information. Relevant guidelines have, in fact, been developed by children's advertisers themselves and modified with the insights of psychologists and educators.

Current Guidelines

I am speaking in particular of the *Children's Advertising Guidelines* of the National Advertising Division of the Council of Better Business Bureaus. This self-regulatory instrument was originally drafted by advertisers themselves in 1972 and issued as the *Children's Television Advertising Guidelines* of the Association of National Advertisers (1972). It was modified by the Children's Advertising Review Unit of the National Advertising Division (1975, 1977) in consultation with a committee of academic advisors, all of them expert in one aspect or another of child development and the media. The 1977 *Guidelines*, broadly supported by the advertising community, state that advertisements directed to children should be truthful, accurate, and fair to children's perceptions. They also include five basic principles, which I will paraphrase here:

1. Advertisers should take into account the level of knowledge, sophistication, and maturity of their intended audience, with special

responsibility to protect younger children from their own suscepti-
bilities.

2. Advertisers should be careful not to exploit the imaginative quality of children nor to stimulate unreasonable expectations of product quality or performance.
3. Information should be conveyed in a truthful and accurate manner with full recognition that the child may learn practices which
   can affect his or her health and well-being.
4. Advertisers are urged to develop advertising that, wherever possible, addresses itself to social standards generally regarded as
   positive and beneficial, such as friendship and justice.
5. Advertisers should contribute to the parent–child relationship in a
   constructive manner, although it remains the prime responsibility
   of the parents to provide guidance.

The *Guidelines*—which closely parallel those of the National Association of Broadcasters (NAB)—also give specific guidance with regard to
presentation styles, use of endorsements, promotion by program characters, or characters from editorial formats, comparative claims, pressure
to purchase, safety, and claim substantiation. Among other things, they
caution against peer competitiveness and representations that might lead
to undue pressure on parents.

During my years as Director of the Children's Advertising Review
Unit (CARU), the guidelines just presented were developed with the assistance of a group of academic advisors, several of whom are also contributors to this book. During this time I and my CARU associates reviewed hundreds of commercials directed to children and talked with
many parents, educators, consumer advocates, and children. From these
activities and my reflections on them in the years since I left the Unit, I
have developed a viewpoint on what is workable, realistic, and desirable
in the future development of children's advertising. It is my own viewpoint entirely and does not reflect in any sense the corporate stance either
of my own agency or of the advertising industry. Nevertheless, I think it is
worth stating—if only as a point of departure for discussions on how
children's advertising should develop in the future.

Creativity

To date, the controversy over the practice of children's advertising
has been so heated, the discussion of whether to advertise to children
such a matter of debate, that too little attention has been given to the *how*
of advertising to children. Guidelines—admirable though they are—have
tended to dwell more on the "don't's" of children's advertising than on
the "do's." I do not lament the existence of guidelines and standards.

They are vitally needed. But often I suspect these rules and regulations—in the minds of the creative developers of children's advertisements—become a list of negative prohibitions. To me, it is little wonder that, within the whole spectrum of advertising, the children's category often seems the least adventurous from the creative point of view.

Yet during the development of the CARU *Guidelines* I had many opportunities to reflect on what good and positive elements exist now within children's advertising that ought to be encouraged further. It is difficult, perhaps even inappropriate, to codify these reflections and insights into rules and regulations. Yet, I often feel that it is these insights on "the good commercial" that most need to be shared with the originators of children's advertising—they being, ultimately, the people who are most able to effect qualitative change in the content of children's advertising.

Socially Useful Teaching

When nonadvertising people talk about how child-directed advertising might be changed for the better, they often seem to be wishing to make advertisements into socially useful teaching units. This thrust in children's advertising—toward the prosocial—was the subject of a seminar for children's advertisers held by the Children's Advertising Review Unit during its first year of operation. Some commercials were singled out as having social value in the eyes of academic experts. I recall in particular a commercial for Ideal's Rub-a-Dub Dolly, which showed a child washing the doll's hair and then showed a mother washing the child's hair. To psychologists this scenario offered positive modeling and wholesome parent–child interaction. Yet the commercial was also "good" in the advertising professional's sense: It represented the product in an attractive and favorable way. Both the commercial and the product had been successful in the marketplace. This seemed to suggest that commercials might be "good" in both ways: effective communicators of desired product information and effective social learning vehicles as well. Indeed, there are dozens of other commercials which do the same sort of thing—a cereal campaign shows families participating in active sports together or children are shown sharing products, helping one another, and taking part in imaginative play.

But I am less inclined now than I once was to want to encourage this line of thought as the best way of looking to the future of children's advertising. When these social learning elements happen naturally in the context of children's commercials, it seems to me all to the good. But I do not believe that children's advertising should be intentionally converted into a vehicle for social learning. This is not to suggest that advertisers should not be concerned about the social content of their messages. I hope that those who are not, will become so and that those who are, will become more so; but, in my opinion, better children's advertising will come from better advertising itself rather than from the social message it bears.

Consumer Socialization

In a document submitted to the Federal Trade Commission in 1978 the Association of National Advertisers (ANA), The American Association of Advertising Agencies (AAAA), and the American Advertising Federation (AAF) presented their case for the practice of advertising to children in these words:

> Perhaps the single most important benefit of advertising to children is that it provides information to the child himself, information which advertisers try to gear to the child's interests and on an appropriate level of understanding. This allows the child to learn what products are available, to know their differences, and to begin to make decisions about them based on his own personal wants and preferences. . . . [Children have] a multitude of different needs and interests in the marketplace, and it is to these individual proclivities that manufacturers address their attention and their efforts. . . .Product diversity responds to these product preferences and ensures that it is the consumer himself who dictates the ultimate success or failure of a given product offering [p. 11].

This chapter also argues that advertising is an instrument for socializing the child as a consumer, one of the many roles she or he learns in childhood and performs in adulthood.

Different Advertising Techniques

It seems to me that this document—taken together with the *Children's Advertising Guidelines*—provides useful direction in thinking about how children's advertising might grow and develop in the future. First, it suggests that advertising is an instrument of diversity. A desirable diversity of product choices is already made available to children through advertising. However, after several years of viewing children's commercials and advertisements, I have come to wonder whether children's advertising—as a special universe within the whole of advertising—has become overly narrow and lacking in creative diversity in the advertising techniques it employs. Is it possible that children's advertisers, singed by the heat of controversy, have become overly conservative and reliant on the past in their approaches to children? Is it possible that worthwhile experiments in style of communications are being overlooked or perhaps inadvertently shut off by the need to conform to rigid codes and their interpretations?

A case in point: One of the most familiar approaches in some kinds of adult advertising, yet one of the most infrequently used with children, is that of the user testimonial in which a presenter with whom the viewer can identify describes his or her real-life experience with the product. At a seminar held by the Children's Advertising Review Unit in 1976, the possibility of child-to-child advertising was discussed at some length. Because of the age-specific ways in which child viewers tend to relate to child performers, child-to-child commercials might involve some risks on the part of advertisers. But is a narrow dogmatism about "what works" depriving child viewers of an advertising style that might be informative to them and fresh—serving the goals of the advertiser as well as those of the child?

A second and related concept to be explored is that of commercials written and produced by children themselves. This has already been done in school classrooms where children are encouraged to invent products, name them, and write advertisements for them as an exercise in understanding the dynamics of television advertising. However, I do not suggest this as an academic exercise, however worthwhile. I suggest it as a way in which child-directed advertising could become even more "advertising to children"—featuring the product points with greatest relevance and meaning to children themselves. Such an approach would recognize a reality: Advertising is already part of the language of children, visual and verbal, one that has created for them mythologies (McDonaldland, for one) that are part of their experience. When children become part of the inventing of such advertising communications, not only do they master the medium for themselves but also they convey to other children the enthusiasm that comes from doing, with authority, a thing previously reserved to adults. This experience, distilled within a commercial, could work both to the child's and the advertiser's advantage.

To date much of children's advertising content has been dominated by fantasy, humor, and product demonstration. Clearly these are effective and worthwhile communications techniques, yet they are only a portion of the advertising spectrum. In a recent viewing of child-oriented entries for the Clio advertising awards, I noted some of these familiar techniques. But there were others that are not often seen in the children's category. One commercial, directed to parents, was written using a problem-solution format. The problem solved was of bored, quarrelsome children, complaining of "nothing to do." Undoubtedly such an appeal strikes a responsive chord with some parents, and a product that offers to alleviate the "rainy day syndrome" addresses itself to a genuine need in children's experience as well. To the extent that commercials speak to real needs and problems they become more effective. At the same time, the reality that they reflect may enhance the child's self-understanding and perception of the world in which he or she lives.

Children's Competence

It is possible, of course, that such advertising departures might not survive the crucible of the marketplace. It is possible that such appeals are already being explored but fail to be aired because they do not perform as well as the more traditional advertising approaches. But it is also possible that much children's advertising is governed by a view of children based on adult suppositions rather than on hard realities. Today's children, to the amazement of their elders, often use television differently than adults; some can actually perform difficult tasks *while* watching television in a way that our adult linear mentalities find hard to grasp. Granting, for the moment, that Piaget is right—that there are certain inevitable passages in child development that cannot or should not be hurried—we should also be aware (through observation, following Piaget) of the media competence that even young children may develop through their involvement with television.

What I am suggesting may sound heretical both to my advertising colleagues and to those critics who view the phenomenon of child-directed advertising with dismay. But I am simply suggesting that in our advertising communications, we should take children seriously as consumers, perhaps even more seriously than we have. Certainly there is a danger in all our communications of talking over children's heads, presenting product information in a way that is confusing to them, being insensitive to their real perceptual bounds. This is a pitfall for advertisers. But in general, most advertising does not err in this direction. Another pitfall may be that of talking down to children, giving them less product information than they can handle, retreating into styles of communication that are based on our own nostalgia and cherished preconceptions rather than on real insights into the child-consumers with whom we wish to communicate.

It is here, I think—and I hope I am not naive in this—that research can play a liberating and genuinely creative role. Too often research has an after-the-fact quality, measuring what has been done (and much too little of that on child perceptions of advertising content); often what research there is has been used to close doors rather than to open them. But research can and should open new vistas in child communications, not only by lending insight into the hardest questions (e.g., "how does modeling take place?") but also by helping to evaluate smaller and more specific possibilities (such as sorting through an array of experimental communications styles or advertising concepts).

Admittedly, much of this may be impractical in the day-to-day arena of advertising and the marketplace, especially when children's advertisers are already faced with a lengthy preclearance process, often neces-

sitating refilming and re-editing of commercial messages before they can
be aired. The system as it stands tends to favor what has been done
before, rather than a previously untried communications style. But innovation, freshness, breaking through the conventional and the hackneyed
—these are the life's blood of advertising and the marketplace. They offer
real benefits to advertisers as well as to child viewers of advertising.

Advertising as a Positive Force

There are two statements about children's advertising, written by
advertisers themselves that continue to haunt me. The ANA, AAAA, and
AAF "Positive Case for Marketing Children's Products to Children" (1978)
says:

> our system of developing products specifically suited for different market segments
> and our ability to advertise them to the intended users is a strong motivator for manu-
> facturers and marketers. It leads to constant search for product improvement and in-
> novation, forcing manufacturers to upgrade and improve existing products in order to
> stay competitive, and providing them with the incentive to discover new products
> which will satisfy evolving consumer needs [p. 11].

And a related statement, in the Children's Advertising Guidelines, (National Advertising Division, 1977) reads: "In the event that a true and
significant advantage may exist in a product which can be readily understood by children, this advantage should be clearly explained [p. 6]."
These statements rest on a presumption that the impetus of the American
marketplace—competition—may work to the interests of children and
other segments of society. Advertising itself may spur the development of
better, more distinctive products. However, mentioning the resulting advantages of a product in an advertisement to children is not often done,
because the National Association of Broadcasters Code—in contrast to the
NAD code just quoted—prohibits such comparative claims. Children's
products may not, in practice, be presented as new or improved. Yet on
Sesame Street one of the oft-repeated learning games sings out, "One of
these things is not like the others," encouraging children to make distinctions based on shape, size, configuration, and other attributes. Might not
advertising also encourage such making of distinctions?

Perhaps it will strike some as an irony, or at the very least a novelty,
to think of children's advertising content not as a fact of life in children's
television—an unavoidable reality, a "fair price to pay" for children's television programs, a by-product of the economic demands of the current
television system—but rather as a potentially positive element in the
whole mix of media directed toward children. Undoubtedly, it is an element that should be monitored and controlled, yet at the same time it is a
form of communication that offers promise of growth and improvement

akin to the growth and improvement we expect in all areas of television communications.

In my own random conversations with children about advertising I have often had the impression that they like advertising more than adults do. Certainly they like the humorous and entertaining elements in advertising, but it seems that they like the product information, too. One second-grader wrote an essay defining advertising as an "entertainment of products." Children sometimes feel that advertising serves their interests: "It tells us what to look for when we go to the store." This statement expresses in childlike terms the "positive case for children's advertising," as defined by the ANA, AAAA, and AAF statement (1978).

Reprise

A contemporary thinker about the rights of children has suggested that as long as there is advertising in our society, children have a right to be advertised to (Farson, 1974). My own thought is that children also have a "right" to the very best kind of advertising. But communications styles improve and grow only through experiment, by making departures, by taking risks, doing what has not been done before. The present heated environment for children's advertising may not favor such innovation. Nevertheless, a serious and honestly self-critical advertising professionalism can bring it about. To my mind, this should be one of the definite, concrete goals toward which the advertising industry moves in the years to come.

With regard to the influence of advertising on the remainder of television content—that is, on the programs they sponsor—it is well to remember that advertisers, in general, do not create and originate television programs. They do, of course, influence their development by the choices they make for sponsorship and by the large audience demands they make in sponsorship. The complaint is often heard, from observers of television, that programs are seen primarily as an "environment for advertising" rather than as content to be evaluated in its own right. Certainly advertisers can establish and maintain high standards with regard to the programs they sponsor. In doing so they serve their own interests—especially in the long-term—as well as those of the children viewing both the commercial and the program.

I am not convinced that the large audience demands which advertisers make are in fact the real barrier to excellence in children's programming. As we have seen, some programs of quality have already been developed and aired, and some have attracted large audiences of children. To date, these programs may seem exceptional. Perhaps, in a medium that demands such a quantity of programming material, such programming will always be the exception rather than the norm.

What I have called the "quantitative" approach to the future of children's television would work to remove children's television from the marketplace. By contrast, the "qualitative" approach would seek to channel the forces of the marketplace toward better children's television. Of the two approaches, the latter seems to me far more promising—and more practical.

References

Association of National Advertisers. *Children's television advertising guidelines*. New York: Association of National Advertisers, 1972.

Association of National Advertisers, Incorporated, American Association of Advertising Agencies, Incorporated, & American Advertising Federation, Incorporated. The positive case for marketing children's products to children. Comments submitted to the Federal Trade Commission, 1978.

Farson, R. *Birthrights*. New York: Macmillan, 1974.

National Advertising Division, Council of Better Business Bureaus, Incorporated, Children's Advertising Review Unit. *Children's advertising guidelines*. New York: Council of Better Business Bureaus, Incorporated, 1975.

National Advertising Division, Council of Better Business Bureaus, Incorporated, Children's Advertising Review Unit. *Children's advertising guidelines* (Rev. ed.). New York: Council of Better Business Bureaus, Incorporated, 1977.

Index

A

AAAA, see American Association of Advertising Agencies
AAF, see American Advertising Federation
ABC (American Broadcasting Company), 103, 119, 136–137, 244, 283
  specials, 34, 341
ACT (Action for Children's Television), 87, 121, 222, 237, 242–243, 326, 341–342
  and FCC, 242–244, 283, 326
  and FTC, 244
  history, 241–242, 323–324, 326
  political strategies, 326–327
Advertising
  activities depicted, 282
  adult concern, 240–241, 245, 325, 330, 344
  adult-oriented, 263–265, 330
  appeals, types of, 260, 279–280, 281–282
  attention to, 308–310, 311
  characters, 281–282, 296
  clustering, 310
  consumer socialization, 347
  credibility, 296, 317
  dimensions for policy analysis, 252–255
  effects, see Advertising impact
  ethical questions about, 281–283
  food, 260–261, 263–265, 276, 295–296
  functions, 344, 347
  guidelines, 237, 244, 261, 344–345
  influence on programs, 37–38, 212, 341, 342–343, 351–352
  information retention, 314–315, 316
  policy issues, 242, 244, 245, 251–266, 269–271, 282–283, 324, 325, 326, 327, 328, 329, 330, 331, 333–336
  policy statements, 256–258, 262, 263
  positive function of, 346–347, 350–351
  products, 275–276, 283, 350
  quality, 339, 344, 346–347
  quantity, 257–258, 340
  recognition, 258, 311, 314–315, 316
  regulation of, 257, 302–303, 331, 332, 344–345
  restrictions on, 274, 278–279, 283, 340
  revenues of, 238–240
  selling intent, comprehension of, 263–269, 313–314
  toys, 275–276, 278
  vitamins, 244, 332
Advertising ban, 262, 283, 332, 334
Advertising guidelines, see Advertising, guidelines; Self-regulation
Advertising impact

acceptance of claims, 288, 289, 317–318
aggression, 301
brand preference, 289–290, 292
child unhappiness, 299, 300
disinhibition, 292–293
expectations, 300–301
individual differences, 307–320
parent–child conflict, 277, 297–298, 300
product dissatisfaction, 300
product preference, 289–290, 294
product requests, 265, 290–291, 318–319
product use, 291, 292–293
Advertising techniques, 258–259, 276, 349–350
animation, 296
attention, 277, 343
disclaimers, 288, 310
disclosures, 278–279, 316
failures, 349–350
fantasy, 278, 348
format, 258–259
humor, 348
premium offers, 277, 293, 294
product presentation, 276–277, 348
program attractiveness, 342–343
qualifiers, 278–279, 316
repetition, 261, 277
sound effects, 277
violent activity, 278
Advertising time, 239–240, 244, 261, 274, 275
Age, 62, 106, 135–136, 168, 186–188, 308–309, 311, 314–315, 316, 317
Agency for Instructional Television (AIT), 14–15, 29, 39, 40, 42, 91, 92, 95, 96
Airborne Televised Instruction, 10
AIT, see Agency for Instructional Television
AMA, see American Medical Association
American Advertising Federation (AAF), 347, 350
American Association of Advertising Agencies (AAAA), 347, 350
American Federation of Teachers, 85
American Medical Association (AMA), 122–123, 222
ANA, see Association of National Advertisers
Animation, see Advertising techniques, animation
Association of National Advertisers (ANA), 344–345, 347, 350
Attention, 52, 310, see also Advertising, attention to; Advertising techniques, attention

B

Baer, William, FTC General Counsel, 336
Balanced breakfast, 296–297
Bank Street School of Education, 41
Batman, 192
Behavioral goals, 22
Big Blue Marble, 51, 59
Bilingual education, 38–39
Bonanza, 38
Bread and Butterflies, 15, 35
Breakfast cereals, 243, 278–279, 292, 293, 294, 297
Burch, Dean, FCC Chairman, 243, 332
Bureau of the Handicapped, 38–39
Buss Aggression Machine, 187, 189, 192

C

CAG, see Children's Advertising Guidelines
Captain Kangaroo, 51
Carnegie Commission, 11
Carrascolendas, 35, 96, 214–215
Carter, James E., U.S. President, 214–215, 333
CARU, see Children's Advertising Review Unit
Catharsis, 120, 130–131, 166–167, 171, 190–191
CBBB, see Council of Better Business Bureaus
CBS (Columbia Broadcasting System), 85, 118–119, 136–137
CCMM, see Council on Children, Media and Merchandising
Center for Science in the Public Interest, 262
Central Educational Network, 15
Cereals, see Breakfast cereals
Change
  in advertising, 215–216, 244, 326, 340–341, 343–352
  in children's programs, 80–81, 215–216, 326, 340–341, 342
  citizen action group role, 14, 83, 87, 327
  in commercial television, 161–162, 201–217, 226–230, 340–341, 342
  in ETV/ITV, 83–97, 99–108
  federal role, 115–116, 123–125, 213–216, 242–245
  industry role, 161–162, 208, 210–212, 342
  parental role, 209–210
  in research, 141–144, 161
  technology, 15–16, 94–97, 101–102, 216–217

in television violence, 123–125, 161–162

Charren, Peggy, ACT President, 326

Children's Advertising Guidelines (CAG), 344–345, 350

Children's Advertising Review Unit (CARU), 244, 259, 331

Children's programming, 87–88, 273

Children's Television Inquiry (CTI), 243, 246

Children's Television Programs, FCC Report and Policy Statement 1974, 326

Children's Television Workshop (CTW), 29, 35, 38, 40, 45, 51, 64, 327

  history, 5–6, 8–9, 11–13

  model, 12–13, 20, 38, 51

Citizen action groups, 14, 83, 87, 121–123, 245, 323–327

Closed-circuit television, 7–9

Cognitive skills, 24, 61–62, 188–189, 263–264, 288

Commercial characters, *see* Advertising, characters

Commercial program development, *see* Program development

Commercial programming, 19, 33–37, 87–88, 150–162, 207, 238–240, 339, 340–341

  change/reform, 154, 211–212, 216–217, 226–230, 239–240

  characters, 151–153

  criticisms, 149–162, 206–207, 211

  instructional uses of, 84, 85, 100, 103

  Saturday morning, 240, 298, 336

  as unplanned education, 71–73, 78–80, 84, 85–86, 100, 103–105, 107–108

Commercials, *see* Advertising

Commercials per hour, *see* Advertising, guidelines; Advertising time

Communications Act of 1934, 214

Congress, 14–15, 114, 115, 118, 124, 214, 325, 328

Consortia, 14–15, 39, 92–94

Consumer Federation of America, 327

Consumer organizations, *see specific organizations*

Consumers Union, 327

Contract, 25

Corporation for Public Broadcasting (CPB), 11, 29, 35, 38, 89, 91–92, 94, 101, 107

Cost per thousand, 153

Council of Better Business Bureaus (CBBB), 244, 256, 330, 345, 350

Council on Children, Media and Merchandising (CCMM), 237, 256, 260, 330

  and FTC, 332, 336

history, 243, 323–324

political strategies, 324–326

Co-viewing, 64–65, 137–138

CPB, *see* Corporation for Public Broadcasting

Cross-cultural, 59, 62, 165–167, 202

CSPI, *see* Center for Science in the Public Interest

CTAG, *see* Children's Advertising Guidelines

CTI, *see* Children's Television Inquiry

CTW, *see* Children's Television Workshop

Curriculum development, 21–22, 78–80, *see also* Educational/instructional programming; Program development and production

D

Davis, Malcolm, U.S. Office of Education, 91

Deceptive advertising, *see* Advertising, dimensions for policy analysis

Disclaimers, *see* Advertising techniques, disclaimers

Disinhibition, *see* Advertising impact, disinhibition; Violent programming impact, disinhibition

Dixon, William, FTC hearing judge, 332–333

Dodd, Thomas, U.S. Senator, 114

Duffy, James E., ABC–TV President, 283

E

Eastern Educational Network, 10–11

Educational Facilities Act 1962, 11

Educational/instructional programming

  distribution, 15, 36, 95

  formal/informal distinction, 19, 20, 35

  funding, 28–30, 38–39, 89–93

  goals, 21–22, 86

  improvements, 10–12, 28, 50, 83–97

  production, 7–8, 20–24, 25, 28, 88

  supplementary materials, 27, 65

  teaching strategies, 7–10, 25, 85–86

Educational/instructional programming impact

  individual differences, 53, 57–58

  instructional limitations, 63, 104–107

  learning process, 60–63, 64–65

Educational/instructional television (ETV/ITV)

  Airborne Televised Instruction, 10

  channels, 6–7

Educational/instructional television (cont.)
  consortia, 14–15, 39, 92–94
  criticisms, 6, 8–9, 50, 83, 99–100, 105
  CTW model, 12–13, 20, 38, 51
  delivery system, 10, 97
  FCC involvement, 6–7
  network formation, 10–11, 15
  and print literacy, 27–28, 85
  problems, 8–11, 26, 27–28
  teachers' role, 7–8, 27
  teaching models, 7–10
  technological advances, 6–8, 15–16, 94–
    97, 101–102
  unplanned, 100, 103–105
  utilization, 86, 101
Educational Testing Service (ETS), 52, 53,
    54, 55–56
Effects of television viewing, see Advertis-
    ing impact; Educational/instructional
    programming impact; Socialization of
    the child; Violent programming im-
    pact
Eisenhower Commission, 114–115
Electric Company, The, 13, 16, 21, 23, 27,
    28, 29, 35, 39, 43, 51, 52, 55–56, 57,
    86, 90, 96
Emergency School Aid Act (ESAA), 35, 38,
    57, 90–91
Engman, Lewis, FTC Chairman, 244, 332
Entertainment, 25–26, 84, 137–144
Entertainment programs in instruction, see
    Commercial programming, instruc-
    tional uses of
ESAA, see Emergency School Aid Act
Ethnicity, 190, 316, 317–318
ETS, see Educational Testing Service
ETV, see Educational/instructional televi-
    sion
Eye-movement technique, see Formative
    research

F

False advertising, see Advertising, dimen-
    sions for policy analysis; Policy is-
    sues, false advertising
Family viewing hour, 124, 213
Fat Albert and the Cosby Kids, 34, 57, 58,
    64, 84
FCC, see Federal Communications Commis-
    sion
FDA, see Food and Drug Administration
Federal Communications Commission
    (FCC), 6–7, 215, 242–243, 245, 274,
    324–325, 333
  and advertising, 257–258, 332
  Children's Television Inquiry and Report,
    242, 243, 246, 255, 257–258, 326, 332
  role in Surgeon General's inquiry, 124
Federal funding of ETV/ITV, 38–39, 89–93
Federal Trade Commission (FTC), 83, 104,
    215, 244–245, 324–325, 333
  and advertising, 215, 244–245, 263–265,
    267, 332, 333–334, 335–336, 347
  hearings, 255, 263, 265–266, 283, 325,
    332–333, 335–336
  Staff Report 1978, 248, 255, 262, 334
Feelin' Good, 16
Ferris, Charles, FCC Chairman, 333
First Amendment, 124, 139–140, 149–150,
    195–196, 213–214, 227–228, 335–336
Flintstones, The, 19
Food and Drug Administration (FDA), 324–
    325
Ford Foundation seminar, 328
Formative research, 12–13, 23–24, 40–43,
    45
Freestyle, 35, 39, 52, 86, 91, 92
FTC, see Federal Trade Commission
Funding, 28–29, 37, 38–39, 89–94, 238–240

G
Gene Reilly Group, Inc., 329–330
Georgetown University Law Center seminar,
    328
GMA, see Grocery Manufacturers of Amer-
    ica
Great Plains National, 96
Grocery Manufacturers of America (GMA),
    335
Gunn, Hartford, Public Broadcasting Ser-
    vice, 97

H
Happy Days, 19
Harley, William, National Association of
    Broadcasters, 97
Holocaust, 85
Host selling, see Policy issues, host selling
Humor, see Advertising techniques, humor

I
I, Claudius, 104
In the News, 84
Independent stations, 274–275

Infinity Factory, 20, 35, 91
Inside/Out, 15, 35, 56, 86
Instructional programming, *see* Educational/instructional programming
Instructional television (ITV), *see* Educational/instructional television
ITV, *see* Educational/instructional programming; Educational/instructional television

J
Jacques Cousteau, 104
Johnson, Lyndon B., U.S. President, 114–115
J. Walter Thompson Advertising Agency, 123

K
Kaye, Evelyn, ACT President, 326
Kefauver, Estes, U.S. Senator, 114
Kennedy, Donald, FDA head, 333
Kennedy, John F., U.S. President, 114–115
Kennedy, Robert F., U.S. Senator, 114–115
Kentucky Educational Television, 25
King, Rev. Dr. Martin Luther, Jr., 114–115
Kirkpatrick, Myles, FTC Chairman, 332
Kramer, Albert, FTC Bureau of Consumer Protection, 333

L
Learning techniques, 60–63, 64–65, 106
Licensing commercial stations, 238
Lion, the Witch, and the Wardrobe, The, 341
Little House on the Prairie, 85
Lucy Show, The, 38

M
MARC, *see* Media Action Research Center
Maryland Center for Public Broadcasting, 107
Measuremetric, 35
Media Action Research Center (MARC), 121–122
Misleading advertising, *see* Advertising, dimensions for policy analysis; Policy issues, misleading advertising
Mississippi Authority for Educational Television, 15
Misterogers Neighborhood, 14, 35, 57–58, 59, 65, 92, 222
Modeling, 71–72, 75–77, 80, 164, 171–174, 288
Mr. Wizard, 19

N
NAB, *see* National Association of Broadcasters
NAD, *see* National Advertising Division
NAEB, *see* National Association of Educational Broadcasters
NARB, *see* National Advertising Review Board
National Advertising Division (NAD), 256, 330, 331
National Advertising Review Board (NARB), 331
National Association for Better Broadcasting, 121
National Association of Broadcasters (NAB), 97, 237, 244, 330
Code, 194, 240, 244, 274, 278
National Association of Educational Broadcasters (NAEB), 97, 114
National Center for Education Statistics, 101, 107
National Education Association (NEA), 84, 85
National Educational Television (NET), 6–7, 11, 16
National Endowment for the Arts, 38–39
National Endowment for the Humanities, 38–39
National Geographic Specials, 104
National Institute of Education (NIE), 38–39, 89, 91, 92, 222
National Institute of Mental Health (NIMH), 222
National Instructional Television (NIT), 14–15
National Parent Teacher Association (PTA), 103, 123, 222, 327
National Science Foundation (NSF), 104, 255, 258, 259, 325
National Telecommunication and Information Agency, 215
National University Consortium for Teaching by Television, 107
NBC (National Broadcasting Company), 118, 136–137
NBC News Notes, 34
NEA, *see* National Education Association
NET, *see* National Educational Television
Networks, commercial, 211, 240, 242, 336, 341, *see also* ABC, CBS, NBC
News, 139–140
NIE, *see* National Institute of Education

NIMH, see National Institute of Mental Health
NIT, see National Instructional Television
Nova, 104
NSF, see National Science Foundation
Nutrition, 262, 295, 316, 324, 332, 336, see also Advertising, food; Breakfast cereals

O

OCD, see Office for Child Development
Office for Child Development (OCD), 103, 222
Office of Education, see U.S. Office of Education
Once Upon a Classic, 342
Ontario Educational Communications Authority, 15, 40
Our Story, 27

P

Parent Teacher Association, see National Parent Teacher Association
Parents, 65, 203, 209–210, 262, 290–291, 297–298, 329–330
Passivity, see Policy issues, passivity
Pastore, John, U.S. Senator, 115, 124
PBS (Public Broadcasting Service), 15, 36, 90, 92, 97, 107
PEAC, see Program Evaluation Analysis Computer
Pertschuk, Michael, FTC Chairman, 333–334
Petitions
    ACT to FCC, 1970, 242–244
    ACT to FTC, 1971–1972, 244
    ACT and CSPI to FTC, 1977, 262
Pilot program testing, 43–44
Pitofsky, Robert, FTC Commissioner, 333
Policy issues, 21, 26, 27, 125, 194, 195–196, 201–217, 251–266, 267, 269–271, 282–283, 333–336
    children as special audience, 194, 202–204
    cost effectiveness of ETV/ITV, 29–30
    false advertising, 254, 268
    funder influence, 37–39, 89–93, 212, 351–352
    government versus industry or parental regulation, 202, 203, 204, 207, 208, 257, 331

host selling, 242, 268
misleading advertising, 254–255, 266–267, 268–269
overcommercialization, 261
parent–child conflict, 262, 265
passivity, 26–27
premiums, 260
print literacy and reading, 27–28
program–commercial separation, 258, 311, 312
proprietary drugs, 260, 291
public participation funding, 334
research role, 205–206, 247, 266–269, 271, 302–303
selling intent, understanding of, 263–264, 313–314
sugar "overconsumption", 265
Polka Dot Door, 16
Premiums, 260, 277, 293, 294
Prime Time School Television, 85
Production techniques, see Advertising techniques; Educational/instructional programming, production; Educational/instructional programming, teaching strategies
Program development and production, 20, 21, 37, 78, 84, 86, see also specific federal agencies; ABC; CBS; NBC; CTW; AIT
    advertiser influence, 37–38, 212, 239–240, 351–352
    audience research, 21, 37, 39–40
    contrasts of school/ITV/ETV/commercial, 36, 78–80, 88–89
    decision makers, 37, 38–39, 87, 88, 92–93
    federal influence, 213–216
    formative research, 23–24, 25, 40–43, 45, 51
    funder influence, 37–39, 89–93, 212, 351–352
    funding, 37, 39, 91–92, 93–94, 238–240
    procedures, 20, 22–23, 33, 40–44, 46, 88
    ratings, 39, 143
    staffing, 20–21, 45, 87
    summative research, 24, 44, 79–80
Program Evaluation Analysis Computer (PEAC), 42
Program–commercial separation, 258, 311, 312
Proprietary drug advertising, 260
Prosocial programming, 56–57, 58, 65, 84
    impact, 57–60, 84, 134–136, 138–139, 141, 169

PSA (Public Service Announcement), 302, 343
PTA, see National Parent Teacher Association
Public participation funding, 334

R
Rebop, 35
Regulation, 177, 227–228, 274, 302–303, 330, 331, see also Self-regulation
Richmond, Julius, Assistant Secretary for Health, 333
Ripples, 15, 56
Roeser, Thomas, Quaker Oats Vice-President, 331
Romper Room, 242
Roots, 85, 104

S
Satellites, 96–97
Saturday Morning Supershow, 16
School House Rock, 51, 84
Script reading, 85
Self Incorporated, 35
Self-regulation, 228–229, 244, 245, 256–258, 331, 344–345
Sesame Street, 5–7, 11–14, 16, 20, 21, 24, 26, 29, 35, 40, 42, 43, 51, 52–53, 54–56, 57, 58, 59, 60, 61–63, 64–65, 90, 92, 95–96, 222, 327, 342
Sex, 135–136, 137–138, 166, 170–171, 189–190
Sheekey, Arthur, USOE, 91
Social class, 53, 72–79, 190–191, 317–318
Social roles, 72–73, 77, 80
Socialization of the child, 71, 167–169, 219–220, 261, 347
Southern Educational Communications Association, 15
SPC, see Station Program Cooperative
Special Projects Act, 90
Star Trek, 38
Station Program Cooperative (SPC), 92
Summative research, 24, 44, 52–53, 55–56, 57–58
Superfriends, 59
Superman, 192
Supreme Court, 213, 214
Surgeon General's Scientific Advisory Committee and Report on Television and Social Behavior, 103, 115–118, 119–120, 123–125, 131–133, 136–137, 141–142, 163, 164, 246, 327–328

T
Tankersley, William, CBBB President, 331
Teacher training, 105–106
Teachers Guides to Television, 85
Technological change, 15–16, 94–97, 101–102, 216–217
Televised instruction, limitations of, 63, 104–107
Television Code, NAB, 240
Television effects research, responses to, 113–125, 221–223, 224–225, 226
Television industry personnel, 210–211, 223–225, 226
Television literacy, 80–81, 103, 161, 349
Television viewing, 10, 150–151, 153–154, 184, 209–210
Thinkabout, 91–92
Toy Manufacturers Association, 278

U
U.S. Copyright Office, 102
U.S. Department of Agriculture, 38–39
U.S. Department of Commerce, 215
U.S. Office of Education, 38, 89–92, 103
USOE, see U.S. Office of Education
Upstairs, Downstairs, 104

V
Vegetable Soup, 35, 39, 57, 91
Videotapes and videocassettes, 94–97
Viewing patterns, 63, 74–75, 241, 308, 340
Villa Alegre, 21, 35, 51, 57, 96
Violent programming, 143, 152, 153, 160, 164
  change/reform, 114–116, 118–120, 121–123, 125, 136–137, 177, 195–196
Violent programming impact, 113–125, 129–144, 159–160, 163–177, 189–190
  behavioral, 118–119, 120–121, 129–144, 164–177, 193
  catharsis, 120, 130–131, 166–167, 171, 190–191
  concerns about, 113, 154–155, 160, 202
  desensitization, 142, 168, 170, 174–175, 168, 170–171, 183–196
  disinhibition, 167–168, 174

Violent programming impact (*cont.*)
  emotional, 105, 142, 157, 158–160, 169–
    171, 175–176
  factors affecting, 140–141, 167, 168, 172–
    173
  individual differences, 137–138, 166, 168,
    170–171, 183–196

W
Warren Commission, 115
Westar I, 96

Westinghouse Broadcasting Company, 283
Westen, Tracy, FTC Bureau of Consumer
    Protection, 333
Wiley, Richard, FCC Chairman, 325
Writers' notebook, 22–23, 41

Z
Zoom, 16, 35